Anthropology and Rural Development in West Africa

About the Book and Editors

Anthropology and Rural Development in West Africa documents the experiences of anthropologists with development in West Africa during the past ten years. It presents case study material to bring out the actual and potential contributions of social science to solving development problems found in Africa and in other parts of the Third World. The book is not a manual that seeks to present solutions; rather it describes some of the kinds of development situations in which anthropologists participated and examines the kind of tensions under which they operated.

Michael M Horowitz, professor of anthropology at State University of New York, Binghamton, is director of the Institute for Development Anthropology, also in Binghamton. **Thomas M. Painter** is a research associate at the Institute and a doctoral candidate in sociology and development anthropology at the State University of New York, Binghamton.

MONOGRAPHS IN DEVELOPMENT ANTHROPOLOGY

Under the General Editorship of
DAVID W. BROKENSHA
MICHAEL M HOROWITZ
and
THAYER SCUDDER

Sponsored by the Institute for Development Anthropology

Anthropology and Rural Development in West Africa

EDITED BY MICHAEL M HOROWITZ
AND THOMAS M. PAINTER

Foreword by Michael M. Cernea

Westview Press / Boulder and London

Monographs in Development Anthropology

Copyright © 1986 by the Institute of Development Anthropology

Published in 1986 in the United States of America by Westview Press, Inc.; Frederick A. Praeger, Publisher; 5500 Central Avenue, Boulder, Colorado 80301

Library of Congress Cataloging-in-Publication Data
Anthropology and rural development in West Africa.
  (Monographs in development anthropology)
  Bibliography: p.
  1. Applied anthropology—Africa, West—Addresses,
essays, lectures. 2. Rural development—Africa, West—
Addresses, essays, lectures. 3. Technical assistance—
Africa, West—Anthropological aspects—Addresses,
essays, lectures. I. Horowitz, Michael M, 1933–   .
II. Painter, Tom. III. Series.
GN397.7.A358A57 1986   307'.14'0966   85-20274
ISBN 0-8133-7149-X

This book has been produced without formal editing by the publisher
Composition for this book was provided by the editors
Printed and bound in the United States of America

10   9   8   7   6   5   4   3   2   1

Contents

Acknowledgments

This book is the result of a long effort by persons within and without the Institute. Acknowledgments of help given by fellow staff members often take the form of blanket thanks to colleagues, but we would like to take exception to this practice and indulge ourselves in this first volume of the IDA Monograph Series. All along, we have benefited from the encouragement of all IDA folk. At numerous points along the way, careful copy-editing and critiques were provided by Michael Painter, Peter Little, and Muneera Salem-Murdock. Vera Beers typed and retyped many earlier versions of the manuscripts, and helped at the end with excellent proofreading. During the final months of the production process, Sylvia Horowitz and Vivian Carlip edited and typed tirelessly, and we cannot thank them enough for their good humor and attention to detail. Curt Grimm assisted with bibliographic research and the preparation of article summaries.

Without contributors there would be no *Anthropology and Rural Development*. Ours have shown extraordinary patience in the face of delays, and have been extremely cooperative with our requests for changes in their manuscripts as the book progressed. We would particularly like to thank them for responding to the idea of making the experiences of social scientists with development programs available to a wider audience.

MICHAEL M HOROWITZ
THOMAS M. PAINTER

Foreword: Anthropology and Family Production Systems in Africa

MICHAEL M. CERNEA

Only a tiny fraction of general anthropological knowledge and research has been used in development, in part because anthropologists have rarely translated and formulated their knowledge into operationally relevant propositions for technical experts, economists, managers, and politicians in development. The present volume undertakes precisely this kind of effort, as it is rooted in empirical field analysis and committed to assist development programs. It demonstrates how penetrating the tools of anthropology can be when aptly applied to development programs and how anthropological findings are translatable into relevant operational guidance.

The 1980s have renewed the focus on the problems and prospects of African agriculture. The "integrated rural development" programs of the 1970s did not produce the hoped-for rates of economic or social growth. Recent evaluations of the African rural development experiences mostly agree that the agricultural sector is in crisis (Eicher 1984; Lele 1984). The crisis primarily concerns production and production-supporting institutions. With 80-90 percent of the continent's population based in rural areas, peasant farming remains the principal source of supply for both urban and rural food needs. As the major economic activity it also supplies a large portion of tax revenues and/or foreign exchange earnings for African governments. Yet the development of peasant agriculture, despite enormous efforts and fashionable remedies, fails to occur. The total volume of agricultural production increases more as a result of expanded acreage than higher yields. Analysts disagree on the causes of the crisis, finding evidence in everything from drought and war to inappropriate pricing policies, over-capitalized projects, and the various political postures of African governments. Lele states, "there is not even much understanding of *what* is required to develop [African agriculture]" (1984:437).

Agricultural development in Africa, and particularly in the sub-Saharan countries, is now given highest priority in international organizations, donor and bilateral agencies, and development research centers, yet there is a recurrent blind spot in the recent literature and rhetoric around most of these agendas: an insufficient understanding of the decisive role, and of the specific operating mechanisms of units of agricultural production in Africa.

Simplistic as it may seem to sophisticated minds, or to designers of complex macro policies, the keys to this understanding reside where they are little searched for: in the small family household or compound. It is precisely this ultimate building block of African agriculture and African economy that is of great concern to the anthropology and sociology of development.

The Economic Commission for Africa (ECA) has characterized the crisis in Africa in graphic but realistic terms. In its preliminary perspective study it says,

> The picture that emerges from the analysis of the perspective of the African region by the year 2008 under the historical trend scenario is almost a nightmare. Bearing in mind that the future of 2008 is the future of the young and unborn children of Africa today, the implications have to be taken seriously. Firstly, the potential population explosion would have tremendous repercussions on the region's physical resources such as land and the essential social services, education, health, housing, nutrition, water, etc. At the national level, the socio-economic conditions would be characterised by a deregulation of the very essence of human dignity. The rural population, which would have to survive on intolerable toil, will face an almost disastrous situation of land scarcity whereby whole families would have to subsist on a mere hectare of land. Poverty would reach unimaginable dimensions since rural incomes would become almost negligible relative to the cost of physical goods and services. The conditions in the urban centres would also worsen with more shanty towns, more congested roads, more beggars and more delinquents! The level of the unemployed searching desperately for the means to survive would imply increased crime rates and misery (ECA 1983).

It is our argument that the family farm unit is the most important and yet least understood piece of the African development puzzle. In the real world, it is this unit of social organization that can make or break every new advance. Any policy or program that sidesteps it is bound to fail.

The centrality of the family-based production unit to any rural development process and the importance generally accorded by anthropologists and sociologists to the kin-group, family, or household as a unit of analysis, accounts for the comparative cognitive advantage of anthropology and sociology in explaining some of the essential mechanisms of African agricultural practice. Sociology and anthropology possess knowledge--more than other social or agrotechnical sciences--of the intricate characteristics of family and kin-based units of production organization in the African economic ecologic contexts. This knowledge must be brought both into the strategy brainstorming sessions and into the savannah and woodlands where the actual laboring for development takes place. In turn, social scientists must deepen and sharpen their knowledge.

The various policies, strategies, and approaches for ameliorating Africa's development ills place their main thrusts most often at the macro level and remain inexplicably remote from the local organizations that fill the everyday life of African small land holders. This is not to say that macrostructural reflection is fallacious, for many worthy contributions are made at this level of analysis. But it is counterproductive not to put equal or more analytical effort into microlevel considerations. The endemic macro-bias that ignores the local scene also ignores the critical linkages that exist between the two areas of concern. Policy makers therefore build up central institutions without appreciating their impact on the grass roots. They court outside knowledge at the expense of indigenous knowledge; outside financial inputs at the expense of a concern for internal savings. Price systems devised at the macroeconomic level are bound to collapse if not checked against what can, or cannot, ultimately be done on-farm and in inter-village markets.

In sum, our argument is that for virtually every *demarche* at the macro level there is a mirror action required at the level of the family household as a basic production-and-consumption unit. The focus of agricultural production is the family farm. There every macro policy, in order to succeed, must catch on. The truth of this fundamental proposition has yet to trickle up. The latest-day "definitions of priorities" that omit this unit of social organization are ill-informed and misplaced.

The complexity and uniqueness of African family production systems makes such neglect particularly consequential. Therefore, a part of our general plea for more sociological knowledge in all phases of development work is the request for more recognition of the special characteristics of African basic farming units, and then for using that knowledge to design projects that better fit the productive organization of the family farm. How can farmers carry out project-supported interventions that do not understand the farmers' own basic units of production?

In rural Africa, the structures of family and household are intricately interwoven with the dynamics of their productive activities. Yet too often these complex interconnections are ignored by planners who substitute europocentric nuclear family models of Western-style "family farms," which frequently misinform development interventions.

A number of myths about African society continue to underlie many project designs: that there is a "traditional African family structure" that has remained the same since precolonial times; that this family unit with its production decisions is largely isolated from other social and geographical networks; that this traditional production group is male-headed and that therefore most decisions about agricultural production, processing, and distribution are made by men; and so forth. Sociological, anthropological, and historical research among African societies across the continent, covering lengthy periods of time, have exposed the flaws in these notions. While there are important similarities

xiii

among African family structures, there are also crucial differences, related to ecological contexts and different modes of production. Colonial as well as post-colonial policies, encouraging settlement in certain areas and forbidding it in others, advocating certain crops and restricting others, promoting schooling, clinics, and piped water, have all influenced household composition, inheritance patterns, and access to fundamental productive resources of land and labor. African families should therefore be understood as contemporary and momentary configurations of adaptive response patterns to the practical, economic, and environmental conditions in which they are enmeshed.

The identification of kinship constellations and their effect on the organization of production, distribution, and consumption in a given area is an important step in understanding the development milieu and is a specific role of sociological expertise in development work. Similarly, the often neglected role of children in African family production deserves more careful attention in planning and analysis of agricultural development programs. Polygyny is a common, if poorly understood, element of African family life. More common among wealthier rural families, polygyny facilitates greater access to agricultural labor, both through the larger number of wives, and in their relatively larger number of children. Recent research in Africa has shown that polygyny tends to increase among wealthier families with the introduction of cash cropping, because cash cropping needs more labor and produces more wealth (Aryee 1978; Orubuloye 1981). It is likely that polygyny will decrease with greater urbanization and expansion of education (Kayongo-Mole and Onyango, 1984).

Understanding these and other characteristics may facilitate the recognition that the family-based production unit is often a set of mini-subhouseholds with rules that regulate both their partial autonomy and their interconnection. The subhouseholds differ from each other. Some center around the food crop plot of each wife of the family head and her children; others are structured around the married sons of the family head. Subhouseholds are mandated for certain operations independently and for others as parts of a whole. Rarely are development schemes tailored with the clear recognition of such structural characteristics. These factors affect such tremendously important processes as the labor allocation at the production unit level between food crops and cash crops. Numerous, unanticipated effects of agricultural projects have been triggered because such differences have not been correctly appreciated in planning, or because planners and policy makers often have not realized that the family's food crops are also cash crops (Little and Horowitz, forthcoming).

The proper appreciation of the structure, role, functions and internal mechanisms of the family-based production unit is only one of the many contributions that anthropological knowledge may make to development thinking and planning. Such knowledge may also help foster the kind of "reversals" that are so vitally necessary to the learning process for inducing development, and which Chambers (1985) aptly called "putting <<last>> thinking first."

However important the family farm unit is, it is not a universe confined to itself. Little appreciated in development work is the enormous importance of farmers' own interlinkages, informal or formal, with wider-ranging structures. Farmers' productive or marketing organizations, which articulate the small farm-units of social organization into larger structures for specific social actions, can be capacity enhancers and synergizers. This is true, for instance, in managing such crucial productive resources as water, by water users associations--or the range, by pastoral associations--or credit, by credit solidarity groups, and so forth.

We are witnessing many programs in Africa strongly concerned with institution building, but still surprisingly disinterested in local organization. Institution building is often advocated in a one-sided, macro-biased manner. Undue attention is channeled to the strengthening of national-level agencies and central macro-organizations, while institution building at the grass-roots level is chronically neglected. In fact, it is at this grass-roots level where there are big gains to reap for development by facilitating the articulation of the small family production units into various types of local organizations. The social sciences are at a comparative advantage in understanding, reinforcing, and constructing these local organizations, as the case studies in this volume demonstrate.

Local organization can be supported in many ways. For instance, despite the fragility and failures of many forms of cooperatives, it has been empirically assessed recently in several West African countries that there is a strong association between functional literacy (that can easily be promoted) and the success of simple forms of village associations that promote local interests. The basis for these associations already exists. African societies have a variety of informal rotating credit and saving societies, cooperative groups, labor-exchange and mutual help groups, and water-sharing groups, many of which provide useful bases for modern institutional development and in fact *are part* of Africa's institutional development. Sociologists and anthropologists may help by articulating and testing methodologies to establish, develop and strengthen various farmers' organizations (Belloncle 1985; Cernea 1985). Many development programs have failed to achieve post-program sustainability precisely because they neglected to build up local organizational capacity. Only if local populations assume an increasing responsibility for program-assisted activities, during implementation and especially following completion, can development programs be sustained. Such responsibility can be fostered by increased degrees of autonomy and reliance on grass roots beneficiaries' organizations.

The incorporation of basic and applied anthropological knowledge into development programs and policies will continue to be a major route to improved design of development programs. Since this view is not universally shared by development agencies and governments, it is incumbent upon the sociological/anthropological communities, and upon institutions like the Institute for Development Anthropology, to persist in their careful analyses, critiques, and arguments.

Introduction: Anthropology and Development

MICHAEL M HOROWITZ
THOMAS M. PAINTER

THE FORMATION OF LINKS

This book documents the experiences of anthropologists with development in West Africa during the past ten years. The selection of West Africa and its emphasis on francophone sahelian West Africa surely reflects the editors' own networks; but the area and the era hold special significance for anthropological involvement in development. During the 1960s anthropologists were conspicuously absent from U.S. government-sponsored activities overseas, although they had had prominent roles both during the war years of the 1940s and in the 1950s when "community development" was a centerpiece of American economic assistance to the Third World (Arensberg and Niehoff 1964). Hoben notes that during the 1950s the International Cooperation Administration, the predecessor of the United States Agency for International Development (AID), was the largest employer of anthropologists in America, but by the early 1970s, "only a handful remained" (1982:354). Their departure was attributed to the rapid expansion of anthropology in universities, to the relative lack of prestige enjoyed by applied as opposed to academic or theoretical anthropology, to a revulsion for American foreign policy engendered by the U.S. role in Southeast Asia and in other parts of the world, and as a reaction to the unsavory involvement of some social scientists in counterinsurgency work in Southeast Asia and Latin America. While these factors served to push anthropologists away from development, neither was there much to pull them toward it. The mainstream approach to development in the 1960s focused on urban and industrial sectors, in which interventions proposed by planners were large- scale, capital-intensive, infrastructural, and centrally planned and administered. In this arena, where rural populations of developing countries were largely ignored, anthropologists were considered to be, at best, irrelevant. Several things happened to bring anthropology back into development, with a central focus on the African Sahel.

The ten years or so of separation saw substantial shifts in anthropological theory and methodology. Ecological and transactive or decision-making approaches to the understanding of social change proved to be analytically more powerful than earlier

1

structural, culturally relativistic, and evolutionary models and more persuasive to non-anthropologists whose skepticism about social analysis had to be disarmed. In addition to modifications in theory and method, anthropologists had to learn more about the nature of public policy and the processes of public administration and economic systems to optimize their usefulness in development. New sub-disciplines, such as economic anthropology, heightened interest in studies of peasant societies in relation to larger economic and political systems, and increased appreciation for the historical elements of the development process.

The anthropology of the 1970s was better prepared than its predecessors to deal with the dynamism and complexity of rural communities, and with the effects on rural systems of the political economies in which they were enmeshed. While much earlier anthropology emphasized the uniqueness of each cultural situation and its structural stability, anthropologists trained in the 1960s and 1970s were more disposed to see both cross-cultural regularities, allowing for comparison, and internal heterogeneity, conflict, and creativity leading to social change. The ecological perspective in anthropology directed students to explore relationships between productive technologies and the environment, and the social, economic, political, and ideological institutions of society. It also facilitated sectoral studies and comparisons, and new specializations became prominent in anthropology, such as river basin development, resettlement, pastoral production systems, artisanal fisheries, and natural resource management.

The mainstream development paradigm was also changing in the late 1960s and early 1970s with the realization among many planners that after 20 years of attempts to recreate Western-style urban industrial societies in agrarian, largely post-colonial dependent nations, a hard-core of countries remained desperately poor despite efforts to increase income and productivity. What is more, the gap between these "least developed countries" (LDCs) and developed nations had actually widened. Within the LDCs the gap between large rural populations living in horrendous poverty and minuscule (often urban) elites had also widened markedly. To deal with these disappointing results, foreign aid organizations and governments in LDCs began to reorient development activities toward the rural poor in an attempt to improve their living conditions in the first instance, rather than rely on the "trickle down" effects of investments in the industrial and urban sectors. A more equitable distribution of income and access to resources was held to be not merely a morally desirable objective but also a necessary precondition for general economic growth. A recent review characterizes the two perspectives as "the economic-growth-and-modernization era" of the 1950s and 1960s, when development was defined as growth in output per capita, and the "growth-with-equity period" from the early 1970s when development planners became more concerned with a fairer distribution of employment, income, nutrition, and health (Staatz and Eicher 1984:3). The shift in emphasis of American Foreign Assistance toward the rural poor, known as the "New Directions" of AID, was legislated by Congress during 1973 and 1975.

The catastrophic drought in West Africa during that time provided the areal focus for these shifts in policy. It was obvious to persons working in rural Niger that 1968 was a bad year, with low grain yields and poor pasture. Since the Sahel experiences considerable annual rainfall variation, no one at that time could know that reasonable rains would not be seen again for half a decade, and that severe drought would continue at least to 1985. Even when in 1969 it became clear to the farmers and herders that they were in serious trouble, the drought evaded widespread attention. Only later, when hungry persons left destitute began pouring into larger towns, physically presenting themselves before government officials and foreigners, did it become generally known that all sudano-sahelian lands were faced with a catastrophe of monumental proportions.

By 1972 and 1973 the dimensions of the drought and the attendant human suffering had become grist for media mills. The American press especially picked up on the story, perhaps because unlike Vietnam, the other great locus of human misery at that time, the United States could play what appeared to be a uniquely positive role: providing relief to a disaster the cause of which seemed not directly to implicate us. (Not everyone, of course, agreed that America was blameless in the affair, as, for example, the Comité Information Sahel 1974 and R.W. Franke and B.H. Chasin 1980). Much of the support for a vigorous U.S. participation in the international relief effort came from the Congressional Black Caucus who saw in the drought an opportunity for a more active American involvement in Africa and a chance to reverse the neglect the continent had received.

Thus West Africa provided the main arena for the New Directions. As the rural areas of the Third World became the principal loci of development programs, anthropologists with first-hand cultural and linguistic experience in these areas were invited to join the economists, agronomists, engineers, and other technicians who staff foreign aid organizations.

There is a certain irony in the receptivity to anthropologists that resulted from New Directions in AID. Planning and financing agencies continued to view the actions of rural peoples as *traditional* (i.e., not rational), and as obstacles to development. They employed anthropologists with the hope that traditional ways could be overcome--changed. Most anthropologists, on the other hand, rejected tradition as an explanatory tool, and looked at it rather as the result of specific opportunity structures in which rural populations were situated. These anthropologists repeatedly demonstrated through their research and analysis that rural communities were neither static nor irrationally opposed to change, but were dynamic, open-ended, and receptive to those changes that promoted their welfare and entailed reasonable risks. Anthropologists argued that the obstacles to development were largely external in nature. These obstacles included natural factors to be sure: climate, soil quality, geomorphologic formation, ecology, etc.; but the obstacles that received the greatest attention were political--the external control of systems and economic decision-making, and their impact on rural populations.

The experiences of Michael Horowitz typify a coming together of these historic strands--the drought, the New Directions, and the tensions that arose between proponents and opponents of New Directions. During the late 1960s he was carrying out an eighteen month program of postdoctoral research on agropastoralism in southeastern Niger. At this time he was one of a very few American anthropologists to have done research in the Sahel, and was the first to do so in Niger. On the basis of this experience, he subsequently accepted a long-term position with AID's West African Regional Economic Development Services Office (REDSO/WA) located in Abidjan, Ivory Coast. This was the first time since the legislation of the New Directions policies that an anthropologist had been hired by AID to help implement these policies in the field. His task was to direct social science research in West African countries under the purview of the regional office and to help ensure that programs financed by AID were socially sound and consistent with the mandate laid out by Congress for AID. Among his activities was the supervision of research within the Mali Livestock project, the first of a so-called "new generation" of AID programs in agropastoralism stemming from the new policy orientations. These projects, unlike their predecessors, were supposed to build upon existing strengths of rural populations who were, in principle, to participate in the planning and implementation of rural development projects as well as benefit most directly from their impact. The field research team in Mali, which consisted of Malian and American social scientists, quickly demonstrated that neither assumption was sound. The project's interventions were out of touch with local realities, and the beneficiaries of the project, it was found, were less likely to be peasant herders than large cattle brokers, government officials, and commercial-scale butchers. The envisioned participation of local populations remained moot.

Horowitz was the first of many. Implementation of the New Directions orientations in development by AID required that all development assistance projects be subject to "social analysis." To ensure this, anthropologists were brought into AID as consultants and as career officers, engaged, in some cases, in the formulation of policy. The great West African drought of 1968 to 1974 also provided openings for anthropologists who were interested in the development process and the potential contribution of the social sciences to more positive consequences for rural peoples affected by development programs. As the United States, along with other bilateral and multilateral donors, mobilized efforts to help the states of the West African Sahel to combat the effects of the drought and reconstruct their rural economies in its wake, it became clear that very little was known about the region as a geo-climatic zone, or about the people who lived there. The need for additional knowledge during this critical period made it possible for more anthropologists to become associated with development programs in Africa, and anthropologists enjoyed some unusual opportunities to carry out research in a multidisciplinary context. Indeed, in some countries where obtaining research clearance for conventional anthropological studies became increasingly problematic after independence, participation in a development research activity constituted privileged entry to fieldwork.

Yet along with enhanced access to the field and unusually generous research funding, development anthropologists commonly faced tensions and frustrations perhaps unknown to their academic colleagues. These tensions and frustrations, some of which are documented in the chapters in this book, derived in part from an unfamiliarity with the rhythms and tempos of government, in which there is tremendous pressure to move to action on the basis of what many social scientists feel is inadequate data and analysis. They also derive from the heavy intrusion of political concerns in the design and implementation of development interventions, so that the championing of the rural poor, exalted in the rhetoric of development, often falls victim to a *realpolitik* in which the benefits of an intervention become captured by the already affluent. A recurrent discovery of anthropologists in development was how rarely the philosophical basis of the New Directions was shared by either host or U.S. government officials.

NOTES ON PROGRESS

The first major review of the role of anthropology and related social sciences in Third World economic development subsequent to the New Directions legislation was held during a conference at AID in Washington, DC, in May 1977. The participants recommended three changes in AID's procedures that would improve the contribution of the social sciences to rural development based on growth with equity (McPherson, ed. 1978).

(1) Anthropology should be involved at every stage of project development: policy formation, identification, design, implementation, and evaluation, rather than late in the design stage ("project appraisal" at the World Bank and "project paper" at AID). This was because the introduction of social analysis late in the final design effort created an adversary relationship between the social analyst and the other members of the appraisal team. By then, momentum on the part of both donor organization and host government to move ahead is great and critical analyses are not welcome. The delaying of social analysis until the engineering, agronomic, or macroeconomic studies are well under way, as is customary, risks a confrontation between the anthropologist and other specialists who often feel personally or professionally attacked by a social analysis that does not confirm their own positions. This is especially the case where the social scientist is the only consultant on a team otherwise composed of career donor organization staff, who may close ranks against an "outsider" who is uncommitted or critical of the organization's need to get on with the business of moving money (cf. Tendler 1975).

(2) Aid organizations should recruit more social scientists as career officers, rather than relying heavily on consultants. There should be established career tracks for these persons, with appointments made at senior as well as junior levels. Conference

participants pointed out that there was little support for social scientists, compared with that given to economists, engineers, agronomists, foresters, and lawyers. In AID, for example, there was no "chief agency social scientist" who paralleled a chief agency economist or engineer, and therefore, it was argued, social analysis lacks both quality control and higher level advocacy for its utilization. As a result, many excellent project social analyses were prepared, but remained as ornamental appendages to project papers, and were not integrated into the main body of the report. Thus, the *requirement* of a social analysis may be satisfied, but its impact on the resultant project is often modest at best.

(3) Host country anthropologists and social science institutions should be more involved in development, both in undertaking social analyses on their own and in collaborating with expatriate scientists. Where qualified persons are few in number and often over-extended because of the demand for their services, it is important that assistance be given to the creation of local personnel with interdisciplinary development expertise. This resource would increase the capacity of LDCs to design, manage, and analyze their own development projects. As these people move up within the administration, they might have a greater influence on local and national policy-making (McPherson, ed. 1978:24).

There has been movement on all of the points raised at the 1977 conference. There are more anthropologists in development positions today, and a few are in reasonably senior positions with some influence on policy. In addition there is a greater involvement of host country social scientists in development. Nonetheless, it would be an exaggeration to claim that progress has been substantial or anywhere near as effective as conference advocates hoped. For all its institutionalization, social analysis remains the weakest element in the project cycle, and development activities continue to be implemented that do not benefit poor populations. As the papers in this volume demonstrate again and again, there is much that can be done, but doing so takes commitments too often lacking in both the donor organizations and the host country ministries responsible for project design and implementation.

THE PRESENT VOLUME

This book presents case study materials that highlight the actual and potential contribution of social science to actions aimed at solving development "problems" found in Africa and in other parts of the Third World. The editors asked the contributors to examine their work and their particular roles vis-à-vis the development process, and candidly to consider issues such as professional preparation (or its lack) for what is often a task involving critical forays into domains of expertise--such as economics-- jealously guarded by their practitioners; to discuss personal research and consulting styles; and to describe the tensions that arise as the social scientist attempts to operate in the gap between the ideas of planners and financers, at one extreme, and those of agrarian peoples, the ostensible beneficiaries, at the other. The book is not a manual. It does not seek to present solutions, but rather to describe some of the kinds of development situations in which anthropologists participated and to examine the kinds of tensions under which they operated.

The articles in the book cover a range of professional involvement by anthropologists and sociologists in African development. Using very practical language, Riall Nolan and Dennis Warren describe how anthropologists have contributed to development training programs--be they for Peace Corps trainees, preparing to work as community development volunteers in Senegal, or government workers in Ghana, being trained for a more effective role in the implementation of national policy.

Dolores Koenig, Robert Hecht, and Allan Hoben are also concerned with practical matters, but they focus more on how social science perspectives can be effectively used to accomplish specific research and evaluation tasks related to development programs. This may entail the redesign of an agricultural development project on the basis of a critical reanalysis of earlier formulations (Hecht, in Guinea); a critique of conventional development wisdom shared by national and international planners in Cameroon about "typical" behavior of troublesome categories of people in rural areas (e.g., mountain dwellers, as discussed by Hoben); or a description of difficulties encountered and solutions proposed to ensure that farming systems research programs being carried out over vast areas of the West African Sahel produce information that is comparable and useful (Koenig, reporting on her experience in Mali).

Essays by Alfred Waldstein, John Grayzel, Thomas Painter, Stephen Reyna, and Michael Horowitz are more critical of the development enterprise overall. These authors draw from their experiences with particular programs to develop more general discussions of issues faced by social scientists and "beneficiaries" in development. They are concerned with the probable payoffs of development projects for affected populations, and with the role of social scientists who seek a practical as well as an analytical link with development. Reyna and Waldstein critically discuss river basin development policies in Burkina Faso and Senegal respectively. Both give attention to the political limits on economic choice faced by governments that are heavily dependent on foreign sources of financing for development programs, and both deal with the leverage applied by donors to influence the particular forms that projects take, and finally the populations they affect. On the basis of work in Niger, Painter addresses what is a strong tendency among national development planners, despite a long history of failures, to build local development organizations on existing socio-economic forms whose attributes are often poorly understood by those who seek to use them as foundations. The papers by Horowitz and Grayzel deal with livestock development projects, and how the implementation of "pastoral development logic" not only fails to increase livestock production, but undermines the capacity of African pastoralists to exploit some of the continent's most marginal lands. They argue that interventions in the area of livestock production often hinder pastoralists in their production strategies and are likely to have a negative rather than a positive impact on the livelihoods of herders. Horowitz addresses several myths concerning herders and their livestock management practices, traces their origins in much government thinking about these "troublesome" people (cf. Hoben's chapter), and on the basis of field work in Niger, demonstrates the difficulties that result when these myths are embodied in multi-million dollar livestock development projects. The argument presented by Grayzel, whose work was done in Mali, is similar. In addition, he makes a minority plea for attention to a factor that is invariably ignored by development planners and social scientists alike--the emotional needs of the rural populations affected by a given project.

A recurrent theme in the essays, and one that can be documented with similar cases from other parts of the world, is that the essential core of the New Directions--*equitable growth based on genuine participation of the rural poor*--has rarely been effectively incorporated into development planning. The fault would seem to lie not with the New Directions themselves, but with the readiness on the part of governments and financing organizations to ignore or even subvert the enfranchisement that such participation implies.

WEST AFRICA

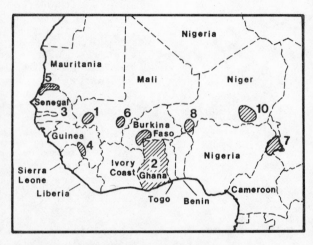

COUNTRIES AND LOCATIONS
DESCRIBED BY AUTHORS

1. Dolores Koenig (Kita, Western Mali)
2. Dennis Warren (Ghana)
3. Riall Nolan (Senegal)
4. Robert Hecht (Faranah and Foulaya regions, Maritime Guinea)
5. Alfred Waldstein (Senegal River Valley, Senegal)
6. John Grayzel (Segou/Bani River, Mali)
7. Allan Hoben (Mandara Mountains/Benoué Plateau, Northern Cameroon)
8. Thomas Painter (Dosso, Southwestern Niger)
9. Stephen Reyna (Volta Valley Region, Burkina Faso)
10. Michael Horowitz (Zinder and Diffa, Southeastern Niger)

Editors' Note to Chapter 1

Why work with peasant smallholders as a means of increasing agricultural production in Africa when larger-scale, more "rational" production is needed? It was a particularly arrogant variation of this vision of agrarian change that informed the Agricultural Production Capacity and Development Project in Guinea described by Robert Hecht. The original project, which he was asked to help redesign, required large transfers of American techniques and equipment to Guinea, even though they were poorly adapted to the capital mix of most peasant producers affected by the project. Through a re-analysis of the rural economy of project areas, Hecht was able to recommend improvements in production techniques for a follow-on project that would not overload smallholders with debt-inducing equipment. Hecht's materials, like those of Waldstein and Reyna, reflect the contradictions and difficulties faced by social scientists in development. Projects are based on considerations of internal rates of return, profit, and rates at which "modern" but often technically inappropriate techniques will be adopted by rural producers. Typically these economic considerations are divorced from the social reality of which they are a part. Under these conditions, it is no surprise that many projects fail. When these difficulties become serious enough, the anthropologist may be called in to salvage a foundering project through an examination of "interstitial" (i.e., social) factors neglected by planners.

1
Salvage Anthropology: The Redesign of a Rural Development Project in Guinea

ROBERT M. HECHT
The World Bank

INTRODUCTION

Salvage Anthropology

During the last several decades, "salvage archaeology" has become a common form of archaeological practice (Gumerman 1973). Ancient sites endangered by the construction of homes, factories, roads, and dams have been excavated by archaeologists in an attempt to save important artifacts from disturbance or destruction. In a similar way, social anthropologists are becoming involved increasingly in "salvage" work in living communities in Third World nations. Anthropologists have played a role in planning, implementing, and evaluating resettlement schemes that have displaced communities in order to carry out dam construction and large-scale commercial farming. Anthropologists have also assisted groups of people facing encroachment, and even genocide, at the hands of outsiders (Chambers 1969).[1] In such cases, they have worked to "salvage," or save, threatened societies. The main difference between these endeavors by anthropologists and the work of salvage archaeologists is that while the latter have sought to preserve an artifactual record, anthropologists are engaged with evolving human communities. The challenge is thus not to preserve the communities as frozen in time,

*The author thanks USAID and, especially, its Regional Economic Development Services Office for West Africa (REDSO/WA) for the opportunity to participate in the redesign of the Guinea project during August-September 1981. The views expressed here are, of course, entirely his own.

[1]Cultural Survival and Survival International are among the best-known organizations fighting against ethnocide.

but to assist them to change and grow in a way acceptable to their members.

Social anthropologists are also being called upon by international aid agencies to help reformulate development projects intended to benefit communities in Third World countries. In this situation they are being asked to "salvage" the work of the development community. Projects may be in difficulty for numerous reasons, including failure to adapt their structure and activities to the existing social, economic, and technological features of the target communities. Anthropologists are playing an important role in improving the projects' effectiveness in achieving their stated goals, such as stimulating national economic growth, enhancing social equity, and raising household incomes. In this context, "salvage" anthropology means extracting the viable elements of a foundering project in its design or operational stage, and combining them with new ingredients in order to arrive at a more effective project. Here, too, the emphasis is not on preserving a living community in an unchanging state; rather, it is on helping the community to evolve in a way that satisfies both local and national aspirations.

Just as salvage archaeology places limits upon the archaeologist's ability to carry out problem-oriented research, salvage anthropology constrains the anthropologist's research framework. Logistically, the short time-span of most development field work may prevent the investigator from carrying out broad statistical surveys, pretesting questionnaires, and becoming intimately acquainted with the project zone. Politically, the foreign aid organizations employing anthropologists may try to influence their analysis and conclusions. Methodologically, the choice of field zone for salvage research generally precedes the framing of a theoretical or empirical problem, which is the opposite of the process that usually takes place in research sponsored by academic bodies.

However, the real differences between applied salvage research and academically sponsored research are less substantial than might first appear to be the case. Applied researchers have done lengthy field stints and employed elaborate survey methods, and all social science research has an intrinsically political and ideological nature (Asad, ed. 1975; Blackburn, ed. 1973). Through a dialectic of theory and practice, the initially practical orientation of applied anthropology can spawn theoretical propositions concerning social and economic change. In other words, there is no reason why salvage anthropology cannot be both theoretical and problem-oriented.

These issues became explicit in the case of the redesign of the Guinea Agricultural Production Capacity and Development Project, a major West African rural development scheme financed by the United States Agency for International Development. The redesign of the project showed how some large development investments may end up being built upon seriously inadequate assumptions about the technical, social, economic, and institutional capabilities of the intended beneficiaries. Such fundamental assumptions most often turn out to be erroneous, due to the ideological biases of the design team personnel or of their lack of knowledge of local socio-economic conditions. In the Guinean example below, the design team operated under the assumption that transfer of advanced, large-scale, capital-intensive technology would be the key to stimulating the country's agricultural development. The team also made heroic--and largely incorrect--assumptions that Guinea's farm extension service and its marketing and price policies were sound enough to provide a conducive environment for disseminating research results to producers.

The redesign effort further illustrated the ways in which anthropology can help to improve agricultural research and training projects. As in the Guinean case, anthropology's contributions can include (1) encouraging broader farmer participation in design, (2) identifying farmers' training needs, (3) building effective communications channels between farmers and research officials, (4) strengthening farmers' local institutions, and, (5) incorporating socio-economic research into the larger framework of proposed "farming systems" research.

USAID INTERVENTION IN GUINEAN AGRICULTURE

The Setting

Guinea's roughly six million persons inhabit 246,000 square kilometers in the western part of West Africa. The country is divided into four main geographical zones. Maritime Guinea, including the capital of Conakry, is a wet (2,500-3,500 millimeters of rainfall a year), low-lying region crisscrossed by saline estuaries and mangrove swamps. It is settled mainly by the Susu ethnic group, who grow rice as a staple crop. Middle Guinea, one of the most mountainous regions in West Africa, with elevations above 1400 meters, receives adequate rainfall for maize and sorghum cultivation, but high population density, intensive farming, and deforestation have seriously depleted soils. The dominant ethnic group, the Fula, consequently subsists on *fonio* or finger millet (*Eleusina digitaris*), a cereal well adapted to the infertile conditions prevailing in Middle Guinea (Derman 1973). The geography of Upper Guinea, extending from the Fouta Djallon mountain range of Middle Guinea in the west to the border with Mali in the east, is strongly marked by the upper stretches of the Niger River, which meanders through the region's vast fertile plain. Upper Guinea is inhabited mostly by the Malinké ethnic group, who grow rice, cassava, maize, and peanuts as food crops under woodland savannah climate conditions (1,250-1,750 millimeters of rain a year)(Hodge, ed. 1971). Finally, Forest Guinea, which shares a border with Liberia and Ivory Coast, has a humid year-round climate (1,500-2,000 millimeters of rainfall) suited to raising cocoa, coffee, and oil palm as export crops and rice as a food crop. The region is inhabited by a number of small ethnic groups belonging to the Southern Mandé group, including Kissi, Kono, Toma, and Guerzé.

Agriculture, the chief occupation of more than 80 percent of Guinea's population, has accounted for around 40 percent of the country's gross domestic product (GDP) in recent years (Department of State 1980). These high figures reflect the undeveloped state of Guinea's industrial and service sectors rather than any significant progress in agriculture. In fact, output in the primary sector over the past two decades has not kept pace with population growth, so that per capita farm production actually has declined since Guinea's independence in 1958 (World Bank 1981a). Food imports have averaged around 100,000 metric tons annually in recent years. Agriculture's share of exports declined dramatically in the 1970s, and currently accounts for less than 5 percent of total export earnings. This partly reflects the rapid expansion of bauxite production during the decade, with the opening of two new mines, but it is also due to a serious malaise in farming. Exports of bananas, once Guinea's mainstay, dropped from 100,000 metric tons in the early 1960s to virtually nil by the end of the 1970s. Coffee exports fell from 14,000 tons to 2,000 tons during the same period.

Stagnation and decline in Guinea's agriculture can be traced largely to a series of postindependence government policies (Hecht 1981). First, the state has enforced a set of official producer prices that are so low that they discourage production. Black-market prices have been two to four times the official levels in recent years. Second, at various times the government has nationalized both wholesale and retail trading and transport of agricultural commodities, resulting in serious inefficiencies and higher costs. Third, less than 10 percent of the government's investment budget has been allocated to the agricultural sector in recent years. This discrimination against farming has placed an additional fetter upon agriculture. Fourth, less than 1 percent of institutional credit in Guinea has been earmarked for farming, with almost nothing for peasant smallholders.

Probably the most important retarding factor in Guinean agricultural policy during the last decade, however, has been the heavy emphasis on large-scale mechanized farming. This policy has encountered major difficulties and yielded disappointing results. Such agricultural experiments are an outgrowth of the government's ideological inclination toward "socialized" forms of production (even when these are ill-suited to prevailing technical, economic, and social conditions), and of its fascination with advanced capital-intensive technology.[2]

Between 1975 and 1978, most government expenditure in agriculture was directed into tractorized and ox-drawn production "brigades," known as *brigades mécanisées de production* (BMP)

---

[2]The government's penchant for large-scale farms and capital-intensive techniques has not been limited to socialized forms of production only: starting in the late 1970s, the Sekou Touré regime appealed to several American agribusinesses for investments in soybean and rice production.

and *brigades attelées de production* (BAP). These were organized at the level of Guinea's more than 2,000 *pouvoirs révolutionnaires locals* (PRL), the country's smallest political units, consisting of several contiguous villages. Members of the BMP and BAP were expected to farm some of their land collectively and to share the tractors, plows, and draft animals cooperatively on the remaining individually held plots.

The early demise of the brigades came in 1978, when most farmers refused to work in the collective fields. In any case, they were inadequately trained to manage such large enterprises. Poor equipment maintenance, lack of spare parts, and shortages of fertilizer and improved seeds were among the problems the brigades faced. Conceived in part by the state as devices for controlling the marketing of farm commodities, the brigades were forced to sell their output at unattractively low official prices.

Starting in 1979, the brigades were superseded by state farms, known as *fermes agro-pastorales d'arrondissement* (FAPA). Several FAPAs were set up at the level of each arrondissement, the administrative unit grouping together eight to a dozen PRLs. The FAPAs were equipped with tractors and staffed by former employees of the government's (largely disbanded) agriculture field services and by recent graduates of Guinea's secondary schools. The government assigned each FAPA a quota of land to be planted in various crops. Typically, this meant 90 hectares of cereals, 20 hectares of cassava, and 20 hectares of fruit trees.

The results of the FAPA program have also been poor (Hecht 1981). Planted areas have generally been less than one-quarter of targets. Output has been even lower, despite the fact that the FAPAs tended to appropriate the choicest farm land in the communities where they were located. Rice yields on the FAPAs, for example, have been consistently lower than on individually-held plots. The reasons are similar to those for the brigades: poor technical and managerial training for state farm employees, major bottlenecks in input supply and marketing, and unprofitable official prices. The Guinean state farm model has been viewed with indifference by the country's peasant smallholders.

Agricultural policies have thus caused Guinean peasant smallholders to be neglected at best (e.g., by credit and investment policies), and otherwise to be harassed and punished (e.g., by the government's stances on official prices and FAPAs). Nevertheless, more than half a million smallholders continue to produce nearly all of Guinea's food and export crops and livestock. The country's economic future is clearly predicated on increasing smallholder farm output. With the approval, in 1980, of the World Bank-financed peasant rice-production project in the Guékédou region, and expressions, in 1981, of government support for a USAID-backed project for smallholder farming in the Faranah region, there were some indications that the Guinean regime at last was interested in trying to dynamize smallholder producers.

The Original Project

The Guinea Agricultural Capacity and Training Project was originally designed by a team from AID in late 1975 (AID 1975a).[3] The purpose of the five-year, $4.9 million scheme was to "train agricultural researchers, extensionists, and administrators and to improve the depth and scope of agricultural research and production techniques." The designers felt that simply by promoting more vigorous agronomic research and expanded training of several echelons of Guinean civil servants connected with agricultural development, the project would lead to increased Guinean agricultural output. There was no perceived need to intervene directly in farm production.

The original project envisioned three main activities:
1. Construction and outfitting of a laboratory at the National Agricultural Research Institute (INRA) at Foulaya, 135 kilometers from Conakry in Maritime Guinea. The lab would be equipped for research in soil science, entomology, nematology, plant pathology, and plant protection. Guinean researchers earning M.A. degrees at U.S. universities in each of these five specialties eventually would staff the Foulaya laboratory. 2. Construction and outfitting of additional facilities for teaching and farm production at the agricultural collège (high school) in Faranah, 475 kilometers from Conakry in Upper Guinea. These facilities included dormitories, classrooms, laboratories, offices, a library, clinic, and cafeteria on the school grounds, plus stables, a piggery, chicken coops, a veterinary clinic, equipment sheds, storehouses, and offices at the nearby collège farm. 3. Construction and equipping of a research sub-station and a demonstration-training farm near the village of Tindo, ten kilometers from Faranah. The Tindo farm would be run by U.S. expatriates with specializations in agricultural engineering, production agronomy, veterinary medicine, rangeland development, and rice culture.

The initial project was heavily oriented toward civil works and provision of American equipment. In all, the project anticipated building more than 60 new structures at the three sites, plus a ten-foot high, mile-long dike in the Niger flood plain at Tindo to protect a 30-hectare perimeter for irrigated farming.

Approval of the original project design in early 1976 was followed by an architectural and engineering study for the sites at Foulaya, Faranah, and Tindo. Two American agronomists on contract to USAID/Guinea in 1977 prepared detailed lists of the equipment and supplies, including U.S. commodities, for the three "legs" of the project. Construction commenced thereafter.

---

[3]All quotes hereafter from the "original project paper," "initial project document," etc., refer to this document.

"SALVAGE" REDESIGN OF THE PROJECT

Identification of Problems

By early 1981, the Guinea Agricultural Production Capacity and Training Project was foundering upon two problems of near-crisis dimensions. First, construction at the three project sites was running more than two years behind schedule, in part due to difficulties in the procurement and transport of building materials. Projected costs had also escalated more than threefold, from $4.9 million to $15 million. Second, with the construction phase limping toward its completion, it was becoming increasingly clear to AID that the *use* of the facilities at Foulaya, Faranah, and Tindo had not been carefully planned. AID had started to realize that detailed programming of research and training, and supplementary financing of this second phase of the project, were imperative to make the first phase pay off.

To deal with the construction problem, in early 1981 AID engineers began to oversee project construction on a weekly basis in an effort to expedite building and cut costs on a number of structures. A special AID administrative and logistics officer also was sent to Conakry, to speed the flow of construction materials and equipment to the three sites. As a result of these measures, the target date for completing construction was moved forward to June 1982, and costs were lowered slightly to $14.4 million.

To solve the problem of inadequate planning and budgeting for the use of the facilities, in August 1981 AID appointed a team consisting of an anthropologist, economist, and agronomist to prepare an identification document for a project to follow the construction phase. This would include training and research and, possibly, farm extension and crop production. The team's first task was to analyze the weaknesses of the original project in order to prescribe appropriate corrective measures. The team perceived that the general weakness of the first phase was that research and training were only vaguely planned. Furthermore, the plans that were made bore little relation to the realities of the existing Guinean farm extension service and of the vast majority of Guinean agricultural producers--smallholders.

In particular, the anthropologist addressed four main shortcomings in the original project. First, the agricultural training component was never specified. The initial project paper, for example, did not mention a curriculum reform at the Faranah collège. Perhaps the paper's authors expected that construction of a demonstration farm at the collège alone would reform the institution's training program. The type of training contemplated for the Tindo farm also was left unspecified in the first phase document, except to say that it would cater to "trainees from Faranah collège, INRA (Foulaya), the Faculty of Agronomy, and extension agents from all over Guinea." Direct training of peasant farmers as village extension workers or demonstrators was not included in the original project, an indication that the farmers were viewed as passive recipients of modernizing technology.

Second, the research needs that were catalogued in the original scheme did not include the social sciences, even though the scheme's designers admitted that social scientific information on rural Guinea was seriously lacking. The scientific specialties listed in the original document were nematology, entomology, plant pathology, plant protection, and soil science at Foulaya, and engineering, production agronomy, veterinary medicine, range development, and rice culture at Tindo. Such areas as agricultural economics, social anthropology, and community development were excluded completely. Yet the authors of the document confessed that their own analyses of the proposed project were "cursory...due to the lack of reliable and current statistics on the Guinean economy, especially the agricultural and education sectors...."

Third, neither the research nor training proposed under the original project considered the state of existing institutions, including extension and national and regional research services. Extension, for example, was in fact poorly financed and under-staffed in 1976, having been neglected because of the advent of production brigades and state farms during the second half of the 1970s. The authors of the project also skirted the issue of identifying the type of production unit (brigade, state farm, or peasant smallholder) to be served, thereby precluding the possible strengthening of the system for delivering the results of agricultural research and training to a specific clientele. At one point, the authors spoke of "transforming peasant smallholder agriculture into more viable, market-oriented operators," yet in another place they asserted that "the optimum size for the [Tindo] farm has been determined by the design team at 110 hectares...the size of 'revolution farms' [i.e., FAPAs] currently being managed by local party units and mechanized work brigades." The peasants versus brigades question was vital for planning research and training, but it was not answered in the original proposal. The choice of relevant production units, for example, might orient research toward mechanized as opposed to ox-plow cultivation. It would also determine a very different organization of extension services.

Finally, there was a tremendous gap between the realities of Guinean smallholder agriculture, which needed to be assisted by the project, and the large-scale mechanized farming by expatriates, which was originally proposed under the project. For example, the teaching farm at Faranah collège anticipated raising 8,000 imported layers and broilers in confined henhouses using imported feed concentrates, while virtually all Guinea's chickens were local breeds roaming freely in the villages and scavenging their food from rubbish mounds. The Tindo demonstration farm planned the cultivation of rice in a leveled, diked perimeter, while Guinean producers, even in the brigades, continued to use uncontrolled flood plain cultivation techniques.

The gap between the original project and the prevailing reality emerged partly because the original project design team's knowledge and understanding of Guinean rural society and economy were limited. The gap also resulted from the team members' fundamental assumption that they did not need to be intimately acquainted with Guinean rural conditions, since modern farm technology, transferred from the United States to Guinea, would be sufficient to transform the rural areas. The "recognized U.S. expertise in agricultural technology" was repeatedly mentioned in the design document as the primary justification for American involvement in the project.

In addition to not tailoring the original project to the pre-dominant farming systems in Guinea, the project planners apparently never consulted the farmers themselves on the project design, nor did they provide for the establishment of mechanisms to enable farmers to participate in the project, such as village associations, cooperatives, farmer training programs, and periodic village surveys. Despite the lip service paid to the "integration" of research and training with extension and farm production, the initial project did not include procedures for channeling feedback from producers to the research establishment; there was no consideration of village-level, adaptive research or the training of villagers as auxiliary extension agents. In other words, the original project did not include the chief agricultural producers of Guinea, peasant smallholders, as participants in the design, implementation, and evaluation of the scheme, or as the intended beneficiaries of agronomic research and training activities. The project had been planned neither with nor for farmers.

Proposed Modifications of the Project

While the authors of the original project began by planning for the wholesale transfer of mechanized farming to Guinea (especially on the Faranah collège farm and at Tindo demonstration site), the three-person AID project identification document (PID) team mobilized in mid-1981 focused initially on the potential of the existing Guinean agricultural system for increasing farm output and improving the living conditions of the smallhold producers. One of the anthropologist's main tasks was to gather information on the social and economic features of the Malinké peasants who made up the vast majority of the smallholders in Faranah region. Proposed modifications in the original project depended on the analysis of this information.

After assembling and reviewing the published data on the Malinké (Cissé 1970; 1972; Person 1968), the anthropologist made a series of village visits and conducted nonrandom interviews of household heads in three communities in close proximity to Faranah: Nialia Centre, Delemara, and Tindo. This yielded additional socioeconomic data. Some of the key results of these surveys are summarized below:

1. Demography. Census samples from three PRLs in the Nialia arrondissement revealed relatively large average household sizes of 8.1, 9.8, and 10.5 persons. This could be explained in part by a high rate of plural marriage, with average polygyny ratios of 1.7 to 1, 2.0 to 1, and 2.1 to 1, respectively. It was also due to a large proportion of complex agnatic kin structures as the basic units of production. In a sample of 20 households, 16 (80 percent) were complex units (seven stem and nine joint

families) with only four conjugal units. This suggested the potential for extended forms of economic cooperation among Malinké kinsmen, in undertaking collective tasks, e.g., building a fertilizer store, and forming producers' groups under the project.

2.   Land.   A household (*lu* in the Malinké language) had rights to farmland based on membership in an agnatic lineage (*babunda*), with several lineages controlling portions of village land.   Distribution of land among households depended on rank among lineages in a village, with autochthonous and chiefly kin groups controlling more territory than outsider and commoner lineages.   It also depended on rank within lineages, with elders managing larger tracts than junior and former "captive" households.   This land tenure system appeared to offer adequate security of tenure to all households; the proposed project was unlikely to disrupt this security.   The project would, however, need to be sensitive to the needs of those at the bottom of the distribution hierarchy, who possessed the smallest plots and least fertile land.

3.   Techniques.   There was only one functioning tractor in the entire arrondissement, and about 10 percent of households used ox-drawn plows for land preparation in lowland rice fields. All other farming tasks were performed with hand tools.   None of the household heads interviewed used chemical fertilizer, insecticide, fungicide, or selected seed.   This suggested that there might be considerable potential for expanding the use of animal traction and fertilizer under the project.

4.   Yields.   Average yields were around 800 kilograms per hectare for rice (upland and swamp), 2,000 kilograms per hectare for cassava, 600 kilograms per hectare for fonio, and 500 kilograms per hectare for peanuts.   These yields, low by West African standards, indicated that there was considerable scope for increasing land productivity under the project.

5.   Labor.   Virtually all farm labor was of a nonwage type, supplied mainly by household members and supplemented by labor prestations from younger agnates, affines, former captives, and reciprocal work-sharing teams (*sere* in the Malinké language) composed of a dozen or more young men from the same age-grade. The main division of farm labor was according to sex.   Men handled much of the heavy work, such as clearing trees and weeds, plowing, and building cassava and sweet potato mounds and fences around kitchen gardens.   Women undertook such operations as planting, weeding, harvesting, and processing crops.   Although most crops required labor inputs from both sexes, peanuts were exclusively a woman's crop, while men attended to the tasks associated with cassava cultivation.   These labor patterns suggested that research and extension efforts for certain crops would require principal participation from female farmers, while work on other crops would involve mainly their husbands.   The absence of a wage labor market also indicated that there might arise serious labor constraints if farmers sought to expand farm size under the proposed projects.

The anthropologist's second task was to assist the other two team members in the collection and analysis of information on Guinean agriculture.   Here, the anthropologist's methodology for conducting village-level household surveys was useful. He helped the economist gather data on the prevailing prices for farm inputs and crops, labor time associated with the various farming operations, and household income and expenditures. He also collaborated with the agronomist in inquiring into current cropping practices, field pests and diseases, soil types and uses, water control systems, and crop-processing and storage practices in the Faranah region.

The three-person team thus put together a broad, composite picture of a prevailing rural economy. What they found was a production system based upon predominantly manual technology, management of land allocation by the kin group and its elders, and nonwage labor recruited largely through kinship ties. Positive trends toward a more productive peasant farming system had been arrested, and even set back, by the Guinean government's policies on farm-gate prices, investment, and credit. The general strategy of the PID team in modifying the original project was to help raise the potential productivity of land and labor through research, and then to increase the actual level of production through extension, farmer training, and the supply of equipment, inputs, and credit sought by peasant smallholders.

The anthropologist formulated four main proposals for modifying the original AID project:

1. Socioeconomic research. It was proposed that a social anthropologist, assigned to the Tindo training and research station, carry out an extensive study of the rural economy and society in the Faranah region. The study would involve the collection of basic information for orienting agronomic researchers, extension service managers, and policy-makers, plus baseline data for evaluating the impact of the project on Guinean agriculture. The socioeconomic research would be carried out during an initial 18-month period, a 6-month midterm evaluation, and at the completion of the 5-year project. The anthropologist also would train Guineans in the collection and analysis of socioeconomic data.

2. Farmer training. It was proposed that the training component of the project be revised to include farmers as a key group of trainees. The teaching curriculum and the demonstration farm at Faranah collège also would be redesigned to correspond more closely to the needs of Guinean agriculture. Farmers destined to serve as extension auxiliaries would receive training at Tindo in techniques of village mobilization, cooperative organization and credit management, and improved farming practices. In this way, the planned training would be directly integrated into extension and production, thus realizing concretely one of the stated goals of the original project. Farm extension and rural sociology would become a part of the curriculum at Faranah collège, complementing the existing courses in the physical sciences. Moreover, the school's training farm would be scaled down considerably from near-monumental proportions--150 cattle, 100 pigs, and 8,000 chickens--to a size that was more technically manageable, financially viable, and appropriate to the level of Guinean smallholder agriculture.

3. Farmer-oriented agronomic research. It was proposed that agronomic research be oriented toward the villages and away

from the research station, in order to involve peasants and scientists in collaborative research. This meant changing the status of the Tindo farm from a substation of the main facility at Foulaya, 340 kilometers away, to a fully autonomous station with responsibility for applied and adaptive research in the Faranah region. It also meant stressing village-level varietal and farm technology experiments rather than on-station testing, as had been envisaged in the original 1975 project. The anthropologist assisted the agronomist and economist in identifying several potentially promising areas of research on an appropriate technical package for smallholders. These included high-yielding varieties of upland and swamp rice developed at the International Rice Research Center (IRRI) (Philippines) and the West Africa Rice Development Authority (WARDA) (Sierra Leone), mosaic-resistant varieties of cassava developed at the International Institute for Tropical Agriculture (IITA) (Nigeria) and in Tanzania, simple water control structures (dams, ponds, leveled perimeters) for wet rice culture and vegetable gardening, expanded use of animal traction, and manually operated rice threshers and de-huskers.

4. Linking extension and production. A small pilot-village farm extension and production scheme in the three PRLs of Nialia arrondissement located nearest to the Tindo station was also proposed. This component, which was not envisaged in the original project, would provide a direct link between the research and training activities at Tindo and smallholder production. Personnel for such a pilot scheme in the three PRLs would consist of about 30 extension auxiliaries or "leading" farmers, 10 extension agents, and a Guinean manager. The extension auxiliaries and agents, trained at Tindo, would meet with participating villagers, conduct field trials, and hold demonstrations. They would also strive to mobilize producers, both men and women, through village associations built upon existing forms of social organization, such as lineages and age-grades.

The four proposals outlined above, plus additional suggestions by the economist (e.g., pricing policy reforms) and by the agronomist (e.g., reorganization of the basic laboratory research program at Foulaya) were embodied in a PID calling for a five-year, $10 million follow-on to the initial AID project (AID 1981). This was submitted to AID in late 1981.

THE LESSONS OF THE GUINEAN CASE

The case of reshaping the USAID/Guinea Agricultural Production Capacity and Training Project summarized above offers lessons concerning the role of anthropological concepts and methods in designing development projects, and on the assumptions underlying foreign aid projects.

Anthropological theory and field methods can play an important role in designing--and redesigning--rural development projects. Once the design team has adopted the approach of gradually modifying existing rural institutions, land tenure systems, and farm technologies, as illustrated above, anthropological field methods can be a useful tool. The authors of the original USAID/Guinea project did not accord importance to understanding rural economic and social structure, since they saw development as taking place through the export of Western farm technology to Guinea. The team assembled to salvage the project, on the other hand, took the study of rural society in the Faranah region as one of the necessary starting points of their work.

Here, anthropology, which seeks to understand socioeconomic behavior intimately and systematically, is particularly well-suited to the task. For the short-term constraints of most project design, the standard anthropological techniques of household surveys, interviews with members of different community groups (women, elders, youths), and observation of daily activities (weeding, harvesting, food preparation) can yield the information needed to formulate a viable project. Through collaboration with other scientists (economists, agronomists, irrigation engineers, soil scientists, plant breeders), anthropological data collection techniques can be applied to other disciplines essential for effective project design. The multidisciplinary or holistic approach usually associated with anthropology, and the emphasis placed by anthropologists on learning from the local population, may even make the anthropologist an appropriate person to serve as a team leader.

The anthropologist can also play a valuable role in enhancing the participation of the people who are the intended beneficiaries. In the design phase, standard skills in organizing household interviews and facilitating community meetings can help to ensure that the villagers' own perceived needs, problems, and proposed solutions are taken into account. The anthropologist can help to design mechanisms for local participation in the implementation and evaluation stages of development projects. Training programs for villagers (leading farmers' courses, adult literacy, nutrition education) and institution-building (farmer and artisan cooperatives, collective works associations) are examples of such mechanisms. One of the anthropologist's prime tasks should be to discover the existing forms of socioeconomic cooperation that could be transformed into new institutions for fostering development.

Each development project is built upon certain assumptions that are inherently ideological. These assumptions can enhance or impair project effectiveness. Neither the foreign aid programs of developed nations, nor the development policies of Third World nations, are ideologically neutral. They express biases toward particular forms of economic organization (individual, collective) and resource ownership (private, state), technical choices (capital- or labor-intensive), forms of participation (broad-based or elitist, single or multi-group), and foreign economic policy strategies (liberal or autarkical). Those involved in international development cannot afford to ignore these ideological biases because they reflect a series of fundamental choices concerning the "good and just" society, and they influence profoundly the shape and effectiveness of development projects.

The original USAID/Guinea project was strongly marked by the belief in the superiority of Western agricultural technology. Foreign aid was thus equated with technological largesse on the part of the donor country, the United States. This view also appears to have been wholeheartedly endorsed by the Guinean president, Sekou Touré, who is said, for example, to have asked for the transfer of American artificial insemination technology to livestock owners in his country.

The United States is not unique in sometimes overlooking socioeconomic realities of the recipient country. Government-owned agricultural schemes backed by the Soviet Union, like Ghana's now-defunct state farms, and labor-intensive, high-yield irrigated rice projects sponsored by the People's Republic of China in Senegal, Burkina Faso, and Sierra Leone, are equally guilty of ignoring local conditions. These foreign aid projects grow out of the prevailing ideology and technical-economic organization of the donor country, and they have also proven inappropriate.

The answer to this dilemma in foreign aid is not for anthropologists to forgo all involvement in development practice. Rather, it is to recognize the ideological nature of foreign aid and to confront the question of what development seeks to achieve. Different visions of what a developed society should be dictate different approaches. It must also be recognized that most rural communities in the Third World today are not standing still; on the contrary, they are changing rapidly. The real question is whether they are changing in ways that meet the aspirations of the local population and of national governments. If not, anthropologists can help to design projects in ways that better realize these aspirations. Anthropologists are well placed to appreciate the fact that prevailing socioeconomic conditions limit the range of possible development project solutions. They should thus strive to elaborate a strategy that identifies realistic goals and a series of project actions to meet them. In this way, the likely outcome of development project choices can be predicted with greater accuracy and the effectiveness of resources invested in foreign aid enterprises enhanced.

Editors' Note to Chapter 2

Dolores Koenig's chapter is based on her work as an anthropologist with a large farming systems research project in Mali. Like Reyna and Waldstein, she presents a case of peasant resistance to state-sponsored development schemes whose aim is to increase cash crop production by smallholders. The resistance manifests itself in efforts by producers in the project zone to promote a diversification of household subsistence strategies rather than increase their dependence on production of crops for sale to state marketing boards. "Stubborn" peasants once again reveal themselves to be strategists in their own right. Their framework in general, however, is not accumulation, but survival. Of course there are exceptions. Koenig's chapter also provides evidence for the argument that development inputs are often appropriated by middle-peasants; this promotes rural differentiation, not a more equitable access to inputs as project planners might wish. She concludes by examining the difficulties of the anthropologist who seeks ongoing contacts with local populations as a research strategy, but who must remain at a distance because of her role as administrator and coordinator for multidisciplinary research teams.

2
Research for Rural Development: Experiences of an Anthropologist in Rural Mali

DOLORES KOENIG
American University

Between 1977 and 1980, I participated in applied research programs within the "West Africa Projects," (henceforth Projects), funded by the United States Agency for International Development (USAID) through Purdue University's Department of Agricultural Economics. The results of the research were to be used by USAID in planning for agricultural development in the West African Sahel. In the following pages I discuss my role as an anthropologist-researcher, some of the research results, and problems encountered by the project.

THE WEST AFRICA PROJECTS

History and Organization

The Projects began in 1976, when the Department of Agricultural Economics at Purdue University received two major

*The research upon which this work is based was funded by USAID contracts AFR-C-1257 and AFR-C-1258 to the Department of Agricultural Economics, Purdue University. I would like to thank N'Golo Traoré, former director of the Institut d'Economie Rurale, in Mali, Abdoulaye Traoré, Assistant Director of the Opération Arachide et Cultures Vivrières (OACV), and Sidiki Maiga, Bouba Diarra, and Yaya Diarra, all of OACV Kita at the time of the study. T. K. White, W. H. M. Morris, and Margaret Saunders made useful comments and criticisms throughout the research, and Ken Jones, Robert Klein, and Chris Picot assisted in computer programming. Allen Fleming, my collaborator on the Kita site, has critiqued my work and assisted me in putting the data into usable form. Tom Painter provided excellent editorial comments on earlier versions of this paper. However, I bear sole responsibility for the interpretations presented here.

contracts from the Sahel Development Program of AID. One contract was for applied research on the socioeconomics of millet and sorghum cultivation in the Sahel, and required descriptive analysis and economic models for use in planning agricultural development programs in sahelian countries. The second contract called for the preparation of a handbook for socioeconomic evaluations of small-scale (less than 1,000 hectares) irrigation projects, including perimeters, irrigated vegetable gardens, and diked and non-diked flood recession fields. The data required for both of these projects were to come from farm management studies done by project personnel at a number of research sites in sahelian countries over a period of several years.

The scale of the West Africa Projects was impressive to an anthropologist accustomed to working alone or with a small team. Data were gathered from at least twelve research sites in three countries (Senegal, Mali, and Burkina Faso) by nineteen researchers during periods ranging from one to three years. Because few researchers remained at any one site longer than a year, sites that were operational for several years usually had several researchers in succession, each supervising a more permanent staff of host-country enumerators. Elsewhere (Chad, Niger, and Senegal), extra support was given to established researchers already in the field, in return for their contribution to the Projects. The Projects also made some pioneering efforts in supplying microcomputers to Malian, Burkinabè, and Senegalese research organizations in order to facilitate data processing in the field (Purdue University 1979; 1980).

The two principal investigators for the Projects, W. H. M. Morris and T. K. White, were agricultural economists. Morris had extensive experience in francophone Africa, while White was new to Africa but had considerable experience with agricultural development in Latin America. Together they developed the general framework for the studies from an economic perspective. Draft questionnaires also were developed, relying heavily on the results of previous work by Norman (1972; 1974a). The principal investigators were receptive to anthropological perspectives and included anthropologists on the research team from the beginning.

The disciplinary backgrounds of research personnel fell into three general groups. Most of the researchers were graduate students in Purdue's master of science program in agricultural economics who had been recruited specifically for the Projects. Knowledge of French was required, and most had previous experience in Africa, often as Peace Corps volunteers. Since they rarely had prior experience with surveys or field research, however, most were placed in structured field situations, working with a senior researcher in the field, a local research institute, or in locations where a previous Purdue researcher already had begun a survey.

The second group of researchers was composed of American-trained anthropologists, three with Ph. D.s and two advanced students who used their research on the Projects to secure data for dissertations. All were from universities other than Purdue. Anthropologists were included in the Projects for several reasons. First, the principal investigators recognized the theoretical importance of sociocultural factors in farmer behavior, particularly in risk avoidance and the adoption of new technology. Second, it was simply easier to find anthropologists who knew how to conduct a survey, could speak French, and were willing to live in isolated areas as field supervisors than it was to find similarly qualified personnel from other disciplines.   The economics students and anthropologists usually spent some time at Purdue during preparation, analysis, and/or write-up phases of the Projects and thus were able to benefit somewhat from comparative perspectives offered by other researchers, but there was no structured encouragement for these researchers to collaborate on their analyses or write-ups.

The final group of researchers was composed of expatriate social scientists, mostly French-trained, who were already located in the areas where they eventually did their Project research. Although contributing significantly to the Projects, they could not benefit from extended collaboration with other researchers because--unlike the first two groups--they spent virtually no time at Purdue, either for preparation or analysis.

In addition to field personnel, there was also at Purdue a small staff attached to the Projects and responsible for centralized data analysis and guidance of student researchers.   At various times this staff included a full-time agricultural economist and/or a full-time anthropologist.   Also included were a librarian, administrative support personnel, and a data processing group.

The principal investigators selected the field sites in light of USAID missions' and host country governments' priorities and in order to observe a variety of representative savanna agricultural conditions.   Thus, for example, of the three sites in Mali, the one at Kita was chosen because the Malian government wanted information on one of its development programs there; the Dogon area was selected because USAID had a local project; and Sikasso was chosen because it was one of the rare areas where flood recession fields had been improved through the use of small dikes.   Once on site, however, the field researchers selected the specific villages to be studied and local interviewers to do the surveys.

Management of the Projects was centralized, and supervision of field researchers was largely the responsibility of Morris, who made trips to West Africa every few months.   Each field researcher was expected to obtain a certain amount of necessary baseline data, but, beyond this, each had a great deal of autonomy in routine, on-site decision-making and selection of supplementary research problems.   Because of their scale, the Projects have produced large quantities of new data on sahelian agriculture, but their scope also raised a number of problems that have required continuous efforts to resolve.[1]

---

[1] I will not deal with the purely managerial problems associated with the Projects, e.g., disbursement of funds, vehicle
(Footnote continued)

Participation in the West Africa Projects

My role in the West Africa Projects began as a field supervisor/researcher at Kita, in Mali, where I worked from June through December 1977. My primary responsibility was to initiate research activities: to gather background information on villages, select the sampling units, choose and train interviewers, and arrange for adaptation of the questionnaire to the local context and its translation into Malinke. While I was in Kita, the research team also pretested the questionnaire, did a complete household and field census in the villages chosen, selected sample families, and began the survey of farm management practices.

Due to other commitments, I was obliged to leave in December, but plans had been made for a student from Purdue to arrive in January and stay for a year to continue the survey during the following agricultural season. These plans fell through, however, and of the original six enumerators, four remained in the field unsupervised until April 1978, when a Malian counterpart who had been trained by a Purdue researcher was sent there. A. Fleming, a student of agricultural economics from Purdue, arrived in Kita to work with the Malian researcher in June 1978 and remained through December.

Under the Malian researcher's supervision, data collection continued through mid-February 1979. Supervisors were not at the site year-round, but were present during the agricultural season (July-November). From this experience it became clear that on a large-scale research project all participants must do their tasks in order to obtain the desired results. This contrasted with my own doctoral dissertation field research, where I alone was responsible for obtaining satisfactory data. Within the West Africa Projects, each level within the personnel hierarchy had to function well to insure acceptable research results, and difficulties at any one level could create problems for the entire project.

Despite the lack of continuous supervision at the Kita site, a large body of data was collected, including a complete census of villages and fields during 1977, and a recensus of most sample households in 1978. From May 1978 through February 1979, 90 sample families in three secteurs de base (village groups that served as units of agricultural extension; henceforth SBs) were visited twice weekly. Information was obtained on agricultural technology and production, time expenditures for agricultural and nonagricultural labor, and household members' incomes and expenditures. Inventories of various items, including livestock, were also completed for the sample families, and all of the fields of a smaller subsample were measured. In two of the three SBs the performance of interviewers was especially good, and it is from

---

(Footnote continued)
procurement, waivers, etc. Suffice it to say that these expanded as the scale of the Projects increased.

these sectors that data have been analyzed. A complementary study of women's roles was also conducted (M. Fleming 1979).

My involvement with the Projects continued after I set up the research site in Kita. I have since participated in the analysis of all data from Kita: data I gathered as well as data collected by the agricultural economist who followed me. In order to avoid unnecessary duplication of work, we initially divided the data analysis on the basis of content. The economist's analyses (A. Fleming 1979a; 1979b; 1980) concentrated on agricultural patterns, including time expenditures, technology, and production, while mine (Koenig 1979a; 1979b; 1980; 1982) concerned census figures, income and expense information, and nonagricultural data. I also plan to analyze data on agricultural labor, thus providing multiple analyses of the same data sets. The data analysis is not yet complete, but the results are relevant for development planning.

RESEARCH IN THE KITA ZONE

The Area

The town of Kita lies approximately 200 kilometers west of Bamako, the capital of Mali, along the railroad from Bamako to Dakar (see Map, Figure 1). The town is the administrative center of the circle of Kita, which is coterminous with Kita Zone of the Opération Arachide et Cultures Vivrières (OACV), the integrated rural development and agricultural agency in the area.[2] The OACV offices for Kita Zone are located in the town of Kita.

The Kita Zone is Mali's major peanut-producing area. It accounts for 50 percent of OACV peanuts and a third of Mali's total production. Sorghum and millet are the major cereals produced and consumed in the area. A wide variety of subsidiary crops also are cultivated in the Kita zone, including maize, rice, and fruits and vegetables grown in irrigated gardens. Throughout its existence, the OACV promoted technical improvements in peanut production, and during the period of research, was promoting techniques to improve grain production.

Kita has a Sudanian climate (900–1,200 millimeters of rain per year), with a long-term annual average rainfall of 1,100 millimeters, giving 135–150 days of useful rain each year (Baron 1976). As a result of the drought during the 1970s, rainfall dropped to 900 millimeters per year during the ten-year period preceding the study. Located between the large, densely populated Niger and Senegal river valleys of western Mali, the Kita

---

[2]OACV was renamed ODIPAC (Opération de Développement Intégré pour la Production Arachidière et Céréalière) after the research was completed.

Figure 1.

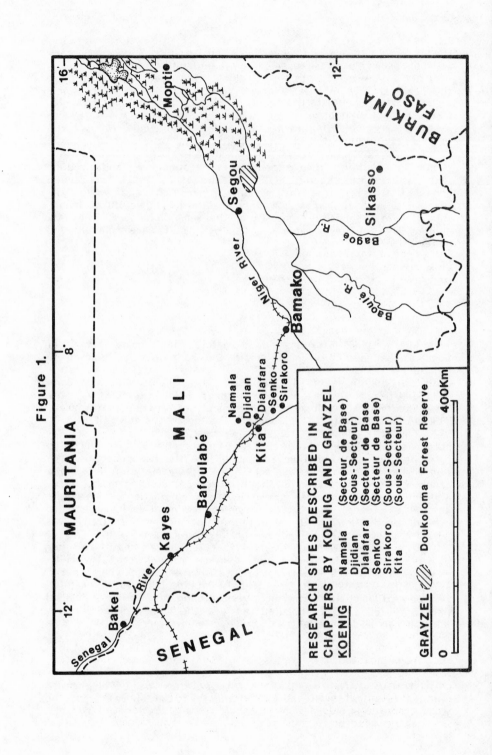

RESEARCH SITES DESCRIBED IN
CHAPTERS BY KOENIG AND GRAYZEL

KOENIG

Namala   (Secteur de Base)
Djidian   (Sous-Secteur)
Dialafara (Secteur de Base)
Senko   (Secteur de Base)
Sirakoro   (Sous-Secteur)
Kita   (Sous-Secteur)

GRAYZEL ▨ Doukoloma Forest Reserve

0   400Km

region has a very low population density--about four people per square kilometer. As a result of this low density, taken together with good rainfall, desirable land is available for agricultural expansion. Under these conditions labor shortages can be particularly acute. Labor scarcity is, in fact, one of the major obstacles to the expansion of agricultural production in the region. Thus, the region has a potential for greater agricultural production if techniques can be found that permit increased output without additional labor.

Selection of Research Sites and Units of Analysis

The villages included in our study were selected with the aid of information provided by the OACV. It was decided to concentrate on the three most accessible OACV subsectors of the Kita Sector of Kita Zone: Djidian, Kita, and Sirakoro (Figure 2). Each subsector was in turn divided into SBs. Each SB included several villages and their dependent hamlets and was staffed by one agricultural extension agent, the SB chief. Because the SB was the basic extension unit, it was adopted as the unit of research. One SB was chosen from each selected subsector: respectively, they were Namala, Dialafara, and Senko.

The three SBs differed in a number of characteristics (see Table 1). Dialafara, for example, showed little adoption of modern agricultural technology, while both Senko and Namala showed significant use. Senko had the highest rate of equipment ownership (plows and multipurpose tool frames), while in Namala people used more nondurable modern inputs (fertilizer, seed dressings, and selected seeds). Dialafara and Senko had significantly better access to unofficial markets than did Namala, which seemed to sell more on the official markets and through the OACV. Persons from Dialafara, only 17 kilometers from Kita town, sold considerable produce there, while villagers from Senko sold in Kita town and at other railroad stations.

For purposes of the research, a household was initially defined as a production unit, i.e., a group subsisting on the produce of the communal fields under the responsibility of one household head. In addition, the household was considered to consist of those individuals who ate from one cooking pot. The first of these two criteria was considered more important if a family did not meet both. The average household in the survey comprised an extended family of 18 persons, of whom 16 were physically present. Persons considered household members commonly included individuals who had migrated, even when they were absent for indefinite or long periods. Two-thirds of the households surveyed reported having members who were absent at the time of the study.

As suggested by data on household size, most households contained extended families, and the typical household head was polygynous. Farm organization was representative of patterns found throughout much of semiarid West Africa: one or several large communal fields are managed by the household head and are worked by most household members. Male and female household

Figure 2

ORGANIZATION OF THE OACV (1977–78)

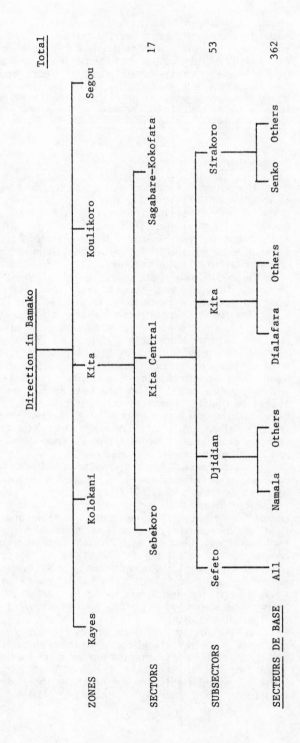
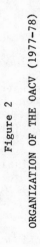

Table 1.   CHARACTERISTICS OF THE THREE SECTEURS DE BASE

Secteur	Rainfall (mm)	Total Population	Number of House- holds	Number of Villages	Primary Ethnic Group	Percent of Households Total	Percent of Households Equipped	Percent of Households Light Themes	Percent of Households No Modern Technology
Namala	737	2,077	154	6	Malinke	100	5	71	24
Dialafara	934	2,313	102	4	Malinke	100	12	48	40
Senko	992	2,293	172	3	Sedentary Peul	100	18	53	29

Source: 1977 Census of Households and Fields. Data on ethnicity and use of technology is self-reported. Rainfall is ten-year average from local meteorological stations.

members may also till individual fields whose produce and resultant cash earnings are theirs. This paper is concerned only with communal fields and their managers, the household heads.[3] It is these fields that produce most of the household's food and income. In the average family of 16 people, there were 4 male and 4 female agricultural workers.

PROJECT FINDINGS

Family Structure and the Adoption of
Productive Innovations by Farmers

Research Findings. The OACV encouraged the adoption of modern agricultural technology, especially in peanut cultivation. This technology fell into two categories: "light themes" (consisting of modern variable inputs), and equipment. The light themes most commonly used were selected seed varieties, seed dressings, and fertilizer. Equipment included an ox-drawn plow, a multicultivator (a multipurpose tool frame), and a seeder.

The farms studied were categorized according to the extent to which equipment and/or light themes were present in agricultural production. "Equipped" farms are those where someone in the household owns equipment. "Light theme" farms are those without equipment, but where someone used at least one of the light themes. "Traditional" farm families neither owned equipment nor did they use light themes: in short, they employed no modern technology in agricultural production.[4] Thus the term "traditional family," used without further qualification, refers only to the kind of agricultural inputs used. More than half (about 58 percent) of the region's households could be classified as light

---

[3]The contribution of women to household production is important; I have treated this elsewhere. See especially Koenig 1979a and 1982.

[4]The sample of farmers for the study was originally stratified according to self-reported information about use of technology. It became evident as the survey progressed that this information was not always accurate, in part because of yearly changes in technology used, and in part because of false reporting. It was generally possible to distinguish people who used light themes from those who did not, even when these people were categorized differently in the initial census. However, it has not yet been possible to differentiate those who simply owned equipment from those who both owned and used it, hence the category of "own" rather than "use" agricultural equipment. A. Fleming (1981) notes that only one farmer from Namala and one from Senko owned but did not use equipment; the situation in Dialafara remains unclear.

theme households (see Table 2); only 127 (30 percent) of the households used no modern inputs. In contrast, relatively few (12 percent) were equipped. In general, equipment and modern inputs were used only by the household head on communal fields, although other men and women sometimes rented or borrowed equipment from a household head.

Cost has been a major barrier to the adoption of equipment. In 1978, the cost of a multicultivator and seeder was about 125,000 Malian Francs (FM), or $305.[5] A subsample of light theme household heads, the group most likely to consider equipment adoption, showed average incomes of 199,000 FM ($486). Since the farmer often had only three years to repay his equipment loan, he would have to pay back 42,000 FM ($102) per year, or about 20 percent of his annual income. In addition, he would also have to provide his own draft oxen. For comparative purposes, it is interesting that this payment of 42,000 FM is higher than the average amount of the largest cash payments (for taxes) reported by light theme farmers--31,300 FM ($76).

Equipped families were more agriculturally productive and wealthier than other families, and they were larger than other households.[6] While the average number of individuals present in all households was 16, this figure for equipped households was 31. On average, 15 persons were present in light theme households, while traditional households averaged eleven.

Equipped households were also more likely to contain extended families. In one extended family pattern frequently observed, the eldest brother is the head, although other adult brothers may remain in the household. Each brother has a wife (or wives) and children, and married children usually remain in the household. Brothers have the option of staying together and forming one farming unit, or of operating independently, with each at the head of his own extended family unit. Our data suggest that among equipped families, brothers were more likely to remain together in a single, larger unit, while among light theme and traditional families they were more likely to have separated.

---

[5]At the time of the study, about 410 Malian Francs (FM) equaled $1.00 US.

[6]The data used here are from several sources. General information on household composition, cropping patterns, and technology use come from the village census of 1977. Income and expense figures are from the study of the Namala SB from May 1978 through February 1979. Production figures are from one interviewer in the Namala SB only, since data from the other SBs were unreliable. Results were corrected for 1978 household size. Therefore, sample sizes used in the text vary widely from example to example. In general, the largest sample with reliable data was used.

Table 2. DEGREES OF AGRICULTURAL MODERNIZATION IN
FARMING AMONG HOUSEHOLDS IN THE KITA ZONE

Household Type	Subclassification	Number of Households	Percent
Equipped			
	Equipped and uses light themes	42	9.8
	Equipped, uses no other modern inputs	9	2.1
Total, Equipped Households		51	11.9
Light Theme			
	Uses three light inputs (seeds, disinfectants, fertilizer)	144	33.6
	Uses one or two of the three light inputs	106	24.8
Total, Light Theme Households		250	58.4
Traditional		127	29.7
Total, All Kita Households in Sample		428	100.0

Source: Census of Households and Fields (self-reported).

There seems to be a feedback relationship between the variables of family size and agricultural production. Large families are able to become more agriculturally productive because they have a larger pool of available labor. Likewise, a more successful family is better able to keep brothers and sons within the family. A younger brother or son in these circumstances may be willing to forgo some of the autonomy gained by heading his own family in return for the material support provided by a more productive extended family.

The major advantage enjoyed by larger families seems to be their absolutely greater access to land and labor rather than their access to different kinds of land, different kinds of labor, or varying proportions of the two. About the same proportions of family members migrated in all categories: 13 percent in traditional, 16 percent in light theme, and 14 percent in equipped families. Likewise, roughly the same proportions of adults were agriculturally active in each family type. The participation of adult males in agricultural production varied from 83 percent in traditional families and 84 percent among light theme users to 88 percent in equipped families. Participation of women in agricultural production ranged from 71 percent in traditional to 75 percent in equipped and 76 percent in light theme families.

The size of land areas cultivated varied according to the number of workers available, regardless of the technology used. The results of analyses done in field size data for our study are not yet available, but researchers observed in a study of Kobiri, a village in Kita Zone, that field size varied directly with the number of workers in the household. Field sizes for all categories of farms averaged about one hectare per worker (Unité d'Evaluation 1977:11).

The larger fields of equipped families result in lower fixed costs of agricultural equipment per hectare of field plowed and per unit of labor. As a result of having access to a greater quantity of human and natural resources, the equipped family has more flexibility over the short term, and should be less likely to suffer from a temporary lack of land, capital, or--most importantly--labor.

The larger family can also be more flexible in the allocation of labor among such tasks as weeding or harvesting during periods of peak labor needs. It may also be better able to deal with labor losses due to sickness. Thus, it is likely that large equipped families not only produce more, but also produce with more reliability and stability from season to season. This hypothesis cannot be confirmed on the basis of data available for a single growing season, but should be evaluated through long-term research.

Looking at the success of equipped families, it is difficult to separate the direct effects of equipment use from those that stem from greater access to labor and land. This would require extended analysis of large equipped versus large non-equipped families, as well as small equipped versus small non-equipped families. However, I shall assume that equipment use does in fact allow a farmer to utilize his resources more effectively, and thus to maintain if not increase his agricultural success within the village.

Agricultural success tended to be viewed by extension agents in terms of greater peanut production and greater cash income. The farmers themselves, however, clearly had a more complex definition of success. First, equipped farmers used equipment to increase cereal rather than peanut production. Although samples were small in both cases, data from our study of the Namala SB, and the study of Kobiri village by the Unité d'Evaluation in Bamako showed similar results. In both studies, the use of equipment was correlated with a much greater increase in sorghum and millet production per capita and per worker (see Table 3). This is shown directly by the ratios of measures of production in equipped families relative to those in light theme families. In both cases, the value is greater for sorghum and millet production than for peanut production. While peanut production increased only slightly in Kobiri village and decreased in the Namala SB, sorghum/millet production increased substantially in equipped families in both places. Yield figures per land unit from Kobiri show the same trend. Peanut yields on communal fields varied from 1,136 kilograms per hectare on light theme farms to 1,165 kilograms per hectare on equipped farms, while millet and sorghum yields were 874 kilograms per hectare on light theme farms and 1,209 kilograms per hectare on equipped farms. Equipped households also were better able to meet nutritional needs than were households using light themes only. Figures from Namala SB show that, on the average, equipped households covered 160 percent of their yearly needs in millet and sorghum, while households using light themes covered 118 percent.[7]

Our data do not allow us to say definitively why the use of equipment should result in greater production differences for grain than for peanuts. However, it appears that equipment may be used to reduce labor time on peanut fields, thus freeing time for grain cultivation. Several factors may be important. First, economic studies in parts of Senegal where the Société de Développement et de Vulgarisation Agricole has programs have shown that plow use does not correlate with an increase in either peanut or millet profitability, but it does in the case of sorghum (Charreau 1974). It is sorghum production that increased most among equipped farmers in Kobiri village, indicating that they are employing their equipment to maximize net return.

Second, because of the rotation pattern suggested by the OACV (peanuts/grain/peanuts/grain/fallow) and commonly followed in the region, increased production of either peanuts or grain often was accompanied by increased production of the other dur-

---

[7]The following requirements were used to calculate nutritional needs: 0.86 kilograms per day for adult males, 0.43 kilograms per day for adult females, and 0.17 kilograms per day for children under 15 (Charlick 1974).

Local Values. Anthropology's concern with local ways of seeing and feeling is a useful and necessary part of development training for several reasons: (a) it improves project planning by taking explicit account of local needs and values, and assigning priority to these; (b) it encourages more insightful examinations of where and how projects go wrong, rather than simply blaming the victim; and (c) it promotes trust, understanding, and respect between change agents and local people.

Language learning, a major point of entry for an under-standing of local ways, received heavy emphasis in program design. We also stressed data-gathering skills, to enable trainees to continue to learn once they were in the field. Thus, for example, we included sessions on how to work with language informants, and how to design, carry out, and interpret communi-ty surveys.

Disassurance. Finally, anthropology--and social science generally--can bring to development efforts what Clarke (1973) has called "disassurance"--a continual calling into question of conventional assumptions and received wisdom. Since questionable notions are not the exclusive preserve of foreigners in Senegal, while we spent considerable time with trainees discussing their own biases toward development and the Third World, we spent at least as much time talking about the biases held by both villagers and government officials. Our goal was not to change those biases, but to understand them, and in so doing, to work more effectively. We did, however, attempt to get trainees critically to examine their own biases, which, as I will note later in this article, proved somewhat difficult.

A variety of anthropological and non-anthropological sources were used in our endeavors to increase the critical awareness of the trainees. The literature made available and used during the training program covered such topics as peasants, community development, field work methods, case study approaches to social change, cross cultural differences and adaptation, and, finally, the political-economic situation of Senegal.[5]

---

[5]Illustrative of the sources we used during the training program are the following by topic:

Peasants: Dalton (1974); Wolf (1966);

Community development and directed change: Arensberg and Niehoff (1964); Brokensha and Hodge (1969); Foster (1973); Goodenough (1963); Huizer (1970); Long (1977); Schwartz (1978);

Case studies of social change: Bernard and Pelto (1972); Brokensha and Pearsall, eds., (1969); Ciparisse and DeGarine (1978); DeWalt (1979); Duvignaud (1972); Hanew and Haney (1978); Paul, ed., (1955); Spicer, ed., (1952); Vengroff (1974);

Discussions of cross-cultural differences and adaptation: Brislin and Pedersen (1976); Freilich, ed., (1977); Hall (1976); Henry and Saberwal (1969); Kimball and Watson (1972);

Writings on development and development anthropology:
(Footnote Continued)

Recognizing the impossibility of covering all aspects of what trainees might feel they needed to know, we concentrated on developing concepts, basic skills and attitudes that would give them a base from which to continue learning on their own.   The literature we selected for the programs provided a background of ideas, facts, opinions and approaches. In some cases, trainees were asked to read and discuss the materials. In others, the training staff read the material, applying ideas and methods to the lesson plans. In direct and indirect ways, therefore, the anthropological approach became one of the bases of program design, as a way of structuring and facilitating the process of trainees' adaptation to their new environment.

Program Structure and Methodology

Training was structured into four overlapping elements: language; cross-cultural awareness; community development; and technical skills. We conducted the ten-week program on a self-contained site adjacent to the regional headquarters of *Animation* in the city of Thies (70 kilometers from Dakar), and followed a tight and intensive schedule.

The first part of each day (8:00-12:00) was devoted to language learning and cross-cultural training. Everyone took French classes, graded according to previous ability. Local languages were taught, first to the few advanced French speakers in the group, and later to everyone. Often a language lesson would be explicitly cross-cultural in content; at other times, separate discussions would be organized on Senegalese traditions, history, manners, and customs. During these sessions, we explored major events in the Senegalese life-cycle, such as birth, circumcision, marriage, and death. At various times, trainees would participate in role-plays; at others, in short field trips to nearby sites. Lunch was eaten Senegalese-style--outside on mats, and with the hands. Afternoons from 3:00 until 6:30 or 7:30 were devoted to technical, cross-cultural and/or community

---

(Footnote Continued)
Belshaw (1974); Bodley (1975); Cochrane (1971), ed., (1976); Pitt, ed., (1976);
Descriptions of fieldwork methods, especially language learning: Glazer (1972); Gudschinsky (1967); Larson and Smalley (1972); Pelto (1970); Samarin (1967); Williams (1967);
Communication and innovation acceptance: Rogers (1962), (1968);
Administration: Schaffer (1973);
Political and economic aspects of Senegalese development: Barker (1977); Cruise O'Brien (1971) (1975).

In addition to these the Peace Corps itself had an impressive collection of cross-cultural training material (see Caplan and Cadden 1976; Peace Corps 1970).

development sessions. Evenings were usually free, except for an occasional film or discussion.

Methodologically, our approach emphasized simplicity, linked concepts, self-pacing, and non-directiveness. For each element of the program, we had a variety of techniques at our disposal: classroom teaching, role-playing, small-group work, practical exercises, independent study, demonstrations, slide shows, guest speakers, field trips, panel discussions, and workshops. In addition, we assembled as much written and visual material as we could (including the sources cited in note 5), creating a small library for trainees to use. Some of the most useful and thought-provoking pieces in the library were essays written by former volunteers describing their work and feelings.

We used two other important teaching techniques. One was the "live-in." On three occasions during the ten-week training program, we arranged to send trainees into rural villages, away from the training site. For each of these "live-ins" we worked with trainees to establish an advance set of learning objectives and arranged feedback sessions afterwards. On the first two "live-ins," each trainee was paired with a volunteer in his or her village; for the last, trainees were on their own in the villages to which they would eventually be assigned.

The other technique concerned the use of the older volunteers already working in Senegal. Older volunteers can have an enormous influence on trainees. While these volunteers are acknowledged by Peace Corps trainers to be extremely useful resource people, their disruptive potential is also recognized, to the extent that in some training programs in other countries, volunteers have actually been barred from the training site.

Older volunteers pose problems for several reasons. Their behavior and physical appearance can be upsetting to trainees, for example. Anecdotal evidence from Senegal indicated that in past programs, more than one trainee left the program because they saw in the older volunteers the image of what they might become if they stayed in the Peace Corps. Older volunteers can also compete with the training staff, by presenting alternative or conflicting information that may confuse or frighten trainees. Volunteers are middlemen or gatekeepers, positioned between the trainees and their new environment; as such, they can to an extent control the type and quantity of information that is transmitted.

Our program design dealt with this in several ways. First, the general outline of training had actually been derived from discussions and interviews that I conducted with several dozen volunteers in the field prior to the start of the program. Second, the core of our training staff was in fact composed of older volunteers. Third, we adopted an open policy toward volunteer visitors to the training site. A steady stream of curious volunteers visited us throughout the program, most of whom stayed a night or two and then moved on. Some were asked to help conduct workshops or discussions with us; all were free to participate in daily activities if they chose. Although volunteers in the immediate area had the most contact with trainees, weekend excursions and live-ins brought more distant volunteers into contact as well.

In these ways, we hoped not only to involve these volunteers in program design, but to ensure that it reflected reality as they had experienced it. This also allowed us to provide some "spontaneous" as opposed to "planned" learning experiences for trainees. We used feedback from the live-ins and from trainee contacts with older volunteers to change the content and the emphasis of the program as necessary. In particular, we used the first live-in to help us structure the community development component, as described below.

Designing the Community Development Component

In effect, trainees themselves designed this program component. Prior to the first live-in, I prepared a short course outline of what I thought trainees should know about project planning and community development, based mainly on three things: (a) my earlier experience as a Peace Corps volunteer in Senegal; (b) my work as a development anthropologist; and (c) interviews with older volunteers in the field. Once the outline was made, I put it aside, to await the completion of the trainees' first live-in experience.

The first live-in matched each trainee with a volunteer in the field, and lasted three days. Trainees were asked to observe as much as possible of the village environment during this time, and to return with suggestions as to what they felt they needed to learn during training in order to live and work in that type of setting. While such a request would have seemed absurd to most of them before the initial live-in, after the live-in they had no problem in generating long lists of topics, questions, and issues.

Trainees and staff sorted these into categories and compared them with the preliminary course outline I had drafted. The two were nearly identical in form; the trainees' list, however, was much more detailed and comprehensive.

Our final outline for the community development component looked like this:

1) AMERICANS AND THE THIRD WORLD
    American world-views
    Ideas of development
    Culture shock
2) THE SENEGALESE ADMINISTRATION
    Government structures and functions
    Resources and support
    The world-views of Senegalese officials
    How to deal with bureaucracy
3) *ANIMATION RURALE*
    The history of the program
    Its basic principles and operation
    Major problems in the program
    Future prospects of the program
4) THE ROLE OF THE VOLUNTEER
    Volunteer activities in the village

       Volunteer roles--what, and with whom
       Working with counterparts
       Role differences between men and women
       Dealing with villagers' expectations
       Role dilemmas

5)   LOCAL-LEVEL CONDITIONS
       Villagers' world-views
       Leadership and authority
       Religion
       Means of livelihood
       Socioeconomic structures
       Major life-events
       Fitting into a village

6)   PROJECT PLANNING AND IMPLEMENTATION
       Project selection criteria
       The project cycle
       Locating and using resources
       Working with people

Here, as in the rest of the program, we emphasized self-awareness and knowledge of Senegal as the keys to success. Recognizing that every village would be in some way unique, we avoided giving cut-and-dried technical "recipes" to trainees as solutions; but laid stress on the identification of group needs and resources as the way to ensure properly planned projects. We showed trainees how to do a community survey in order to gather and analyze information, and we underlined the necessity for local participation, forward planning, consultation with government officials, and provision for the eventual departure of the volunteer as key ingredients.

Teaching methods were basically the same as for the other parts of the training program--lectures, discussions, small-group work, readings, site visits, guest speakers and panelists. Rather than teaching people how to do specific projects, we attempted to impart a certain way of thinking about and planning what one did in the field, why, and with what results. In essence, the community development component was based on the idea that knowledge of the local situation and one's own relationship to it was the most important factor in successful work. And this, of course, was explicitly anthropological in terms of its approach.

REACTIONS TO THE PROGRAM

Trainees, Peace Corps staff, and Senegalese officials all evaluated the program in very positive terms. The success was due to a combination of things: high levels of motivation among trainees, an extensive reservoir of effective teaching materials and methods developed by the Peace Corps office in Dakar, and an experienced and highly competent Senegalese and American training staff. The anthropological perspective that I brought to the program would not have been particularly effective without these other factors.

In the absence of follow-up evaluations or control groups, it is not possible to say very much more about the effectiveness of training, other than that it was *perceived* as effective by all of the groups concerned. What can be discussed in some detail, however, are two related aspects of the way in which the program unfolded. The first of these has to do with the mood of the trainees as they moved through the program, and how this was evidenced in their interaction with older volunteers. The second concerns a number of problem areas that developed as training proceeded, and how we dealt with these.

Trainee Reactions

There were three distinct phases of training, each with its dominant mood or atmosphere.

Phase One: Anxiety and Enthusiasm. The initial phase was marked by a high degree of trainee enthusiasm, coupled with general anxiety. This phase lasted between one and two weeks, ending for most trainees with the successful completion of the first live-in. Staff efforts concentrated on making trainees comfortable and maintaining a reassuring environment. For their part, trainees were intensely curious about everything, and directed a constant stream of questions at staff and visiting volunteers.

This interaction between trainees and older volunteers was one of the most interesting aspects of the program. The two groups, ostensibly from the same cultural background, found each other odd at first. "They move like they're under water," a trainee said to me one day, commenting on the older volunteers' languid pace. Older volunteers found trainees equally strange. "Jogging?" muttered one as he watched a group of trainees head down the road in the early morning. "Where do they get the energy?"

Trainees lost much of their initial apprehension with the first live-in, however. They had lived in a village--however briefly --and had experienced the world "out there." They were eager to explore this new environment, but now realized that they lacked certain basic skills. They therefore returned to the training site with even more questions than before; but this time, questions with a sharper focus.

Phase Two: The Doldrums. The climate, the change of diet, the heavy training schedule, and the onset of minor ill-nesses began to take their toll. It was hot, there was no rain, and a dry wind carried dust everywhere. Trainees grew listless, and complained of the heat and the long hours. Excitement and energy turned to weariness and irritability. The end of training seemed a long way off, and little progress was apparently being made in learning languages that had seemed so exotic and interesting a few weeks before. Some trainees complained of being discouraged.

It was evident to the staff, however, that trainees were making good progress, whether or not they themselves were aware of it. Their language ability, for example, was improving rapidly. This in turn was opening new doors for them; they could now travel and explore on their own, bargain for things in the market, and make Senegalese friends. At the same time, they were developing finer discriminations; trainees were beginning to focus on specific aspects of their environment, instead of simply being overwhelmed by it all.

Frustration reached a high level during this phase, however. Many trainees still expected direct, yes-or-no answers to their questions, and grew impatient when no clear replies were forth-coming. They also grew impatient with the training process in general.

The war stories and gratuitous advice offered by older volunteers began to grate, as trainees increasingly wished to become volunteers on their own terms. They resisted staff suggestions that they were still unprepared to fend for them-selves. The second village live-in took place during this tense phase; once again, the trainees spent the weekend with older volunteers in their villages. Significantly, many trainees re-turned from this live-in with a number of critical observations about the life-styles and working methods of the volunteers in whose villages they stayed. These included claims that some volunteers were too directive in their work, or too insensitive to villagers' real needs. Other trainees questioned whether villagers would be able or willing to continue their projects after the volunteers left. More than anything else, these comments demon-strated to us how far trainees had come in their ability to make sense of their new environment.

Phase Three: Departure. Phase three began around the time of the third and final village live-in. Trainees were now expected to spend the weekend on their own, in the village to which they would eventually be assigned. The mood of the group returned to what it had been initially--enthusiasm mixed with apprehension. Apprehension, because it was time to leave the now-familiar training site for the world of the village; enthusiasm, because many trainees now recognized that they had made substantial progress, and were eager to test their skills on the outside.

The excitement and anxiety increased after the final live-in, as the time for final departure drew near. Training ended with a swearing-in ceremony, followed by a celebration that included a dinner and a series of highly entertaining skits presented by the "new" volunteers. The next morning, an exhausted staff stared dully at each other as the noise of the last departing bush-taxi echoed within the confines of the now-deserted training site.

Staff Assessment. After training was over, the staff held a week-long post-mortem. While the training was evaluated by everyone as highly successful overall, a number of issues did inevitably emerge. Four of these were particularly noticeable during training. All but one of them ceased, in effect, to be a problem by the end of the program.

1) Lack of Structure. Somewhat to our surprise, trainees did not object to helping plan the training program. Many of them were initially dismayed, however, by the discovery that the *Animation* program for which they were destined had low govern-ment priority and provided very little in the way of concrete guidelines for action. Trainees rightly wondered whether they were needed in Senegal, and just how effective their work was

likely to be. Understandably, most trainees wanted structure.
For some of them, this was the first time they had ever really
been on their own; for almost everyone, it was the first experience working in a foreign country.

Discussions on this point managed to convey the staff's view
that lack of structure need not be a disadvantage, since it allowed wide latitude to individual volunteers, enabling them to
respond to truly local needs instead of following a national plan
that might be inappropriate locally. Trainee observations of older
volunteers at work during the live-ins also gave them a sense of
the range of possibilities inherent in their work situation. By the
end of the training program, few if any of the trainees continued
to be bothered by this lack of structure.

2) Non-Directiveness. The non-directiveness of many parts
of the program bothered some trainees; they initially resisted the
idea that they should assume prime responsibility for their
experience in Senegal. This was especially true of the community
development component, which was regarded as less "technical"
than other program components. There were correct and incorrect ways to use language, appropriate and inappropriate
manners, and right and wrong ways to mix cement, but there
seemed to be no clear-cut recipe for doing community development
and planning projects.

Trainees tended initially to seek clear and unequivocal
answers to their questions, resisting suggestions that there was
no single explanation or course of action that would be right in
all circumstances. As it was our intention to provide an orientation rather than a set of rules, we resisted trainee demands for
precise answers where we felt none existed. Instead, we urged
trainees to apply basic principles and discover answers for themselves. The trainees were surprised to find that the older volunteers from whom they sought answers were, if anything, even
more vague than the staff. Gradually, with the rise in confidence that the village live-ins gave them, better feedback from
older volunteers, and improvement in language ability, trainees
came to depend less and less on staff, and to be more willing
--and able--to strike out on their own.

3) Working within the System. Here, problems centered on
several aspects of the Senegalese work environment, in particular
those relating to administrative structure and protocol, and local
attitudes to time. Trainees complained that instead of conducting
meetings in a straightforward fashion, speaking to the point, and
answering simple questions directly, Senegalese officials tended to
be excessively formal, long-winded, and elliptical in their replies
to direct questions. They noted with frustration that officials
preferred to talk about how the government system was *supposed*
to work rather than about how it *really* worked.

Trainees also encountered the frustration of working within
an unfamiliar set of bureaucratic rules. Administration in Senegal
is highly centralized and hierarchical; top-down decision-making
is the norm, with elaborate rules governing contacts between
offices. One result of this is that there is little room for independent initiative at the lower echelons. Although the lack of
structure in their program allowed volunteers considerable

personal leeway, trainees soon realized that in their official contacts with government, they occupied the lower rank. They therefore had to accept the importance of established procedures, of following the Senegalese administrative *voie hierarchique*, and of according the proper deference to both the procedures and the officials involved.

The problem was compounded by the fact that most trainees had had little experience with bureaucracy of any kind. To the extent that many of them arrived in Senegal with other administrative models in their minds--models that were often highly normative and sometimes wholly theoretical--they felt uncomfortable with the Senegalese system.

We dealt with this directly, and in a decidedly anthropological fashion. As we described the structures and functions of the Senegalese government system to the trainees, we also laid stress on understanding the world-view of the officials in the system. After meetings with officials, we held feedback sessions where trainees discussed their perceptions and reactions. Our training staff--especially the Senegalese members--responded with insights and interpretations of what had happened. Although we were careful to avoid giving the impression that trainees must *agree* with administrative arrangements, we urged them to first *understand* how officials saw themselves and their work, and to accept the necessity of working within the system to the greatest extent possible.

Although by the end of training few trainees had accepted "the system" wholeheartedly, their contacts with older volunteers had shown them that it was necessary to work within the existing framework, and had also taught them some practical strategies for doing so.

Finally, trainees had some problems with the Senegalese approach to time. Western ideas about time have been often mentioned, of course, as an aspect of cross-cultural adjustment. Alverson (1977) for example, has examined differences in perceptions of time between Peace Corps volunteers and rural Tswana. Senegal's trainees experienced the same general sorts of difficulties as those discussed by Alverson in making the transition from time as quantity to time as event.

Questions such as, "How long will it take to do this?" "When will the meeting start?" and "When will the governor come?" were typical of trainees' wish to order events along familiar lines. They were initially frustrated when they found that few other people--either volunteers or Senegalese--were willing to give them precise answers. From volunteers, the reply was usually, "It'll happen when it happens." Senegalese, if pressed, would sometimes provide a precise--but inaccurate--answer out of politeness. Here again, exposure to the quite different attitudes of older volunteers gradually made trainees more accepting of different ways of thinking about time. By the end of training, a considerable modification of some trainees' own attitudes was evident.

4) <u>Attitudes to Development</u>. This was the area where, at the end of training, there was still a gap between what we intended and what we accomplished. The gap appeared most

noticeably in the community development component of the program, where, among other things, we attempted to uncover and discuss assumptions that trainees held concerning development and the Third World.

Inviting the trainees to examine their assumptions in this regard proved a difficult task. Our training evaluations brought this out, as trainees indicated that they found this part of the community development component to be less relevant and useful than the others.

To an extent, of course, our efforts might have been improved through better teaching techniques. I tend to think, however, that we were less successful here because our examination of American attitudes directly confronted trainees' self-concepts, and may have actually increased rather than diminished their anxiety and uncertainty. Although the trainees were highly enthusiastic about the volunteer experience, they were reluctant --initially at least--to examine certain of their attitudes and motivations.

Trainees initially assumed that what Senegalese peasants needed was somehow identical with what they as volunteers had to give; that American know-how was both superior and relevant in this context; and that this know-how would be perceived as such by the Senegalese and accepted rationally, once communication had been established. Many of them also assumed that any changes that took place during their volunteer experience would be in one direction only--from them to the Senegalese.

These attitudes were reinforced to some extent by Peace Corps recruiting propaganda and by the very nature of the work environment. Since most trainees came to the program with a "project orientation"--a need to "do something" as a volunteer, projects became not only a way of structuring their experience and legitimating their presence in Senegal, but also an important final step in self-definition, of becoming a "true volunteer." If anything, the structure of our training program probably lent additional emphasis to this concern.

Given this situation, it is not surprising that trainees' attitudes were slow to change, but training was only one part of a much longer process of change in attitudes and orientations, one that lasted throughout the volunteers' two-year term of service.

TRAINING PROGRAMS AND ANTHROPOLOGY

Anthropology has much to contribute to the design of training programs such as the one I have been describing, and these programs, in turn, have something to say to anthropology. One of the clearest examples of this concerned the changes that trainees went through as they became volunteers, and how these were accomplished. There is a potentially rich field for investigation here, centering on the process of transition that volunteer groups undergo during their training and subsequent service. For the rest of this section, I would like to discuss several aspects of this transition, and what they may tell us about the overall process of cross-cultural adjustment.

It is generally agreed by volunteers and staff that the Peace Corps experience is a time of profound personal change for most volunteers. Non-volunteers, moreover, are generally assumed to be unable fully to comprehend the nature of the changes that volunteers undergo in the field (Alverson 1977). If it is obvious that volunteers undergo some fairly important changes during this time, it is not at all clear what these changes consist of, and how and why they occur.

For our trainees, the process involved both individual changes and the development of a group awareness incorporating shared points of view and shared norms of behavior--in other words, a subculture. Only part of this subculture came to them directly through the efforts of the training program; a significant --and perhaps major--portion came from the group of older volunteers with whom they were in daily contact. In this trainee-volunteer interaction, the training program per se provided a venue, a framework, within which an essentially "volunteer subculture" was transmitted to newcomers.

According to our trainees, many of them joined the Peace Corps expecting to find out at first hand what overseas life is like. To a greater extent than many of them realized, however, this first-hand experience was actually accomplished and mediated through a group. Our trainees made a transition, not from American to Senegalese culture, but to a third, volunteer culture (or more accurately, subculture), that was transmitted to them through the networks they established with older volunteers.

What are some of the main features of this volunteer subculture? Volunteers modify their language usage, for example, to include a variety of French and local terms.[6] They adopt varieties of Senegalese dress--*pagnes* for women, *khaftans* and Moslem trousers (*chaaya*) for men.[7] Many volunteers also wear

---

[6] I am not speaking here of language *use* within the volunteer group itself. All volunteers in Senegal learn to speak both French and local languages (principally Wolof) with a generally high degree of fluency, and use these languages daily in their contacts with Senegalese. Older volunteers, however, speak a language among themselves known as "Franglof," consisting of an English base plus large numbers of French and Wolof terms and constructions. In its most developed form, Franglof can be virtually incomprehensible to uninitiated Americans. This specialized vocabulary serves, among other things, as a means of marking group boundaries.

[7] The clothing preferences of Senegal's volunteers give them a particular "look" that distinguishes them from other foreigners. Like language, dress provides an easy means of group identification, and like language, it was one of the first things
(Footnote Continued)

teere, the Koranic charms made by local marabouts. Volunteers assimilate Senegalese attitudes toward work and time, becoming more task- and event-oriented, more relaxed, and more un-hurried. Key features of Senegalese daily life--gift-giving, hospitality, greeting, visiting, sharing--assume more importance among them.[8] To some extent, they also absorb other, more diffuse attitudes from the Senegalese around them--local stereo-types of other ethnic groups, distrust of government officials, and regional pride, for example.

Other aspects of Senegalese life are usually rejected by volunteers, however. Few of them become Moslems, for example, and most do not observe Ramadan or the various dietary prohibi-tions. Few volunteers marry Senegalese. Volunteers do not usually accept Senegalese notions of causality or the supernatural (although in an ethnographic sense, they may know a great deal about these). Thus, while many volunteers may indeed believe--or hope--that their *teere* charms will help bring them good for-tune, few of them believe that a powerful *teere* will prevent a knife or bullet from entering the skin, although many Senegalese believe this. Volunteers, in other words, keep their Western "scientific mentality" more or less intact, adding to it bits and pieces of Senegalese lore. In the same way, volunteers generally do not modify their original concepts of health or disease causa-tion to conform to those of the Senegalese.

The subculture created by volunteers thus contains both Senegalese and American elements, while remaining distinct from either. The process of transition to this subculture begins in training, and continues over the term of the volunteer's service, as new elements are added. Eventually, many volunteers begin to see more and more of a perceptual, philosophic, and behavioral gap between themselves and other overseas Americans such as diplomats, tourists, businessmen and AID officials.

(Footnote Continued)
trainees noticed about older volunteers. "Did it ever occur to you," a trainee said to me one day as we watched a group of male volunteers playing volleyball, "that all the *Animation* volunteers look alike?" The volunteers in question were uniformly dressed in *chaaya* and rubber sandals, and were bare-chested, tanned, bearded, and had short-cropped hair. In addition, each volunteer wore one or more *teere* charms attached to an arm or leg.

[8]A small but significant example of this concerns eating habits. Eating alone, eating in front of other people, or refusing food are frowned upon in Senegal. At best, it is considered very impolite; at worst, it may indicate witchcraft or mental illness. Volunteers learn these attitudes, and some of them internalize them to a surprising degree. I left the Peace Corps in 1968, but even today, I find it hard to eat in front of other people in a room without at least offering to share my food. Numerous other ex-volunteers from Senegal have told me of similar feelings.

To judge from anecdotal evidence, many volunteers change even more in relation to people living in the United States itself. The "re-entry shock" that volunteers returning from the field sometimes experience can be more severe than initial culture shock overseas. To my knowledge, however, no in-depth studies of the re-entry phenomenon exist.

This volunteer subculture is transmitted to newcomers through informal networks that develop during the training program, where the transition is most directly visible, and slowly draw the two groups together. At the start of the program, trainees and older volunteers regarded each other warily. In my early conversations with trainees, some of them expressed misgivings about the Peace Corps based largely on what they imagined the experience had done to the older volunteers they were now seeing. Trainees seemed to know intuitively that the older volunteers were the sort of people they would eventually become if they stayed with the program. Thus, trainees paid close attention to—and commented on—older volunteers' dress, attitudes, and speech patterns. Older volunteers, in turn, commented on the naivete of trainees, and their obsession with irrelevancies such as clean toilets, cold beer, and hot water. Trainees' questions were difficult to answer; volunteers' replies not clearly understood.

As training progressed, this began to change. A turning point came soon after the first live-in. Not only did trainees' self-confidence grow enormously as a result of this, but there was a markedly greater acceptance of trainees by older volunteers from this point on. Two weeks after their arrival, the trainees produced a series of skits where older volunteer attitudes and mannerisms were ingeniously lampooned. Everyone was impressed by how acutely perceptive these sketches were.

As the trainees learned enough of the volunteer context to make communication easier, the two groups began to interact more easily. Trainees began to adopt some volunteer mannerisms; they bought Senegalese clothes, began to use local expressions, and stopped worrying so much about the toilets. Trainee questions and volunteer answers now seemed to make more sense to both groups. Inevitably, the decisive shift in trainee consciousness came when they began to refer to living in their assigned village as "getting out into the real world"—a notion many of them would have found outlandish two months previously.

The third village live-in included a key ritual, that of "adoption" into a Senegalese family living in the village. This arrangement has evolved over the years, and is now part of Peace Corps policy in Senegal. Volunteers join a village family, sharing their house, their food, and—inevitably—their concerns. They contribute a part of their living allowance for family expenses. They are given a Senegalese name by their family, and are addressed by the appropriate kin terms. Volunteers and staff agree that this arrangement greatly contributes to the ease with which most volunteers adapt to Senegalese life.

Soon thereafter, training ended with an official American ceremony at which trainees were "sworn in" as volunteers, and a celebration[9] during which another series of satirical skits was presented.[9]

The transition described above was for me one of the most striking aspects of training. Why does such a subculture come into being, and what purposes does it serve? On the one hand, of course, the structure of the training situation itself could be said to promote the creation of such a subculture. Trainees are temporarily segregated from the larger Senegalese world, in a situation where, initially at least, their main sources of information about the "outside" come from staff and older volunteers.

At the same time, trainees have literally no choice about whether or not to "adapt" to Senegal; it is part of what it means to be in the Peace Corps. Although volunteers have some latitude as to the type of adjustment they make, individually and as a group, their resources and work assignments make it inevitable that they live and interact as close to the grass roots as possible.[10]

On the other hand, however, the volunteer subculture is not simply an artifact of the training situation; it exists "out there" among the volunteers, and is functional in training in several important ways:

---

[9]Classically-minded anthropologists would, I think, be impressed with the degree to which this process resembles Van Gennep's three-phase breakdown of a rite of passage. In the first, or *separation* phase, "initiates" were taken from their families to a strange place where none of their previous knowledge or skills were deemed useful by the strangers who assumed control over their lives, and who were designated their "teachers." In the second, or *transition* phase, initiates became highly dependent on these teachers, for they could not grasp the totality of what was happening to them, did not know how to ask the right questions, and felt inadequate and insecure. At various stages in this phase, secret knowledge was transmitted to the initiates, drawing them closer to the stranger/teachers who now formed their main reference group. Eventually, the initiates perceived themselves as having changed; during the third, *incorporation* phase, this perception was confirmed by their teachers. Initiates were welcomed into the new group in an elaborate ceremony, which included feasting, demonstrations of their new abilities, and poking fun at their former teachers. Initiates now dressed, talked, and behaved differently, and assumed new names.

[10]This is in marked contrast to certain other groups of foreigners--US diplomats and AID officials, for example--where government policy concerning salary levels, living conditions, and logistic support seems designed to maintain people in an essentially self-contained American environment while living overseas. Tendler (1975) provides an interesting and detailed discussion of how this works for AID staff overseas.

1) The subculture provides *support* for trainees during their initial phase of anxiety. Trainees are reassured by the presence of Americans who possess certain strategies for "making it" in the new environment. Although communication between the two groups is difficult at the early stages, trainees are very interested in learning what these strategies are.

2) The subculture provides an *ideology* for trainees, replacing or modifying their original expectations and imaginings, few of which are confirmed or reinforced in the new environment. Trainees often remarked to me that Senegal was different from what they had imagined (or been led to believe by Peace Corps) while in the United States. The volunteer subculture helps explain to them who they are, why they are doing what they are doing, and what the future will be like. It provides, in other words, a context for much of the learning that takes place.

3) Finally, the subculture provides not only support and a context, but detailed *information* to trainees about the many unfamiliar and sometimes threatening things in their new environment. In a process similar to that by which novice drug users learn to experience an unfamiliar drug from others, trainees literally learn how to experience Senegal.

I suspect that the role played in training of this kind by such subcultures is more important, and occurs more frequently, than most trainers realize. Peace Corps trainees most emphatically do not learn about Senegal "first hand"--at least, not initially. Instead, they learn a *version* of Senegalese reality through interactions with older volunteers. And although individuals are free to learn on their own following training, training sets the initial parameters within which much of this subsequent learning takes place.

One would have to observe this process over time and in several Peace Corps contexts to know more about the role of such subcultures. It seems clear, however, that many of the difficulties in adjustment to local conditions described, for example, for volunteers in Botswana (Alverson 1977) are coped with in Senegal by means of the volunteer subculture. Rather than being at odds with Senegalese life, the subculture accepts important aspects of it, and provides support, information, and direction to newcomers. By so doing, it encourages and enables volunteers to adapt relatively easily to local conditions.

This is not to say, of course, that volunteers in Senegal are without adjustment problems, but merely that these seem less severe than in several other countries where I have observed volunteer life. In particular, Senegal's volunteers do not constitute a group whose overt attitudes and behavior run counter to accepted Senegalese standards, as has sometimes been the case elsewhere.

More work is therefore needed to answer the question--which is well outside the limited scope of this paper--of why and how subcultures vary in the degree to which they promote cross-cultural adaptation. It seems probable that not only do subcultures vary from one situation to another, but also that they may change over time within a single context. A variety of factors are undoubtedly at work here, whose range and importance could only be assessed through comparative research.

In Senegal, the cross-cultural transition seems to involve changes at several levels, over an extended period of time. Fairly superficial, external levels of change, such as in eating habits, dress, and vocabulary, occurred first. Other changes, such as attitudes to time, were beginning to occur by the time the training program ended. Deeper changes in attitudes and values, however, either do not occur at all--as in the case of ideas of causation or of the supernatural--or they take longer to appear than the ten-week period allowed.

A good example of a deeper change that *does* occur, but only after some time, is that of volunteer attitudes to development and Third World. Earlier, I noted that this presented an area of some difficulty during the training program, and that, in contrast to the other problem areas I observed, trainee attitudes did not seem to change much during the program.

This problem has been noted by Rhoades (1978), who characterizes Peace Corps volunteer attitudes as an idealistic "Albert Schweitzer Complex," originating in an ethnocentric model of development deeply rooted in American society's notions of inherent superiority and encouraged by Peace Corps recruiting tactics. Rhoades blames this complex for many of the frustrations and difficulties encountered by volunteers overseas, and urges an end to recruiting propaganda and an increased dose of realism in training.

Rhoades is correct when he says that volunteers enter the Peace Corps with unrealistic notions of what development work is about. He is also correct in claiming that this is exacerbated by Peace Corps recruiting procedures. It is therefore not surprising that trainees did not lose the "Albert Schweitzer Complex" during training, for that would have entailed shedding a heavy load of assumptions, values, and preconceptions, many of them bound up with personal self-image.

What Rhoades does not mention, however, is that volunteer attitudes *do* change over time. Most volunteers--in Senegal, at least--undergo distinct attitudinal changes on the subject of development as a result of their village experiences following training. They gain a deep and unique understanding of one small segment of Third World life at the grass roots, and as a result, they often become increasingly critical of the context within which much development work takes place. This was quite noticeable during training itself, as trainee world-views confronted those of older volunteers. It was also evident in what older volunteers wrote for us on the subject of development. Here, for example, is what one two-year volunteer had to say:

> From work and thought I advise only this--if you think of your coming to Africa as a means of uplifting an underdeveloped people, then unpack your bags and remain at home. The smacking condescension of many Westerners here stands as one great insult to a very dynamic people with a rich culture and a heritage as deeply felt as any. Still, the experts from the powerful nations pour in--all with the same

paternal attitudes, full of misplaced sympathy and even a
personal distaste for the life of the common man. No wonder
that so many development efforts have gone awry, being
based on such ignorance. Come, then, to work with your
brothers and equals--it's very satisfying. (Peck, n.d.)

CONCLUSIONS

Successful development involves intense and sustained interaction between people. Where foreigners are involved, their
effectiveness in this interaction depends to a great extent on
their cross-cultural adaptation. This article has discussed how
this adaptation took place for Peace Corps trainees, and how
anthropology was used to facilitate this process.

While anthropology is indeed useful in training program
design, it is only one part of what promotes cross-cultural transition. Equally important is the informal network of information,
values, and relationships that I have termed the "volunteer
subculture." Let me conclude by offering some thoughts on the
significance of this fact.

Although largely unrecognized in the literature, such subcultures will be familiar to anyone who has lived in an expatriate
community. They probably exist in a variety of cross-cultural
situations, and play an important role in them as a means for
transmitting information and attitudes to newcomers, and for
defining and maintaining group boundaries. It would be interesting, therefore, to identify and learn more about such subcultures
and how they operate within such groups as the diplomatic corps,
the overseas business community, and the large aid agencies;
situations where, in each case, cross-cultural sensitivity is presumed to be necessary for effective performance. Findings could
be compared with what we already know about such topics as
ritual, socialization, and acculturation in other contexts.

Although subcultures such as the one I have described can
promote cross-cultural adaptation, they may also operate as
"counter-cultures," and work against it. Anthropologists know
that development agencies have cultures and structures just as
the recipients of agency programs do; we also know that, like
other cultures, agencies have both "normative" and "pragmatic"
rules. Subcultures may, therefore, diverge considerably from
more "normative" agency values--to the extent that they even
become subversive. Since the information and values they trans-
mit will have a significant effect on the ways in which new members adapt, it seems important for anthropologists to determine
how and why such subcultures arise, what functions they perform, and whether they promote or discourage cross-cultural
adaptation.

Finally, subcultures have implications for training program
design. Programs reflecting only "normative" ideologies will
inevitably be undermined, if an alternative "pragmatic" view
comes across through more informal networks. In Senegal volunteer subculture was not at odds with agency policy, and therefore
functioned as an important and positive factor in the success of

training.   To the extent that a serious discrepancy in views exists, however, trainers will have to decide whether to restructure the training program to include such alternative viewpoints, or whether to isolate the trainees, distance the dissidents, and attempt to block the operation of the informal network.   Since attitudinal change in trainees continues long after the end of a training program, such attempts to prevent "contamination" are probably doomed to failure.

Although the material I have presented here is specific to the Peace Corps in one country, the mechanisms and processes observed there will have wider relevance. Any development agency operating in a culturally different environment will need to pay close attention to the conditions under which the attitudes and orientations of its personnel persist or are modified in response to that environment.   Training--especially if grounded in an anthropological approach--can be of great value, but the role and importance of subcultural networks also needs to be recognized and dealt with, to ensure a successful transition.   The volunteer experience--in which this cross-cultural transition is both explicit and dramatic--has considerable relevance for development work in a variety of contexts.   It deserves more attention from anthropology than it has received thus far.

Editors' Note to Chapter 5

The chapter by Abe Waldstein describes strategies of peasant settler households to deal with the overweening presence of a Senegalese state corporation (SAED) for developing the delta region of the Senegal river. SAED is the result of a state strategy to increase production of rice and other crops. SAED decides what crops will be planted and where, and provides seeds, insecticides, credit, and other inputs, to be reimbursed to SAED at harvest time. SAED decides when settler labor will be used for key operations, and when and for how long crops on the perimeters will be irrigated. Finally, SAED insists that settlers' production be sold to SAED alone, and closes the bargain by imposing prices lower than those paid elsewhere. The appropriation of basic decision-making in production, which is the hallmark of river basin development schemes in Africa, is also described by Reyna in his chapter. What are the alternatives to these expensive, autocratic structures? Waldstein proposes that the scale of intervention be reduced. If these projects were smaller, he argues, producers would have greater flexibility, and reduce their dependence on capital-intensive techniques that alienate peasant knowledge from its application to local conditions of production in light of local limitations. Waldstein goes on to argue that the interests of SAED planners and settlers on the schemes are fundamentally opposed. These lines of argument raise important issues about the consequences of continued dependence on outside sources of financial and technical support, whatever the size of the program. Under these circumstances, is smaller really better?

5
Irrigated Agriculture as an Archetypal Development Project: Senegal

ALFRED S. WALDSTEIN
United States Agency for International Development

For several generations, governments in the West African Sahel have been casting covetous eyes on the waters of the great hydrological systems of the region. The governments have wanted to tame these waters in the hope of transforming the regional subsistence economy into an active part of the world market economy, in the expectation that this will result in greater material security for the Sahel.

These desires have taken form in efforts to develop irrigated agriculture in the basins of the several major river systems of the region. Created in 1932 to develop the interior delta of the Niger River in Mali, the *Office du Niger* administers the oldest projects of this kind in West Africa. It has never achieved the goals set out for it. De Wilde (1967) and Hammond (1959, 1960) discuss the shortcomings of these schemes from technical, economic, and social points of view.

In more recent years, interest in extending irrigated agriculture in the Sahel has been growing, in spite of the questionable social and economic records such projects have established. One of the areas where interest has been strong since the end of European rule has been the Senegal River Valley. In January 1965, the Senegalese government created the *Société d'Aménagement et d'Exploitation des Terres du Delta* (SAED), which was given a mandate to develop all aspects of irrigated cultivation in the Senegal River Delta, from construction of hydro-agricultural works to marketing the harvest. In 1975, the Senegalese government extended SAED's authority to include the hydro-agricultural development of the entire length of the Senegalese bank of the Senegal River. In the meantime, the Mauritanian government had created its counterpart to SAED to oversee the hydro-agricultural development of its bank of the river.

Irrigation projects raise a number of important issues for the producer. Most important is the question of what are the objectives of those sponsoring hydro-agricultural development. Assuming the goals are multiple and not in logical conflict, the question becomes what producer interests must be addressed in order to achieve these objectives. This question turns on the

more abstract issue of how plans for hydro-agricultural articulate
with theoretical approaches to development in general.

The research on which this paper is based was conducted in
the zone of Kassak in the Senegal River Delta (Waldstein 1983).
This field experience in an irrigated agriculture project along the
Senegal River led directly to the author's recruitment by a large
engineering firm with a contract to do the environmental impact
analysis for the proposed integrated development programs of the
Senegal River Basin. The author was responsible for the socioeconomic analysis volume of this study (Gannett, Fleming, Corddry and Carpenter, Inc. 1980). The Senegal River Delta research was also the basis for a general study of agricultural intensification projects across the Sahel focusing on the question of
who are supposed to be the beneficiaries of development projects
(Waldstein 1980). This study was commissioned by the Regional
Economic Development Services Office for West Africa of the United States Agency for International Development (AID). The author has also participated in the design of irrigated rice projects
in Guinea-Bissau and in the Casamance Region of Senegal.

The present paper focuses on the role of irrigated agriculture in the overall subsistence strategy of the households in the
zone of Kassak in the Senegal River Delta. This role has evolved
through an interplay between producer interests with the ecological, technical, economic, and administrative constraints of the
project and the terms of production within it. Producers in the
scheme deploy whatever means they have at their disposal to optimize their access to and hold on material resources. They must
provide for the welfare of their families and seek to do so with
the greatest margin of security possible. However, such producer goals are not necessarily congruent with the goals of donor
agencies seeking to realize an acceptable return on their investments. Linkages that exist between donor agencies and national
institutions determine the parameters of production in a particular
instance and terms of access to them. As a result, the linkages
with donor agencies and national institutions are the single most
disruptive factor to producer household subsistence strategies in
affected areas.

GENERAL BACKGROUND

The Senegal River Delta Milieu

The Senegal River Delta is an almost featureless plain, de-
void of all but the hardiest vegetation. It owes its formation in
the last 15,000 years to the retreat of the sea under pressure
from progressive alluvial deposits brought by the river from the
interior (Diagne 1974). The soils of the delta are high in clay
content and laced with salt. The high salinity has prevented
cultivation of all but one-twentieth of the total 188,000 hectares in
the delta.

Before 1964, the delta was occupied only by several groups
of transhumant pastoralists and about a dozen fishing villages.

Hervouet (1971) estimates that in 1964, before the construction of the irrigation works, the population density of the delta as a whole was 5.4 people per square kilometer, with a composition of two-thirds Wolof, one-sixth FulBe, and one-sixth Maure.

Prior to the construction of the irrigation works, the delta was subject to the annual post-rainy season river crest, which inundated much of the area and flushed away some of the accumulated salt deposits. However, by January, the retreat of the high waters left the delta subject to salt water infiltration.

Rainfall is sparse and irregular in the delta area. Between 1944 and 1973, the average annual rainfall for Saint-Louis-du-Sénégal, at the northwestern extreme of the area, was 323 millimeters. In Dagana, at the southeastern extreme of the delta, it was 297 millimeters per year over the same 30-year period (Diagne 1974:188). During the rainy season of 1976, the administrative district of Ross-Bethio, which includes the zone of Kassak, recorded 212.3 millimeters of rainfall.

SAED

SAED was founded through a series of laws and decrees in early 1965. From the beginning, SAED was charged with developing land for hydro-agricultural production; controlling, transforming, and marketing produce; and promoting cooperative organization among the peasants working on its lands (République du Sénégal n.d.). SAED is defined as a public establishment in Senegalese law, a corporate person of special public right, given its own endowment and financial autonomy, and not benefiting from any private participation. Its operations are overseen by the Ministry of Rural Development and Hydraulics.

During 1965 and 1966, SAED created five villages in the Middle Delta to cultivate the catchments in the area that it had prepared for irrigated agriculture. Among them were Kassak Nord and Kassak Sud. Since that time, the works have evolved through three levels of technical refinement. Primary irrigation works are those in which a relatively simple cultivable catchment basin has been constructed. In secondary works, the catchments are ringed by a protective dike. Within each catchment there is a maximum difference of 25 centimeters between the highest and lowest points, and the catchment is irrigated and drained by a canal entering at the point of mean elevation. Tertiary works are those in which pumping stations have been installed to allow better control over the level of submersion in the catchments than is permitted by gravity-fed secondary works.

Each technological advance in the irrigation works has resulted from the failure of the simpler technological forms that preceded it to live up to expectations. However, not even the most technologically refined works have solved all the technical problems associated with the project. For example, the main drawback of the secondary gravity works was that the level of submersion in the polders is a function of the magnitude of the river crest. The particularly low crest of 1968 restricted cultivation to only 10 percent of the improved land that had been seeded. SAED attempted to solve this problem by construction of three large pumping stations at Ronq, Thiagar, and Diawar, with smaller pumping stations at the head of the main canals feeding the different polders.

Supplementing the secondary gravity works with pumping stations has not, however, resolved other problems of the secondary gravity works. The 25-centimeter gradient between the extreme points in a polder is still too great to insure proper submersion of all the rice in the polder. Use of the same canal for irrigation and drainage has limited the repertoire of irrigation operations. For example, it has been impossible to execute the rapid pre-irrigation soaking and drainage sequence.

The Zone of Kassak

There were several good reasons for SAED to begin its career by resettling producers to work irrigated perimeters it created in the delta. The delta was a large, sparsely populated area that was, in a sense, demographically virgin territory. The creation of the irrigated perimeters would disrupt the socioeconomic life of only a few thousand transhumant pastoralists. Opposition from the local population was not expected to be strong. A direct confrontation with the complex land tenure system reigning upriver and the politically powerful landholding class it maintained (Boutillier 1963) could be postponed. Adaptation of the local modes of production to the agro-industrial production system would present few difficulties since there was little crop production. Moreover, it appeared that underutilized labor from other parts of the country could be attracted to the delta to begin to exploit the resource potential of its underutilized land. The delta was perceived to offer an excellent opportunity to supplement national food production by adding to the net total of cultivated land. The technology to do this seemed, in 1966, to be simple and relatively inexpensive. The delta is conveniently located along the main paved road connecting Dakar with Nouakchott. Finally, SAED hoped to build upon the lessons of the Richard-Toll plantation and other irrigated cultivation experiments conducted between the 1940s and 1960s. More study and thought had been put into the development of the delta area than anywhere else in the Senegal River Valley, and first-rate documentation already existed for the area.

Kassak Nord is 22 kilometers northeast of Ross-Bethio, following a dike that begins at the northern extremity of Ross-Bethio and leads to Ronq, on the banks of the Senegal River. By dike the distance between Ross-Bethio and Kassak Sud is six kilometers. If one could travel directly, crossing the Kassak Creek and some of the polders of Kassak Nord, the distance between them would be two kilometers. FulBe encampments, their number and location varying according to the season, are scattered along a ten-kilometer stretch of the paved road beginning at the Kassak Sud turnoff.

In 1966, when Kassak Nord was created, about 200 household units settled there. Two years later, Ndiaye (1968) found 176 households containing 1,044 people, of whom 681 were able-bodied adults. In 1976, the vice president of the cooperative estimated that 187 households retained cultivation rights in the village polders, although a number of them do not reside in the village. Almost all of the families in the village are Tukulor or FulBe from the Department of Podor in the Middle Senegal Valley. The few non-Tukulor and non-FulBe from the village have almost all left Kassak Nord. Fulfulde, the common language of the Tukulor and the FulBe, is the language of the village. Almost all the men are proficient in Wolof as well. Virtually everyone in the village follows the Tijani practice of Islam.

The most striking social characteristic of Kassak Nord is the pattern of caste affiliation of its inhabitants. Tukulor society is stratified, as is the case with all Senegalese peoples north of the Gambia River (Boutillier et al. 1962; A. B. Diop 1965; M. Diop 1972; Wane 1969). There is a disproportionately high number of fishermen and artisans in Kassak Nord when compared with the figures on caste distribution among the Tukulor in general. At the same time, there is a disproportionately low number of nobles and warriors in Kassak Nord when compared with Tukulor society as a whole (Boutillier et al. 1962:54). It appears that Kassak Nord tended to attract people from land-poor castes in the Middle Senegal Valley. A number of recruits also came from villages along the Senegal River, near sites that had witnessed the development of small polders under various agencies in the 1950s and 1960s.

Kassak Sud was similarly settled by approximately 200 households in mid-1966. Ndiaye (1968) found 162 households in Kassak Sud, including 850 people, of whom 451 were able-bodied adults. In a 1976 census, SAED counted 215 households with 650 able-bodied adults who had cultivation rights in the polders of Kassak Sud. This number included 58 FulBe households who had acquired rights to cultivate there.

These original settlers of Kassak Sud were veterans of the Senegalese and/or French armies. The veterans had been pressuring the government to show its gratitude for their public service. They were attracted to Kassak Sud by government promises of ample housing, generous subsidies, a full range of social services, and the means to secure a livelihood. Close to half of the settlers remaining in Kassak Sud in 1976-1977 were Tukulor. The remainder was divided about equally among the FulBe, the Serer, the Wolof, and individuals from a number of groups from the Casamance Region of Senegal. The Wolof have come mainly from the areas around the cities of Louga and Thies. Wolof is the *lingua franca* of the village.

A number of FulBe also have cultivation rights to the zone. Fifty-eight households from two distinct FulBe groups were joined together to form the *Association d'Intérêt Rurale* (AIR), a precooperative, of Kassak Sud Peulh. The members of the AIR have cultivation rights in the irrigation works lying between Kassak Sud and several FulBe encampments. Rights to these works are shared with the inhabitants of Kassak Sud. Defining these shared rights in particular instances is a source of tension among the members of Kassak Sud and Kassak Sud Peulh. The Hururbe groups, who claim to have been occupying the zone for several hundred years, comprise two-thirds of the membership. The other third of the membership is Wodaabe, who have been moving into the middle delta from the lower delta since the late 1940s. Although all the FulBe are Muslim, the Hururbe usually follow the Tijani practice, while several of the Wodaabe follow the Quadiri formula. There is considerable tension between the two groups. SAED fiat is the only force preventing a rupture of the AIR.

THE PRODUCTION SYSTEM

Rice is generally sown by scatter seeding in July, after the rains have had a chance to soak in and soften the ground. The fields are flooded around September 10, and weeding begins ten days to two weeks later. Harvest is in November and December. SAED estimates that 40 person-days of labor are required for proper cultivation of a hectare of irrigated rice, although many people are able to put in only 20 to 25 person-days and still get a respectable harvest.

Tomato seedlings are generally planted around August 15 in a special plot. After about 45 days, the seedlings are transplanted into the polders. After 60 more days, the vines begin to bear fruit. They bear from mid-December to mid-April. Tomato cultivation requires much more labor time in an absolute sense than rice cultivation, and it demands much more attention than rice cultivation. While weeds flourish among the tomato plants, rice, cultivated under water, is less susceptible to weed growth. From the first herbicide spraying, near the end of October, to final harvest, tomato plants require almost daily attention.

Access to factors of production in its polders is controlled tightly by SAED. Every year the administration of the delta perimeter, headquartered in Ross-Bethio, decides what sections of a village's polders will be cultivated in what crop. It periodically charges its agents to conduct a census of the households in the village in order to enumerate the able-bodied adults, male and female, that heads of households claim they have to support by irrigated cultivation.

The land designated as available for cultivation is divided by the number of able-bodied adults claimed to be dependent on the works for their livelihood. In Kassak Sud, in the 1976-1977 cultivation season, families were allocated 0.23 hectares per able-bodied adult. The board of directors of the cooperative then takes the extension staff and the membership of the cooperative into the polders to make the physical division of the land cultivated. Locations of plots are determined by lot, and the board of directors of the cooperative makes all decisions regarding land allocation. The physical measuring may be carried out by the extension agents or the board of directors. The extension agents represent SAED's interests, and SAED will rely on them in cases of disputes that the board of directors cannot settle.

Each SAED perimeter has a quartermaster's department designated to oversee the sale of equipment, agricultural supplies, and cultivation services for each zone in the perimeter. An officer from the quartermaster's department delivers equipment, supplies, and services to the polders; tallies up the account; and bills the cooperative. In fact, SAED delegates to the quartermaster's departments the right to inspect the cooperative books and prevail upon the cooperative to take action it deems appropriate in cases of members who do not pay their share of the cooperative debt.

Table 1 presents the average charge to the producer for cultivating a hectare of rice in Kassak Nord, in Kassak Sud, and in Kassak Sud Peulh for three recent seasons. With the conversion to tertiary works, SAED estimates a producer cost of $427.56 at 1976 prices to cultivate a hectare of rice (République du Sénégal 1976a).

Table 1.
AVERAGE PRODUCER CHARGE TO CULTIVATE
ONE HECTARE OF RICE

	1974-75	1975-76	1976-77
Kassak Nord	$117.79	$134.05	$149.96
Kassak Sud	$117.79	$134.05	$152.36
Kassak Sud Peulh	$117.79	$134.05	$152.36

A household gains access to the land in the polders of Kassak through membership of its working-age males in the village cooperative. The cooperatives are administered by a nine-man board of directors. The cooperative structure that existed in Kassak up to 1976 was adopted for the sake of consistency with the structure then generally in use throughout the peanut-producing regions of the country. With this structure, producers in Kassak were assured access to credit.

While satisfactory for peanut production, this structure has had difficulty accommodating rice production because rice producers accumulate higher debts than peanut producers, and rice is grown in specially developed works instead of family plots chosen by the cultivator. Because rice is a staple food in Senegal, people can consume almost all their production if they decide to postpone payment of their debt, and they can sell as much as they want through informal channels or on the parallel market, and avoid passing their produce through official circuits.

The president and the weigher of the cooperative had too much power for a situation where production for the cooperative represented a family's total livelihood. This led to much intragroup conflict and factionalization. Cooperative members would not work together in the polders. In Kassak, they hardly knew one another; yet, they were forced by the technical design of the works to labor side by side. Extension agents found supervision of the cooperative membership an insurmountable problem under these conditions (Cissokho 1974). It was not possible in this structure to assure a high rate of debt repayment.

Tertiary works are so expensive to develop that a more efficient system of labor management has had to be found in order to
achieve normal investment returns in world financial markets. To
alleviate these shortcomings, SAED has been promoting the subdi-
vision of the cooperatives into producer groups together with the
development of the tertiary works (République du Sénégal 1976b;
Cissokho 1974), which are defined as follows:

> The producer group is a small agricultural undertaking con-
> taining an average of twelve to twenty cultivators placed in
> works with complete mastery of water, that is to say
> equipped with advanced works. It is constituted from social
> affinities among previously selected peasants working in the
> same hydraulic mesh....This has necessitated the intensi-
> fication of the extension network, being one agent for two
> producer groups (about 24 to 40 persons) (République du
> Sénégal 1976b:2).

The objective of organization by producer groups is to enable
SAED to police the labor in its tertiary works and to get the
yields and debt repayment that will enable it to justify the expansion of its operations to the international financial community upon
which its future growth depends. Kassak Sud was organized in
producer groups for the rice cultivation of 1976. While rice was
always cultivated individually, tomatoes always had been cultivated in collective groups. The producer groups there grew out of
the tomato cultivation groups of the previous several years.
   By adding another layer to the supervision of production in
its irrigated perimeters, SAED hopes to improve the efficiency
and increase the return to its operations. The producer groups
introduce divisions into the cooperative structure, diluting the
power of the president and the board of directors, and thereby
reducing the chances for abuse of power at this level. The scale
of the group is small enough that its internal dynamic unfolds in
daily person-to-person contacts that follow the principles of small
group behavior laid out by Homans (1950, 1961) and Mills (1967),
fostering a high level of group solidarity. SAED expects group
solidarity to insure that work is done well and that debts are
repaid promptly. Only by meeting these standards could a producer hope to maintain the esteem of his affinity group.

PRODUCERS' RETURN ON PRODUCTION IN THE ZONE

In the course of fieldwork for this study, 70 households in
Kassak Nord, 50 households in Kassak Sud, and 38 households in
Kassak Sud Peulh were interviewed. This represents 37.4 percent of the households believed to retain cultivation rights in
Kassak Nord, 31.8 percent of the households believed to retain
cultivation rights in Kassak Sud, and 65.5 percent of the households belonging to Kassak Sud Peulh AIR.
   Rice production data were obtained by asking informants how
many sacks of rice they remembered harvesting in a given season. The sacks are a standard size and are assumed to contain

Table 2.

NET AVERAGE RETURN PER HOUSEHOLD FROM RICE CULTIVATION
IN KASSAK

Season	Location	Gross production (tons)	Official x price (dollars per ton)	Costs per household (dollars)	Net return per household (dollars)
	Kassak Nord	3.048	184.44	269.90	292.27
1974-75	Kassak Sud	2.955	184.44	209.05	335.97
	Kassak Sud Peulh	1.819	184.44	153.74	181.76
	Kassak Nord	1.613	184.44	301.60	- 4.10
1975-76	Kassak Sud	0.415	184.44	162.75	-86.21
	Kassak Sud Peulh	0.510	184.44	133.79	-39.73
	Kassak Nord	4.477	184.44	386.81	438.93
1976-77	Kassak Sud	0.774	184.44	127.03	15.73
	Kassak Sud Peulh	0.774	184.44	127.03	15.73

80 kilograms of paddy. At harvest time virtually the entire harvest is put into sacks at one time, either for transfer to SAED or for storage by the household. Only a small amount is eaten, traded, or sold before it is sacked. Producer memories are probably fairly accurate for the three most recent harvests.

Tomato production data are probably more reliable than rice production data. Since tomatoes are produced in collective groups, it has been possible to reconstruct the net return per producer from tomato production for all the years that tomatoes have been grown in the zone by cross-checking the reports of the different members in the group.

Table 2 derives the average net yield per household from rice cultivation in the zone in three recent seasons. The average gross production comes from interviews with the household heads. The official price is set by the Senegalese government. The production cost per household was determined by multiplying the cost of production per hectare, as presented in Table 1, by the size of the average household plot as calculated from the reports of the household heads.

The general rate for agricultural day labor in the delta area during the period of field research was $1.90 per day. Meanwhile, under Senegalese law of that time, unskilled manual labor in the formal sector had to be paid a minimum of $3.65 per day.

Table 3 compares the labor input at 40 person-days per hectare with the net return to producers given in Table 2. Table 3 expresses the net return in terms of days' paid agricultural labor, as days' paid manual labor in the formal sector, and as kilograms of paddy converted at the rate of 18.44 cents per kilogram.

Table 3.

NET RETURN PER HOUSEHOLD FROM RICE CULTIVATION
EXPRESSED AS DAYS' LABOR OR FOOD

Season	Location	Days' Labor per Plot	Produc- tion (net Value)	=	Days' Paid Farm Labor	or	Days' Manual Labor	or	Rice (kg)
1974–75	Kassak Nord	128.0	292.27		153.8		80.1		1,585
	Kassak Sud	92.8	335.97		176.8		92.0		1,822
	Kassak Sud Peulh	60.8	181.76		95.7		49.8		986
1975–76	Kassak Nord	130.8	− 4.10		0		0		0
	Kassak Sud	56.0	−86.21		0		0		0
	Kassak Sud Peulh	40.4	−39.73		0		0		0
1976–77	Kassak Nord	147.6	438.93		230.0		120.3		2,380
	Kassak Sud	28.8	15.73		8.3		4.3		85
	Kassak Sud Peulh	28.8	15.73		8.3		4.3		85

Table 3 demonstrates several important conclusions. The 1974-1975 season was one of the very best for all of the cultivators in the zone. In that year the average household in all three groups in the zone got a better return for its expenditure of labor on rice production than if it had allocated the same labor to paid agricultural day labor in the area. However, only in Kassak Sud did the return approach the minimum level of compensation for unskilled manual labor in the formal sector.

In Kassak Nord the average household has 6.1 members. It needs about two tons of paddy to meet its annual food requirement. In Kassak Sud the households are somewhat smaller, averaging 5.2 members. These households need 1.7 tons of paddy to meet their food needs. In 1974-1975, the average household in Kassak Nord was still not able to meet all its food needs from its rice production after clearing its debts, while the average household in Kassak Sud was able to do so. It was not possible to make an estimate of the paddy rice needs of the FulBe households. The return to the FulBe probably did come close to meeting their consumption needs in rice.

The 1975-1976 season was a disaster for all. The average household was not able to clear its debts in any of the three groups, let alone have some surplus for household consumption. In all three cases the return to labor would have been higher working for wages in agricultural day labor than in rice cultivation in the SAED works.

There is reason to believe that the figures for Kassak Nord have improved, but that the figures for Kassak Sud and Kassak Sud Peulh are worse than they were. By SAED figures, the 1976-1977 season was quite successful in Kassak Nord (République du Sénégal 1977). Once again it proved to a household's advantage to devote its labor to rice production rather than to look for agricultural day labor. However, the net return to rice production was still not high enough to make rice production preferable to the lowest level of unskilled manual labor in the formal sector. This year production in Kassak Sud and Kassak Sud Peulh was only marginally positive after clearing the cultivation debt. Either kind of paid labor outside the polders would have yielded a better return than rice cultivation.

The 1974-1975 season was the most successful for which data were gathered. Yet even then a household would have been acting rationally to invest labor in entry-level unskilled manual labor if it could find an opening. Only in Kassak Sud in 1974-1975, Kassak Nord in 1976-1977, and, possibly, in Kassak Sud Peulh in 1974-1975 was the average household able to earn enough from the sale of rice to meet its consumption needs for the year. Moreover, there is no dependable pattern to returns from production. A good year was followed by a disastrous year, which was then followed by a bad year for some and a good year for others. In such circumstances a rational household has to turn its attention elsewhere to assure its material security.

---

[1]A disclaimer is in order so that these tables do not lead to an overly pessimistic conclusion. The tables calculate net returns as if the producers were paying off their debts in their entirety and marketing rice only through official channels. In fact, most producers usually escape paying a large portion of their debt. During the 1976-1977 season in the delta, SAED reported that only between 35 percent and 60 percent of the debt was paid in the different cooperatives (République du Sénégal 1977:60). Producers' effective net return is larger than it appears on the tables.

Table 4 presents the history of tomato production in Kassak Nord. It focuses on how many days of labor members of the reconstructed groups had to supply per season to earn their shares of the group's net return. It then evaluates the return to labor for each day of the member's labor responsibility, as well as the return for each month of the season the member continues to produce tomatoes, during which time the pursuit of other economic activities must be forgone. Virtually all tomato production is marketed. The vast majority of the members of a group know only their net return from cultivation during the season. They do not know how much the group produces, how many hectares the group cultivates, or how high is the group cultivation debt. Sometimes even the group leader cannot help on these questions. On the other hand, since tomato cultivation is a group effort, the data for the three sites are not inferential. Rather, they reconstruct total production for the three sites.

Table 4.

NET RETURNS PER HOUSEHOLD FROM TOMATO CULTIVATION IN
KASSAK NORD

	1972–73	1973–74	1974–75	1975–76
Average return per household	$ 46.98	$124.11	$ 23.60	$ 28.77
Hectares cultivated	6	17	16	24
Total labor requirement (@ 90 person-days/ha.)	540	1,530	1,440	2,160
Total work force	54	84	83	66
Days' labor per household	10.0	18.2	17.4	32.7
Net return per day's labor	$ 4.70	$ 6.82	$ 1.36	$ 0.88
Net return per month of season	$ 5.87	$ 15.51	$ 1.95	$ 3.60

Table 4 illustrates all the problems that have been plaguing SAED tomato cultivation since its inception. The net return per day of labor was higher during the first two years than producers could have earned doing agricultural day labor or unskilled manual labor outside the zone. However, producers were so underemployed that they could have earned more per month compared with a prorated net return from tomato production if they had worked only a few days in any kind of job elsewhere. For this reason, large numbers of people in Kassak Nord have been choosing not to participate in tomato cultivation. Increasingly, those who cultivate tomatoes hire sharecroppers to take their place in the polders. Other households have their sons cultivate

tomatoes while the head of the household pursues economic interests outside the delta.[2]

Only one household head in the 70-household sample in Kassak Nord expressed an interest in tomato cultivation in the 1976-
1977 season. The lack of interest is partly a reflection of people's experience of the two preceding years. It is also a response to SAED's expressed intention to concentrate most of the
tomato production in the delta in a new polder some distance from
Kassak Nord.

Table 5 presents the data for the history of tomato production in Kassak Sud. Since the beginning of tomato cultivation
there, participation has been high. This record, in itself, implies that the producers in Kassak Sud feel themselves to be more
successful in tomato cultivation than do those of Kassak Nord.
While tomato cultivation in Kassak Sud has been more successful
than in Kassak Nord, the problem remains that the tomato cultivators are underemployed. The net return per work day for producers has, for most years, been above the minimum wage level
for unskilled labor in Senegal. But tomato production requires
producers to commit their time for the entire eight-month cultivation season, so that, when computed on a seasonal basis,
their monthly salaries are still quite low. As a result, a number
of tomato cultivators in Kassak Sud hire sharecroppers to take
their place while they look for wage labor elsewhere.

The FulBe of Kassak Sud Peulh have been the least successful with tomato cultivation. Yet the number of tomato cultivators
grew substantially between the 1975-1976 season and the 1976-1977
season. The Wodaabe, as a group, began tomato cultivation in
1976-1977. Table 6 presents the evolution of tomato production
for the two years for which production figures are available for
Kassak Sud Peulh.

The FulBe may not be discouraged by this low productivity
because they are not yet satisfied that these two years constitute
a pattern. If their low productivity in tomato cultivation continues, they may begin to have second thoughts. They also may
feel that, even at low levels of productivity, tomato cultivation
supplements their economic well-being without making excessive
demands on their labor during the dry season when they must
confine themselves to the zone in order to oversee their interests
in livestock.

---

[2]Casted fishermen do not cultivate tomatoes. The most
productive season for coastal marine fishing begins around rice
harvest time and continues until a month before rice planting.

Table 5.

NET RETURNS PER HOUSEHOLD FROM TOMATO CULTIVATION
IN KASSAK SUD

	1968-69	1969-70	1970-71	1971-72	1972-73	1973-74
Average return per household	$ 6.50	$100.00	$250.00	$135.00	$138.00	$259.00
Hectares cultivated	18.	13.	22.	33.	40.	40.
Total labor requirement (@ 90 person-days/ha.)	1620.	1170.	1980.	2970.	3600.	3600.
Total work force	65.	32.	57.	116.	155.	157.
Days' labor per household	24.9	36.6	34.7	25.6	23.2	22.9
Net return per day's labor	$ 0.15	$ 2.73	$ 7.21	$ 5.27	$ 5.95	$11.31
Net return per month of season	$ 0.81	$12.50	$31.25	$16.88	$17.25	$32.38

Table 6.

NET RETURNS PER HOUSEHOLD FROM TOMATO CULTIVATION
IN KASSAK SUD PEULH

	1974-75	1975-76
Average return per member	$ 44.44	$ 15.56
Hectares cultivated	2.8	2
Total labor requirement (days)	252	180
Work force	14	12
Days' labor per household	18	15
Return per day	$ 3.17	$1.30
Return per month	$ 5.56	$ 1.95

FACTORS LIMITING THE PRODUCER'S RETURN FROM PRODUCTION IN THE WORKS

Part of the explanation for the low return to producers working in the SAED irrigation projects lies in factors that have limited total production. The most important factor is ecological. As explained earlier, the environment of the delta does not lend itself readily to cultivation. Moreover, high concentrations of grains in the otherwise barren area attract insects, birds, and rodents. The problem is even more severe during the tomato season, when the tomato plants are about the only green vegetation in the area. However, the decisions regarding where and how to develop Kassak were based on political rather than ecological considerations.

A second factor limiting production is technical. The irrigation works require major departures from customary production practices in producers' home areas. Producers owe the conception, design, construction, maintenance, and conditions of operation of the works to decisions negotiated at higher levels of integration of the world economy.

A socio-historical factor that also limits production is expressed in the social disorganization characteristic of resettlement (Scudder 1976). To some degree it is expressed in the difficulties people have in accommodating themselves to the unfamiliar technology and system of production in the zone. Here too the socio-historical factor results, albeit indirectly, from decisions made at the political center. The socio-historical factor is also represented in the persistence of political and social relations that have evolved in the Senegalese environment over a long period of time. It is the social context in which the producers continue to make their behavioral choices. While physically located in the delta area, producers take steps to preserve their interests and options in their home areas and elsewhere. Settlement in the irrigated zone has not meant exclusive commitment to irrigated production. The new settlements of the delta have not become communities in the sense of people maintaining social relations based on many-stranded exchanges and interdependencies. On the contrary, people in the irrigated areas are limited almost entirely to cooperation in the work place. However, it is difficult to assess to what degree this situation is a cause of low absolute production in the works and to what degree it is a result.

The final factor is the impact of the world economy on daily life in the zone. This factor is not so much a constraint on absolute production as a factor limiting the net return on whatever the producer harvests. The irrigation works and all of the infrastructure that enables the producer to exploit them have been created in collaboration with institutions of the world economy. This has led to the imposition of technical and administrative structures to which the producers must adapt in order to maintain their rights in the works. Moreover, the peripheral position of the delta producers in the world economy places them in an even more precarious position because they owe their livelihood to an installation created through a development option that depends on heavy expatriate participation. They are in a subordinate position vis-à-vis the driving forces that have provided their means of production.

The interests of SAED as a Senegalese national institution are different from those of the people who work in its perimeters. To understand the divergence of interest one need only examine the linkages between SAED and the world economy. Large-scale irrigation schemes such as those in the zone of Kassak take tremendous infusions of foreign investment capital. A 1976 estimate (République du Sénégal 1976a) put the cost of replacing secondary works with tertiary works at $1,555.55 per hectare at then current exchange rates--if the polder already had a pumping station at the head of the main canal. Investment requirements for areas that were completely unimproved ranged from four to six times as high.

The Senegalese government cannot afford to underwrite SAED expansion at the rate necessary to keep pace with national food needs. It cannot afford the hardship such a policy would cause for government administrators, for administrative functions, and for the general population. It must, therefore, appeal to international financial institutions to provide the funding to realize projects like SAED. However, investment capital at the periphery of the world economy is a very expensive import.

The appeal to international financial institutions requires a disposition to subordinate SAED programs to the requirements of the world economy. The public institutions, such as the World Bank, USAID, Fonds d'Aide et de Coopération--the French government foreign assistance agency--or Fonds Européens de Développement--the European Common Market assistance organization--that have been financing SAED must require a prospective aid recipient to demonstrate the financial viability of the project under consideration. No financial institution can

afford the risks of withdrawing from policy discussion regarding
the allocation of funds it is making available. It appeals to a
project analysis methodology to enable it to determine the most
efficient allocation of its scarce financial resources among infinite
possible recipients (Franco 1975). The keystone of the project
analysis methodology is an examination of the economic viability of
the project on the institutional level, from a cost-benefit or
cash-flow point of view.

International financial institutions are reluctant to make
funds available for projects that they believe may fall below a
threshold of sustaining themselves economically. Therefore, SAED
must show a structure of operations that gives a reasonable promise of economic viability when it is courting international financial
institutions. However, international financial support is a Trojan
horse which, despite its innocuous appearance, permits outside
institutions to intrude upon internal political affairs. These donor institutions have a politico-economic worldview that they encourage recipients of financial support to accept through the stip-
ulations that accompany loans and grants. SAED's structure is
oriented more to the requirements of international capital markets
than to the normal behavioral patterns of the people that both
SAED and the financiers avow to be the project beneficiaries.
The project thus overlooks the primary interests of its produc-
er/participants at several critical points.

Meanwhile, SAED must be ready to guarantee its underwrit-
ers that their investment is secure. This is done in part by
commissioning costly feasibility studies from expatriate consultants
before embarking on any project. Second, a condition for the
disbursement of some funds may be that a certain number of
expatriate advisers be hired to fill administrative posts in the
organization. A third guarantee lies in the financial control over
SAED retained by the central government. The SAED
administration has very little latitude in allocating funds. While
this situation has been criticized as a handicap to efficient
operations, it minimizes the chances for financial irregularities
and assures potential investors of SAED's responsibility.

SAED translates these abstract considerations into a concrete
framework for producer activity in its works in several ways.
For example, SAED determines the crop or crops to be cultivated
on a particular parcel. All of the harvest from SAED land, other
than that authorized for home consumption, must be surrendered
to SAED at a price set by the central government. The price has
always been considerably lower than that prevailing on the free
market. SAED recoups part of its high investment and administrative and production costs through the low price it offers producers. It appropriates a designated portion of production in
order to recover the cost of field operations. In the SAED system, each producer contracts a debt to be repaid in kind at harvest time. The debt is calculated on the mechanical services,
seeds, fertilizer, pesticides, hand tools, and, in the tertiary
works, water that are put at the producers' disposal during the
growing season. The mix of these factors used by each producer
is computed individually when calculating his debt. The advantage to SAED is that, even in years of low production, the

accounts will be able to show it clearing its operating costs, despite the fact that it may not be able to collect these costs from the producers. The advantage of this system to the producers is that they have an evident incentive to increase their production. Once they clear their debts they may keep for themselves the full value of their production at the official price. The disadvantage to the producers is that they are almost always in debt. Their debt remains a fixed cost whether they produce one grain or several tons. Only under exceptional circumstances, such as during the worst years of the recent drought, does the Senegalese government absolve producers of their debts. By and large, the government shifts the major part of the risk to the producers.

Membership in a corporate cooperative organization is required of producers in SAED's perimeters. The cooperatives are organizations of producers created at the behest and under the direction of SAED. Cooperative members are assigned to exploit fields in a common zone, and they inhabit the same village or group of villages in the zone. The cooperative organization serves the interests of SAED much more than those of the producers. The cooperative cannot act as a unit to put pressure on produce buyers, since SAED exercises monopsonistic control over produce marketing. It cannot exert price pressure on suppliers because SAED has a monopoly over sales of supplies, materiel, and cultivation services in its perimeters.

Accounting procedures prevent cooperative members from reaping the benefits of collective work. Each household is allotted a plot according to the number of able-bodied adult members. The head of the household is its representative in cooperative councils. The debt contracted in cultivating its plot is contracted in his name, and the cash return to its effort is paid directly to him. The largest unit of collective work allowed by the cooperative is the household, which for practical purposes means the nuclear family. This system assaults the role that women, married and unmarried sons, and extended families historically have played in the local economy.

The cooperative seems to be little more than an instrument to buttress SAED's economic viability. It provides a framework to integrate the producers into the organization, localize them in space, establish their position in a hierarchy, facilitate communication, establish a structure for conducting training and extension work, and ease the arduous accounting responsibilities of the administration.

The Senegal River Valley is typical of much of Africa, inasmuch as most families in the area combine several different activities in their subsistence strategies. They have shown a general unwillingness to become completely dependent on only one activity to meet their material needs. Families spread their subsistence risks over several different sectors. However, SAED is under pressure to demand a major change in the producers' risk-distribution strategy. SAED must insist that producers devote their energies to production of a narrow range of commodities within the SAED perimeters.

To demonstrate its economic viability, SAED must control producer performance in its perimeters in several ways. While these steps do not necessarily limit production in the works in an absolute sense, they do limit the producers' returns to their efforts in the works. SAED must determine the crops grown, the prices paid for them, and the charges to cultivate them. It must have virtually complete control over the produce. It also must organize, train, supervise, and discipline the work force. It must appropriate virtually all of its workers' productive effort. Only under these conditions can SAED hope to demonstrate to the international financial community that it is a bankable agro-industrial undertaking.

PRODUCERS' ADAPTATIONS TO THE ECONOMIC SITUATION IN THE ZONE

As indicated above, producers would be earning higher revenues by allocating their labor to entry-level, unskilled manual labor in the formal sector or even to itinerant agricultural day labor than by continuing to cultivate in Kassak. Yet people have not entirely abandoned their efforts to produce in the zone. In spite of the precarious situation, the irrigation works offer a net advantage to the FulBe of Kassak Sud Peulh. They have been able to adjust their herding patterns without a great deal of difficulty. The works represent a far better secondary economic pursuit than any they previously had enjoyed. The works only minimally disturb their primary economic pursuit of stock raising. Few of the FulBe have any economic pursuit other than stock raising and cultivation within the SAED perimeters. The general rule is that married men cultivate, while unmarried men herd. Of the three groups treated in this study, only the FulBe of Kassak Sud Peulh AIR show any prospect of long-term stable residence in the zone. Since the FulBe will be staying in the area for reasons primarily connected with their stock-raising activities, and since they are already engaged in economic activities that commit them to the zone, the opportunity cost of irrigated agriculture will remain quite low for them.

The villagers of Kassak Nord and Kassak Sud are far more inclined to look for employment outside the works. There seems to be a large number of laboring jobs available in the delta, especially during the dry season. This is the period when construction work to develop the polders is undertaken. During the cultivation season, SAED itself is generally the employer. The veterans of Kassak Sud usually have the advantage in competing for these jobs because they tend to be more experienced wage laborers.

By far the most important means of supplementing the revenues earned working in the irrigation works is a range of absenteeism strategies. This study found that 47 percent of the members of the households interviewed in Kassak Nord do not live in the village. Fifty-two percent of the females are absent, while only 40 percent of the males are absent. In Kassak Sud, 43 percent of the members of the households interviewed do not live in the village. Male absenteeism, 39 percent, is not significantly different from the rate in Kassak Nord, while female absenteeism in Kassak Sud is only 46 percent.

The particular form of absenteeism adopted by the settled villagers in the zone might be called itinerance. In the context of Kassak, itinerance means seasonal movements—linked to the agricultural calendar—of settlers between the irrigation works in the zone and sites outside the zone that offer opportunities to supplement the returns to irrigated cultivation. While itinerance is a commonly used strategy in both Kassak Nord and Kassak Sud, the sociological distinctiveness of each population has led to distinctive patterns of itinerance in each village.

In Kassak Nord there are three general patterns of itinerance for household heads. In the first, the household head leaves his family in the village while he moves out of the area. Often the household head becomes a peddler in the rural areas in the Senegal River Valley. Except for irregular visits when his affairs take him into the neighborhood, he is with his family only during rice cultivation season, when he activates his rights in the irrigation works. He does not cultivate tomatoes. Fishermen and clerics follow this pattern. Among the 70 households in the Kassak Nord sample, 18, or 25.7 percent, were found to be practicing this itinerance strategy.

In the second pattern, the household head removes his family from the village and relocates it, usually in its area of origin in the Middle Senegal Valley. The household head, nonetheless, tries to retain his cultivation rights in the works. Every year he returns to Kassak Nord—after having sown his rainfed crop in the Middle Valley but before sowing his flood recession crop—to sow rice. He may stay in Kassak Nord to do a weeding. He then returns to the Middle Valley, going back to Kassak Nord only at harvest time. He does not cultivate tomatoes. His harvest, for lack of proper care, is often smaller than average but it is a handsome supplement to his other resources at minimal cost. This study found 21 of the 70, or 30 percent, of the households in the Kassak Nord sample to be of this type.

Only 18, or 25.7 percent, of the total households in the Kassak Nord sample have heads who are residentially stable. Among these households, three heads worked as laborers for SAED or for construction companies in the Middle Delta, three heads are weavers who still are able to sell their wares in the area, one is a tailor, one is a military pensioner, three earn money carting, and several others seem to depend on absent working-age sons for supplemental income. It is probable that the number of stable heads of households recorded in the sample overrepresents the actual number. Insofar as people saw the present study as a subterfuge for carrying out a much-resisted census, they had an interest in portraying themselves as more stable than they are. They would fear expulsion from the works as a result of an honest account of their itinerance.

The scheduled interviews in Kassak Nord elicited the names of 77 householders who had removed their families from the village since 1966. The peak years of removal were 1968 and 1969, immediately following the first of the series of disappointing harvests, and between 1972 and 1975, the most difficult years of the

drought. All but 23 of the departing families seem to have returned to their home areas in the Middle Senegal Valley. The 23
exceptions went to urban areas, where many seem to have found
employment.

In Kassak Sud the patterns of absenteeism are somewhat
different. The heads of households who leave their families behind tend to be latecomers, men who acquired their own rights in
the works by sharecropping for one of the veterans. They are,
by and large, itinerant clerics or peddlers during the dry season. They do not cultivate tomatoes. Several in this group are
young, literate men, mostly single, who have their own plots in
the works but spend a lot of time in urban areas working or
looking for work. Of the 50 households interviewed in Kassak
Sud, 10, or 20 percent of the total sample, were engaged in this
first itinerance strategy.

The second itinerance strategy, in which the householder
removes his family from the zone while he himself returns during
the cultivation season, also occurs somewhat less frequently in
Kassak Sud than in Kassak Nord. Twelve households in the
Kassak Sud sample, 24 percent of the total, engage in this
strategy. Most of these people come to Kassak Sud for the rice
cultivation season only. They try to hire sharecroppers to take
their place in tomato cultivation. Most of these householders are
urban residents. They carry out what few operations they
perform on the rice crop during time off from their urban
employment.

The third pattern of itinerance, the split family strategy, is
almost nonexistent in Kassak Sud. Only three households, 6 percent of the total sample, practice this strategy. In contrast with
Kassak Nord, 25 households, fully 40 percent of the total sample,
are headed by men who are residentially stable. In this group,
however, five household heads have military pensions, six are
paid laborers for SAED or one of the public works firms active in
the Middle Delta, two earn money as carters, another is a tailor,
and another is the village baker. As in Kassak Nord, several of
the remainder may be itinerant as well but feel it in their interest
to mask their movements.

The scheduled interviews in Kassak Sud elicited the names of
61 heads of households who have removed their families since
1966. As in Kassak Nord, the peak years of removal were 1968
and 1969 and from 1972 to 1975. Only 9 of these 61 households
settled in rural areas. All the rest went to urban areas.

The difference between Kassak Nord and Kassak Sud in their
approaches to absenteeism lies in the rural orientation of the latter. For the itinerant cultivators of Kassak Nord, the irrigation
works have become simply a part of the land they cultivate that
is separated by considerable distance from their other holdings.
Irrigated cultivation is one of a group of seasonal activities
pursued in a range of geographically separate places. A household head maximizes the economic security of his family by jug-
gling this range of activities as adroitly as he can to his advantage.

For the householders of Kassak Sud, the irrigation works
have taken the place of cultivation rights long since abandoned

by people whose military service has taken them all over the world. They are similar to the cultivation rights retained by many Senegalese urban dwellers as part of their subsistence strategies. Many urban dwellers, even those with relatively secure middle-class incomes by world economic standards, spend part of the cultivation season every year in fields they have either inherited or rented. For the residents of Kassak Sud, irrigated agriculture is a secondary activity which is a far better supplement to their primary activity than any other option available to them.

The long-term prognosis for residential stability in the zone does not depend solely on the choices made by the original settlers. It depends, probably to a greater degree, on choices made by members of the following generation. This study identified a total of 127 offspring over the age of 14--the putative threshold of economic independence--of the settlers of Kassak Nord. Of these, 105 were judged to have made their long-term commitments for adult residence. Overall, 60 percent have made commitments that preclude long-term stable residence in Kassak Nord, and 72 percent of the males and 55 percent of the females have made choices that will keep them out of the village.

The prospects are either that these two villages will become seasonal labor camps for the successors of the original settlers in the next generation or two, or, as has already begun in Kassak Sud, the successors of the original settlers will gradually be replaced by a poorer and poorer underclass of dispossessed rural labor that acquires its rights in the works by sharecropping. Even the replacement of the original settlers by these latecomers cannot hold out the prospect of long-term residential stability, unless there are some fundamental changes in the nature of the system of production of the zone.

The villagers who settled in Kassak Nord and Kassak Sud are having to resort to several forms of itinerance to make up the difference between their annual material requirements and their ability to meet their requirements in the irrigation works in the zone. One rationale for the creation of the irrigation works in the delta was the hope of decreasing the rate of rural exodus from the Senegal River Valley by offering a secure, dependable, and ample source of income in the area. The project has betrayed its economic and social promise, and has become a support for itinerance as a fallback subsistence strategy for producers. It has served to stimulate emigration in the Senegal River Valley.

AN ALTERNATIVE PROPOSAL TO MITIGATE THE BURDEN
OF PRODUCTION IN THE WORKS

Limited options face those who must decide the future of agricultural development based on irrigation in the Senegal River Valley. One is the technical improvement option. This is the option chosen by the *Office du Niger* (de Wilde 1967: vol. 2) when it could not find enough labor to produce an adequate return to its investment. The rationale is that greater technical refinement is required to increase the return to investment in the project. As the *Office du Niger* example shows, this option entails several problems. Technology and the expertise to use it efficiently are especially expensive in the periphery of the world economy. Moreover, intensive use of more and more refined technology merely increases the costs of production the administration must recoup before the producers can realize a return. Finally, the cost of technology is rising much faster than the value of the produce it yields. A project that locks itself into the high-technology option risks alienating its producers by the gradual reduction of their net return.

A second possibility is the administrative reform option. There are indications that Senegal is choosing this option at the present time. The rationale behind this option is that the fundamental problem with the project is in its administration, narrowly defined. The view held by proponents of this option is that responsibility for the situation goes no further than one or two levels of administration. No serious attention is given to the institutional links that have shaped social life among the producers in the works. This study has concluded that exercise of the administrative reform option is shortsighted because it is blind to the reality of the structure of the world economy. The administrative reform option is meaningless unless there is a major change in the systematic relationships of world economic structure.

In a sense, the administrative reform option is a form of scapegoating. SAED is most certainly not to blame for most of the problems it inflicts on producers in its works. It is not above criticism in some areas over which it has autonomy of action. However, it is grossly unfair to look at SAED as the culprit in the continuing history of Kassak. SAED has been an instrument of other institutions. The poor decisions SAED may have made have been only peripheral to determining the fate of the producers. SAED is a "foreman" doing its job in the world economic structure. The crucial decision, made at higher political levels, is to follow a development option relying on heavy influxes of finance capital from expatriate sources.

This study concludes that the most attractive development option is the localocentric option. This option places its primary reliance on the efforts of the local population. It aims at reducing reliance on capital investment and, by extension, on the institutions of the world economic system. This option gives local people the greatest latitude in determining the appropriate responses to local conditions.

Coward (1979:28) has argued that solutions to the organizational problems associated with many modern irrigation projects may be found in "...the numerous examples of locally constructed and operated systems that exist in a variety of natural and socio-political settings." One hypothesis of the present study is that the politico-economic vulnerability of people working in large-scale, capital-dependent irrigation works exists for participants in any kind of large-scale, capital-dependent development project. In contrast, smaller-scale, simpler, more labor-dependent projects come close to ideals of egalitarian distribution of political power and equitable distribution of economic benefits.

The most important measure to mitigate the political and economic vulnerability of producers in the Senegal River Valley in particular, and in irrigated development areas in general, would be to place a priority on the development of what SAED calls small perimeters. The Senegalese village perimeters usually cover from 25 to 50 hectares. The most important diagnostic trait for small perimeters is not the raw dimensions of the perimeter but the manner in which the development is underwritten. A major component in building a small perimeter is the investment of labor by its intended beneficiaries. For that reason, the financial cost per hectare of creating a small perimeter has been estimated at 60 percent of the cost of developing a hectare of a large perimeter (OMVS 1977:37).

Small perimeters are located conveniently to villages or areas where there are high concentrations of people. They are constructed on level ground, on the high banks that define the main channel of the Senegal River. These high banks offer limited surfaces of lighter, sandier soil than do the catchments that lend themselves to large-perimeter development. This makes it possible to cultivate small-perimeter plots with minimal modification of the hand methods to which the producers are accustomed.

The development of such small perimeters still requires the intervention of an outside institution. Local producers are essentially dependent on outside expertise for the design of their works. The construction, however, is generally carried out by local labor on a voluntary basis. Therefore, the design must not require too much technological mastery for realization. Imperfections will be corrected by local efforts. The producers can thereby reduce their dependence on outside agents for creating and adapting the works they use.

Works developed in this way need far less capital investment than large-scale works requiring heavy machine equipment manned by expatriates. A reduction in the need to import investment capital can have a positive impact on producers. SAED, or whatever official agency is responsible for administering the project, can relax some of the restrictions placed on these producers. It thereby passes on to them some of the benefits of its reduced capital requirements.

Insofar as the administrating agency has lower cash-flow requirements to meet its obligations in world financial markets, it should be able to permit the producer latitude in the crops cultivated. Producers will still be required to reimburse the administrating agency for the cultivation debt they incur, and the reimbursements will have to be in a crop prescribed by the agency. However, producers may be permitted their choice of crop on part of their plots. In addition, the administrative agency should be able either to raise the price it offers producers or to permit producers to sell a significant portion of their harvests on the open market.

As the producers become more responsible for building the irrigation works, supplying the cultivation inputs and field labor, and marketing the output, they should begin to approach the status they now hold in the customary cultivation system. In the small perimeter system, producers retain a certain degree of political and economic autonomy, albeit mitigated by their integration in an economic development project. However, the agency still has to supervise construction and maintenance of the works. In addition, it has to make available extension personnel to consult for cultivation of new crops under new conditions with new technology.

In small perimeters, producers should be able to have a certain latitude to determine a social organization of production appropriate to their particular circumstance. If debt repayment requirements fell, SAED could afford to be more flexible in the forms of social organization of production it accepts.

A final advantage of small perimeters is the flexibility the option gives producers to pursue other activities. Producers can meet all their financial obligations in a small perimeter more easily than in a large perimeter. Small plots do not absorb the entire labor supply of the plotholder's production unit, and SAED can relax the labor requirement per production unit in the small perimeters. Producers would, therefore, be free to pursue other economic activities according to their evaluations of the local economic situation. Maintenance of this flexibility is a form of anticrisis insurance strategy similar to that followed by the FulBe of Kassak Sud Peulh AIR. The viability of such a strategy holds some promise of a moderation of emigration rates. It is in producers' interests to indulge in a range of activities to minimize risk in case any one activity should give a disappointing return. Small-perimeter development is promising for the modesty of its pretensions: it does not seek to transform socioeconomic life in the area, but to supplement what is already there.

This paper ends on a question. Can the argument be extended from irrigated development projects to development projects in general? Assuming project beneficiaries are rational people, their interests would best be served by structuring a project so that they have the widest possible range of free choice. The only way to do that is to keep outside institutional intervention to a minimum. Projects would, therefore, be designed for minimal reliance on capital and other resources that are locally scarce and for maximum reliance on a more plentiful local resource--labor. If this approach to development proves itself, it may be possible to accomplish more with less.

Editors' Note to Chapter 6

John Grayzel argues, no doubt to the discomfort of many development socio-economists and planners, that attention to the emotional needs of beneficiaries is necessary in the planning of development projects. His position is that emotions be addressed not as an "extra dimension," but as the missing factor that may explain the response--or lack of response--of local people to projects that otherwise look good on paper. It is probable that many ethnic groups briefly described by project designers under the rubric "charactistics of project zone populations," have equivalents to the FulBe pulaade described by Grayzel: Their Way. There can be little doubt that this shared socio-psychological reality influences the reactions of local populations to projects whose designs ignore if not actively impede the fulfillment of cultural, hence individual, satisfactions. If readers, even the most hard-headed, will grant for a moment that this is the case, they may also concede that it is just as surprising that these issues are never addressed in project plans. If anthropologists, in particular, continue their involvement in development, they should become better attuned to these affective, nonobjective factors that may matter a great deal to people enclosed in project zones. It is also possible that the concerns of Grayzel are key issues in a useful approach to the much discussed but ineffectually handled "participation problem." They have everything to do, after all, with respect for human dignity.

6
Libido and Development: The Importance of Emotions in Development Work

JOHN GRAYZEL
Agency for International Development

> . . . many writers in development economics . . . often [refer] to the reform and modernization of sectors, activities, beliefs and institutions. But what is actually under discussion is not the reform and modernization of this sector or that activity, but of the people engaged in them; and not the institutions but of those who participate in them. The subjects of the transformation are people, that is persons and groups of people, not abstract entities such as activities or sectors.
>
> P. T. Bauer, *Dissent on Development*, p. 189

INTRODUCTION

Humanity: A Neglected Factor in Development

Most people will admit when forced to do so that the world is a complex place. Even those who tend to favor one overriding theory of history because of its superior explanatory power, be it dialectic materialism, environmental determinism, sociobiology, or even divine intervention, would be hard pressed to advance their preferred framework to explain the myriad of decisions and actions that occupy most of our daily lives. Similarly, most development agents and anthropologists who work with macro theories and models would reject the notion that their perspectives and actions serve to deny the basic importance of the individual, or that their approaches are dehumanizing. Anthropology is after all

---

*The opinions in this article are entirely those of the author and in no way are meant to reflect the opinions, beliefs, or policies of the U.S. Agency for International Development.

supposedly the study of man, and the millions of dollars spent yearly on development are purported to serve some human purpose.

Many thinkers emphasize processes over individual actions, not because they consider the individual unimportant, but because they feel that without an understanding of a person's place within larger systems, we cannot institute reforms that affect large groups and successive generations, as opposed to a lucky or privileged few. The value of opinions such as Bauer's, quoted above, is that they remind us once again that in searching for the bigger picture we often lose sight of the individual and of the individual's capacity to determine his own state of existence.

An example of this is the ongoing refusal within development theory and practice to accord significance to one of the most basic elements of our humanness--our emotions. Ethnographic accounts and development "PR" may occasionally use emotion-laden scenes to invoke the reader's attention and involvement, but rare are the anthropologists and development theorists who allow their analytical or operational schemes to become clouded by such considerations. The closest they come is to discuss their own or other people's values. While the "value" concept can be useful in discussing emotions, it is not synonymous with emotions. By "values" we mean external norms of behavior, proclaimed through speech or action; by "emotions" we mean internal feelings, knowable in others only through empathy.

Emotions and the Organization of Development

This chapter deals with emotions and development.[1] Many development efforts fail because they are based on faulty

---

[1] The anthropological literature on human emotion, let alone emotions and economics, is rather scant. One unusual exception is Robert Brain's *Friends and Lovers*. In discussing the virtual taboo against emotions in Anglo-American social science, Brain cites how "the combined scorn of all Anglo-Saxon structuralists and functionalists was poured onto the unbowed heads of two American sociologists when they seriously and interestingly suggested that the important relationship between a nephew and his uncle might have a sentimental basis" (p. 13).

Another exception, more relevant to development concerns, is J. Binet's *Psychologie Economique Africaine* (1970). Binet writes, for example:

Tout cela concourt à montrer qu'il existe un monde du "bon plaisir" ou l'on pose des actes pour l'agrément que l'on en attent et sans grand souci de leurs conséquences économiques....Les valeurs y sont éminement subjectives, difficilement comparables les unes aux autres....On peut donc
(Footnote Continued)

assumptions. In some cases, these assumptions may be valid at higher levels of abstraction--the macrolevel, where planning decisions are made, yet have little relevance or validity for implementation at the microlevel. At this second level the forces of individual emotion may be as important or more important as causal factors than political, economic, or social structures. Despite its importance, however, the emotional dimension is neglected in development planning, and is one of the most underutilized tools in implementation of development plans.

The focus of this chapter is intentionally bifurcated. It seeks first to demonstrate that the emotional context of a development activity, meaning the feelings of members of a particular population toward an activity that will affect them, can be critically important to understanding and predicting their response to changing circumstances. Second, it argues that development planners and implementers can understand these feelings only if they themselves are willing and able to become emotionally involved with and committed to the populations they affect with their plans. Through the use of case study materials, we will endeavor to demonstrate the importance for successful project design and implementation, of attention to the emotions of intended beneficiary populations, and the need for greater emotional involvement of the development workers themselves. Thereafter, we will highlight several current obstacles to such an approach, and finally, we will suggest several changes to improve the situation.

(Footnote Continued)

difficilement trouver les lois applicables à cet univers morsélé et changeant. Tout est affaire d'intuition personnelle. Le désire de prestige joue un grand role....

(All this serves to show that there exists a world of "good times," where one does things for the pleasure they bring without caring as to economic consequences. The values applicable there are fundamentally subjective and difficult to compare to others....It is therefore difficult to discern any rules that govern that fluid and fragmented universe. Everything is a question of personal intuition. [Though] the desire for prestige plays a large part....)

For a very different, more biological, approach to the importance of emotions in explaining human behavior, there exists E. Chapple's provocative book, *Culture and Biological Man: Explorations in Behavioral Anthropology* (1970).

A CASE STUDY: THE DOUKOLOMA FULBE

The Research Setting

In 1973 I received a grant from the Research Foundation of the State University of New York to conduct a study of the adaptive strategies of a pastoral population in a region near Segou, Mali, where the United States Agency for International Development (AID) was planning to undertake a livestock development project. (See Map, p. 34.) My wife and I settled in a small hamlet south of Segou, on the Niger River. About sixty-five kilometers to the south was the village of Douna, and another river, the Bani. Beginning at that point, and extending twenty-six kilometers east along the river's bank, was a government protected forest, the Doukoloma Forest Reserve (Grayzel 1977).

The area was inhabited principally by Bamana (Bambara) agriculturalists, and several thousand FulBe herders who lived in small, scattered villages. The Doukoloma forest was supervised by an agent of the Malian Waters and Forestry Service (Service des Eaux et Forêts), who was responsible for regulating the use of the area for farming, grazing, and wood-gathering. At the time of the study, farming within the forest reserve was limited to a small area. Grazing rights were open to all, subject only to regulation of wood cutting, and a prohibition against fires.

Prompted by the devastation of range land by a prolonged drought, AID had authorized funds for a project to convert the forest into a managed grazing area for cattle, and to encourage local farmers to gather forage for animal-fattening. My task, and that of my colleagues, John Van Dusen Lewis and Dangui Sissoko, was to study the area's populations and their use of the forest's resources.

Methodology

It was initially assumed that persons who were cattle owners and used the forest would also be most concerned by a reallocation of its resources as a result of the project. Therefore a survey was made of herds in the forest during the months of maximum use--October and November--and on the basis of information concerning the owners' home villages, the initial geographical limits of our study were drawn. The area involved was about 40 x 15 kilometers in size. Some 35 villages and hamlets, whose total population was 7,500 to 8,000, fell within the area boundaries. Inhabitants were herders, farmers, and fishers. These specialties corresponded closely with the area's three ethnic groups: FulBe (also referred to as Peul, Fula, or Fulani), Bamana (Bambara), and Somono (principally Bamana who had adopted fishing

as a way of life).[2]   Each of the three researchers settled into a
community located within an area of ethnic predominance (myself
with the FulBe, Lewis with the Bambara and Sissoko with the
Somono), and pursued their research goals.[3]

In order better to understand the various activities in the
area as well as to obtain the data needed for my research, I
hired several teenage research assistants.   They criss-crossed
the area on bikes every five to ten days.   We identified individual cattle owners and the markings on their cattle, and were
thus able to trace almost all animal movements in the area without
resorting to the kind of direct questioning that invites guarded
responses and flawed information.   Another research assistant
spent time at the local cattle market, located about 25 kilometers
northwest of my home village.   By carefully listening in on the
haggling that precedes most animal sales, he was able to obtain
fairly accurate information on the number of sales and the prices
paid, once again, without direct questions.[4]

---

[2]There also existed an important intermediary population of
people called Foroba Fula ("public fula") who were supposed
descendants of slave herders of the former Bamana kings.   As
they were oriented to the pastoral life, they generally sought to
integrate themselves into the FulBe life style and communities.

The ethnic identity factor represents a complex situation.
In much of the Sahel, and certainly in this area of Mali, a persons's way of life (farmer, herder, fisherman), his or her basic
values, and productive system (e.g., individual producer, collective family enterprise, intrafamily cooperative production),
were in many respects multiple facets of the same phenomenon.
Thus in the Doukoloma area if you earned your living as a fisherman, you were probably called, and called yourself, a Somono
even if your father had been a Bamana farmer.   If you were a
FulBe, you were brought up in an atmosphere stressing qualities
that predisposed you to take up herding, (e.g., independence in
decision making, the individual possession of capital rather than
rights to cultivate land, greater knowledge of animal husbandry
than agriculture).   Lastly, being a member of an ethnic group
that possessed a way of doing things already structured one's
relations to others in such a way that, all else being equal, it
was easier, and usually more productive, to continue doing things
as they were done, than individually to deviate.

[3]For reports by the individual researchers, see Eskelinen et
al. (1979).

[4]I might note the overwhelming economic justification of such
low-level research.   I was able to collect a full year's market and
migration data on a graduate stipend of $600 a month, the loan of
a USAID vehicle, and $120 a month for four teenage assistants.
The average cost to AID for an outside consultant is $10,000 to
$12,000 a month in addition to in-country logistic support.

Information from these activities was supplemented with data gathered through the use of less structured participant observation while living among the people and following their daily actions.   My observations in the area over a period of one year produced quantitative data on herd composition, cattle sales, and herd movements.   While my findings were not based on a large random sample, they provided, I believe, an accurate description of the situation, and did so with considerable depth.   My participant observation also provided information that in turn made possible the explanation of several critical inconsistencies and enigmas.

Quantifiable Findings

Analysis of the quantifiable data revealed some very clear indicators on the nature of the pastoral system in the area. Herds were generally composed of 24 to 35 percent male animals; of these, 19 to 23 percent were steers of up to six years of age. While most informed observers at the time of my research supported a belief in the basic economic rationality of African pastoralism,[5] there remained numerous dissenting voices.   These critics of traditional pastoral enterprise continued to stereotype traditional herders as non-economic beings who accumulated ever-greater numbers of animals for prestige, or because of an insatiable need for security.[6]   At first glance, the data we obtained on herd composition seemed to support the contention that, indeed, not enough animals were being culled.   However, when these data were interpreted in light of market prices and the production strategies of individual herders, the case proved otherwise.   Cows were kept only as long as they were promising breeders, and were generally sold for slaughter after two years without calving.   Given that grazing resources were free, profits

---

[5]An excellent review of present thinking regarding pastoral people is available in M. Horowitz's *The Sociology of Pastoralism and African Livestock Projects,* AID Program Evaluation Discussion Paper No. 6 (1979).   See also Horowitz's chapter in this volume.

[6]For example, N. Nestel's comment, "Herdsmen maintain animals for motives of prestige, not economics.   The herdsman lives outside or on the fringes of a monetary economy and usually he attaches greater importance to the number of his stock than to their productive efficiency" (quoted in Brokensha et al., 1977, p. 18).   Another perspective is expressed by J. Caldwell, "The nomads are not ranchers; their aims are to live in the country rather than to make their fortunes out of it; their chief concern is not to profit out of the good times but to survive the bad times and to see that their families and society remain intact" (Caldwell 1975:34).

were not maximized if male animals were sold before they reached full size at the age of four or five years. The optimal moment of sale for each seller was determined by a combination of factors which, in addition to weight, included immediate access to market, seasonal variations in the herder's need for cash (e.g., taxes and celebrations), and price fluctuations for both cattle and alternative cash produce (sheep, goats, and cereals). In all cases, however, by age six all males except oxen for use or rental and necessary breeding bulls, were sold.

Most males kept beyond six years of age were used as plow oxen, supplemented by a small number of breeding bulls. Herders were not engaged solely in livestock production, but in a diversity of remunerative activities, including meat production, crop cultivation, and rental of plow oxen to other cultivators. Surprisingly, the largest percentages of male animals were found in the herds of the predominantly agricultural Bamana who had no emotional attachment whatsoever to cattle, not in the herds of the cattle-oriented FulBe. The one group that did seem to possess excessive numbers of older males (four to five stud bulls per one hundred animals) were the wealthier FulBe. Once again, however, from *their* perspective, this was not excessive, since it provided a margin of insurance in case one or two should die. Some of the older males were occasionally loaned to people who owned only a few animals or who didn't have any bulls, and, purportedly, the presence of these males in the herd makes it easier to control the cows on the long treks between grazing areas.

Management practices, particularly in relation to annual transhumance, were clearly reflected in the data obtained on herd movements to and from the area. Some FulBe herds regardless of size, left the area each year on transhumance to more distant pastures. The data also showed that no Bamana herds with fewer than 100 animals went on transhumance; but that all FulBe and Bamana herds larger than 100 animals went on transhumance. These differences were caused by constraints on herd management. Owners of large herds found themselves faced with several major problems: the difficulty of locally feeding and watering the herds during the dry season; the need to spend a great deal of time caring for the herd or to pay someone else to do so; and finally, the need to deal with the jealousy of neighbors. Since one hundred head of cattle constituted the basic unit a herder could handle during transhumance, and, as a corollary, since their care was a full time job, it made little sense for a herder to stay around his community doing less remunerative, part-time agriculture while paying another to care for his herd.

Implications for Project Design

The above information clarified the logic of specific pastoral practices in the area, and bore testimony to the basic rationality and adaptiveness of the existing livestock production systems. This is not to say that the systems could not be improved, but it did indicate that the imposition of an entirely new system was unwise.   Unfortunately, the livestock project being planned for the area would do exactly this.

The project called for the creation of a single, geographically delimited area for year-round grazing and annual fattening operations. This feature of project plans persisted even though our research revealed a rational system of pastoral production whose real problems were elsewhere. These consisted of bottlenecks in the organization of animal transport to northern markets during the spring; poor quality seasonal grazing areas; counterproductive governmental policies such as depressed price schedules for animals, unpredictable closures of trade routes for political reasons; and finally, a system of yearly taxes on cattle regardless of their value or use.

On the basis of my findings I argued that a multifaceted, mobile, flexible system of production called for a similarly flexible response on the part of project planners. Instead of a single improved grazing area, efforts were needed to improve the carrying capacity of the entire system. This was possible by encouraging continued seasonal transhumance, a pastoral strategy that allowed grazing areas to be used when their nutritional value was greatest, and by encouraging efforts to improve pasture quality in those areas known to be unsatisfactory during the annual transhumance cycle. At the same time, government services, in particular the livestock service, should have assumed the responsibility of continually evaluating the effects of decisions by other government agencies--regarding taxes, prices, and import regulations--on livestock production activities.

Unanswered Questions

The situation described above highlights the rationality of FulBe livestock practices. We should be careful, however, to avoid the over-glorification of "traditional" rationality that has replaced earlier denunciations in some circles.[7] Barring drastic change, most production systems that have survived in a specific environment for any length of time are those that have proven adaptive. Given this situation, one must beware of clustering quantified data in ways that only emphasize major consistencies, while slighting potentially important inconsistencies. The data that revealed the trends discussed above also indicated broad variations in behavior among individuals that were not economically, managerially, or environmentally adaptive. Some practices made no contribution to sustaining maximum livestock production, while others appeared to have negative effects.

In the case of the most carefully studied herds, where the average rate of off-take was 9.1 percent, there were always a few

---

[7]A qualification of the now popular view of pastoralists as completely rational producers is expressed in Brokensha et al., 1977, p. 6.

Table 3. AVERAGE PRODUCTION OF PEANUTS
AND SORGHUM/MILLET IN COMMUNAL FIELDS
IN RELATION TO DEGREE OF AGRICULTURAL
MODERNIZATION: NAMALA SB AND KOBIRI VILLAGE

	Peanuts		Sorghum/Millet	
	Kg/Capita	Kg/Active Worker	Kg/Capita	Kg/Active Worker
Namala SB				
Light Theme (n = 9)	250	365	202	283
Equipped (n = 4)	185	343	232	382
Ratio: Equipped/ Light Theme	0.74	0.94	1.15	1.35
Kobiri Village				
Traditional (n = 2)	75	164	90	199
Light Theme (n = 2)	166	297	140	251
Equipped (n = 4)	170	330	230	447
Ratio: Equipped/ Light Theme	1.02	1.11	1.64	1.78

Source: Kobiri Village, from Unité d'Evaluation (1977). Namala
SB, 1978 farm management study (one interviewer only).

ing the following year. Yet farmers continued to plant larger
communal grain fields. In Kobiri village, the only site for which
data were available, the average size of fields cultivated in grain
(4.0 hectares) was larger than the average for fields cultivated in
peanuts (3.2 hectares) for all categories of farmers (Unité

d'Evaluation 1977:11). The most extreme difference was found among traditional households which, on average, cultivated 2.1 hectares in grain and only 1.1 hectares in peanuts.

Social considerations reinforce economic ones. Greater peanut production can only increase income, but more grain makes possible a variety of returns, only one of which is increased income. Moreover, even from an income perspective, earnings from grain sales have the advantage of being spread out over the year. Since grain was more often sold privately than through official marketing channels, the farmers could sell to merchants as they needed money rather than all at once, which they had to do if they sold peanuts to the OACV. They may also choose to sell at a time when prices are higher rather than lower, thus maximizing their returns. They do, however, risk being unable to find a suitable buyer who will pay an acceptable price when they want to sell. For example, after a bumper crop, parallel-market grain prices fall below the official ones, and if farmers need to sell grain to obtain cash, they must sell at the low price offered by middlemen. Since they cannot predict at planting time what the crop year will be like, it makes sense for farmers to plant some combination of peanuts, which provide a secure income through fixed prices, and grain, which, in terms of income, is more speculative.[8]

Grain may also be used to fulfill intra-village social obligations and to increase an individual's influence within the village community. If not sold, increased grain production can be used to add to household grain stores. This not only helps insure the continuation of the household by providing subsistence during bad crop years, but the presence of that insurance also increases the household head's ability to attract members (i.e., potential labor). The accumulation of grain reserves permits redistribution in various ways to increase influence within the village community. Intra-village political power is gained primarily through redistribution rather than accumulation, and grain is more usefully redistributed than are peanuts.

The redistribution of grain is also important in obtaining and keeping a wife, since it ensures allies who will supply a man with a reliable woman (Lewis 1978:41). This is valuable because the ability to secure wives is a way of building one's household and increasing one's influence. A significant tangible reward for men who remain in the household is women. Equipped families clearly contained a higher proportion of women: there were 1.3 adult women for each adult man in equipped households as compared with 1.1 women per man in light theme households and 1.0 women per man in traditional households. The value of women is two-fold. First, they contribute added labor power to the family, working on communal fields and growing a variety of crops in

---

[8] Peasants elsewhere have been shown to value sporadic over yearly lump sum incomes (cf. Champaud 1970).

their own fields. Second, they produce children, thereby increasing the household's size and adding to its social and economic resources.

Family grain is also distributed directly to other members of
the village. Successful families in the villages studied often gave
one-tenth of their production to the poor as the *diaka*, a traditional Moslem gift (A. Fleming 1979a:7). This increases the
influence of the giver as well as providing help to the poor.

The increased proportion of grain produced by equipped
farmers may also be directly related to strategies they have
adopted to avoid risk, which are different from strategies used
by non-equipped farmers. To understand these strategies, it is
useful to compare the cash incomes of equipped and light theme
farmers.[9] Figures from Namala SB (Table 4) show that heads of
equipped households had substantially higher cash incomes than
did heads of light theme households, earning, on average,
433,000 FM ($1,056) and 199,000 FM ($486), respectively. Although absolute earnings of equipped household heads from
peanut sales were higher, the proportion of their total earnings
accounted for by peanut sales was much lower than for heads of
light theme households, amounting to 50 percent and 81 percent
of total earnings, respectively. Equipped farmers were substantially less dependent on peanuts as a source of income and were
able to rely to a much greater degree on other sources, which
varied considerably from farmer to farmer. One farmer earned
over 300,000 FM ($732) from the sale of millet/sorghum; another
earned 133,000 FM ($324), and a third earned 72,500 FM ($177)
from livestock sales. A fourth received 22,500 ($55) for contrac-
tual services, and another 40,000 FM ($98) from private credit.
There is evidence that another equipped farmer, who went into
large-scale trade, showed gross income of 488,000 FM ($1,190)
from the sale of imports, with expenses of 362,000 FM ($883),
thereby earning a profit of over 100,000 FM ($244).

It is well known that sahelian farmers attempt to minimize
risk from the natural environment through intercropping different
cultivars (Norman 1974b), and also try to reduce risk from the
political environment by first growing enough to feed themselves
and only then turning to cash crop production. The more affluent farmers in the area have taken this same general pattern of
adaptation and transposed it to another level, diversifying sources of cash income to avoid dependence on one income source. In
so doing, they have decreased their direct dependence on rainfed

---

[9]Income and expense figures must be viewed with extreme
caution, for they are surely underestimated. B. Stomal, another
Purdue researcher, has suggested that farmers tend to forget to
tell interviewers about major expenditures (e.g., bridewealth,
livestock purchases, school fees) when they become used to
remembering and reporting small daily expenses [personal
communication]. The use of mean values also tends to hide great
variation among individuals in any one category.

Table 4. MEAN INCOME AND EXPENDITURES FOR HOUSEHOLD HEADS: NAMALA SB

Household Type	Income			Expenditures			
	Source	Amount (FM)	Percent of Inc.	Item	Amount (FM)	Percent of Inc.	Exp.
Light Theme (n=12)	Peanuts	161,238	81	Repay OACV + other inputs	17,434	9	12
	OACV credit	13,226	7	Livestock	1,920	1	1
	Gifts	4,965	2	Taxes	31,318	16	21
	Other	19,655	10	Kola nuts	15,585	8	11
				Imports	13,756	7	9
				Gifts	26,407	13	18
				Other	40,517	20	28
Totals, Light Theme Households		199,084 ($486)	100		146,937 ($358)	74	100

Inc. - Exp. = 52,147 (excess)
($127)

Equipped (n=9)

Peanuts	216,747	50	
OACV credit	19,489	5	
Gifts	17,886	4	
Other	178,804	41	
Repay OACV	0	0	0
Other inputs	7,997	1.5	4
Livestock	13,722	3	6
Taxes	57,742	13	26
Kola nuts	29,361	7	13
Imports	49,992	12	22
Gifts	59,182	14	26
Other	7,647	1.5	3

Totals, Equipped Households   432,926   100
($1,056)

Totals   225,643   52   100
($550)

Inc. - Exp. = 207,283   (excess)
($506)

Traditional (n=6)

Peanuts	6,613	14	
Millet/sorghum	17,938	37	
Gifts	10,918	23	
Other	12,806	26	
Livestock	2,083	4	4
Taxes	7,300	15	13
Kola nuts	14,726	31	26
Imports	11,833	25	21
Gifts	16,537	34	30
Other	3,351	7	6

Totals, Traditional Households   48,275   100
($118)

Totals   55,830   116   100
($136)

Inc. - Exp. = 7,555   (deficit)
(-$18)

Source: 1978 farm management study, Namala SB only.

agriculture by moving into other arenas; they were simultaneously increasing their links with the outside world, particularly through greater trade and livestock transactions. At the same time, they continued to assure their own role within the village by providing their own and other families with food.

What do these patterns of differentiation among farmers imply for the future? Both equipped and light theme farmers have entered the national economy, but in ways that have different consequences. Wealthy farmers were benefiting from the exercise of entrepreneurial skills despite government policies to discourage this. They were widening their control of productive resources through diversification within farming and livestock production, and also were beginning to control rural exchange networks through trade. This is in contrast to light theme farmers, who lacked the resources of their equipped neighbors and had to obtain the funds they needed solely through cash crop production. The consequence was an extreme dependence on peanuts as a source of cash. Traditional farmers entered the national economy only minimally. They sold a small amount of their production to earn money for taxes and manufactured goods, but remained more dependent on village neighbors than on national marketing systems for their survival.

The implications of this intra-village differentiation for longer-term processes of stratification are still unclear. The strong position of wealthy farmers could lead to their greater political domination: they alone have links outside the village that could be used to develop a power base independent of the village, allowing them to become more exploitative of other villagers. This had not yet happened, however, because the lines of kinship that join families of different economic levels and the ideology of village equality have decreased differentiation on explicitly economic grounds. The dominance of wealthy families remained primarily political, and was achieved through economic redistribution rather than through economic exploitation. Unfortunately, the design of the study made it difficult to secure data on relationships between families. The unit of analysis was the family and the family farm; therefore, information on transactions between families was not systematically collected. In retrospect, it is clear that a research strategy that took the village rather than the household as a unit of analysis would have allowed us to answer questions more satisfactorily about relationships among villagers and the implications of such relationships for processes of economic differentiation.

Practical Implications of Research Findings. As a means of increasing cash incomes for peasants, the OACV was a relatively successful program. Light theme households in Namala showed an average per capita income of 19,400 FM ($47) in the 1978-1979 season, compared to 7,100 FM per year ($17) in 1972 for all of southern Mali (CRED 1976). Even after allowing for inflation during the intervening years, the typical light theme family was doing well in rural Mali. Yet an examination of the equipped farmers' situation suggests that the OACV's main contribution has been to assure a market for the local cash crop, and that the development program has done little to encourage local autonomy or more equitable distribution of resources.

A comparison of income sources for equipped and light theme household heads underscores the dependency of light theme families on peanut sales and the vulnerability of their cash incomes should any problems arise in peanut production or marketing. It is not clear what will happen to peanut production or marketing in the future. The World Bank has discontinued its funding for the OACV as it existed in 1977. Interim financing of some components was continued through French technical assistance, and the World Bank will probably finance some projects in the region through ODIPAC (Opération de Développement Intégré pour la Production Arachidière et Céréalière), which replaced OACV.[10] In 1982, the Malian government stopped official peanut marketing, and it became difficult for farmers to sell all their peanuts. The immediate effects of this move on farmers are unknown, but during the 1960s peanut production in the region declined drastically when there were no effective marketing channels (Jones 1976:368). As these data show, wealthier farmers have access to other sources of income in such circumstances, but farmers who use only light themes have few alternatives.

The failure of the OACV to transform rural society is related to the fact that the aims of development programs have often been to provide foreign exchange for national governments and cheap food for urban consumers, rather than development for rural areas. Yet, the trend toward integrated rural development projects and agricultural development projects that stress subsistence over cash crops suggests that the explicit goals of rural development projects have changed. For example, the World Bank has said that it would orient new projects toward the least favored rural inhabitants, and that these projects should be run in a decentralized way in order to permit participation of the rural poor in the process of planning and execution (World Bank 1975a: 38, 69). The New Directions policies of AID stressed the same goals.

If these goals were to be taken seriously, data of the kind presented here suggest that planners need to recognize that rural societies in Africa already include a number of groups that have unequal access to labor, land, and capital. Larger farmers who already have greater access to these resources are more likely to benefit from programs as they are currently designed. Therefore, if a project has limited resources, it would probably be more fruitful to design it specifically to benefit smaller rather than larger farmers. My experiences with development projects and with farmers lead me to believe that larger farmers have the capacity to manipulate the components of any project for their benefit, while small farmers do not.

---

[10]The World Bank subsequently renewed some funding of ODIPAC, and the resulting project promoted diversified farming and supported farmer cooperatives (World Bank 1981b).

Projects such as the OACV have often been planned to serve all farmers within a given region uniformly. The OACV in its very design was biased toward larger farmers, since farmers were required to have a minimum of ten hectares of land (the average farm size) and own a pair of draft oxen in order to obtain credit for a plow. Therefore, the OACV could not serve poorer farmers or encourage a more equitable distribution of benefits. Thus OACV's programs very likely promoted already existing inequities.

A single agricultural project cannot change national or worldwide processes of social stratification. However, a project can be planned in such a way as not to exacerbate existing inequities. There are some straightforward ways to deal with these problems. Project designers should take into account differences in resources available to farmers, and their different needs in light of these resources, and plan specific subprojects accordingly. If resources are too limited to design separate subprojects for different groups, projects might be directed toward some middle-range of access to resources, rather than using figures for holdings or household size that, in fact, reflect characteristics of better endowed segments of society (cf. Mencher 1977).

Implications for Theory Building. There should not be a split between applied and academic interests in anthropology, and one researcher can often have both. The study of agriculture in Kita had distinct practical goals, but it has also contributed to our knowledge about the relationship of social organization to agricultural change and the adoption of new technologies. Indeed, the large number of studies being done in conjunction with development projects in the West African savanna offer a rich opportunity for relatively controlled cross-cultural comparison. I would like to suggest what seem to be useful directions for the future by pointing out some contrasts between my results and those of Lewis (1978; 1979) and Weil (1973), who discuss the problems of agricultural development in ethnically similar Mande-speaking groups in Mali and Gambia respectively.

In Kita, households with the most traditional family structures (polygynous, extended, with collateral branches) were also the ones most likely to adopt new agricultural techniques. In contrast, among Bambara farmers in the region near Segou, to the east of Bamako, those most integrated into traditional social relationships were the least likely to adopt new equipment (Lewis 1978).[11] Moreover, traditional forms of labor cooperation were used to discourage adoption of equipment in the Segou region by cutting off access to exchange labor of farmers who used

---

[11]Lewis and I do use somewhat different indexes of insertion into traditional village-based social structures. I rely primarily on family size and the kind of extended family present, while he relies more directly on genealogical connections among families. A more definitive discussion than that presented here would examine the degree to which these two indexes correspond.

equipment. Lewis (1978:40) suggests that the reason for this lies in the degradation of the region's heavy clay soils, due to the deeper plowing made possible by farm equipment. Thus, equipped farmers would need to fallow more often and use more land per capita than nonequipped farmers. A comparison with the Kita situation suggests the importance of demographic pressure in this response.

Assuming that soils in the Kita region may be exhausted somewhat sooner by plowing, [12] Kita farmers can be less concerned about limits on access to land because more land is available. Kita is known for its low population density, lower than that of most other inhabited areas of Mali, including Segou. One index of population density is the length of the fallow period. Lewis (1979:119) reports that few farmers placed land in fallow for 20 years, yet A. Fleming (1979a:10) observed that some farmers fallowed for as many as 30-40 years in Kita, and that 10-20 year fallows were relatively common. Moreover, enough free land is available so that if there were a localized land shortage, a family could move out to clear new land in a nearby agricultural hamlet. Smaller farmers in Kita need not worry that greater land use by equipped farmers will jeopardize their own access to land in the short run. Thus, population density plays a role in determining whether or not a given innovation affects traditional social relations.

A comparison of the two cases also suggests the importance of relative location in state systems. Present-day Mali was the site of a number of precolonial empires. From around the thirteenth century A.D., the Niger basin was a significant territory held by those empires, and was passed in turn from Mali to the Songhay to Segu. Meanwhile, peasants in the region--which included the village studied by Lewis (1979)-- had the choice of paying tribute to the latest conquerors or being enslaved. Lewis suggests that the strong egalitarianism found in Bambara villages is directly related to a productive strategy that could be used to provide tribute and avoid enslavement. Although Kita town served in the sixteenth century as the head of one of the smaller successor states of Mali (Levtzion 1973:99), it has generally been a backwater of the empires. It lies between the two major Malian river valleys, the Senegal and the Niger; it is hilly and infested by flies carrying onchocerciasis. [13] Lacking the agricultural and transport importance of the Niger valley, and having a very small population, the Kita region was probably less consistently

------

[12]This is not necessarily an accurate assumption, as the degree of degradation also seems to depend on the heaviness of the soil (Lewis 1978). However, it is the most conservative assumption in this case.

[13]Distance from major trade routes as well as the presence of the onchocerciasis disease vector probably contributed to the Kita area's low population density.

pressured to pay tribute. In fact, the formation of small, isolated villages far from major trade routes was a Malinke strategy for avoiding payment of tribute (Brasseur 1968). The Malinke villages in the Kita region seem to have had less need to provide a united front to invaders by virtue of being more isolated, so there were fewer internal constraints to the development of stratification. Thus we see that historical factors can be important in forming present-day cultural values, which may in turn aid or impede the adoption of new social or technical patterns.

Although the manner in which they have remained so differ, both Malian areas appear quite traditional when compared to the Gambian village of Bumari described by Weil (1973). There, large extended families had disappeared and small families were the major productive units. At least some agricultural production had become more intensive, and the division of labor had changed so that women rather than men were the primary food producers. Men grew peanuts, but less millet and sorghum. Women continued to grow the rice they had always grown, but it had become an important staple rather than a subsidiary one. The greater changes found in the Gambia are again related to its location within a state system. As Kita was isolated from the main areas of the Malian empires, so was Mali from the European colonial empires based on the sea. Although affected by colonialism, Malian peasants, far from major colonial ports and urban centers, were less likely to be drawn directly into colonial trading patterns. In particular, they were not called upon to provide food for urban and port centers.

Present political constraints are also important. More affluent Malian peasants continue to strive both for traditional rewards (greater intra-village status and power, more wives, livestock) and for more modern rewards (consumer goods, education). Modern rewards do not replace traditional rewards at least in part because they have not been reliably available. In Mali, the socialist policies of Modibo Keita, from 1960 until his fall in 1968, increased rural poverty and isolation. Villagers had few possibilities to earn income, to increase their power or influence outside the village, or even to purchase basic goods. Jones (1976:302) notes that very few consumer goods were for sale in rural areas through the late 1960s. Only in the south, where cotton was produced for export, could official programs obtain even simple agricultural implements for sale to peasants. The lack of goods, high consumer prices, and low producer prices led to a fall in peanut sales from 56,000 metric tons in 1958-1959 to 10,000 metric tons in 1968-1969 (Jones 1976:368). The present government has reinstituted more effective marketing channels, but Malian peasants still cannot depend on the national economy and must look to structures of reciprocity and redistribution within their home villages for security.

The data from these three sites suggest that an understanding of the limitations on adoption of new agricultural technologies cannot be derived from a general model that emphasizes one or two independent variables as the keys to understanding social change. The above analyses of comparative change among Malian and Gambian villages have stressed ecological factors (e.g., soil quality, demography), and factors stemming from the larger political economy (e.g., the role of both traditional and modern empire building). While these two sets of conditions may be the principal determinants of how people structure their societies, they cannot by themselves explain a particular social form in a particular village. One must examine how the different factors interact in specific circumstances in order to understand the social structure of a village, hence the ways in which it is likely to react to a development program.

This observation is not new. Stavenhagen (1975) shows how the processes of colonization interacted with different varieties of traditional social organization to form distinctly different patterns of social stratification in Mesoamerica and in the Ivory Coast. It needs to be emphasized that while general models of social change can be valuable guides for the anthropologist, they cannot explain particular social forms in the detail needed for development planning. This underlines the importance of the anthropologist in providing specific analyses for particular projects. It also suggests that anthropologists will never generate a model of change refined enough to be satisfactory for every situation. A model is useful for orienting the researcher in approaching a situation, but not sufficient to understand that situation.

THE ANTHROPOLOGIST AND THE WEST AFRICA PROJECTS: SOME PROBLEM AREAS

Data Collection and Analysis

In my work with the Projects I played two roles: development specialist and anthropologist. While not incompatible, these roles placed different demands on me. As a development specialist who would like to see Malian peasants live better, I wanted the results of the research to have some immediate impact on the design and implementation of a project. As an anthropologist, I was concerned about the quality of the data and have reservations about drawing too many conclusions from them. Concerns about data quality are many: my field time was too short; the data were collected by others; I could not contact enough farmers because of my administrative responsibilities; and some important questions were left unasked. Although a great deal of quantitative information is available to me, as are the anthropological studies of many who have previously worked in the West African savanna, I did not have an opportunity to engage in careful, extended fieldwork of my own. Thus, as an anthropologist, I view the findings outlined above as hypotheses for further investigation rather than definitive conclusions. What I have argued seems to be valid, based on the quantitative data and literature, but it requires further validation that can come only from more extended ethnographic fieldwork with farmers.

From an anthropological viewpoint, the inadequacy of the data is directly related to the research design and methodology, the bulk of which was prepared by non-anthropologists. Unlike many situations where anthropologists must design or evaluate projects in four to eight weeks, time was not a problem. The research continued for about 18 months, a period clearly sufficient for adequate field research. The major problems stemmed from failure to ask some of the right questions and the distance of the research supervisor from the people being studied.

Attempts to analyze the field data have made it clear that certain important questions left unasked during the survey can no longer be pursued. As noted above, for example, very little information was obtained on relationships among villagers and their implications for economic and political stratification. Some of these unasked questions are the normal result of research: one is never thorough enough and more information can always be collected. In other cases, e.g., concerning intra-village relationships, the lack was caused by a research design that did not use an anthropological approach. The absence of this approach was notable in our assumption that the relevant unit of analysis was the family farm. Most anthropologists would have been more tentative about the appropriate unit of analysis, letting villagers themselves define appropriateness in a given situation.[14] An approach that allows villagers themselves to define the problem can uncover important information that otherwise would have been ignored.

The failure to ask the right questions is also tied to the second problem, that of distance between the research supervisor and the interviewee/informant. The approach that allows informants to participate in defining the important questions also presupposes close contact between the anthropologist and villagers who will discuss many different issues. Yet much development research is organized in such a way as to make this close contact very difficult--and so it was for the Africa Projects.

This organization resulted in part because traditional anthropological research posed problems for development planners. The major problem was that of representativeness of findings and the capacity to generalize from the data collected. The smaller data base often used by anthropologists was not considered representative by planners, who saw it as failing to provide them with the basis they needed to design projects for large populations. Therefore, development research designs tend to use large samples--too large to be interviewed well by one individual. To deal with this, a hierarchical research organization was developed, in which a research supervisor (anthropologist, agricultural economist, etc.) supervises a number of lower level personnel who actually do the interviewing and have contact with informants.

---

[14]I am not arguing for a totally emic approach, but simply against rigidly defining the universe of investigation before entering the field. Applied researchers can learn from the experiences of Hill-Burnett (1978), who effectively combines etic and emic perspectives.

While research supervisors make important decisions about research design, they must also serve as administrators, and it occasionally happens that supervisors have virtually no contact with villagers because of administrative demands. On the other hand, research supervisors who wish to reduce the distance between themselves and their informants must take active steps to establish such contacts. In this project, for example, supervisors were not encouraged to live in villages (rather than in towns), nor were they encouraged to learn the local language, or to spend time in informal discussions with farmers and their families. In my case, living in a village remained an unrealized goal. Because of my administrative duties, it became possible only after my contract terminated, when I was ready to return to the United States.

While contact with villagers is crucial, the field time and conditions need not be the same in a research project as during traditional fieldwork done by the lone anthropologist. First, the research project anthropologist has available considerable supplementary data. Second, because of additional human and technical resources, research questions can be better designed, allowing the anthropologist to use the limited time more efficiently.

Interviewers can be used more effectively. Presently, interviewers, who often have little formal education, tend to be assigned to well-defined, repetitive tasks that leave little room for error. Many research designers assume that less educated interviewers are incapable of more complex tasks, but my experience suggests that this assumption is incorrect. On the contrary, work that consists only of repetitive tasks stifles those who could be the best and most productive interviewers. To supplement such duties, they could be taught the rudiments of participant observation and given a list of relevant questions and notebooks in which to record their observations. The resulting observations could be discussed by interviewers and supervisor and may be added to the data base and/or suggest the formulation of new questions. Careful and consistent supervision of the interviewers is essential, of course.

Microcomputers also may prove to be a valuable field tool once such practical issues as provision of spare parts and voltage regulation are solved. Effectively used, they enable the researcher to do preliminary tabulations of results in the field. Such early quantitative results, when combined with qualitative information, may usefully indicate inadequacies in the survey techniques and suggest directions for further research.

Two examples from the Kita study are illustrative. First, analysis in the United States of data from budget questionnaires indicated that most individuals have incomes substantially greater than expenditures (see Table 4). The data also showed almost no livestock purchases among the peasants studied. Yet peasants rarely keep cash, and livestock is known to be a common form of investment for savanna farmers. It is likely that farmers were hesitant to reveal certain kinds of investment information and/or that survey techniques were inadequate to uncover it. Had it been known while interviewers were still in the field that anticipated data were missing, informal interviewing could have been used to supplement the survey and find out why we learned nothing about livestock investments. Preliminary tabulations of results on a microcomputer in the field would have allowed us to discover this gap before returning to the United States.[15]

Quantitative results can also point to new areas for research, especially if local patterns differ from those found elsewhere. Literature on female earning power suggests that women beyond childbearing age or with no children have greater earning opportunities than do younger women (Weil 1973). Yet, the Kita results suggest that first wives of household heads earn more than other female household members, regardless of their age or the number of their children. Further field study could have provided useful insights into the constraints on women's economic opportunities. We should be willing to make better use of the labor resources and new technologies available to us, for they may help us to make better use of the limited time we often have for participant observation.

Interdisciplinary Collaboration

Development projects commonly include applied research teams made up of several technical personnel having different professional backgrounds. The Projects I discuss here fit this pattern to some extent, because both economists and anthropologists were hired, and sites were often staffed by persons from each discipline. There was little cooperation, however, among personnel with dissimilar training. No systematic attempts were made to have individuals from different disciplines follow one another as consecutive site supervisors. Whoever was available at the time was sent. When, by chance, two researchers having different backgrounds staffed a site, the project lacked a structure that would encourage collaboration.[16]

As a result, individual researchers have written about what they considered most important. Topics treated by anthropologists have included migration; the role of women; the role of the extended family and land tenure; and the social organization of

---

[15]The West Africa Projects did install a microcomputer at the Institut d'Economie Rurale in Mali, but too late to be of use for tabulating data from Kita.

[16]At several sites, particularly in Mali, anthropologists followed economists or vice versa, yet they rarely found themselves in a position to collaborate. It should be noted, however, that the longest term collaboration between an anthropologist and an economist on the Projects occurred between a project anthropologist in Burkina Faso and an economist from another organization who were able to work together over a period of several years. For the results of their work, see Murphy and Sprey (1980a; 1980b; 1980c).

production, including attention to the distribution of access to resources and the division of labor. Economists studied a variety of topics appropriate to their interests: the relationship between the use of cultivation equipment and increased agricultural productivity; production increases gained through extensive rather than intensive cultivation; and the development of linear programming models. Although most project researchers produced new information relevant to development, the possibilities for integrating individual results into a regional multidisciplinary analysis are limited. This is an important point because it was one of the major goals of the research project. While reports from individual researchers at single sites can be useful, they tend to present a limited perspective. Factors of considerable importance that might come only from a multidisciplinary analysis or from comparing different sites are ignored.

The problem can be partially solved by simply bringing individuals together at some single place and time to write. But this would have been difficult, because people from different disciplines were not at the research sites simultaneously. Greater opportunities for collaboration should have been part of the research design. In making site assignments, for example, care should have been taken to have people from different disciplines succeed one another at research sites, and some overlap should have been planned. Thus, when the last researcher from a site was engaged in data analysis, there would have been some possibility of researchers from that site working together on at least part of the final report. In cases where a site was staffed by one person, individuals from differing disciplinary backgrounds who had worked at sites having similar characteristics could have met to collaborate in writing a joint paper. Of course, practical problems could foil such possibilities: for example, the first person to work on the site might already have left for another job. Still, some collaboration in writeup would have been possible if the project organization had provided for encounters of this kind.

Eventually the Purdue Projects endeavored to bring people together by organizing large workshops over several days. Nevertheless, there is also a need for much smaller groups to meet and discuss analyses over a longer period of time, if a final report is to be a synthesis of various perspectives. Moreover, the problems of organizing even small workshops were magnified by the scale of the West Africa Projects.

The Scale of Project Operations

The problem of operational scale reflects the large-scale, regional view of agricultural development adopted by the Projects. If data already exist, a review of existing literature can provide a comprehensive picture of a situation. The assumption of the principal investigators, however, was that needed micro-level data did not exist. Thus, they felt that data collection at many sites was required to reach a satisfactory understanding.

Data collection on such a large scale led to unforeseen problems. Major daily logistical problems arose from the need to secure information from and provide money to as many as ten researchers working in relatively inaccessible locations throughout West Africa at any given time. Difficulties with data processing occurred. The farm management studies, which entailed repeated interviews on daily labor time, yielded an enormous quantity of data. In an attempt to handle this mass, microcomputers were introduced at some field sites midway through the program. For most researchers, though, the microcomputers arrived too late; they were obliged to return to the United States with boxes and trunks full of forms for coding and key-punching prior to analysis.

Project staff spent several months trying to design a coding form that would render data from different sites directly comparable. Because of great variation among sites, however, the effort was finally abandoned. A large staff was hired for coding, punching, and programming operations, but it always seemed insufficient.

There are no easy solutions to the problem of scale. One, obvious, entails the design of smaller scale projects. But this seems infeasible because of the nature of donor organizations. In AID, for instance, the problem of scale is linked to the Agency's propensity to fund expensive projects, which, in turn, is related to a tendency to base professional staff advancement on the capacity to "move money." Tendler (1975) notes that in the 1960s, when only import costs were funded, expensive dams and power plants were frequent projects. Since then, policies within AID have allowed financing of costs other than imports, but the change has not altered the tendency to base advancement on "money moving." Now AID employees find themselves in the position of having to plan projects that are on an "appropriate" scale and aid the poor, yet still spend large sums. One way to accomplish this is to replicate a simple project at many sites (e.g., dig 200 wells rather than 20), or to design an umbrella project (e.g., an integrated rural development project) that contains a large number of small-scale projects.

For research programs like the West Africa Projects, if the problems of scale do not interfere with project implementation it is only because there is nothing to be implemented. But the same kinds of problems do occur in development projects, and for similar reasons. Large scale makes the logistics of projects unduly difficult, and it also makes them less likely to succeed. Large-scale projects are less able to respond quickly to varying needs among local populations, or to involve local populations in project decision-making. Smaller projects may be better able to achieve such goals, but small-scale projects are infrequent, given the present constraints within donor organizations. Policy changes at the highest levels within these donor organizations will be necessary if development projects are to be organized to encourage local participation and responsiveness to local needs.

CONCLUSIONS

The experience and the results of the work discussed above are drawn from my role as an independent consultant. While this is only one of many roles that anthropologists may play, it is one frequently assumed by technical experts who become involved in development work. Persons considering work as consultants should be aware of several aspects of this role.

Consultants may have a significant degree of autonomy, but they rarely have any institutionalized power. At best, they may enter a situation where an outside expert is expected to tell planners what to do in order to save them from a sticky situation (cf. Tendler 1975:13). Often the consultant's capacity to influence those who plan and implement projects depends as much on prior contacts with insiders as it does on disciplinary expertise. It is the insider, the staff member, finally, who defines general development strategies and the goals and structure of specific projects. Consultants must accept this fact of life--and limitation--before they agree to an assignment.

Relative isolation is another problem common to the independent consultant. It is not unusual to be the only anthropologist on a given project, and there is often no one with whom to discuss anthropological problems that arise. This problem is exacerbated by the lack of literature available to the practitioner, since results of development work often appear only in internal reports and are not easily available to the general public. People who do not know about a previous project often have a difficult time learning about it, and then obtaining relevant information about it. Moreover results are often focused on the particular needs of the projects, and broader issues, such as methodological problems or "lessons learned" are not explicitly addressed.

All this makes it very difficult for individuals to learn from the mistakes or successes of others. I have myself seen the problems discussed above (interdisciplinary collaboration, data collection, scale) repeated in similar form on another project in the recent past. The obvious solution is to encourage more communication among those doing independent consulting, but this too is extremely difficult since consultants are spread all over the world and many do not have the free time necessary to write additional papers.

The disadvantages of independent consulting are, however, balanced by its advantages. The consultant's autonomy, which exists on several levels, can serve to balance his/her lack of power. First, a consultant often has autonomy at the level of the project organization. On the Purdue Projects, once the major survey was under way, researchers had a great deal of autonomy in choosing supplementary projects. They also had freedom as to how they chose to write up data and reports. Project descriptions are often fuzzy, and employers far away, so that consulting personnel frequently have a significant amount of freedom in deciding how to carry out their assignments within general limitations of finances and time.

Autonomy also goes beyond the individual assignment: as consultants become established, they usually have a greater choice among projects. The consultant can choose projects that use a particular methodology or development strategy, deal with a particular problem or sector, are located in a certain country, or meet personal goals. For example, I have largely confined my work to Mali and Cameroon. This has allowed me to use and expand my general knowledge of these countries, do a better job on projects, and deepen my understanding of the issues involved. I have also been able to work more often on long-term projects that have the potential of providing data more satisfactory to an anthropologist. Finally, I have been able to work during part of the year while teaching during the remainder.

Not all consultants will have the same goals. However, independent consultants, once they are established, have the possibility of structuring their lives around individual sets of priorities. One reason for this has to do with another aspect of consulting--the blurring of lines of authority. The consultant is hired by a contractor who may or may not be directly involved with the project. With USAID projects, consultants work more directly with, but not for, personnel in the country mission, with host country counterparts, and, sometimes, with AID Washington staff. The possibilities for securing future work often depend more on relationships with these latter groups than with the employer, since employers often change. In the same vein, contractors often have difficulty locating personnel, and turn to AID missions or Washington for suggestions. Missions will recommend those they have worked with and know well. The blurring of lines of authority encourages and even forces autonomy and independent decision-making by consultants, who must nevertheless be able to make recommendations acceptable to those with whom they work. Acceptable recommendations do not mean total agreement, but they must be feasible for the situation.

Because of my experience as a consultant and because of these features of independent consulting, I have stressed the points made in this paper. The advantages (access to relatively large amounts of data; autonomy in research design, analysis, and dissemination of results) and the disadvantages (inability to ensure that results will have impact on future project design, definition of the general structure of research by persons more central to project planning, isolation) I have discussed arise from the situation in which the work is done. Anthropologists who choose to become independent consultants, particularly on long-term projects, can expect to find rewards and constraints similar to those treated here.

Editors' Note to Chapter 3

Anthropologists sometimes have reputations for being pro-peasant and anti-government. What, then, can anthropology offer to state planners? Dennis Warren illuminates the possibilities as he describes his participation in efforts to promote decentralization and a more active role for regional government workers in Ghana in the planning and initiation of local development programs. Like Nolan (Chapter 4), Warren draws from anthropological and interdisciplinary perspectives, in this case to train, or re-train, Ghanaian government workers in the organizational techniques needed for effective decentralization. Among these is the capacity to overcome obstacles to effective communication that frequently hinder the planning and implementation of development efforts. Warren and his co-workers had the task of transforming bureaucrat-administrators into initiators of development programs reflecting local needs and interests. Their experience in Ghana made Warren and his associates at Iowa State University particularly aware of a need to provide interdisciplinary training for anthropologists and others for more effective work in development programs.

3
Anthropology and
Rural Development in Ghana

DENNIS M. WARREN
Iowa State University

THE CHANGING ROLE OF ANTHROPOLOGY IN GHANA

During the past decade, I have accepted assignments with the United States Agency for International Development (AID) on seven occasions, including five short-term assignments (from several days to three months), and two two-year assignments. These have included the design and presentation of general rural development models and the identification, design, and social soundness analysis of specific development projects, as well as their implementation and evaluation. These activities have been carried out in several sectors, including health, agriculture, co-operatives, integrated planning, and development administration.

In this paper I will describe the changing roles that anthro-pologists have played in Ghanaian rural development. Then I will discuss my own involvement in the long-term design and imple-mentation of rural development activities in Ghana. This includes my participation in the Economic and Rural Development Manage-ment Project (ERDM), a complex, national effort to facilitate the decentralization of development planning and budgeting from the central government in Accra to the nine regional and 68 district capitals in Ghana, and my involvement with the Primary Health Training for Indigenous Healers Project (PRHETIH). The link-ages that the ERDM project afforded me with all Government of Ghana departments and USAID/Accra officials in several sectors provided me with the additional opportunity to utilize my prior knowledge of indigenous healers in Ghana in helping to design and implement the PRHETIH project in the Techiman District. Finally, the paper describes how these processes of cross-fertil-ization have led to the development of new programs at Iowa State University that will more effectively prepare students and faculty for international development assignments.

---

*The author thanks Bill Berg, Jerry Wood, and Bill Fuller of AID, and the team members of the Economic and Rural Develop-ment Management Project (ERDM) and the Primary Health Training for Indigenous Healers Project (PRHETIH). R. E. Welch and Tom Painter provided critical editorial comments, and Audrey Burton assisted in typing drafts of this paper.

As an anthropologist, I have found that my knowledge of culture change, cross-cultural and cross-disciplinary communication models, and specific Ghanaian cultures, coupled with experience of using ethnoscientific techniques, contributed significantly to success in the design and implementation of both the ERDM and PRHETIH projects. My work was anthropological fieldwork of an experimental nature: an attempt to facilitate cross-cultural and cross-disciplinary communication through the development of culturally relevant training materials. These materials helped project participants understand the function of values, norms, and attitudes, and of emic and etic perceptions of phenomena in either fostering or hindering the types of communication necessary for truly successful rural development projects.

Earlier Roles for Anthropologists in Ghana

My involvement as an anthropologist in USAID development efforts in Ghana is linked to important shifts in AID policies caused by the New Directions legislation of 1973.[1] However, earlier links between anthropology and the government in Ghana can be traced to 1921, when the British colonial administration established the position of Gold Coast government anthropologist. The position was filled first by Robert S. Rattray, in 1921, and subsequently by Margaret J. Field, who assumed it in 1938. The government anthropologist facilitated colonial development efforts, recorded Ghanaian cultural histories, and compiled ethnographic data that could be used by government officials to further their understanding of local populations and institutions.[2]

---

[1] On May 30, 1973, 26 members of the House of Representatives Foreign Affairs Committee introduced a series of amendments to the 1961 Foreign Assistance Act that were designed to incorporate a strategy for increased local participation in development efforts into United States foreign aid policy (Owens and Shaw 1974:xiii). The amendments stated that U.S. development assistance should give highest priority to projects submitted by host governments that directly improve the lives of the poorest segments of their populations and increase their ability to participate in the development of their countries. In the past, the priorities of foreign donors had been concerned with increasing the pace of overall economic growth rather than with helping the poor, so the amendments represented a radical policy change. The amendments were signed into law by President Nixon on December 17, 1973 (Mickelwait et al. 1979:2-3).

[2] Brokensha (1966a) presents a thorough summary of the shifts in emphasis among anthropologists working in Africa. The controversy surrounding the roles of colonial anthropologists is

(Footnote Continued)

For a decade following independence in 1957, anthropology was viewed negatively in Ghana as a discipline that focused on ethnicity ("tribalism") and tradition ("the primitive past"). Ghanaian officials saw anthropologists as

. . . reactionaries and romantics who want[ed] to concentrate their studies on the primitive undeveloped Africa, who [were] unconcerned with pressing economic, social and political problems, and who also [were] so wedded to the prevalent equilibrium theory that they deplore[d] such revolutionary changes as [were] happening in Africa (Brokensha 1966a:15).

Sociologists, on the other hand, were viewed popularly as scholars actively supporting Ghana's efforts in the march toward modernity. For more than a decade after independence, some anthropologists felt it politically prudent to call themselves sociologists.

This image of the anthropologist has changed dramatically in the past decade, in part due to efforts by such Ghanaian anthropologists as K. A. Busia, Kwame Arhin, and Kweku Nukunya, and by expatriate development anthropologists teaching in Ghana, including David Brokensha, David Tait, David Butcher, Leo Barrington, and G. Lumsden. Butcher, Barrington, and Lumsden were involved in the Volta Resettlement Scheme.[3] Current AID policies require social soundness analyses for development projects, and have involved a growing number of Ghanaian anthropologists and sociologists--among them P. A. Twumasi and K. Nukunya--in development programs.

(Footnote Continued)
discussed in Asad, ed. (1973), Berreman (1968), Gjessing (1968), Gough (1968), Lewis (1973), Magubane (1971), and Owusu (1975; 1978).

[3]Brokensha has worked both as a colonial administrator in East Africa and as a development anthropologist for AID in Kenya. His interest was in intermediate-sized urban areas in Ghana (1966b). David Tait worked among the Konkomba peoples of northern Ghana until his untimely death. David Butcher, Leo Barrington, and G. Lumsden all were involved in the planning of the Volta Resettlement Scheme, a relocation of 80,000 Ghanaians whose towns were inundated by the Volta Lake after the closing of Akosombo Dam. Patrick Twumasi, a medical sociologist at the University of Ghana, has conducted social soundness analyses and evaluations of several USAID projects in Ghana, including the MIDAS project in Atebubu. Kweku Kukunya, a social anthropologist at the University of Ghana, has participated in the evaluation of USAID projects in Ghana, such as the DANFA project.

The Impact of 1973 AID and World Bank Policies on Anthropology

> [In 1973] . . . the United States became the first of the
> rich countries to shift away from a "trickle-down" to people-
> oriented development. Redirecting our efforts toward the
> poor who make up the overwhelming majority of people in the
> developing countries conforms to the instinctive concern of
> Americans that past foreign aid programs have not reached
> the people we have wanted to help (Owens and Shaw
> 1974:xiii).

AID continues to stress this new development strategy. At about
the same time, the World Bank began to stress the need to involve local people in planning, decision making, and implementation of development projects (World Bank 1975b:7, 37, 75).
These policy shifts by AID and the World Bank provided a
challenge and a mandate for the participation of anthropologists in
development efforts. Both AID and the World Bank soon realized
that it was one thing to stress the need to promote participation
of host-country nationals in the identification, design, and
implementation of development programs, and to require that
projects contribute to a more equitable distribution of economic
and political resources; it was quite another to translate the
rhetoric of new policies into reality.[4]
    At this juncture, anthropologists successfully argued that
development programs could benefit from anthropological knowledge, methodologies, skills, and sensitivities in project design,
implementation, and evaluation (Cochrane 1971; 1977; 1980). In
1974, AID organized the Development Studies Program, which included anthropological training for AID personnel, required that
social soundness analysis (SSA) be a part of all project design
efforts, and set up permanent anthropology staff positions both
in AID/Washington and in the Regional Economic Development Services Offices (REDSO) located in Abidjan and Nairobi.
    AID's requirement that social soundness analysis be an inte-
gral part of project design has had an important impact on development anthropology.[5] First, it has involved anthropologists from

---

[4]Many problems exist in the attempt to institutionalize the
New Directions legislation at AID, some of them discussed at
length in Mickelwait et al. (1979); Rondinelli and Palia (1976)
provide a useful survey. A growing number of texts is available
to assist in improving project management according to New
Directions guidelines. These include Cleland and King (1975),
Daines et al, (1979), Delp et al. (1977), Rondinelli and Ruddle
(1976), and Goodman and Love, eds. (1979).

[5]Social soundness analysis addresses three distinct but
related issues: (1) the compatibility of the project with the
sociocultural environment in which it is to be introduced
(Footnote Continued)

the United States and from such host countries as Ghana. Second, it has shown anthropologists and other social scientists what they must do to function effectively within the severe time limitations characteristic of development projects in order to produce useful social analyses.[6] It has also demonstrated to AID how important social analysis can be in avoiding expensive errors in project design and implementation. Now required as a complement to technical, economic/financial, and institutional/administrative analyses at both the Project Identification Document and Project

---

(Footnote Continued)
(sociocultural feasibility); (2) the likelihood that new practices of institutions introduced among the initial project beneficiary population will be diffused among other groups (spread effect); and (3) the social impact or distribution of benefits and burdens among different groups, both within the initial project population and beyond. Readers interested in a complete outline of the specific sociocultural analyses and factors required by AID for such analysis are referred to AID (1978b:1-12).

[6] As more anthropologists and other social scientists work on short-term project design and evaluation assignments for AID and international agencies, greater attention has been focused on the development of social science methodologies that allow a consultant to produce an effective SSA in a relatively short period of time. Useful sources include Ascroft (1974), Chambers (1974; 1980a; 1980b; 1983), Cochrane (1979), and Brokensha et al., eds. (1980). A conference on Rapid Rural Appraisal held at the Institute of Development Studies in Sussex, United Kingdom, produced 44 relevant papers, which may be obtained by writing to the Institute for Development Studies, University of Sussex, Brighton BN1 9RE, UK. Of these, Honadle (1979) is particularly useful and may be obtained through Development Alternatives, Inc., 1823 Jefferson Place NW, Washington, DC 20036. AID evaluation publications include several invaluable series begun in 1979, among them: (1) Program Evaluation Discussion Papers; (2) Evaluation Reports: Program Evaluations; (3) Evaluation Reports: Project Impact Evaluations; (4) Evaluation Reports: Special Studies; and (5) Program Design and Evaluation Methods. *The Manager's Guide to Data Collection*, No. 1 in the Program Design and Evaluation Methods series (November 1979), is very useful (see Hageboeck 1979). Documents in these series are available at no cost through the Office of Evaluation, Bureau for Program and Policy Coordination, Agency for International Development, Department of State, Washington, DC 20523. Other sources include the Monograph Series of the Rural Development Committee at Cornell University, of which Uphoff et al. (1979) is highly recommended. The materials developed for use in the Development Advisory Team Training Program are available as an unpublished training manual (Warren 1981) through the University Bookstore, Memorial Union, Iowa State University, Ames Iowa 50011. See also Horowitz, ed. (1976) and Horowitz (1979).

Paper stages in the process of project design, social soundness analysis requires that a sociocultural feasibility study be done (AID 1978b). The Economic Rural Development Management (ERDM) Project was one of the first to include a serious social soundness analysis in the project design (Klonglan 1976). As will become clear in the description of the ERDM and PRHETIH projects, both fit philosophically within the format of the New Direction policies.

AID policies stressing participation and equity have been strengthened by the requirement that AID field missions prepare an annual Country Development Strategy Statement (CDSS) (AID 1978a). Thus, since 1979, each mission has been expected to demonstrate through the CDSS how its development assistance programs are designed to foster equitable growth and meet basic human needs within the country; to show how well macro- and micro-analyses have been conducted to identify the causes and characteristics of poverty from sociocultural, political, and institutional perspectives; to specify how effectively the program has dealt with women's roles in development; and to indicate the extent to which potential environmental impacts have been recognized. AID/Washington evaluates the CDSS to determine the mission's capacity to deal with these issues. The host country is also rated, in terms of economic need as well as in terms of the government's commitment to foster policy and institutional changes to allow such programs to bear fruit. I had the opportunity to participate in the preparation of the first CDSS for the Ghana Mission and, through the Institute for Development Anthropology, to evaluate the second CDSS for Ghana.

Development Alternatives, Inc., on contract to AID to identify bureaucratic and administrative constraints within the Agency that hinder implementation of the 1973 New Directions policies, provided recommendations for policy and organizational changes that could foster improved implementation of New Directions (Mickelwait et al. 1979). Bryant (1980) has provided more recent suggestions for internal organizational improvement. These recommendations will further foster the utilization of anthropologists in development efforts.

THE ECONOMIC AND RURAL DEVELOPMENT MANAGEMENT PROJECT (ERDM)

Project Background

In 1971, Ghana passed the Local Government Act, which provided for decentralization of the government's development functions toward its 68 constituent district councils. The councils were given the right to collect 88 different types of rates, fees, and tolls, and to retain these revenues for purposes of funding development projects designed at the district level.[7] The membership of each council was to be composed of the following:

1. district councillors, two-thirds of whom are popularly elected to represent the town and village development committees within the district;
2. the heads of decentralized government departments within the district;
3. the district chief executive; and
4. the council chairperson, elected by the councillors from among themselves for single-year terms.

The Local Government Act changed the district council from an essentially administrative body to one whose primary emphasis was on development. In 1977 the Local Government Act remained a paper document, and the government was eager to identify ways to hasten its implementation. The act was regarded with considerable interest within the AID mission to Ghana, since it emphasized the need for increased participation by district-level populations in their own development. Town and village development committees were to have their local interests represented by their popularly elected district councillor.

In the initial planning stages of ERDM, USAID/Accra and the Ghana government envisaged a project to facilitate implementation

---

[7] Prior to the enactment of the 1971 Local Government Act, district council authorities were required to collect numerous types of revenues within the district administrative area. Most were forwarded to the central government at Accra, where decisions were made concerning the redistribution of these revenues. Because most of the monies collected within a district were not to be used for development in that district, revenue collectors lacked motivation for collecting all the potential revenues in their districts, particularly in remote areas. Moreover, a number of mechanisms emerged at the district level to retain revenues before they were forwarded to the central government. Since these retained revenues could not be entered on district account books, most were channeled into individual ventures, frequently of a personal or commercial nature and hence without any particular economic multiplier effect for the district. A combination of individual advantages gained from this system by a small number of district revenue collectors and officials, and a lack of knowledge and understanding among district inhabitants of the 1971 Local Government Act, have allowed this behavior to continue, at the expense of the districts and their development plans. One of the first activities of the training sessions was to enumerate the sources of revenue that districts have at their disposal. None of the districts had a complete list, and total potential revenue available to each district was invariably higher than any official had imagined. This exercise considerably increased interest in the Local Government Act by showing district officials that they could obtain resources for useful projects.

of the 1971 act. According to the Project Identification Document, USAID/Accra felt ERDM should be tried on an experimental
basis in two or three districts of Ghana. The Social Soundness
Analysis by Klonglan (1976) included emic analyses of the concepts "development," "participation," "coordination," "planning,"
and "social change" as used by local groups, government officials, and elected officers; organizational analyses of the role of
coordination among government departments; and analyses of communication strategies among government departments and between
them and local populations. Partly as a result of this analysis,
the Ministry of Economic Planning requested that USAID/Accra
expand ERDM and support a government-wide effort to institutionalize decentralized planning and decision making in all 68 districts across Ghana.[8]

USAID/Accra personnel on the ERDM project were expected
to work with Ghanaian counterparts and to help implement the
1971 act. As stated in the project paper, the purpose of the
ERDM project was to create the institutional capacity to provide
training and consultancy services in planning, coordination, and
management for district and regional level officials and council
members. The ERDM project was formally inaugurated in the fall
of 1977 as a joint venture between USAID/Accra and Ghana's Ministry of Economic Planning. ERDM objectives included the following (personal communication from Robert Gardner, former Commis-
sioner of Economic Planning):

---

[8]Klonglan presents an extensive social soundness analysis in
the Economic and Rural Development Management Project Paper
(Asiedu-Ntow, et al. 1976). He includes "an ethnoscientific analysis of Ghanaian beliefs about development, participation, coordination and planning" (p. 28). He also discusses the Local Government Act in an historical framework that includes colonial administrative structures that have continued through the present,
and he provides an overview of indigenous administrative structures, in order to specify participatory mechanisms that could
facilitate the decentralization process. Klonglan also considers
the district-wide impact of a program that would emphasize the
initiation, rather than solely the implementation, of integrated
rural development activities.

Klonglan found considerable interest for participation in the
proposed program among villagers contacted: 75 percent of the
district and regional heads of government departments and 80
percent of the district councillors interviewed responded favorably
to such a program.

He recommended that various communication strategies, including the adoption-diffusion model, be worked into exercises for
ERDM training programs in order to increase participation and
encourage spread effects. The potential impact of an apparent
shift in power from the central government to district administrative units is discussed in the section on social consequences
and benefit incidence.

1. increase emphasis on the development of rural resources;
2. facilitate the decentralization of development planning, coordination, and decision making toward district levels of authority;
3. increase the effective involvement of rural people in the development process, and hence enhance the creation of local projects and activities as a result of the effective application of improved ideas and techniques from ERDM training programs; and
4. provide institutional capacity for the development of coordinated district plans, executed jointly by district councils and district development departments working as integrated district development teams.

The objectives were a large order. An historical overview of decentralization efforts in Ghana indicates that a number of commissions had been set up since World War II to make recommendations for more effective local government. Most of these commissions, as well as the legislative acts based on their reports, emphasized the need for administrative decentralization. The 1951 Local Government Ordinance, the Greenwood Commission of 1956, the 1961 Local Government Act, the Siriboe Committee and the Mills-Oddoye Commission of 1967, were followed finally by the 1971 Local Government Act, amended in 1974. However, ERDM was the first serious effort to organize the decentralization process.

Incorporation of New Directions Policies into the ERDM Design

Although my formal role in the ERDM Project did not begin until the summer of 1977, my short-term assignments in international rural development project design (dating back to 1974) had an impact on the design of the ERDM project. These assignments were designed to provide guidance to AID officials seeking to promote greater participation and equity in development planning through more effective use of data and methodologies from the social sciences, particularly anthropology and rural sociology. The three-and-one-half-year sequence of events leading up to my participation in ERDM may be an indication of the speed at which innovations diffuse through a bureaucracy as complex as AID's.

The step-by-step account begins in January 1974, when I prepared a "Proposal for an Applied Anthropological Component for the Iowa State University AID Project Designed to Increase the Production of Cereals and Legumes in Ghana." The proposal aimed to demonstrate to colleagues in other academic disciplines at Iowa State University (ISU)—particularly those in technical areas like agriculture—and to officials at AID, the potential contribution that provision for an applied anthropology component could make to a cereals/legumes project. Among the enumerated contributions were:
1. a description of the sociocultural and politico-economic systems of client populations, in order to foster

understanding and communication between change agents and local groups;

2.   a description of the values, premises, and assumptions held by the innovators and the innovating organization, and how national, professional, and bureaucratic structures may affect decisions in the implementation of a program for direct change;

3.   a definition of development problems and their possible solutions from the perspective of local populations, as a complement to definitions used by change agents;

4.   facilitation of successful interaction and communication between members of the innovating organization and populations to be affected by their innovations.

The list of potential contributions was based, in turn, on several premises:

1.   often, the difficulties experienced by innovative programs stem from discrepant perceptions by innovators and local populations concerning the nature of the problem;

2.   there are no absolute or universal solutions to technical problems in cross-cultural situations;

3.   appropriate solutions to culturally defined problem areas are a function of the local milieu and the larger context of which that milieu is a part (Warren 1974b).

This proposal circulated through AID, arriving after some months at the office of Edward Hirabayashi, the Human Resource Officer for the Africa Bureau. Many of the points raised in the proposal interested him, and he traveled to ISU for a visit during which he encouraged a broader attempt to define issues of participation. This contact motivated more than 20 ISU social and technical scientists who had been involved in international development programs to meet together for a weekly seminar. One result of this seminar was the document, "A Communication Model for Active Indigenous Involvement in Rural Development and Nonformal Education," which was presented to AID/Washington by Klonglan, Warren, and Owen in May 1974 and later, during the summer of 1975, by Warren at the East-West Communication Institute in Honolulu (Warren 1976).

The model was designed to suggest mechanisms for more effective communication and collaboration between indigenous populations and national and international development agencies. One such mechanism was a process for comparing a problem that had been defined by a foreign adviser or a host-country counterpart--be it in the area of family planning, improved health delivery, or increased agricultural production--with the problem as perceived by local groups. A second mechanism aimed to facilitate communication links between the beneficiary group and the change agency through systematic delineation of areas of indigenous knowledge (for example, disease or soil classification systems), as well as indigenous decision-making processes. Having delineated a given folk model, the outside adviser can better understand how a given problem viewed from the perspective of a development agency might articulate with indigenous models of knowledge and reasoning (Warren 1974a).

This collaborative, multidisciplinary, international effort to specify obstacles to the implementation of AID's New Directions policies continued. Correspondence and visits to ISU linked faculty there with faculty at the University of Ghana, Ghana's Academy of Arts and Sciences, and the University of Ife. The results of these efforts were presented by Hirabayashi, Warren, and Owen during August 1974 in a special session of the Fourteenth World Conference of the Society for International Development in Abidjan (Adegboye et al. 1974).

A human resources development model, written in an inter-disciplinary style, was presented as "The Indigenous Network Communication Model." It compared the rhetoric of participation and equity within development agencies with the realities of many development projects in which neither participation nor equity was successfully pursued. The basis of the model was an "understanding and formalization of indigenous knowledge systems along with active indigenous involvement in rural development" (Hirabayashi et al. 1976:60).[9] With the presentation of the model went the following message:

> Problems in a social [change] situation, especially at the local level, are characterized by the manner in which they constantly transgress and spill across the "boundary lines" of agencies, associations and other types of social sub-divisions. Therefore, problem-solving is best achieved through a collaborative style with a common approach of working together--in a problem-oriented trans-organizational system (Ibid. 1976:63).[10]

A second seminar on the Indigenous Network Communication model was presented at AID/Washington by Klonglan and Warren in December 1975. Klonglan was then asked to conduct the social

---

[9]The Indigenous Network Communication model embraces five dimensions: (1) ethnoscience; (2) problem-oriented trans-organization; (3) transfer of technology; (4) evaluation and attitude and behavioral change; and (5) training institutes in communication of human learning (Hirabayashi et al. 1976:60).

[10]Such a collaborative, problem-oriented approach transcends specific organizations or sectors and assumes (1) that it incorporates the priorities as defined by local communities into the development planning process; (2) that the managerial strategy focuses on a problem in its total context rather than on just a part with which a particular group or agency might be concerned; (3) that there exists equitable involvement by all those participating in problem-solving; (4) that greater redistribution of decision-making occurs through a system of incorporating local participation in problem-solving; and (5) that all units work for a better distribution of the benefits of development programs (Hirabayashi et al. 1976:63-64).

soundness analysis on the ERDM project design in Ghana in March and April 1976, and to present the results of the analysis to AID's Development Studies Program in June 1976 (Klonglan 1976). The project manager, Bill Berg, then came to Iowa State to interview me for a possible position on the ERDM project. This was followed by a request for a temporary assignment in order that I might work on the final stages of the ERDM design in Ghana during the summer of 1977. I was thus in a position to further incorporate these approaches to the practical application of New Directions principles into the structure of the ERDM project.

The AID Technician Roles

The nine weeks spent on temporary assignment for AID in Ghana to assist with the design of the ERDM project ended with the signing of a bilateral project agreement by USAID/Accra and Ghana's Ministry of Economic Planning. I then spent considerable time negotiating the implementation of the program with regional commissioners in each of Ghana's nine regions. I also assisted with the selection of the remaining members of the American technical team, each of whom had had considerable long-term work experience in Ghana as well as high levels of language proficiency and an excellent knowledge of Ghana's history, culture, and administrative system.[11]   In addition, I had to locate housing for

---

[11]On September 4, 1977, the American ERDM team arrived in Ghana. It was composed of Wilfred Owen, Jr., Moses Thompson, Geraldine Brooks, and me. Owen, on leave from the African Studies Program, University of Illinois, had worked during four years in Ghana as a teacher and researcher on development topics, had a thorough knowledge of the history and administrative system of Ghana, and was married to a Ghanaian. Moses Thompson, former head of the African Program for Operation Crossroads Africa, had been to Ghana on 13 different occasions to set up Crossroads rural development projects and knew the country very well. I had been a Peace Corps volunteer in Ghana, had spent a total of six years in the country, and was married to a Nigerian born in Ghana. The three of us had known each other for over a decade. Geraldine Brooks, the fourth member, was a management consultant who had worked with Peace Corps training programs in Ghana and had years of experience with the design and implementation of training programs in Africa, the Caribbean, and the United States. The project manager was Jerry Wood, a former Peace Corps volunteer in Thailand, who had spent the previous six years working with AID as a trainer in management, consulting, and planning. He had been instrumental in establishing the Institute for Agricultural Management at Kwadaso, near Kumasi, Ghana--another USAID program--in 1975-1977.

The five of us were to work as a national team, with each
(Footnote Continued)

the technicians in the regions where they would be based and to prepare an outline of the initial job descriptions for Ghanaian trainer-consultants and for district council training programs.

From September 1977 through August 1979, I helped administer the ERDM program in 18 districts within the Brong-Ahafo and Ashanti Regions. USAID/Accra gave us considerable freedom with our roles and with the design of the ERDM program. I had the opportunity to be acting national project manager on several occasions when the project manager was out of the country. With the other three American technicians, the American project manager, and the Ghanaian project director, I assisted in the following tasks:

1. selection and training of 27 Ghanaian regional trainer-consultants, three-person teams being assigned to each of the nine regional capitals;
2. design and completion of the first cycle of ERDM training in 18 district and 2 regional capitals, in collaboration with two of the Ghanaian regional ERDM trainer-consultant teams;
3. design and specification of expected results of the ERDM district council training sessions;
4. design of follow-up training sessions with district councils;
5. design and funding by USAID/Accra of a master's degree program at Kumasi University of Science and Technology, to train district-level economic planning officers beginning in 1980;
6. establishment of a self-sustaining Ghanaian capability for management and development-planning training and consultancy in two of Ghana's nine regions;
7. promotion of program objectives among regional decision makers and clientele groups, in order that those objectives would be shared and internalized by that clientele; and
8. assure the availability of adequate facilities, staff, and other resources needed to support the achievement of program objectives.

The nature and structure of the ERDM program made each American field technician a liaison officer between district,

---

(Footnote Continued)
being responsible for the coordination of efforts in two of Ghana's regions. I lived in Kumasi and coordinated ERDM efforts in the Brong-Ahafo and Ashanti Regions; Owen lived in Tamale and organized the Upper and Northern Regions; Brooks worked out of Koforidua for the Eastern and Volta Regions; and Thompson was based in Takoradi to coordinate the Central and Western Regions. Wood was national coordinator on the American side; he worked with George Cann, the Ghanaian project director based in the Ministry of Economic Planning, with the National Coordinating Committee and National ERDM Secretariat in Accra, and assisted with training programs in the Greater Accra Region.

regional, and central government officials; between the Ministry of Economic Planning and USAID; and between ERDM regional secretariats and the national coordinating committee in Accra.

Design and Implementation of the ERDM Training Program

Once the 27 Ghanaian trainer-consultants had been selected, it was necessary to make a strong, functional team of these individuals and the five American USAID project personnel. The Ghanaians were of diverse ethnic and professional backgrounds. Among them were members of the Buem, Ewe, Fante, Ga, Ashanti, Akyem, Brong, Gonja, Dagarti, Mamprussi, and Adangbe ethnic groups.[12] One senior trainer-consultant had served as a district councillor.

All ERDM trainer-consultants and American technicians went through an intensive nine-week training session that emphasized team-building, management and development planning, and experiential training techniques. All members were required to absorb the necessary background material, personally experience this approach to training in a non-threatening atmosphere, gain experience and confidence in handling experiential training, and redesign training materials in order to make them more appropriate culturally for the first cycle of ERDM training sessions in each of the regional and district capitals. We also attempted to identify obstacles to implementation of the Local Government Act and to design training materials that would help improve the situation.

Among the obstacles identified were the extreme variability of physical, natural, and human resources among the districts; the complex ethnic mix of some districts; and the membership of most district councils. Strained relationships between traditional and district councils, between decentralized and centralized departments and ministries, between district officers and district councillors, between the district chairperson and the district chief executive, and finally, between the district councils and international development technicians from abroad were cited as obstacles to ERDM implementation.

---

[12]Trainer-consultants came to ERDM from the Agricultural Development Bank, the Technology Consultancy Centre, the Department of Cooperatives, the Ministry of Economic Planning, the Ministry of Health, the Department of Social Welfare and Community Development, Ghana Educational Services, the Ministry of Agriculture, the Industrial Development Board, the Department of Town and Country Planning, and the Ministry of Local Government. A wide spectrum of ages and of junior and senior officials entered ERDM, with an equally wide range of educational backgrounds (including some trainer-consultants with degrees or diplomas obtained in the Soviet Union, Germany, Britain, Canada, the United States, Israel, Zambia, Cameroon, and the Netherlands).

There was more enthusiasm for ERDM within districts than in the central government. ERDM was a tangible example of a shift in power from Accra to the district level, and it marked a change in emphasis--away from centralized planning for districts and toward collaborating with districts in their development planning. Attention was given to more effective utilization of human resources as opposed to an emphasis on infrastructure. District officers were included in project planning rather than simply ordered to implement programs planned by others. Uncoordinated projects were brought together within integrated rural development programs, characterized by an effort to coordinate the planning efforts of district, regional, and central levels of government.

In initial surveys we found that, while earlier decentralization efforts (noted above) were designed to change the emphasis of district council functions from administration to development, no training opportunities had been provided for district-level officials in order to equip them for the change. Most in-service training programs in Ghana were not based on experiential modes of training, and central government officials conveyed negative attitudes about the capacities of district-level officials to plan and manage decentralized efforts. Among the difficulties encountered at the district administrative level were severe conflicts within councils, between councillors and district officers, and among district officers; duplication of efforts; insufficient communications; poor cooperation and integration; insufficient planning data; and a lack of planning objectives. Interethnic conflicts among district-level officials were also a problem, particularly in cases where the chief executive assigned to a district happened to be a member of an ethnic group looked down upon by the predominant ethnic group under his administrative responsibility.

Many of the problems we identified were common to all districts, including the following:
1. inadequate organizational structures;
2. lack of exposure to management and development planning techniques;
3. lack of basic knowledge of the Local Government Act and the new expectations of district administrations based on the act;
4. lack of planning objectives or district-level data for planning;
5. lack of control and accountability structures;
6. departmental and ward orientation as opposed to district orientation;
7. district officers still operating as implementers of centrally planned programs instead of being initiators of programs; and
8. lack of cultural and linguistic knowledge of local populations among many officials transferred to unfamiliar districts.

Our role was to design training programs that could transform disparate department heads and district councillors into effective district development teams, and to facilitate cooperation and coordination across departmental and ward lines for district councillors. We focused on integrated development for the district as a total unit, based on a clear understanding of available internal and external resources and a clear identification of the problems and potential solutions. We sought to establish a program that would permit key actors within districts to identify and understand the obstacles they had faced in pre-ERDM attempts to promote district development.

After the first nine weeks of intensive training and planning by the Ghanaian and American ERDM personnel, it was decided that each three-person Ghanaian regional team of trainer-consultants should be able to:

1. prepare and conduct periodic training seminars and workshops on management and development planning for regional and district-level heads of government departments and elected district council members;

2. provide mobile consulting services in the districts for rural development planning, implementation, monitoring, and evaluation;

3. reassess and redesign training programs to better meet the expressed desires and needs of each individual district council;

4. coordinate actions required to implement the new development role assigned to the district councils; and

5. assist in the practical field training of district-level economic planning officers who were to begin master's degree training at Kumasi University of Science and Technology in 1980.

Initial ERDM training goals included updating and improving the managerial and planning skills of elected district councillors, district heads of government departments, and district chief executives and acquainting the combined district council with a broad range of management and planning tools and techniques. These were translated into specific learning objectives that we hoped participants in ERDM training programs would achieve. Thus (see Warren 1980b; Warren and Blunt 1984), participants were asked to:

1. become aware of their own style of management and method of leadership, and learn to practice management style flexibility;

2. develop greater skill as managers in handling inter- and intra-group dynamics;

3. build an awareness of communications difficulties and provide tools for increased accuracy and effectiveness in communications, at the individual and group levels;

4. develop an understanding of motivational factors, particularly as they relate to staff development and productivity;

5. plan and program work more effectively on the basis of sound and measurable objectives;

6. develop the ability and initiative to gather and utilize information required for finding creative alternatives in the problem-solving and decision-making process; and

7. understand the structural characteristics of productive, effective   organization   and   diagnose   unhealthy,

unproductive organizational characteristics and develop constructive alternatives to them.

The Design of Culturally Appropriate Training Materials

Cycle I of the training program began with district (three-week) and regional (one-week) sessions, using the principle of experiential training--a learning method based on the assumption that trainees learn and retain best what they directly experience. Participants in a council training program would be divided into five- or six-person teams at the start of a training session, with membership cutting across ethnic and professional lines, mixing civil servants and elected councillors, and heads of both decentralized and centralized departments. The main objective of such mixed, and potentially volatile, groups was to create effective district development teams composed of both elected officials and civil servants. During each training module, teams competed in performing exercises designed to apply course materials to relevant district problems. Many of these exercises were based on anthropological approaches to cross-cultural and cross-disciplinary communication. The principles embodied within each exercise were explained in discussion sessions following the exercise (Schein 1969).

The Cycle I training programs centered on providing trainees with a thorough understanding of the 1971 Local Government Act. Teams of trainees were asked to identify constraints to effective implementation of the act and to recommend measures to deal with those constraints. Training focused on teaching management techniques--with sessions on group dynamics, team building, communications, problem identification, setting priorities and developing alternatives, situational management, decision-making techniques, and motivation and productivity--and on providing planning skills, such as Gantt charts, managing by objectives, logical frameworks, project evaluation and review techniques, critical-path method, budgetary processes, and understanding the nature and role of data in planning.

Sessions on team building, group interaction, and group dynamics were interspersed throughout the training program. Exercises were designed to give participants insights into the different sets of beliefs, values and norms, premises, assumptions, and biases that result in either cooperation or conflict within a group of individuals. We stressed the role of sociocultural and cognitive structures in influencing and, sometimes, determining the behavior of individuals within groups. The district and regional training sessions were usually the first opportunities for all government department heads and district councillors to meet and become acquainted.

We began by dividing the participants into dyads that interviewed and then introduced one another to the total group. We would then ask one department head to enlighten the group about the goals and objectives of another department. The vast majority had little or no information about the objectives of any other department within the district or region, in part--as it became painfully clear--because most departments had no objectives. District councillors tended to find this exercise quite amusing, since it supported their stereotype of district officers as being ineffective and lazy. Their amusement usually ended abruptly when a councillor representing one ward was asked to enlighten the group about the main problems and projects across wards.

Many councillors viewed district department heads as adversaries: as individuals attempting to thwart efforts of district councils. A principal reason given for uncooperative attitudes was ethnicity, for in many cases the officials came from other parts of Ghana. These sessions were the first forum in which district officers could make clear to district councillors the vertical constraints they faced when their regional superiors viewed them as implementers of programs planned in either Accra or the regional capital, without regard to problems, needs, and desires identified by the district councils. Once district councillors understood the bureaucratic constraints on district officers' activities, opportunities emerged to discuss ways of working around the constraints. Role playing was used in many instances, with district councillors asked to play the role of district officers and vice versa. Many of the exercises were designed on the basis of situations in specific districts. Frequently, during our preliminary contacts in district capitals for purposes of organizing the training sessions, problems existing within the district had been aired, and these were incorporated into exercises in as nonthreatening a manner as possible. Exercises in conflict resolution were very important in most districts.

Throughout the training program, communications exercises were conducted. One-way and two-way communications exercises included rumor clinics (Pfeiffer and Jones 1974, 2:12-15) and sessions on organizational communications in centralized and decentralized modes (Finch et al. 1976a:43-47). Training materials adapted from Foster (1969) stressed the different premises and biases attached to different ethnic, national, and academic backgrounds, and the character of communications between officials and district populations. The nature of sociocultural and value systems, of processes of change, and of adoption and diffusion of innovations were covered.

Recommendations and results of each training session were compiled in lengthy reports that were distributed to all participants, all regional officers in the relevant region, and the ERDM national secretariat for use in Accra. This approach has resulted in the collection of a large body of data from different regions and districts of Ghana in which obstacles to decentralization are described. Many districts have taken the initiative and have acted on their own behalf to improve their situations, and examples of improved cooperation, coordination, and productivity have been recorded throughout Ghana (Warren 1980; Warren and Blunt 1984). Participants throughout the country helped design what they felt would be the most useful format for the second cycle of training.

Cycle II began in spring 1980, focusing on financial and budgetary aspects of decentralized planning, as well as dealing with other managerial and planning issues. Five cycles of training have now been completed. Within a year of the signing of the ERDM project agreement, the Establishment Secretariat of the Government of Ghana made the ERDM Project a permanent feature of the Government of Ghana, a tribute to its tremendous impact.

PRHETIH: An ERDM Dividend

The ERDM Project took me back to Techiman District in the Brong-Ahafo Region, where I had served as a biology teacher in the Peace Corps during 1964–1966, and where I spent 1969–1971 doing my doctoral research on Bono ethnomedical systems. My position with USAID/Accra gave me ready access to the Regional Medical Officer of Health and his personnel in the regional capital of Sunyani as well as to the district officers in Techiman. I also maintained direct contact with the National Health Planning Unit in Accra, which had been organized with USAID help. The data they were collecting showed that tertiary (specialist) health services were absorbing 40 percent of the Ministry of Health's annual budget but servicing only 1 percent of Ghana's population. Secondary (hospital/clinic) services were absorbing 45 percent of the annual budget and servicing 9 percent of the population. This left 15 percent of the budget for primary (preventive and promotive) health services to cover the remaining 90 percent of the population, most of whom live in 46,000 small towns and villages (Ghana 1977:53).

In Techiman District, two private hospitals exist, one run by the Medical Mission Sisters and one by the Ahmadiyyan Muslim Mission. Both are very heavily used and understaffed. In the ERDM training session in Techiman, it was possible to have participants consider National Health Planning Unit data as well as the data I had collected on indigenous healing systems (Warren 1975; 1982c). Included in the council training were hospital personnel and heads of the various Ministry of Health units (community and public health nurses, medical field units, health inspectorate, and the district medical officer of health), as well as the regional secretary for the Ghana Psychic and Traditional Healers Association. Training participants recognized indigenous healers as a resource that had not been fully utilized. My data helped to improve the negative stereotypes of indigenous healers held by many district officers, particularly those from the Ministry of Health. In role-playing sessions, where a priestess-healer and the head public health nurse changed roles, these stereotypes surfaced and were discussed at length.

Based on earlier successful training programs for traditional birth attendants in the district, a parallel training session was discussed by ERDM participants that would capitalize on the presence of herbalists and priest/priestess-healers in rural areas of the district, where Ministry of Health personnel only rarely had the time and inclination to visit. It was decided to set up a coordinating committee to bring together heads of the various units representing both the Ministry of Health and the indigenous healers.

The regional head of the Ghana Psychic and Traditional Healers Association, the district heads of the herbalists, *mallam* healers, priest-healers, priestess-healers, the paramount chief of the traditional council, the head of the traditional birth attendants, the head of the health inspectors, the district medical officer of health, the hospital administrator, and the head of both the community health and public health nurses comprised this committee. The head of the nutrition unit of the Rural Health Training School at nearby Kintampo was added because of his active interest in dealing with kwashiorkor cases through indigenous healers. A Peace Corps volunteer played an active role as liaison between the Ministry of Health and the indigenous healers. Negotiations with the Bishop of the Sunyani Diocese and various regional Catholic medical personnel regarding the training of non-Christian healers were successfully concluded. Liaison relations were established between the coordinating committee and Oku Ampofo's Center for the Scientific Research into Plant Medicine, funded in part through USAID, with Techiman herbalists going for in-service training at the Center and then participating in improving herbalists' skills upon their return to Techiman district.

USAID's office of Health, Population, and Nutrition maintained an active interest in the project. When they asked me to conduct a social soundness analysis for a large, multidonor primary health care program for Ghana, I was able to include the potential role of indigenous healers in primary health care, including the PRHETIH project in Techiman. The PRHETIH project was formalized and inaugurated on June 7, 1979--with national television and radio coverage--by the Regional Medical Officer of Health, the paramount chief of the Techiman Traditional State, and other dignitaries. Meetings of the coordinating committee have made use of many of the principles of cooperation and coordination presented during the ERDM training program. Stereotypes held by personnel from the Ministry of Health about indigenous healers, and vice versa, are less severe, and one now finds a considerable amount of positive interaction between the two groups. Both are concerned with the quality of health in the district, and they feel they can be more successful by working together than they could by continuing to work separately.

Training sessions for indigenous healers were designed with active participation by the indigenous healers on the coordinating committee. Response to the first set of seven training sessions was excellent, and the first two training groups (including priest/priestess-healers, herbalists, and *mallams*) have now completed their training and received certificates of award from the Regional Medical Officer of Health.

For me, the design and implementation of PRHETIH is an example of putting ERDM principles to work in an area of deep personal concern--rural health care. The various negotiations and the disparate types of organizations, belief systems, and behavioral patterns dealt with were complex, but the end result was well worth the effort. PRHETIH is a tribute to the rational approach to problem identification, it provides recognition of indigenous healers as valued human resources (particularly important given the serious limitations of the national health delivery system), and it results in improved cooperation between the Ministry of Health and local healers. PRHETIH is also a tribute to the effectiveness of the ERDM training program.[13]

LESSONS FOR DEVELOPMENT ANTHROPOLOGY
FROM THE GHANA EXPERIENCE

Partly as a result of first-hand experience with AID and other development agencies, anthropologists are meeting the challenge of working across disciplinary boundaries by extending their own anthropological background and knowledge. They now have working abilities in other academic areas important in development, particularly in agricultural economics, rural sociology, public administration, social psychology, and management and planning. Training skills necessary to foster effective and efficient teamwork are being acquired. These experiences have resulted in several graduate anthropology programs in this country being reformulated to meet the academic and training needs of anthropology students intending to work in development.[14] At Iowa State University, I am using my development experience in Ghana to expand our applied program in three directions.

The first direction is a new course I have developed and taught through the graduate program in technology and social

---

[13]For detailed descriptions of the PRHETIH (Primary Health Training for Indigenous Healers) Project, see Warren (1980), Warren and Tregoning (1979), and Warren et al. (1982). A documentary film on the project, Bono Medicines, 1982, is available through White Pine Films, Inc., P.O. Box 76, Lone Rock, Iowa 50559.

[14]Anthropology departments with programs in applied and development anthropology have increased in number during the past decade, due in part to the hiring of anthropologists with international development experience. Some programs make provision for a specialization in development and applied anthropology, while others have formal graduate degrees in the development area.

Departments with development and applied anthropology programs include those at the University of Kentucky, the University of South Florida, the University of Arizona, the University of California at Santa Barbara, State University of New York at Binghamton, Iowa State University, Boston University, and the University of Florida. Departments that include applied and development anthropology emphases in formal medical anthropology degree programs can be found at the University of California at Berkeley and the University of California at San Francisco, Case Western Reserve University, Michigan State University, and Southern Methodist University.

change. The course takes integrated rural development as a focal
point for learning international development design and evaluation
procedures, formats, and policies for AID. This type of training
provides the student with background in development lexicon
(jargon), procedures, and expectations, prior to possible participation in an international, multidisciplinary team that has from
three to six weeks to produce a viable study and document for a
project or program. The course approach combines a lecture
format with experiential training. Participants are organized into
multidisciplinary, multinational teams and experience many of the
same exercises we used in the ERDM training program. The
response has been very positive.

The second direction is a new twelve-month master's degree
program in international development studies. Recognizing the
multidisciplinary nature of development, we encourage our master's-level students in anthropology to remain at Iowa State for a
third year to obtain this second, cross-disciplinary master's degree, which combines work in three different development study
areas to complement the students' major field. The three areas
are selected from a list of 25 participating departments and programs. An anthropologist, for example, can focus on community
and regional planning, agricultural economics, and development
communications, or choose from several other areas of recognized
excellence on this campus. Students from disciplines other than
anthropology may combine development anthropology with two
other disciplines.[15]

The third direction is designed to make better use of Iowa
State University faculty members who have experience in international development. To this end, I have initiated the development
advisory team training program, which is being sponsored by our
World Food Institute and the ISU-AID Title XII strengthening
grant. The development advisory team concept is based on AID's
New Directions policies, which require that international development projects funded entirely or partially by federal monies be
designed and evaluated from a multidisciplinary focus that includes social soundness analyses, economic and financial analyses,
and technical analyses appropriate to the sectoral focus of the
project (such as primary health care, agricultural extension, nutrition, or highways).[16]

AID and other international agencies frequently award contracts to international consulting firms for the provision of teams
to perform such analyses. More often than not, team members
come from different universities and agencies and have never met
prior to the assignment. They sometimes find it difficult to work
together effectively as a team. Sorting out different approaches
to development planning, different personalities, and different

---

[15]Details of this program are available in Warren (1982b).

[16]Details of this program are available in Warren (1982a;
1983).

ideologies can be a wasteful and frustrating venture when the team has three to four weeks to produce and deliver a design or evaluation document that may have a dramatic impact on the local population.

Many of us at Iowa State University who do consulting work for AID, the World Bank, and the United Nations have experienced such frustrating team efforts. After much discussion with ISU's Technology and Social Change Program, the World Food Institute, and various international consultants on campus, it seemed that we could make better use of our international human resources and do so at minimal cost. Our feelings were supported by a recent study conducted by Development Alternatives, Inc., which discussed the composition of the design team. They stated:

> When outside consultants were used, it was invariably preferable to put together a team that shared a common approach to development and had a common institutional base, or had at least worked together in the past, rather than assemble individuals whose paper qualifications rated them as experts but who might not be able to work together as a team.... At least one member of a design team should have sufficient technical background to judge the appropriateness of different technological packages, but the critical skills needed on a design team were found to be not so much technical in nature as those that contribute to a sensible project in a particular political, economic, social and cultural milieu.... In most of the design exercises, a core group consisting of a rural development specialist, an anthropologist or rural sociologist, an economist (usually an agricultural economist) and an agriculturalist proved to be effective. It was desirable that at least one member of the core group also have experience and expertise in project management arrangements. In many of the design exercises, the participation of female professionals was found not to be simply desirable but necessary (Mickelwait et al. 1979:141-142).

The development advisory team project encompasses the following objectives:
1.   identify potential development advisory team members from Iowa State University faculty and staff who are multidisciplinary in perspective, knowledgeable about the region of the world in which they are to work, and focused on the particular project about which they are to provide expertise;
2.   survey the knowledge of potential team members concerning project design and evaluation, and assess their perceived training needs;
3.   design and implement a six-day intensive training program for ISU development advisory teams that focuses on team building and the acquisition of cross-disciplinary approaches to project design and evaluation according to AID procedures, with ERDM training program

materials forming the basis for the development advisory
team program;
4.   redesign training courses as regular university courses
and as intensive summer training sessions for cross-disciplinary development planning teams of international
students doing graduate work at ISU;
5.   design training courses for local government and community action programs in the State of Iowa.

More than 250 Iowa State University faculty, staff, and
graduate students, from 59 departments and every college, have
participated in the first five development advisory team training
sessions.   The first session of a second cycle of training was
held in May 1983.

Development work has given me the opportunity to gain a
more fundamental understanding of the nature of communication
across cultural and disciplinary boundaries, of values, norms,
and attitudes, stereotypes, prejudices, ethnicity, and the nature
of emic and etic perceptions of phenomena.   Through the new
training programs at Iowa State University I hope to translate
these insights and understandings into a format accessible to others interested in working in rural development--anthropologists
and individuals from other disciplines as well.

APPENDIX: ERDM TRAINING EXERCISES

We designed a series of communications exercises to complement those used for many years during training programs for
management/planning in the United States, described in the
Finch, Jones and Litterer texts (1976a; 1976b), and in the training handbooks by Pfeiffer and Jones (1974).   One exercise began
with a series of quotations from nineteenth and early-twentieth
century social scientists (such as Herbert Spencer [1877] and
Vernon Blake [1927]), which portrayed Ghanaian and other Third
World ethnic groups in very negative terms.   The purpose was to
portray the importance of perception and differential (emic vs.
etic) depiction of events in cross-cultural situations.   We stressed
the role of the consultant in the transfer of skills and abilities by
focusing on the problem as it is perceived and identified by a
client, thus releasing the client's creative and productive poten-
tials.   Innovations should be based on the client's felt needs.
Using a systems approach to the communications process, we
stressed that effective communication across ethnic or professional
boundaries (e.g., between the Ministry of Health and the Ministry
of Agriculture) or between levels of a bureaucratic hierarchy frequently are distorted, due to varying perceptions of a given
event or phenomenon.   Examples of gross distortions of Ghanaian
culture by an outsider were taken from A. B. Ellis (1966), who
stated that the Akan (Twi-Fante) language has 350-400 words,
none of them abstract, and that Ghanaians are able to count to
ten only by using the fingers.   Ellis, having missed the linguistic
features of tone, nasalization, and terminal vowel length, stated
that one word had to serve for several meanings.   To Ellis, *pápá*
(good), *pàpá* (father), and *pàpà* (fan) were all the same word.

He also declared that Ghanaians could not distinguish between present and past tense, evidence that he could not perceive the difference between *kã̃* (speak) and *kã̃ã̃* (spoke). Moreover, *ǹsá* (hand) and *ǹsã̃* (palm wine) were said to be the same—because nasalization as a phonemic feature was missed. Spencer stated that

> We forget that discriminations easy to us, are impossible to those who have but few words, all concrete in their mean-ings, and only rude propositional forms in which to combine these words....By such undeveloped grammatical structures, only the simplest thoughts can be rightly conveyed. We learn that among the lowest men inadequate words, indef-initely combined are also imperfectly pronounced (Spencer 1877:149).

Such writings tended to evoke strong and indignant reactions from the participants against the authors. Having set a volatile stage with these statements, teams read an adaptation of Horace Miner's Nacirema article (1956). Each team was then asked to present three adjectives to the whole group which they felt best described the Nacirema, and to describe the degree to which they felt the Nacirema would be receptive to their own district devel-opment programs. Invariably the descriptive terms used by teams were as negative (e.g., superstitious, primitive, inhuman, magic-ridden, bush, uncivilized, isolated) as the terms used in nine-teenth century descriptions of Ghanaian ethnic groups. Most teams felt it would be a waste of time to try to promote change programs through the Nacirema, since they would be extremely resistant to change and were very secretive. The impact of this exercise on participants when they realized that the Nacirema represented a biased, outsider's view of certain American phenom-ena was important in bringing about a more thorough understand-ing of differential perceptions and definitions of district develop-ment "problems" according to variant ethnic and academic per-spectives.

The Nacirema exercise was reinforced by exercises in which interethnic teams were expected to delineate the terms used by each ethnic group represented on the team to describe other eth-nic groups, and to assign these terms semantic weights with re-spect to negative, positive, or neutral factors. For members of dominant ethnic groups it became strikingly clear that "minor" ethnic groups described the dominant groups by terms just as negative as those used by the dominant groups to ridicule the less-dominant. This had a startlingly sobering effect on the self-perception of members of both dominant and less-dominant ethnic groups.

Examples of terms and phrases which the Ga use to describe other ethnic groups include the following: the Ewe are described as competent thieves; the Fante as "breezes" (i.e., good-for-nothings: people who do not build houses but sleep on the beach-es, preferring to spend most of their money on food); the Kwahu as stingy (those who use only the head of the herring to make their soup); the Northern Ghanaians as slaves; the Ashanti as bat-eaters; the Sierra Leoneans as those whose hands are not free to greet but who have their spoons ready to eat as soon as invited; the Zabrama as donkeys (individuals who carry goods to earn their living); the Ibo as crickets (those who chatter late into the night); the Portuguese as those who smell like onions; and the Ga from Labadi as those who are salt makers and never bathe. Adangbe speakers, closely related to the Ga, describe the Ga, on the other hand, as small thieves and the Ewe as big thieves, and the Ashanti and other Akan as uncircumcised. Abusive labels are used by definable groups among the Adangbe themselves: e.g., the Krobo subgroup call the Ningo those who use bad juju, while the Ningo refer to the Krobo as head-cutters.

The intra-ethnic classifications were designed to discover the terms used by members of a given ethnic group to define and classify members of their own society who are regarded as progressive, as opposed to individuals who are less exposed to outside forces or those regarded as less ready to adapt to changing circumstances. All ethnic groups had such terms--for example, "bush" (i.e., rural) as opposed to urban. Different perceptions again became evident. Urban Adangbe refer to rural folk as bush and unenlightened and to themselves as urban and enlightened, while rural Adangbe refer to the urban Adangbe as those who are usually hungry--and equally unenlightened. Stress in the exercise was placed on the role, functions, and nature of ethnicity, stereotypes, and prejudices, and on their role as constraining forces in inter-ethnically composed district councils.

It was discovered that extension officers had never been exposed to training in ways to formalize indigenous knowledge systems. One could find agricultural extension officers from southern Ghana posted in districts of the upper and northern regions of Ghana, and vice versa. None had any knowledge of ways in which local farmers defined and classified types of soils and other agricultural phenomena. Moreover, given the stereotypes held by southern Ghanaians of northerners as "simple" and relatively "primitive," one-way communications frequently prevailed. Officers from the Ministry of Health were expected to operate in outreach programs in parts of Ghana where they did not understand the local language and also had minimal knowledge of ways in which diseases were locally perceived, defined, and classified, and how such classification systems were linked to behavioral patterns to treat and prevent diseases. We designed exercises based on Western negative perceptions of Ghanaian indigenous healers and compared these with my research on the complexity of Akan disease classification systems (see Ademuwagun et al. 1979). Similar exercises were based on Western statements about Akan art as being based on a "primitive state of mind" (Segy 1975:10) and "the product of primitive mentality or primitive reason" (Ibid:6). We next compared these statements with the complex artistic taxonomies worked out by Kweku Andrews and myself (see Warren and Andrews 1977). Each group then was asked to delineate an ethnic knowledge system in skeletal taxonomic formats (e.g., soils, crop varieties, crop pests, diseases). It rapidly became clear that many of these systems were far more complex than had been anticipated. This exercise had a dramatic effect upon members of all ethnic groups (see Brokensha et al., eds. 1980; and Warren 1984).

Exercises in inter-ethnic proxemic and kinesic communications difficulties also were designed, particularly in districts with international agency involvement. It was clear that the Ghanaian equivalent to the American "finger" was the American sign requesting a lift from a passing motorist. Differences in individual space/territory needs and in basic gestures, expressions, and postures, and their role in communications were enumerated and discussed.

Further exercises in differential perceptions of the "same thing" were conducted, using such well-established training exercises as the 24 matchsticks or the nine dots exercises (see Pfeiffer and Jones 1974, 4:99-103). The relationship between a person's control of communications and information flow and the power of the individual was examined through power play exercises. Exercises readapted for use in a Ghanaian format and context included broken squares (Pfeiffer and Jones 1974, 1:25-30), one-way/two-way communications (Pfeiffer and Jones 1974, 1:13-18), rumor clinic (Pfeiffer and Jones 1974, 2:12-15), force-field analysis (Pfeiffer and Jones 1974, 2:79-84; Finch et al. 1976a:262-264), power relations (Pfeiffer and Jones 1974, 3:46-48), and numbers simulation (Finch et al. 1976a:32).

Team-building exercises adapted included lego man (Finch et al. 1976a:207), Berkshire dominoes (Finch et al. 1976a:63-68), and role plays (Finch et al. 1976a:107-123). One very illuminating exercise we designed focused on problem identification. An example used in the Ashanti Region is as follows:

> For a long time, the most important product of Lake Bosomtwi has been a small fish called *apatre*. *Apatre* are caught by the indigenous Ashanti fishermen using small hooks and nets, working by day and also by night with the use of kerosene lanterns. In 1975 kerosene and nets became scarce and costly. The catch diminished but the supply was still sufficient to meet the demand of the small nearby markets and the local population. Suddenly Zabrama aliens arrived with their larger nets. These nets were used to sweep through the lake bringing out even the most tiny creatures living there. The Ashanti fishermen feared that sooner or later there would not be any living creatures left in the lake. The aliens, besides having access to better storage facilities also had a wider market for their fish. A bitter dispute broke out between the two groups. The Zabrama, in the meantime, had established cordial relations with the lakeside chiefs--who seemed to be solidly behind the Zabrama fishermen.

Teams were asked to read the passage and identify the primary problem in this set of circumstances; to describe how the problem might be perceived and defined differently; and to define who or what was causing the problem; who was being affected by it, and how the problem might be resolved and what alternative solutions might be defined for it.

This was an excellent exercise to show differential perception of both a problem and solution. Those officers trained in technical approaches to identifying and solving problems (e.g., heads of the Highways Authority, Electricity Corporation, Water and Sewerage Corporation, Department of Town and Country Planning) tended to focus on the technical advantage of the Zabrama; individuals trained to view problems in social terms (e.g., heads of the Department of Social Welfare and Community Development, Department of Rural Development, Ghana Educational Services, Ministry of Health) tended to focus on the social relationships, on power and economic relationships, and on ecological perspectives. The fact that it was difficult to come up with a "primary" problem and solution was due to the difficulty most individuals faced in viewing the various academically oriented perspectives as being complementary, not necessarily conflicting, views of a set of phenomena, views that should be regarded as a rich human resource in the district. This explained many of the conflicts in the council, where an individual would fight to have his or her view recognized as *the* correct one, with other views being considered wrong or insufficient.

Techniques introduced to improve decision making in complex groups were brainstorming (see Pfeiffer and Jones 1974, 3:14-16; Delp et al. 1977:3-5), nominal group technique (see Delp et al. 1977:14-18), and consensus (see Pfeiffer and Jones 1974, 4:51-65).

Another exercise involved understanding that one's self may be part of a given "problem." This led us into the design of training modules for situational management, motivation, and productivity. Many of these materials were adapted from McGregor's earlier theories of X and Y (1960), followed by Reddin's material (1970, 1973), including the three-dimensional management style diagnosis text that matched participants' perceived managerial behavior with eight ideal types: four effective (bureaucrat, developer, benevolent autocrat, and executive) and four matching ineffective styles (deserter, missionary, autocrat, and compromiser). This examination produced dramatic results in terms of personal insights into one's managerial style. It was also used to provide feedback to regional heads of departments, particularly in instances where a majority of the district heads were operating in ineffective styles, especially the least effective style (deserter). In districts where district officers appeared to have been forced into the deserter mold, we expanded the exercise to identify district officers' attitudes toward themselves, their bosses, and their subordinate workers (see exercises in Finch et al. 1976a:99-105). In eight district council training sessions the majority of the terms used by district officers to describe their technical officers were negative (e.g., lazy, hostile, unproductive). District officers saw their own regional officers as corrupt, arrogant, and selfish, and themselves as humble, hardworking, punctual, and kind! In feedback sessions we could show district officers that their regional officers viewed them in the same negative way as the district officers viewed their own technical officers. We discussed the possibility that technical officers might view their district officers in ways as negative as those in which the district officers viewed their regional bosses. The emphasis was based on the Johari Window exercise (see Finch et al. 1976a:169-171), improving one's insights into the way outsiders view oneself. Motivation and productivity studies dating back to Maslow and up through Drucker and Herzberg were discussed (see summaries in Finch et al. 1976a, 1976b).

Considerable time was spent learning to write measurable objectives (see Mali 1972), gaining background in Gantt charting (see Delp et al. 1977:252-259), Log Frames (see Delp et al. 1977:260-264; AID 1973, 1974a, 1974b), and CPM and PERT (see Delp et al. 1977:241-251). The role of data in planning was stressed in several practical exercises designed to: (1) define the resource base of the district from all perspectives; (2) begin the production of a district development handbook; (3) set up a district economic planning operations room where data from all departments could be displayed for council planning; (4) write the first draft of an integrated district development plan and budget; (5) organize a revenue collection control exercise; and (6) produce monthly reports by district officers and district councillors, based on Management by Objectives, which would be distributed to all other heads of departments and councillors. Emphasis in training was placed on gathering solid data, from a systems perspective, to understand Ghana's difficult economic situation. Participants discussed the future of decentralization efforts, given the following: (1) a rapidly growing population; (2) a decline in agricultural productivity; (3) a decline in cocoa production (which provides 60 percent of the foreign exchange for Ghana), as land for cash crops is being shifted into subsistence crops; (4) the rapid decline in Ghana's timber resources (which currently provide 30 percent of the country's foreign exchange); (5) the role of the civil service--nearly 300,000 strong: a tremendous burden on the national treasury, but very unproductive.

District revenue control exercises indicated vividly that not a single district had an accurate idea of its potentially available revenues. Estimates made in the training sessions made it clear that no council treasury in Ghana was receiving more than 20 percent of its potential revenue, suggesting a sizable internal financial loss for the districts.

The three-week training sessions finished with a complex, two-day exercise--the Rural Road Construction exercise--created by Bill Berg and Jerry Wood of AID. Designed to simulate a managerial and planning situation as complicated as those which occur in reality, it forced teams to put into action all of the managerial and planning techniques covered during the previous days.

Editors' Note to Chapter 4

Riall Nolan describes a training program he directed for Peace Corps volunteers in Senegal who were preparing for work with the service of Animation Rurale *in community development. He highlights the rewards and frustrations of this kind of training, and raises important issues for anthropologists who are interested in cross-cultural training programs and development work. First, newcomers to Senegal are not simply trained for their work as volunteers. They are also influenced by a subculture of veteran volunteers, complete with its own ideology. This subculture has a critical impact on the attitudes of the new volunteers, and affects their subsequent actions. Second, Nolan notes that the training program had only a slight impact on volunteer's perceptions of the development process. It is very possible that the trainee's reticence to grapple with this issue was rewarded in part by the volunteer subculture. Within this value system, a greater premium is given to adjustment than to an examination of development "problems" and the relation of Peace Corps volunteers to them.*

4
Anthropology and the Peace Corps: Notes from a Training Program

RIALL W. NOLAN
Georgia State University

INTRODUCTION

The behavior and attitudes of local change agents, long recognized as important to the success of community development efforts, are especially crucial when the change agents are foreigners who must adapt to an entirely different culture. Peace Corps volunteers provide a particularly interesting example of how this adaptation is achieved.

In 1979, as director of a Peace Corps training program for rural development volunteers in Senegal,[1] I was able directly to influence the transition from middle-class America to rural West Africa and observe accompanying changes in attitudes and behavior. This article discusses three main aspects of that training program: how anthropology was used in program design to structure and facilitate this cross-cultural transition; how trainees actually made the transition; and (c) the implications of this process for further work and research.

PEACE CORPS IN SENEGAL

Senegal's Peace Corps program (emphasizing English teaching and rural development) dates from 1963. Most of the rural development volunteers work in the government's *Animation Rurale*

---

[1]The training program ran from March 23 to June 3, 1979, and included 34 trainees. A number of people contributed to the success of the program, and I would like to thank them here. They include Madelise Blumenroder, Star Campbell, Boubacar Diallo, Yoro Diallo, Patricia Dia, Xadi Diop, Gary Engleberg, Susannah Evans, Lisa Gaylord, Pierre Halpert, David Hunsberger, Isma Faye, Cheikh M'Bodj, Ami Niang and Koumba Taiba Seck. Patrick Dumont and Thomas Painter read and commented on early drafts of this article, made many helpful suggestions, and provided background materials.

program. *Animation*, as it is usually referred to, seeks to build skills and satisfy felt needs at the village level through self-help projects supported by government agencies. Cissé (1964) provides a clear summary of *Animation*'s methods and objectives. Begun in 1960, *Animation* was once the cornerstone of Senegal's rural development policy (Hapgood 1964). Since then it has been relegated to an increasingly minor role, for a variety of political and technical reasons (see Schumacher 1975 and Barker 1977 for a discussion of some of these). Although *Animation* survives today, rural development in Senegal is now dominated by large sectoral projects run through parastatal agencies, whose goals and methods are quite different from those of *Animation*. These agencies --and the projects they carry out--depend heavily on foreign finance and technical assistance.

In spite of this shift, however, Peace Corps/Senegal remains a strong supporter of *Animation*. In 1979, virtually all of *Animation*'s village-based personnel were Peace Corps volunteers, and this had been the case for some time. Senegalese staff prefer to remain in the larger towns and cities, emerging periodically to offer advice and assistance to villagers and the volunteers who live and work directly with them.

Volunteers thus work in a relatively unstructured environment, in a program that has low national priority. They are "resource persons" helping villagers define and meet their needs through a variety of small-scale projects usually limited to a few specific areas--gardening, health, water supply, and simple construction. These limitations on scale and scope reflect the realities of the local situation: that most Senegalese villages have the same basic needs; that volunteers, as a rule, have somewhat limited technical skills; and that both local resources and external support are largely lacking. Although some of these projects are highly successful, they have limited impact, and are not linked to overall rural development policy in any coherent way.[2]

Given these constraints, how successful are Senegal's volunteers? This cannot be directly measured, since no hard guidelines or standards exist, and few studies of volunteer

------

[2]Peace Corps/Senegal's continued involvement with an essentially moribund program having little national impact is, I believe, based on several pragmatic considerations. One is the type of person typically recruited as a volunteer--the "BA generalist"--who has little or no relevant training or experience. The rudimentary skills which most volunteers have, in other words, precludes their involvement in more complex undertakings. Another consideration is essentially diplomatic. Keeping volunteers in visible but non-threatening jobs allows both the Peace Corps and the Senegalese government to satisfy their respective constituencies, while at the same time avoiding any serious examination of either volunteer effectiveness or of national development policy.

performance have been carried out.[3]   Although many of their
projects "succeed" (in the sense that they are completed with
village support), such projects have never, to my knowledge,
been extensively evaluated.

In the absence of hard criteria for volunteer success, therefore, Peace Corps/Senegal places great emphasis instead on how
well volunteers adjust to life in Senegal. Indeed, for most Peace
Corps staff members, volunteer success is defined *primarily* in
terms of cross-cultural adjustment, defined and measured largely
through subjective means, including self-report.[4]

In the case of Senegal's volunteers at least, an emphasis on
cross-cultural adjustment seems to work, for they have relatively
low dropout rates compared with some other Peace Corps programs, and a high overall proficiency in local languages. On the
whole, volunteers in Senegal enjoy living there, and form close
relationships with their Senegalese friends, neighbors and colleagues. Former volunteers speak very positively of the country
and their experience there, and many of them eventually return
to work or visit, often for long periods of time. A major emphasis in training program design, then, became that of promoting a "positive" cross-cultural adjustment.

A secondary focus was on the doing of "projects." An
essentially Western concept applied with vigor to non-Western
areas, it is by no means clear that projects are the best way to
promote change-for-the-better, given the indisputable fact that
many have unforeseen or negative effects on people, social institutions, and the environment. In one sense, projects are merely
a bureaucratically convenient way of organizing people and resources. But all of this notwithstanding, Peace Corps, like so
many other agencies, promotes a "project orientation," implicitly
in its recruiting literature, and explicitly in its training
programs. As a result, potential recruits tend to accept
"projects" as the way to do development work.

My task was therefore to design a program to reflect these
two major emphases. It is to a discussion of this design phase
that I now turn.

---

[3]This is hardly surprising, since most community
development agencies prefer to define their goals and working
methods in fairly loose terms. By avoiding a clear definition of
what is actually being attempted, or of what constitutes
satisfactory performance, agencies can then claim that whatever
they managed to do was both successful and appropriate.

[4]Thus, Jones and Popper's study (1972) of volunteer
behavior and host country characteristics defined performance in
terms of ten criteria, grouped into categories of "attrition,"
"performance," "satisfaction," and "language proficiency." Eight
of the ten criteria were determined by volunteer self-report, one
by staff judgement, and one from service records.

DESIGNING THE TRAINING PROGRAM

The Peace Corps asked me to design a training program that was specifically anthropological in orientation. I was fortunate to have available to me a group of professional Senegalese trainers, specialized in language and cross-cultural work, and six currently-serving Peace Corps volunteers to serve as technical trainers and program administrators. This group became our training team, and worked with me to design and carry out the program. Previous training programs in Senegal had evolved an effective methodology for teaching language, cross-cultural awareness, and technical skills, and so these became major program components, to which we added a fourth: "community development," which dealt with the mechanics of project planning and implementation.

The Anthropological Approach

Given the fact that we began with a clearly-defined structure and an experienced staff, what was specifically anthropological about our approach to program design? I had no intention of training people to be anthropologists, but did attempt to give trainees an anthropological perspective--a conceptual approach to living and working in Senegal that would ease their transition into the new society and guide and structure their future learning. Although this was most explicitly set out in the community development component, it underlay all aspects of training. Four aspects of anthropology's overall approach guided training program design.

Holism. Anthropology's holistic orientation views cultures as integrated ensembles, and seeks wider meanings in isolated acts. Such an approach is very useful for developing cross-cultural awareness and exploring the linkages between aspects of everyday life in Senegal. In our program design we were at pains to show trainees how social, economic, and religious aspects of life were reflected in everyday behavior. We also treated the topic of values holistically, showing how villagers' concepts of the good life (i.e., development) were tied not only to their socio-economic arrangements, but also to historical experiences, such as the influence of both Islam and French colonialism.

Cultural Relativism. Cultural relativism is another powerful tool for coming to grips with a new culture. Unlike holism, however, relativism may directly threaten trainees' self-concepts; and must therefore be carefully introduced and used. The notion that other cultures have good reasons for doing apparently outlandish things leads quickly to the discovery that one's own ways may appear equally outlandish to others. Ultimately, relativism fosters the realization--uncomfortable for some--that there may in fact be no single best way of doing anything (marrying, learning, making a living, improving). In program design, we therefore discussed differing value-systems and world-views, and what they implied for volunteer work.

producers is simply impossible, due to near-catastrophic conditions (e.g., drought) or situations where producers refuse en
masse to reimburse their loans.

A second feature of the inflexibility of state credit agen-
cies--and consequently of the local cooperatives that are their de
facto extensions in rural areas--has been a consistent refusal to
provide the short-term cash loans most needed by Niger's peasantries. Credit for development purposes is *invariably* tied to
the acquisition of state-recommended production techniques, commodities, or such inputs as selected seeds, chemical fertilizers,
and animal-drawn plows and implements. This rigidity has produced a number of anomalous situations in which peasants have
repeatedly illustrated their ingenuity in order to obtain the cash
they need but which the state will not provide. Thus, for example, cooperative members may take out loans for cultivation equipment or other commodities promoted by government extension
programs, and once having obtained delivery, sell them at considerably less than their value in order to mobilize needed cash.

Third, the "creditworthiness" of applicants for agricultural
loans is determined by village notables in conjunction with representatives from the government services concerned, who are invariably outsiders. This leads to a situation where allocation of
credit is likely to go to persons whose acceptability is judged not
in terms of the need to break out of a cycle of low productivity,
but in terms of perceived ability to reimburse the credit. Under
these conditions, persons most in need are excluded. Recipients
of state agricultural credit are often wealthier peasants.

Fourth, for cooperative members who are persuaded to try
new methods on their fields and are granted commodity credit,
there is no guarantee that the government will be able to deliver
the inputs they request, either in sufficient quantities or on
time. Local cooperatives cannot exercise effective control over
policy in the aforementioned problem areas, and they have no
means of resolving the difficulties arising from them. Once in
debt to the state for agricultural inputs, they are also totally
dependent on the state's capacity to deliver.

Fifth, the importance of women as producers highlights
another aspect of the inflexibility of state-sponsored cooperative
programs in Niger. Despite their potential need for a range of
assistance in the area of production credit, women very frequently are excluded from Niger's rural cooperatives (Painter 1979:12;
see also Barrès et al. 1976:28, 40-41, 44; Painter 1980b:16-17).

Finally, interest charged for state agricultural development
loans may be quite high, particularly for seed loans, where two
sacks must be returned for every sack borrowed in order to build
up cooperative seed stocks. Development planners and critics of
development programs make much of the usurious interest rates
charged by wealthier peasants who grant loans in cash or kind.
Planners promote state credit schemes as a means of insulating
the peasantry from rapacious elements in rural society. Not only
is this promotional line another instance of what may be termed
development ideology, it also is sociologically naive. It fails to
address the local networks of patron-client relations within which
a variety of resources may be mobilized, and which provides the

context of so-called "traditional" credit. A closer examination of
the situation is likely to reveal that those elements whose interests are opposed to the peasantry nonetheless provide access to
credit under conditions far more flexible than those offered by
the state, which, through the reproduction of development ideology, presents itself as a promoter of peasant interests (Bachard
1976:51-52; Goussalt 1973, 1976; Nicolas 1974).

While far from exhaustive, this listing suggests some of the
limitations on the capacity of state-sponsored cooperative structures to alleviate risks that accompany productive innovation in
agriculture, and the basis for an ongoing lack of interest or commitment to cooperatives by Niger's peasants. State agricultural
development programs have inherited their emphasis on increased
production of a marketable agricultural surplus from the colonial
period. This is reinforced by a continuing heavy dependence on
a very few agricultural experts as a source of foreign exchange.
A keen awareness of this orientation, well established in the
peasants' thinking, plays an important role in shaping their
attitudes about development programs. The result is considerable
circumspection whenever a new agricultural development "package"
is presented to them.

An understanding of these factors throws new light on the
widespread reluctance of Niger's peasantry to embrace modern
productive innovations of the kind promoted by the Dosso project.
Peasant conservatism may be considered a two-pronged strategy.
First, it helps to assure reproduction of the basic production and
consumption unit over time under conditions where the subsistence base has eroded, in terms of both production and exchange.[21]   Second, it acts to insulate the integrity of this unit
from incursions by the state in the production process.   In
short, what some consider peasant conservatism may be more
accurately considered a form of resistance (Hutton and Cohen
1975:105-106; Nicolas 1971).

Peasant producers in the Dosso region are being encouraged
to innovate in agricultural production, but under conditions that
make state expectations of them unreasonable. Given a worsening
crisis of simple reproduction (Painter forthcoming: Chapters IX
and X; Shenton and Lennihan 1980) among many peasant households in the Dosso region and the perceived opportunity costs of
innovation and added investment in rain-fed agriculture, increasing numbers of the region's households are obliged to participate
in seasonal migrations of hundreds of miles yearly to the Guinea
Coast states in order to ensure the precarious continuity of the

---

[21]Concerning the region under discussion, see Beauvilain
(1977), Guillaume (1974), Painter (forthcoming), Poncet (1974),
and Raulin (1963). Cf. Faulkingham (1977a and b) and the work
of Nicolas and Raynaut listed in the references cited. For
perspectives on erosion of the Nigerien peasantry's position in the
sphere of exchange, see Berg (1975:119-127), Cohen et al.
(1979), and Derriennic (1977).

subsistence economy at home (Painter 1979:47-54, 1980a, forthcoming).

Considerations of risk-taking in productive innovation oblige
us to realize anew that rural development schemes such as the
Dosso Project do not operate in a vacuum. Those who plan development "interventions" (the term used by development assistance agencies) in sahelian agriculture must view the innovations
they promote in the context of the overall socioeconomic environment and their feasibility in the eyes of producers, *regardless* of
their presumed technical superiority. In so doing, one sees that
Nigerien agriculture is clearly not conducive to widespread
changes in comportment of the kind repeatedly promoted by
agricultural development programs throughout the country.
Casual examination of the national investment structure in Niger
will doubtless reveal that aside from government development
projects, rain-fed agriculture, which accounts for the vast majority of Nigerien crop production, is the least favored of all investment areas (Nicolas 1974:739,765; cf. Arnould 1982:351-352).

The Structure of Cooperative Organization

There has been a great deal of rhetoric since the mid-1960s
about the "cooperative movement" in Niger, but cooperative
organization has occurred in rural areas as a result of state
development planning, and not of peasant initiatives. This pattern of state intervention in marketing and agricultural production
has occurred throughout West Africa, as postcolonial states have
attempted to cut into areas of capital accumulation based on
agricultural marketing where metropolitan trading companies
(e.g., the Compagnie Française de l'Afrique Occidentale), Levant-
ine, and to a lesser extent, African, merchants have long enjoyed
privileged access (Goussalt 1973; 1976). These interventions
have taken the form of state marketing boards and the creation of
rural marketing cooperatives that are allowed (in principle if not
in practice) to sell solely to the boards. The result has been
greater state involvement in agricultural marketing processes at
minimal cost, without any expansion of peasant control. The
credit function of the cooperative was aimed at increased production, hence increased sales.

While the state has benefited substantially from its enhanced
control and coverage of crop production and marketing processes
and the subsequent accumulation made possible by local cooperatives, benefits to cooperative members have been far less impressive. Prices paid to peasant producers in Niger are much higher
now than ever before, but it is important to recall that the price
increases were a long time coming. The severe drought of 1969-
1974, the subsequent famine, and the resultant coup d'état were
necessary before producer prices were increased (Higgott and
Fuglestad 1975:389-390 and passim).

All of this is not to say that some form of cooperative organization, the result of peasant initiatives, cannot serve to better
defend "peasant space" (Holmquist 1980) in Niger. Rather, it is
to emphasize that cooperative structures introduced by the state

have not been the result of peasant initiatives, nor has the state allowed them to function in this manner. A good deal more than rhetoric and repeated emphasis on traditional communalism will be required. Some genuine devolution of power will be necessary.

Recent cooperative orientations in Niger, embodied in the government's Development Society, may afford these local organizations the clout they must have if they are to be anything more than an inexpensive means for promoting wider state penetration into Niger's rural economy behind a facade of self-management. Concerning these possibilities, our optimism must be guarded, for overcoming the inertia of more than half a century of colonial and neocolonial development will be difficult.

SOCIOLOGY AND THE DOSSO PROJECT

The Contribution of Sociology to the Dosso Project

A Cautionary Contribution. Development planners and short-term consultants, like those who employ them, are driven to recommend interventions. Crudely put, they are being *paid* for recommendations (Tendler 1975). As our two weeks in Dosso quickly passed, I became increasingly convinced that in the absence of so much obviously needed information on agrarian structures and processes of change in the Dosso region, it was far better to acknowledge the gaps in our understanding of key issues, face up to the impossibility of resolving them on the spot, and press for clearer formulation of questions in the future. These could be answered under appropriate conditions: if not under the rubric of "sociological follow-up" within the Dosso Project itself, then by national or expatriate researchers who were willing and able to spend time in investigation.

Given that the performance of rural development projects in West Africa has been generally poor (World Bank 1978b), the strategy seemed appropriate, although, from the Bank's perspective, it may have seemed ill-timed. Assuming that the Bank was serious about its plans for sociological follow-up during the period of Project operations, there was clearly much to be done. Answers to the numerous questions submitted to the Bank in my working paper (Painter 1979) would be useful for the specific purposes of the Project. They would also contribute to our understanding of rural social formations in this part of Africa, the nature of agrarian change, and the possibilities for the promotion of more generally beneficial development.

In the section of my working paper containing recommendations for sociological follow-up within the Project, I argued that collaboration be solicited from Nigerien social scientists. These recommendations were omitted from the French-language version of the working paper subsequently circulated among government staff connected with the Project. This is not surprising, for there is a marked preference among international development agencies to use their own nationals or third country social scientists for this type of research.

A Late Contribution.   The reasons for the tardy association
of a sociologist in the pre-operational phases of the Dosso Project
remain unclear.[22]   On the basis of an earlier project preparation
paper drafted by the Bank in conjunction with Nigerien development planners (République du Niger/Banque Mondiale 1978), one
can only surmise that, as the Project took shape in the minds of
Bank planners, a sufficient number of unexplained, potentially
troublesome issues of a nontechnical nature remained by late 1978
for them to decide it was better to have a sociologist late than
never.   Indeed, better late than never, but better earlier than
late.   I would argue thus, however distant sociological considerations may be to planners, who seem singularly inclined to look at
technical matters as issues largely divorced from the social organization of agricultural production and the risks faced by peasant
small holders in Africa.   The technicist position is inaccurate in
the extreme.

General Issues Arising from the Dosso Project

The Poverty of the Sociology of Cooperation in Niger.   The
inability to provide the basis for a satisfactory bridge between
introduced cooperative organizations and spontaneous forms of

---

[22]In this respect the Dosso Project is not atypical, for social
scientists are not often associated with development programs
during the early stages of their elaboration.   Less often still are
they involved on a continual or long-term basis.   There are
exceptions.   The USAID-Niger government-financed Niger Range
and Livestock development project is one.   Other cases can be
found described in Foster et al. (1978).   The need for a more
thoroughgoing involvement of social scientists in the identification
of problem areas, and in the planning, implementation, and evaluation of rural development programs has been a consistent concern of the Institute for Development Anthropology (IDA).   See
Brokensha et al. (1977); Horowitz (1979:85-94); Horowitz, ed.
(1976:iv-vii); McPherson (1978); and the Institute profile published in the Anthropology Newsletter (1980).
    The nature, terms, and appropriateness of participation by
social scientists (particularly anthropologists) in internationally
planned and financed rural development programs are topics of
considerable debate, and relevant articles occur with increasing
frequency in, among others, Human Organization, Current Anthropology, Practicing Anthropology, Anthropology Newsletter,
and Culture and Agriculture.   In addition to numerous papers
presented at the 1980 Annual Meetings of the American Anthropological Association in Washington, D.C., and the citations above,
see Almy (1977); Atta-Mills (n.d.); Belshaw (1976); Brokensha
and Pearsall, eds. (1969); Cochrane (1971; 1979; 1980); Frank
(1975); Glick Schiller (1981); Gough (1968); Stavenhagen (1971);
and Thompson (1976).

cooperation in Niger was a troublesome leitmotif during my efforts to respond to the Bank's terms of reference concerning the specific case of rural cooperatives in the Dosso region. Neither the ethnographic materials available prior to my work in Dosso, nor the majority of written materials on Nigerien cooperatives, nor, finally, the meager complementary information I was able to garner from interviews, planning documents, and other sources during my stay in Dosso were sufficient to afford a satisfactory portrayal of the situation there. I was obliged to extrapolate on the basis of research and planning activities among hausaphone populations in the south central regions of the country, and to do so with such circumspection that clear-cut policy recommendations for the Bank were not forthcoming. Insofar as recommendations did emerge, they were at odds with the planning priorities of both the Bank and the Nigerien government. My prognosis for enthusiastic participation of Dosso region peasants in Project cooperatives was not optimistic. This conclusion was based on considerations of the political economy of the Dosso peasantry. No amount of ethnographic or sociological data would have altered it.

The continuing popularity of rural cooperatives among Nigerien and international development planners despite a generally poor performance record and doubts concerning the future viability of all forms of local cooperation in rural Nigerien society, serves to underscore the necessity for careful study. Such a call for more research will not surprise readers. Unlike much of the work done to date, however, we require studies that focus on forms, processes, and contexts of spontaneous cooperation and the possibilities for buttressing these local forms, if this strategy is considered viable. As importantly, this research must seek to avoid conceptualizing local forms as situated within a rural society largely undifferentiated, undynamic, and for all practical purposes, isolated (Painter 1981).

I am not advocating more loosely focused sociological inventories of the kind called for by international development agencies in order to amass even greater quantities of (unused) "baseline data." However valuable basic research may be in the long run, the continued generation and accumulation of data in this manner is a luxury we cannot afford. More theoretically informed and/or problem-oriented research is needed. I would suggest that the significance of the issues raised in the foregoing discussion on spontaneous and introduced forms of cooperation provides a suitable point of departure for needed rethinking, conceptual clarification, and inquiry on the nature of agrarian change in southwestern Niger.

The sociological perspective is particularly well-suited to promoting a better understanding of spontaneous and introduced forms of cooperation, and a better grasp of the promise and perils that reside in attempts by development planners to link the two. That this perspective has not yielded greater insight to date concerning the Nigerien case is lamentable, but the situation need not remain so.

The Necessity for a Critical, Interdisciplinary Perspective.
The social scientist who becomes involved in various phases of development planning, implementation, and evaluation, eventually

must address a complex set of issues whose scope frequently surpasses narrow considerations of village life or the features of a specific development program or project. What is more, these considerations are very likely to surpass the limits of the disciplinary perspectives developed as a graduate student and reinforced during professional life. Thus, social scientists must work to cultivate an appreciation of relevant issues in fields outside of their specialties. In so doing, they must accept the risk of being considered intruders in areas of specialization and professional ideologies frequently considered by practitioners as highly technical preserves (e.g., agronomy, agricultural economics, management). In addition, they must develop the capacity to do so competently and critically.

In the case of the anthropologist, for example, a grounding in political anthropology, however valuable, may not suffice as preparation to grapple with the nature of the postcolonial state, the class interests promoted and hindered therein, and the complex, dynamic relations between these factors and the success and failure of rural development programs. This is not to minimize the importance of low-key politics, an understanding of which is central to clarity concerning rural cooperation and the fate of rural cooperatives (Charlick 1974; Painter 1981), but to suggest that it is only part of a larger picture. Indeed, there is need for a critical awareness of the nature of the relation between rural producers in Niger and the state, interstate, and international structures that determine their access to credit, technology, education, health services, and the like.

The development social scientist's concern for the modalities whereby women may be "further integrated into development" is an inadequate approach to a problem that is hardly one of integration. Indeed, African women *are* integrated in the development process, however poorly this integration may fit liberal definitions of autonomy and self-sufficiency. The crucial issue then is not how women may be further integrated into development, but how they are in fact included, and how proposed development programs might adversely affect their current and evolving situation (Barrès et al. 1976; Institute of Development Studies 1979; Roberts 1979). Women must be considered as critical actors within the basic unit of production, consumption, and investment in rural areas--the peasant household.

The responsibility of the social scientist in development includes considerably more than the careful study of structures and processes at the local level with reference to specific development programs (i.e., projects). It is also necessary that *the very nature* of the development process being mediated by state and international development planners and their consultants be more adequately understood and subject to continuous and critical examination.

The latter requirement, for a continual, critical perspective on official policies, approaches, and justifications, is of particular importance. One is reminded of the debunking function described by C. Wright Mills (1943) as carrying great significance in the social scientist's role in society. I submit that the importance of this critical, debunking activity is multiplied manyfold in the case of the social scientists who endeavor to engage in international development. For many readers, it is readily apparent that the context of development and underdevelopment is the expansion of world capitalism. This view of the development process may not be shared by persons and agencies directly engaged in development planning, for whom such readers work. With exceptions, to be sure, development planners are ill-inclined to accord serious consideration to these "exogenous," not to mention "historical," features in which they may have little interest, and, in any event, over which they have little control. As I have suggested earlier, as professionals whose futures depend on proof of their capacity to intervene (i.e., to spend money), they are less likely to consider *why* problems arise than they are "what to do about them" in a narrowly technical sense.

Finally, suggestions by social scientists that development planners and their programs may have wrongly understood the problem for which they are concocting solutions, or that the solutions may be contributing to other, more fundamental yet unidentified problems, may not be warmly received by planners. In my view, it is extremely important that these criticisms be made, although in doing so, one runs a personal and professional risk. For individuals who have decided to work within the problematics provided by development agencies, this risk may be too great. The bearers of bad news may discover that their welcome wears thin. This is particularly the case of "independent" (free) consultants.

The perspective loosely termed development anthropology endeavors to promote socially sound interventions within development programs through critical examination of the assumptions underlying such programs, as well as the relation between their anticipated and unanticipated consequences. This task is not possible in the absence of a perspective in which more than strictly sociocultural issues are considered. Such a perspective should enable the social scientist so engaged to penetrate and better comprehend the oversimplifications, blind spots, obfuscations, ideologies, and errors contained in and reproduced by official definitions of problems and their solutions.[23] In addition,

---

[23]An analysis of ideologies, shared and promoted among development planners and technicians in international and national development assistance organizations, and the consequences of these ideologies for conceptions of development "problems" or "intervention areas" and their "solutions" in the form of specific programs ("interventions") has yet to be done and would make a valuable contribution to our understanding of underdevelopment and the relations of development agencies to it. *Grosso modo*, Tendler (1975), Mills (1943), and others (cf. Ruther 1979), have provided us with useful groundwork in this area. "Development-ese," the peculiar language that fills official development documents and peppers the verbal accounts and explanations given by

(Footnote Continued)

and here is an area where many, particularly radical, social
scientists are likely to hedge, there is a responsibility to develop
alternative strategies, to act as well as critically analyze.

The Social Scientist "in" Development. Only recently have
international assistance agencies become aware of and responded
to the need for more than perfunctory attention to sociological as
well as narrowly defined economic and technical considerations
most often accorded top priority in the elaboration of development
programs. While there are certainly no grounds for complacency
or misplaced eagerness, it is encouraging to see that the critical
participation of social scientists in some aspects of development
programming has increased. The social scientist, whose role was
long restricted to that of the troubleshooter or coroner, performing post-mortems on failed projects in order to pinpoint "nontechnical" causes, has inched ever so slightly into a position of offering constructive expertise earlier in the planning of development
programs.

The promise that this situation offers is attractive and problematic. Whatever the extent to which social scientists eventually
are integrated into development, and however handsomely they
are paid for their services, it is essential that they retain their
critical wits about them. The scenario that comes to mind when
one imagines a situation where critical participation gives way to
co-optation is a somber one, and the line of demarcation between
the two may be fine indeed.

(Footnote Continued)
development planners, is more than simply jargon. It is the
social reproduction of shared definitions of the situation, which,
in a real and normative sense, obscure more than they reveal.
This is not by chance, but reflects the models-in-use by most
planners, and the organizations for which they work. The role
of ideology in development planning deserves considerable
attention.

Editors' Note to Chapter 9

*Steve Reyna is concerned with development and class forma-
tion. He uses case study material from Burkina Faso and the
Volta Valley Authority (AVV) to illustrate how the specific nature
of development choices in a dependent state of sahelian West
Africa produce particular patterns of class formation. The AVV,
like SAED as described by Waldstein, is the mechanism for extension of state and donor control over peasants' decision-making on
settlement schemes. An important point of Reyna's presentation
is that, in addition to control over the means of production and
the product, control--what he calls meta-control--over the decisions of how the means of production are used and the production
organized, is a critical issue in understanding processes of class
formation linked to state intervention in river basin agricultural
development. Yet the AVV itself is the result of a "least unattractive" development strategy by the Burkina Faso government,
forced to make development choices that are influenced by the
policies of external sources of development investment.*

9
Donor Investment Preference, Class Formation, and Existential Development: Articulation of Production Relations in Burkina Faso

STEPHEN P. REYNA
University of New Hampshire

INTRODUCTION

This chapter examines the influence of donor development assistance investments on class formation processes in the West African nation of Burkina Faso. Further, it introduces the notion of existential development to characterize the direction in which these processes have moved some segments of Burkinabè society.[*] A great deal of the literature on class and stratification in Africa tends toward ex cathedra pronouncements. Non-Marxist observers declare their inability to discern classes in Africa (Hill 1972; Jackson 1973; Kimble 1962; Lewis 1965; Lloyd 1966; Zolberg 1966), while Marxists report that classes are growing rapidly (Amin 1976; Leys 1975; Magubane 1976; Meillassoux 1975; Rey 1973; Wallerstein 1973, 1977).[2] On several points, however,

---

[*] Burkina Faso, the name adopted by Upper Volta in 1984, is used throughout this paper, even in references to the country before that year.

I should like to thank D. Aronson, R.E. Downs, J. Gregory, M. Herold, T. Painter, E. Skinner, and R. Talbot for helpful comments on earlier versions of this paper.

[1] Substantive conclusions are derived from two sources. The first consists of a variety of published and unpublished documents. For a discussion of the quality of these data, especially concerning the Autorité des Aménagements des Vallées des Volta (the AVV) see Reyna (1980). The second source of information is participant observation and interviews conducted during three missions to Burkina Faso, made while I was the Regional Anthropologist for the Regional Economic Development Services Office/West Africa (REDSO/WA) of the United States Agency for International Development (AID), based in Abidjan, Ivory Coast. The views presented here are not those of the Agency for International Development.

[2] W. Arthur Lewis, for example, states that "West Africa is simply not a class society on Marxist lines. In a class society
(Footnote Continued)

these divergent perspectives seem to agree--that the systematic study of inequality in Africa is off to a "shaky start" (Wallerstein 1973:375), and that it is full of "conceptual confusion" (Tuden and Plotnicov 1970:2-3); the resultant state of class analysis has been described by Dunn as "exceedingly confused and inconclusive" (1978:11).[3]   In these circumstances, a strategy favored by many anthropologists is a return to fundamentals, that is, to studies of change that are carried out at the local level, followed by the development of interpretations that account for local-level observations.   This approach to the analysis of class formation informs the present discussion.

This introductory section identifies two fundamentally different patterns of preference for the investment of development assistance in Burkina Faso: one in river valley areas, and one in interior areas. This section also suggests an approach to the analysis of the impacts of these patterns of donor investment preferences upon class development.   The second section, on arenas of class formation, presents data from studies in the riverain and interior areas and suggests that donor investment in riverain areas contributes to the development of what are termed state class relations, while donor investment in the interior catalyzes varying rates of what is termed private class formation. Two variations of private class formation are identified: one occurs in relation to elites, the other in relation to various traditional structures.   The third section, on the growth of a bureaucratic gentry, goes on to argue that findings from studies in the riverain and interior areas indicate processes of dual class formation, and seeks to explain these processes as the result of the articulation of distinctive production relations in each area. Finally, the term "existential development" is introduced to characterize the direction of Burkinabè development.   Existential development is the creation of opportunity structures all of whose 'opportunities' are negative. Support for this interpretation is provided through the analysis of class consumption-level data from the riverain and interior areas of Burkina Faso.

(Footnote Continued)
political power resides in a few people who own the instruments of production" (1965:18).   No data are advanced to support this assertion.   In a similar vein, on the basis of their survey of the literature pertaining to dependency and African inequality, Shaw and Grieve speak of the "pervasiveness of inequalities" (1979:230) in the absence of any supportive data.

[3]The literature on class formation is growing rapidly.   Useful reviews can be found in Katz (1980) and McClelland (1979). Of particular interest to students of the West African situation is the work of Shenton and Lennihan (1980) and Shenton and Watts (1979) on northern Nigeria.

Patterns of Donor Investment Preferences

Burkina Faso, a landlocked state roughly the size of Colorado, had 5.7 million inhabitants in 1976. Except for a small part in the north of the country that is sahelian in climate (included within the Sahel Regional Development Organization), where pastorally oriented Fulbe or Tamachek speakers predominate, Burkina Faso is best described in bio-climatic terms as savanna or guinea-savanna, and is inhabited by Voltaic speakers (Murdock 1959). For purposes of development administration in the country, the Burkinabè government established Regional Development Organizations (henceforth ORDs), each being distinguishable in terms of habitat and history.

The ORDs in central Burkina Faso are located on the Mossi Plateau. This area, the seat of the precolonial Mossi kingdoms, today has the highest population density in the country, containing about half the national population. The area east of the plateau, as far as the border with the Niger Republic, is included within the Eastern ORD. Inhabited by the Gourma, the Eastern ORD contains the nation's lowest population densities. The ORDs to the southwest and southeast of the Mossi Plateau have population densities intermediate to those of the plateau and the eastern regions. Acephalous peoples, largely Busani and Bisa in the southeast, and Lobi, Bobo, and Senoufou in the southwest, inhabit these areas. Within this savanna zone, two distinct geological zones can be identified: the river valley or riverain lands near the Volta Rivers and their tributaries; and the interior lands, little influenced by the passage of the rivers. In general, riverain soils are more fertile than those of the interior.

McFarland has described the economic prospects for Burkina Faso as bleak and argues that the economy generates little capital for financing industrial expansion (1978). Some 91 percent of the national population lives in rural areas, and per capita income during 1979 was estimated to be $159 (USAID 1980:36). The country has almost no industry or mining and lacks public and private domestic capital for investment in development. From 1972 to 1974, 80 percent of all investments originated from foreign governments, and total foreign assistance amounted to about $60 million (Dumont 1978:276). This situation persisted through the late 1970s, when it was estimated that international development assistance in 1979 would be greater than the national budget for the same year (USAID 1980:25). According to AID, the 1979 budget showed "disproportionately larger increases in non-developmental spending, including...military and internal administration" (1980:19). Investment capital from private foreign sources is very limited and has little impact on development.

Thus Burkina Faso's development is heavily dependent upon the investment preferences of external donor agencies, and considerable regional skewing of investment preferences has been observable since the early 1970s. Donor agencies have shown a marked preference to invest in the riverain areas of Burkina Faso, as will be described below. The Autorité des Aménagements des Vallées des Volta (AVV), for example, is a Burkinabè parastatal organization created for resettlement and the production of cash and food crops in the Volta River valley area. The AVV is financed by French, German, Dutch, and European Economic Community (EEC) development assistance. Details on the organization, program, and agricultural packages of the AVV have been described elsewhere in considerable detail, and will not be repeated here (cf. Bei Agrer 1978; Murphy and Sprey 1980c; and ORSTOM 1979:280).

During 1980, the proposed budget for the Government of Burkina Faso amounted to $191 million (USAID 1980:25). Of the amount budgeted for the government, about a fifth was allocated to rural development, and roughly a fifth of all foreign assistance was used for the same purpose. Thus some $76 million was invested in rural development during 1980, and fully one-fifth of that (about $15 million) went to the parastatal AVV. In 1978, according to Sorgho and Richet (1979:4), the AVV had about 3,750 hectares of land in production. Assuming that the AVV's land areas in production increased to about 4,000 hectares by 1979, approximately 20 percent of Burkina Faso's total rural investment was being spent on 40 square kilometers of the country's 274,000 square kilometers of surface area. Elsewhere in Burkina Faso, donor investments have also been drawn to parastatal agro-enterprises in river valley areas of the country (Ouedraogo 1979:555).

Analysis of Class Formation in West Africa

The literature on West Africa reports three types of changes having implications for class formation. The first is the growing influence of government bureaucracies. During the early days of independence, Ly (1958) and Dumont (1962) signaled what they believed was the emergence of a new bureaucratic class in francophone West Africa. The view today of some sources is that there exists in West Africa an "organizational bourgeoisie" (Markowitz 1977). Others take a more cautious approach to these developments, as does Meillassoux after a review of the evidence from Mali. He speaks of a bureaucracy having some of the characteristics of a social class that exercises control over the economic infrastructure of the country and its peasantry (1970:106-107). The second type of change, observed during the mid-1960s by Amin (1967:277) is the emergence of a bourgeois planter class. Amin was concerned with the Ivory Coast, but other studies in the forest areas (Campbell 1974; Hill 1963; Stavenhagen 1969) and savanna zones (Ernst 1976; Jones 1976, and Cruise O'Brien 1971) of West Africa reveal that increasingly, private individuals, with state support, are gaining control over land and labor, and are producing staple and cash crops for domestic and foreign markets. A third change is the proliferation of parastatal organizations that, since independence, have played an important role in the organization of agricultural development (Hermann 1981:11; Gaud 1968; and Lavroff 1979). Those who know the Gezira scheme in the Sudan are familiar with Barnett's analysis which examined the control exercised by the scheme's managers over the organization of production (1977:179). Thus, bureaucrats, parastatal managers, and private landowners are three groups who exhibit attributes of class.

Some conceptual definition is needed in order to proceed. Production relations are relations between individuals resulting from their relations to the means of production and the product. In certain production relations, individuals exhibit differential control over the means of production and those with greater control appropriate the product in some form of surplus labor from those with lesser control. These are class production relations.[4] Class formation analyzes both: how differentials in control and appropriation emerge; and how classes come to exhibit common action--i.e., how class consciousness develops. This essay does not consider development of class consciousness. Private class relations are those in which private individuals appropriate a surplus. State class relations are those in which either individuals or positions within a hierarchy of state offices appropriate a surplus. Bureaucracies, parastatals, and private landowners are interpreted as attributes of a dual process of state and private class formation. This process is in turn explained using an articulation of modes of production approach most persuasively argued by Rey (1971, 1973).[5] Articulation is used in Wolpe's sense as: "...the relationship between the reproduction of the capitalist economy on the one hand and the reproduction of production units organized to precapitalist relations and forces of production on the other" (1980:41).

Articulation theorists view articulation, rather than dependency, as the "...fundamental cause of underdevelopment" (Meillassoux 1975). Underdevelopment, low productive force productivity, is a characteristic of precapitalist domestic economies in a 'phase' of the articulation of these with capitalism where the latter 'maintains' the former in order to derive certain resources necessary for its reproduction (Rey 1973). This essay contributes to the articulation programmatic by exploring systems of articulation in a time period--the postcolonial--less well represented in the literature. The following section describes the riverain and interior arenas of class formation.

---

[4]This study conceptualizes classes in terms similar to those of Giddens (1974:28), rather than along the lines provided by Dahrendorf (1959:23); that is, emphasis is placed on *control over* as opposed to *ownership of* the means of production.

[5]The articulation perspective is developed in Dupré and Rey (1980); Rey (1973); Meillassoux (1972; 1975); Althusser and Balibar (1970); Poulantzas (1973); and Bettelheim (1972). A review of this literature can be found in Wolpe (1980:1-45). For particular attention to Rey's (1973) perspectives, see Bradby (1980:109-118).

ARENAS OF CLASS FORMATION IN BURKINA FASO

Riverain Zones

The French bilateral development assistance agency, Fonds d'Aide et de Coopération (henceforth FAC), recommended in 1971 that a parastatal organization be created with responsibility for the development of the newly accessible river valley areas along the Volta Rivers then being cleared of onchocerciasis (river blindness). The idea was that the parastatal would enable the government of Burkina Faso to attract the funds it needed from donor agencies for development programs in the river valleys (FAC 1972).

Burkina Faso accepted the FAC recommendations, created the AVV by presidential decree in September 1974, and transferred formal ownership of all Volta River valley land to the state. By 1979 the land area included by this transfer amounted to about 30,000 square kilometers, or roughly 12 percent of Burkina Faso's total land mass. A subsequent decree in 1976 formalized sweeping changes in the control over land use in AVV areas. How land was to be productively used was to be determined by the AVV's development plans. The decree further specified that the rights of settlers on AVV lands were conditional on their performance of agricultural activities required of them by the AVV managers. Thus, the 1976 decree provided the juridical basis for a specific type of class formation in Burkinabè society. It authorized state control over access to and use of the means of production.

The AVV is the largest agricultural parastatal in Burkina Faso, and when it began operations, total investments in the organization were expected to range from $143 million to $236 million (Bei Agrer 1978). As a result of its actions, an estimated 20,000 families would be resettled into river valley areas to produce cotton and grain. By 1979, with 85 percent of its activities financed by foreign development assistance, the AVV had settled 1,700 families.[6] The following section examines reasons for the AVV's creation.

_____

[6]AVV is presently divided into a headquarters and different agricultural perimeters. Authority is centralized, so that most decisions are made at the headquarters. Perimeters are in principle composed of sectors (80,000 hectares), divided into blocks, and further subdivided into villages. Four or five blocks are planned for each sector, and within each block there should be 400 families residing in 8 to 16 villages of 25 to 50 families (ORSTOM 1979; Reyna 1980).

AVV migrants must apply an agricultural production package designed to intensify land use, maintain soil fertility, and introduce cash cropping. These goals are to be furthered by allocating to each planned, mean farm family of five laborers, ten hec-
(Footnote Continued)

Colonial Incorporation and Post-colonial Conjuncture

The decision to establish the AVV resulted from a conver-
gence of EEC and the Burkinabè government interests that had
been maturing since the colonial period.   During the early
twentieth century, French colonial policy in West Africa was dominated by Albert Sarraut's insistence that the colonies help France
to recover from World War I (Sarraut 1923; Skinner 1980:126).
The specific strategy followed in the case of Burkina Faso was
based on the view that the area was not viable economically
(Songré et al. 1974:126).   As a result, productive investment in
Burkina Faso was minimal; private and public capital were di-
verted to more attractive areas, largely along the Guinea Coast.
The role of Burkina Faso, from early in the 1920s, became that of
a reservoir of cheap labor for enterprises in the coastal areas
(Londres 1929:126).   At about the same time, Burkinabès were
obliged to grow and sell cotton at low prices because the French
textile industry was seeking a reliable, inexpensive source of this
raw material.   France provided no new inputs so that cultivation
continued   using   existing   productive   forces   (Ossendowski
1928:276).   Colonial investments in Burkina Faso were limited to
interurban road and rail links, and some urban infrastructure,
which were all intended to speed labor and cotton from Burkina
Faso toward the Guinea Coast.   French merchants offered, under
near-monopoly conditions, expensive consumer goods produced by
French industry.
These policies helped to nudge Burkina Faso into the French
corner of the capitalist system.   Existing agrarian productive
forces were burdened with additional labor requirements, while
labor was rushed to more lucrative areas of investment. Hence,
commoditization of production and labor was accelerated under
terms of trade where Burkinabè producers sold labor and commodities cheaply, while paying high prices for French goods.[7]

(Footnote Continued)
tares, of which at any point in time six hectares should be
farmed.   Farmers are obliged to cultivate cotton on 40 percent of
their fields.   The first two goals are furthered by altering and
adding to the factor mix utilized in existing systems.   First,
labor is intensified.   Second, new inputs are added, including
selected seeds, pesticides (DDT), chemical fertilizers, and animal
traction.   Third, new agricultural practices are introduced,
ranging from planting seeds in straight lines to new crop
rotations.   Soil fertility is maintained by insisting upon fallows
two years out of every six, introducing nitrogen-fixing plants,
and using chemical fertilizers.   The package was developed under
experimental conditions, so that its ability to attain its major
goals is unproven.

[7]A satisfactory history of the incorporation of West African
savanna regions into the capitalist world economy remains to be
(Footnote Continued)

For the first decade after independence, the development strategy of the Burkinabè government continued colonial patterns. Rural investments were few, and what little agricultural development there was, was implemented by French enterprises: the *Compagnie Française pour le Développement des Fibres Textiles* (CFDT); the *Société d'Aide Technique et Coopération* (SATEC), and the *Compagnie Internationale de Développement Rural* (CIDR). The colonial emphasis on the cultivation of cash crops through the use of minimally improved productive techniques and reliance on existing forms of organization continued (Marchal 1977:85). French firms in Burkina Faso left the adoption of minor productive innovations up to Burkinabè farmers (Gregory 1979; de Wilde 1967). Thus the CFDT was able to effect some increases in cotton production, but other successes were small. Productivity generally stagnated or declined, and ecological problems on the Mossi Plateau worsened.

This situation affected the Burkinabè bureaucracy in two ways. First, stagnating and declining production in agriculture lowered government revenues, threatening bureaucratic incomes. Second, as conditions on the Mossi Plateau continued to deteriorate, the Mossi petitioned their bureaucracy for assistance (E. P. Skinner, personal communication). These pressures on the Burkinabè bureaucracy intensified during the 1972-1974 drought. By the early 1970s, then, it was in the political and economic interest of the Burkinabè bureaucracy to seek agricultural improvements.

In 1973, the World Health Organization began to implement a program to control the blackfly, *Simulium damnosum,* the vector for onchocerciasis. The effectiveness of this program made the riverain areas of Burkina Faso more attractive, for with the river blindness vector under control, valley areas could be resettled and used to increase agricultural production (Berg 1978).

France and other EEC nations were interested in the development of these new river valley lands. During the first decade of independence, the CFDT demonstrated that it could grow cotton. Not only would the textile interests of the EEC countries benefit from Burkinabè cotton, but European agro-industrial farms could potentially sell their goods and services to Burkina Faso's cotton schemes. On the basis of projections of the AVV's investments and operating costs, conservative estimates indicated that EEC firms could easily do business worth $125 million in setting up the AVV parastatal for the production of cotton in the valley areas. It was estimated that another $3.5 million could be realized each year through sales of farm equipment and supplies to the AVV once operations

---

(Footnote Continued)
written. What appears to distinguish Burkina Faso is the absence of a flourishing cash-crop sector as is found in northern Nigeria (Shenton and Freund 1978) and Senegambia (Copans 1980), and the very early institutionalization of Burkina Faso's role as a labor reservoir for the forest areas of the Guinea Coast.

had begun (Reyna 1983:215). On the other hand, European agro-industry could not count on selling a great deal to the impoverished farmers of Burkina Faso, and earlier experiences in which reliance was placed on Burkinabè farmers voluntarily to adopt new productive techniques in agriculture had been disappointing (Gosselin 1978). The creation of an agricultural parastatal resolved this problem because--according to one expatriate adviser on the AVV--the parastatals could *impose* the new techniques and *oblige* producers to adopt them.

The AVV promised additional markets and an increased supply of cotton to EEC industries, while it held out the promise of higher government revenues and greater bureaucratic incomes to Burkinabè bureaucrats. The FAC mission that proposed the organization of the AVV informed the Burkinabè government that revenues would amount to about 3.7 billion CFA francs over a 25-year period as a result of the parastatal's operations. To these visions of billions, the mission added that as many as 150,000 individuals could be resettled from the Mossi Plateau into the parastatal's domain, thus alleviating the growing problem of overpopulation on the Plateau (FAC 1972). Thus, it appeared that creation of the AVV would consummate certain EEC and Burkinabè needs, and so they rushed off to a common bed--which was of course the AVV.

Differentials in Control over Land Use

Land control differentials are indicated by the percentage of land-use decisions made by different classes in a class relationship, and by which class bears what risks resulting from these decisions. The following decisions concerning farming techniques are controlled by AVV management: field size and location, type of soil preparation, crop type, seed variety, rotation system, sowing dates, and cultivation techniques.[8] Annual variable production cost decisions made by AVV or other officials include those of seeds, fertilizers, insecticides, and seed treatments. Annual fixed cost decisions made by AVV or other government agencies include those for small equipment (hoes, shovels, etc.) and animal traction (oxen amortization costs, oxen maintenance costs, equipment amortization costs, equipment maintenance costs). The following cotton distribution decisions are made by AVV or other agencies: sale date, sale price, and farmgate

---

[8]Just as industrial workers know nothing about decisions concerning production techniques made by management, so tenants do not always follow AVV farming directions, report Murphy and Sprey (1980c). The point remains: in the domestic mode of production farmers make all major agricultural decisions, while on the AVV they may obey or disobey, but they may not decide.

price.[9]   AVV tenants make none of these major production and distribution decisions.

Next, AVV tenants are compared with agrarian wage laborers and sharecroppers in terms of their protection against income losses consequent upon resource utilization decisions to show how risky this lack of control renders their well-being. Chadian agricultural wage laborers with whom I am familiar generally make no decisions affecting production costs, but they don't bear these costs. They make very few decisions concerning production techniques or product distribution. Further, their incomes are usually sensitive to production fluctuation, because land owners, experiencing poor rains and knowing that harvests will be poor, stop employing wage laborers. Recent research indicates diversity in sharecropping systems (Robertson 1980), but generally sharecroppers participate in production-cost decisions, costs which they often share with landowners (cf. Scott 1976). Sharecroppers normally make substantial technical production and distributional decisions. Finally, their income, however, is somewhat protected against production fluctuations as the 'share' appropriated by the landlord decreases with output declines, and because landlords have been known to reduce the percentage which they considered their 'share' with such declines (ibid.).

In sum, AVV tenants bear a portion of production costs, like sharecroppers; however, like wage laborers, they formulate no major land utilization decisions. Thus their control appears even riskier than that of wage laborers, who--like AVV tenants--lack mechanisms insulating their incomes against production losses and make no decisions concerning land utilization, but who bear no direct production costs. AVV tenants must contribute financially to uncertain decisions they do not control, and are given no protection should these go awry.

AVV managers enjoy greater *de jure* control over land use than private landowners. Conditions of tenant land access are regulated in Burkina Faso either through custom or government action. Private landowners must conform to customary or governmental land utilization rules. Article 2 of the 1976 Presidential Decree delegated AVV the authority to contract, and alter in mid-contract, conditions of access. This gives AVV even greater control over its land than private landowners, who must conform to existing rights and duties applying to individuals using their land, while AVV managers can formulate and reformulate these rights and duties. This places AVV in a situation of meta-control over its tenants. Party X exhibits control over Y when societal

---

[9] It may be objected that the ordinary farmer theoretically works under similar distribution constraints, and that AVV merely reflects governmental marketing policies. There is, however, a difference. The normal density of extension agents in Burkina Faso is about one or two per agricultural sector. In AVV settlements there is one agent for every two to five families. The AVV is *dirigiste*.

rules allocate X authority to make decisions over Y. Party X enjoys meta-control when it also makes the *rules* defining its authority over Y (Baumgartner et al. 1975). The managers seen most often by AVV tenants are extension agents, often teenagers from urban areas who wear platform shoes while explaining farming techniques they don't understand. Given AVV's meta-control, is it any wonder that tenants are described as exhibiting an "insécurité fondamentale" (Kattenberg 1979:40)?

Appropriation

AVV is one of three structures integrated vertically within a larger system of appropriation in Burkina Faso. Each structure has a specific function: the production of commodities, the marketing of commodities, and finally, control of the resources used for production. The AVV is the first of these structures. The second is the *Société pour le Développement des Fibres Textiles* (SOFITEX), and the third is the Burkinabè government itself. Tenants on the AVV produce cotton and are required to sell their production to SOFITEX, a monopsony, 51 percent of which is owned by the government and 49 percent by the CFDT. SOFITEX gins and sells the cotton--most of it (about 90 percent in 1978) being exported to France (Sorgho and Richet 1979:26)--and appropriates the difference between the prices it pays AVV tenants and those it receives on the world market. Of this amount, an undisclosed portion is absorbed by costs. The remainder is transferred to the Burkinabè government's *Caisse de Stabilisation des Prix des Produits Agricoles*. It is then redistributed in part to other government agencies through budgetary allocations, a portion being used to pay government salaries. Thus the surplus appropriated by SOFITEX from AVV tenants through its monopsony and subsequent dealings in the world market is used in part to pay government bureaucrats, including the AVV managers who make risk-free decisions concerning the use of land by AVV tenants.

Estimations of value appropriated, based on 1978 conditions, are possible. AVV tenants were paid 50 F CFA/kg in 1978 for their cotton (Sorgho and Richet 1979:29). If the average farm cultivated 1.5 hectares of cotton per farm, with yields of 1000 kg/hectare--as planned and achieved by AVV managers (Bei Agrer 1978)--the mean gross tenant income from cotton would be 75,000 F CFA. SOFITEX would reduce these 1,500 kg of cotton by ginning to approximately 555 kg of cotton fiber--assuming 37 percent of the original weight to be left after ginning (Sorgho and Richet 1979:33). This fiber would have then sold at prevailing 363 F CFA/kg world market price. Hence, in 1978, 1,500 kg of cotton would generate 201,485 F CFA, of which approximately 63 percent would be transferred to the state. Under these conditions, the rate of labor exploitation for 1.5 hectares of cotton is calculated as 166 percent during 1978-1979 (Reyna 1983). The exact percentage devoted to salaries for the bureaucracy is unknown.

Wallerstein (1976:6) suggests that consequent upon capitalist core expansion, "coerced cash-crop" classes emerge in the periphery "...where the peasants are required by some legal process enforced by the state to labor at least part of the time on a large domain producing some product for sale on the world market." A defining feature of such class systems is that state actions directly set the rate of surplus value appropriation, meaning that appropriation is through primitive accumulation. Wallerstein was largely referring to *encomiendas* in Hispanic America and the "Second Serfdom" in eastern Europe. The AVV tenant class works a vast domain--riverain land. It produces a commodity for the world market--cotton. It is legally coerced in ways controlled by state actions to cultivate this commodity. What distinguishes AVV from 16th century "coerced cash-crop" systems is that in the former, the state owns the means of production. Thus, because of the participation of the state in production relations, it is appropriate to speak of state, "coerced cash-crop" class relations on Burkinabè lands. Formation of private class relations in the interior is explored in the following section.

Interior Zones

Little capital is available in the interior because of riverain donor investments. Fertilizer and other inputs are allocated first to agro-parastatals.[10]   Interior incomes are exceptionally low, which means that farmers cannot anyway afford those few inputs that are available. Agricultural technicians are disproportionately assigned to agro-parastatals, which reduces the quality of agricultural services available in the interior. If an increasing supply of agricultural inputs and services is necessary for increases in productivity, an opportunity cost of favoring parastatals is stagnation in interior agriculture. Below, it is shown how stagnation, in the presence of population growth, harms both the environment and farming systems, driving people from their land, with consequences for class formation.

---

[10]A large percentage of agricultural inputs and services goes to the AVV, while of the remainder a fair amount was destined-- at least during the mid-1970s--for use in cotton production in the southwest (Elliott 1975:46). Thus very little is left for interior zones. For example, in 1977-1978, the Eastern ORD, sole distributor of fertilizers in the eastern part of the country, distributed a total of only 36,000 kilograms of chemical fertilizers for use in cotton cultivation in an area of over 50,000 km^2. None appears to have been distributed for use on food crops (ORD de l'Est 1980:101).

"Demographic Enclosure"

Burkina Faso appears to be in the first phase of a demographic transition. Mortality has decreased about 10 percent since 1960, while fertility has continued at previously high levels. As a result, the rate of natural growth has been high: about 2 percent per annum since 1975 (USAID 1980:7). According to Marchal, much of this population growth occurred before mortality rates began to decline, and he estimates that the Burkinabè population doubled during the period 1925 to 1973 (1977:75).

One explanation for this growth may reside in policies initiated by the French colonial administration. The French required that Burkinabè farmers cultivate cash in addition to food crops, but provided no labor saving implements to meet the increased work load. In addition, they increased the nonagricultural work required of farmers by forcibly recruiting them for *corvée* labor. At the same time (from the early 1920s), they acted to reduce the size of the available labor pool by organizing migrations to the Ivory Coast (Skinner 1980). The result was a significant intensification of labor demands on rural dwellers (Suret-Canale 1976). Some scholars have argued that the demand for child labor in agriculture, and hence fertility, is likely to climb with decreasing agricultural productivity due to overexploitation of the land and male out-migration (Cleveland 1979; Faulkingham 1977a; Handwerker 1977; Reyna 1977; Deere 1978; and Javillonar et al. 1979: Chapter 2). Population and emigration increased during the colonial period in Burkina Faso while mortality and immigration remained roughly constant, implying an increase in fertility. During this time span, labor demands intensified. Such evidence is consistent with the view that increased labor demand resultant from colonial policy contributed to Burkina Faso's population growth.

Consequent upon this population growth were density increases on the Mossi Plateau (Marchal 1977:75), which have been documented to restrict access to farmland in Burkina Faso (Boutillier 1964; Kohler 1971; Swanson 1979). Kohler describes a sequence of tenure changes he observed among Mossi at Dakola. As density increased, land ownership passed from lineage to individuals, with control over land passing from lineage to household heads (1971:151). These household elders should not deny access to household members, but can and do exclude non-household, lineage members. Access to land is thus narrowed, because individuals are deprived of guaranteed access to former lineage lands.

Density increases imply decreasing per capita amounts of arable land. This land scarcity, in the absence of new technology, leads to soil deterioration and productivity declines, which is the case on the Mossi Plateau where the declines are known to be considerable (Marchal 1977). Under demographic conditions prevalent on the Plateau, households are thus faced with less arable land and restricted access to alternative lands due to changes in the land-tenure system.

The frequency of land borrowing provides some indication of these land shortages. Table 1 presents data on the relation

Table 1.   Burkina Faso: Incidence of Land Borrowing
in Relation to Population Density

Area	Density	Percentage of Borrowing
Eastern ORD		
Pama	$0 - 5/km^2$	23% of all households borrow fields
Gobinangu	$15 - 30/km^2$	44% of all households borrow fields
Mossi Plateau		
General	$46/km^2$	50% of cultivated fields are on borrowed land

Sources: Population density. Pama and Gobinangu: Upper Volta
1979. General, Mossi Plateau: Courel and Pool 1973:994.

Percentage of Borrowing. Pama and Gobinangu: Swanson 1979:30-31. Mossi Plateau General: Boutillier 1964:97.

between population densities and the quantity of land borrowed.
Not surprisingly, in areas where densities are greater, the incidence of land borrowing is higher.

As land becomes scarcer, households are left with holdings
insufficiently large to satisfy their subsistence needs, given their
techniques of agricultural production. The result of this process
is the sloughing-off of elements of an agrarian labor force searching for land or for some other means of satisfying their subsistence needs. The process is a "demographic enclosure," for
demographic rather than legal events trigger separation of people
from their land. Finally, "demographic enclosure" results in a
supply of labor in need of land.

Migration from the Mossi Plateau can be interpreted as an
indicator of the magnitude of "demographic enclosure." There is
a relatively large literature concerning Burkina Faso's migration
reviewed in Gregory (1974), and Piché, Gregory and Coulibaly
(1980), which establishes three points. First, the volume of
intra- and international migration is great, including perhaps 12
percent of the total male Burkinabè population (Courel and Pool
1973:1013; Upper Volta 1979). Second, migration is highest
among male, productive age-groups in the most densely populated
regions (Piché, Gregory and Coulibaly 1980; Smith 1977:282).
Third, the literature indicates that migrants are motivated to

leave Burkina Faso either to augment incomes (Courel and Pool
1973:1002; Piché, Gregory and Coulibaly 1980:36-38) or to avoid
the consequences of population pressure (Kohler 1972). In the
absence of services and inputs to modernize farming, these
explanations suggest the following argument. The need to supplement income results from declining productivity consequent at
least partially upon increasing population density; therefore, population movements, in part, may be said to be a "response to
declining availability of arable land" (USAID 1980:7). The higher
the migration, the greater the "demographic enclosure," which is
consistent with Gregory's observation that "...migration is the
principal process by which Africa is being proletarianized"
(1979:82).

Influences on the Type and Rate of Private Class Formation

Labor sloughed off the land through "demographic enclosure"
is available to others who control land. Some goes to supply agricultural parastatals, including the AVV (Murphy and Sprey
1980c); the majority, however, goes to private individuals. Before proceeding, it is important to identify what requires emphasis concerning interior, private class formation. The available
social science literature rarely reports private class relations.
Their absence is noted (Gregory 1974:317). Studies are reviewed
below in different interior areas which suggest how donor investment preference may have at the same time stimulating and re-
straining implications for rates of private class formation.

The Eastern ORD is an area of low demand for agricultural
commodities according to data collected by the Michigan State University farm-level agricultural survey (personal communication: G.
Lassiter). Few individuals purchase large quantities of staples,
and though the government wishes to purchase cotton, it does so
at unattractive farmgate prices. Nevertheless, Swanson observes
that "Traders and functionaries in large communities...use their
influence and wealth to secure for themselves valuable property
[e.g., land]" (1979:6; insert added for clarity). This land is
then worked by wage laborers, usually paid in kind, mainly to
produce foodstuffs demanded in local markets. Individuals ac-
quiring land in this manner are government officials, traders,
"traditional" rulers, or veterans who have greater access to financial capital. Land is often acquired by asking for its donation
from an individual with authority over its disposition. Land authorities are usually only too pleased to oblige in expectation of
future services from the donee. Exchanges of this kind exhibit
characteristics of what Sahlins has termed generalized reciprocity
(1972:194).

---

[11]The reciprocity appears more generalized than balanced,
because "direct exchange," required for the latter form, is lacking (Sahlins 1972:194).

Only a very small percentage of the farms, however, employ wage labor. Preliminary results from a three-year, farm-level, agricultural/cultural survey by Michigan State University of Eastern ORD households suggests that 10 percent of the labor supplied to farms is some form of wage labor (personal communication: G. Lassiter). Sharecropping is not reported. In Fada N'Gourma, for example, which is the largest town in the Eastern ORD, an informant estimated there to be 20 to 30 farms of from 20 to 30 hectares employing wage labor. If we very generously assume that there are 20 farms of the same size as those in Fada N'Gourma in each of the other large towns in the Eastern ORD, then there are 500 such farms occupying a total of 125 square kilometers, meaning 0.25 percent of the Eastern ORD's 50,000 square kilometers are given over to private land-owner/wage-laborer farming. Thus classes based on wage labor are slowly emerging in the Eastern ORD.

The Mossi Plateau is also a region of relatively low demand for agricultural commodities, but one of far greater population density than in the Eastern region. Evidence suggests that class relations are forming here, but involving a different land acquisition mechanism. During the late 1960s and early 1970s, Gerard Remy, who studied farming in the densely populated region of Nobere, showed that those with more high quality farmland were from founding lineages and/or lineages with lower growth rates, while those with lesser amounts of fertile land were from more recently arrived lineages (1972:87-95).[12]

A second study from the Plateau, that of James Smith, permits speculation concerning some possible effects of differential land endowments. He suggested that:

> ...the decision to grow or not to grow a cash crop clearly distinguishes two types of household. The first has more than enough resources to assure its survival and growth, while the second is closer to the subsistence level (Smith 1977:88).

With these additional resources, this first household:

> ...hires more labor and owns more equipment than the average household. It appears they feel less constricted in selling their food crop since they sold a larger proportion of it than other households (ibid.)

The second household type allocated "...its resources to subsistence activities and probably also to the internal village labor market..."(ibid.:88-91).

---

[12]Marchal reports the same phenomena for the portion of the Mossi Plateau around Yatenga: "The first arrivals were able to take possession of the best land...while the late arrivals were left with the gravelly soils..." (1977:76).

Smith and Remy have thus shown how individuals with greater amounts of land come from earlier arriving lineages which occupied the most and best land, and whose lineages then proceeded to expand at slower rates. Individuals with lesser amounts of
land are those from later arriving lineages with higher growth
rates. Advantaged individuals tend to hire labor to grow cash
crops. These class relations are thus at least partially formed as
a result of differentials in lineage land occupation and growth
rates.

Officials and traders also use their position to acquire land
and form class relations on the Plateau as in the Eastern ORD.
This occurs near large communities where the demand for foodstuffs is greater. For example, there is a small dam at Mogtedo,
80 paved kilometers from the capital, Ouagadougou, where according to Dumont "...more than half the dam's irrigated fields were
the property of urban dwellers..." (1978:308) and were worked
by wage labor. At Boulbi, immediately south of Ouagadougou, a
dam was constructed and irrigated rice cultivation begun. Fields
were originally allocated to local farmers, but, according to
Dumont, "...their plots were given to someone else who was in
reality the figurehead for a bureaucrat" (1978:308).

Dumont reports on the situation from around Banfora and
Bobo Dioulasso in southwest Burkina Faso. This area has lower
population densities than the Plateau, but, due to proximity to
Ivory Coast markets, has a stronger demand for agricultural commodities. He states:

One sees appearing more and more orchards, often of
mangoes...planted above all by those with money: urbanites,
bureaucrats, soldiers. These new non-peasant farms are
thus the work of a new category of absentee landlords...
who have land "attributed" to them by customary authorities.
These developing enterprises create a new category of
workers, proletarians, detached from their means of
production: agricultural wage laborers, often paid 100 F CFA
plus a meal (1978:309).

Finnegan observed the existence in southeastern Burkina
Faso at Tenkodogo of "several" mango orchards of perhaps 80
trees per orchard. He further reports that orchard owners experienced difficulties in finding a market (1980:317). This is in
contrast to the vast mango plantations seen in Dumont's area.
Such contrasts suggest that a brisk demand for a cash crop may
catalyze class distinctions.

There is a final arena where Burkinabè labor migration ac-
celerates class formation. This is in the forests, first, of Ghana
and today, largely in the Ivory Coast. Perhaps a sixth of
Burkina Faso's inhabitants reside in these coastal countries. A
1960 survey found that most were agricultural workers (Courel
and Pool 1973:1003). Campbell documented the growth of an
Ivoirian "planter class" that expanded from an estimated 300 families in 1950 to 20,000 wealthy families who "...controlled about
one-fourth of cultivated land, [and] employed two-thirds of salaried labor..." in 1965 (1978:72-73). This labor was supplied by

foreign migrants (ibid.:102) drawn almost exclusively from
Burkina Faso (Foltz 1965:47). Changing demand for agricultural
commodities in the form of "rising coffee and cocoa prices" has-
tened the emergence of this class because "after 1946 [it] encouraged an increase both in the total output and in the land area
cultivated of these two crops" (Campbell 1974:72), which was
largely farmed by the wealthy families.

An additional stimulant to the development of class distinctions is the availability of financial capital. During the 1970s,
Burkina Faso lacked major loan funds and institutions with the
capacity to inject significant quantities of credit into the interior
areas of the country. This situation contrasted sharply with
northern Ghana, where, according to Goody (1980:38), government policy was to make capital available to members of elites
through such state agencies as the Agricultural Development
Bank, the national bank (the Ghana Commercial Bank), and commercial banks (Standard and Barclays). In the interior areas of
Burkina Faso, individuals can secure control over land, but little
financial capital is available to permit access to higher-yielding
crop varieties, fertilizer, or farm implements. Thus, those who
control land are able to do little more than satisfy the demand of
nearby towns for staples.

These studies suggest the emergence of two types of private
class systems, which are distinguished by how control over land
is obtained. First, there are class relations in which appropriation is the role of members of elites: control over land is secured
by officials who take advantage of their privileged positions within the state. These I have called "elite class relations." What I
have termed "traditional class relations" develop when individuals
gain greater control over land as a result of the specific history
of land occupation by lineages of which they are members. Evidence suggests that the market for agricultural commodities and
the availability of financial capital affect the rate of private class
formation. In areas where the demand for agricultural commodities is greatest and profits can be realized through agricultural
production (as in southwestern Burkina Faso and in the Ivory
Coast), class relations emerge rapidly. In areas where effective
demand is lower (e.g., the Mossi Plateau, the Eastern ORD,
etc.), the emergence of class relations is a slower process. The
two factors that influence the rate of private class formation are
themselves conditioned by the nature of the Burkinabè state's
relation to the larger world economy. Burkina Faso lacks, as it
did during the colonial era, a product for which it enjoys a comparative advantage vis-à-vis world demand.

Finally, some labor does not migrate, but remains and is
absorbed within the domestic economy. Evidence suggests that
the productive structures that are the constituent elements of the
domestic economy are in the midst of a "profound disorganization"
(Ancey 1977:6), and that important changes are occurring in communal production relations. The individualization of land tenure,
described in the Dakola region by Kohler (1971), and the observations by Ancey that 40 percent of the fields around Koudougou
are individually held and worked largely by women whose husbands are away on migrations, suggests a breakdown of

production relations that might have been characterized as communal in the past.

THE GROWTH OF A BUREAUCRATIC GENTRY; REPRODUCTION AND THE ARTICULATION OF PRODUCTION RELATIONS

The remarks below will summarize the evidence that has been presented thus far on processes of dual class formation, and will combine the two aspects of the process within a single model--that of an emergent bureaucratic gentry.

Dual Class Formation

We have seen that Burkina Faso is heavily dependent on international donor agencies for the capital it needs to invest in development. The formula of an agro-parastatal organization, of which the AVV is an instance, has been elaborated as a response to the interests of suppliers of investment capital and the interests of the Burkina Faso government, which needs investment capital. The investment priorities of the agro-parastatals are in river valley areas that have been cleared of onchocerciasis, as areas fit for the production of cotton. Thus Burkina Faso's dependence on exterior sources for the investment capital it needs and the development of the parastatal formula for the administration of capital made available by the EEC have led to a preference--a skew--in investment toward the river valley areas at the expense of the neglected interior areas of the country.

The consequences of these investment preferences by donors are two. In the riverain areas they are the result of development programs financed by donors of capital; in the interior, they are the result of an absence of investment capital. Capital investment in the riverain areas has led to the creation of parastatals and the creation of legal structures having consequences similar to those described elsewhere as enclosure. The existence of agro-parastatals and the effects of legal enclosures provided the conditions for the emergence of what I have termed state class relations.

In the interior areas, the absence of investment capital is a continuation of a situation having origins in the colonial period. The lack of investment blocks the accumulation of capital in agricultural production, and thus impedes improvements in agricultural productivity through the use of improved techniques. Given the lack of access to credit for technical inputs, populations of the interior areas have placed greater reliance on local labor supplies. This reliance on population growth as a means of increasing the pool of agricultural labor, the only available means of increasing production, can be traced in part to policies promulgated during the colonial period. The result of continued population growth, combined with severely restricted access to production inputs, has been greater scarcity of land. The outcome, as population densities increase relative to arable land, has been an increase in out-migration. This is "demographic enclosure." The labor freed by the effects of "demographic enclosure" then becomes involved in processes of class formation, having different rates in each of the two zones. More specifically, four situations of class formation can be distinguished. First, where the demand for agricultural commodities is considerable and there exist sources of capital for investment to increase production--as, for example, in the forest areas of the coast--this freed labor becomes engaged in rapidly emerging private class relations. Second, under conditions where the demand for agricultural commodities is weak and there is little, if any, capital for investment in agriculture--as in the Eastern ORD and the Mossi Plateau of Burkina Faso--private class relations emerge that are based on access to resources through membership in elites or through traditional links. In a third situation we have seen, some labor squeezed from lands in the interior feeds production on the agro-parastatals, and thus becomes involved in what I have termed state class relations. Finally, some of the freed-up labor is absorbed by existing structures of domestic production that function under increasingly marginal conditions.

On the basis of the evidence and interpretations presented above, the conclusion follows that class formation in Burkina Faso is affected by its heavy dependency on donor investments, but in a manner more complex than that suggested by stating that dependency stimulates the formation of social classes. This dual class formation process is explained in the next few paragraphs in terms of changes in peripheral production relations due to core tactics to facilitate the expanded reproduction of capital.

Expanded reproduction occurs when there is a succession of periods of production that result in increased social wealth. Thus the combined value of each period is greater than that of the period before. Under these conditions, net investment and the accumulation of capital are possible (Marx 1970:579). The policies of the colonial administration in Burkina Faso, and the current, postcolonial policy of the Burkinabè government of channeling investments through parastatals, are strategies to further the incorporation of Burkina Faso within the capitalist world economy in a manner beneficial to expanded reproduction in the core states of the economy.

The government policies described in our discussion of colonialism and neocolonialism in the riverain areas have supplied cheap labor for the production of inexpensive primary commodities for French industry. At the same time, these policies insured a monopoly over the sale of French goods to Burkinabès. In sum, the effects of the policies were to favor expanded reproduction by French enterprises. A continuing conundrum of postcolonial states is how to retain control over production once direct political authority has been lost. The scale of operations is often so great in the case of parastatals such as the AVV, that governments like Burkina Faso's lack the capacity to manage them. This requires that an affiliation be formed with agencies of core states, thus facilitating the direct influence of the latter in the organization of production in the periphery. Furthermore, as indicated above, the rate of remuneration given to labor on parastatals like

the AVV is low.   These organizations tend to produce commodities
required by the industries of the core states in Europe, and to
offer them at low prices because of low levels of labor remuneration.   At the same time, the scale of the parastatal operations and
the   techniques   they   promote   permit--even   require--substantial
purchases of commodities produced by European industries.   Thus
the colonial and postcolonial policies that affect the dual process
of class formation can be seen as strategies for promoting expanded   reproduction: initially--during   the   colonial[13]   period--in
France, and presently within the EEC member states.

These strategies, employed by core states in conjunction
with the Burkinabè government to promote the expanded reproduction of capital, affect production relations in Burkina Faso by
squeezing domestic production and encouraging the articulation of
novel production relations in the country.   Bernstein has used
the concept of a simple reproduction "squeeze" to help explain
what often happens to domestic economies as a result of commoditization (1977).   Simple reproduction, as distinguished from expanded reproduction, occurs when there is a succession of periods of production with no resultant increase in social wealth.   All
capital and natural resources consumed in the process are replaced; all surplus value is spent on consumption goods; all
wages are spent on consumption.   Under these conditions, there
occurs no net investment and no accumulation of capital (Marx
1970:567).   The economy simply reproduces itself through time.
A squeeze on simple reproduction occurs when the reproduction of
the system through time becomes problematic, and continuity is
seriously threatened (Bernstein 1977:64-65).

What has been described elsewhere as "demographic enclosure," and treated as a set of purely ecological relations between
population, soil structure, land tenure, and labor supplies, is an
instance of such a squeeze.   In the case of Burkina Faso's interior areas, the squeeze has been induced by strategies employed by core states to promote expanded reproduction.   The
result has been an imbalance between soil fertility and population
such that the capacity of the domestic economies to maintain social
welfare at replacement levels is jeopardized.   Soil fertility declined as techniques formerly used to maintain soil quality deteriorated under increasing demographic pressure.   Yet population
growth can be considered as a response to declining soil fertility
through the production of labor for the cultivation of larger areas.   The capacity of the system to reproduce itself is endangered because under present conditions the contradiction between
techniques of production and population growth is so great that

---

[13]The position taken here differs from that of Meillassoux
(1975), who argues that capitalism is unable to reproduce its own
labor power, and must consequently exploit domestic modes of
production to secure labor.   No position is taken on the complicated issue of whether core capitalism can or cannot reproduce
its labor.

each production cycle brings with it more consumers and decreased productivity. The squeeze results from the tactic used to promote expanded reproduction: high fertility has been promoted under conditions where the consequences for minimal soil fertility are severe, yet access to improved production inputs has been limited.

There is a tendency to view the simple reproduction squeeze as arising from the process of commoditization under conditions where prices received by producer households for their commodities continue to decline, while prices for the necessities of simple production increase (Bernstein 1977:64). This situation developed during the colonial period in Burkina Faso. The prices paid to producers of agricultural commodities were deliberately depressed; meanwhile, the costs of production and consumption goods increased (Piché, Gregory, and Coulibaly 1980:82-84). Increased fertility among populations of the interior areas may have been one response to this situation. Thus, the apparent enthusiasm of Burkinabès for neo-Malthusian solutions appears to be related to a squeeze on simple reproduction, whose origins can be located in policies originating in the colonial period. By the postcolonial period, however, this solution had both changed and intensified the squeeze by provoking serious deterioration of soil fertility and the mechanisms previously used to maintain it, further depressing already low levels of agricultural productivity.

The strategies employed by the core states to promote expanded reproduction have created the basis for the articulation of domestic, private, and state production relations in the savanna and forest areas. First, the nature of investment by the core in the Burkinabè economy has given rise to conditions from which private and state classes emerge. The emergence of what I have termed state classes is due to investment by donors in agro-parastatals, and the resultant juridical and institutional structures that have promoted the appropriation of surplus value produced by tenants on the parastatal schemes, where relations of production involve a form of primitive accumulation. The formation of what I have termed private classes occurs in areas where the comparative advantage for the production of agricultural commodities required by core states is particularly great. The structure of demand for these commodities and the availability of capital serve to catalyze the formation of private class relations. The flow of surpluses within such production relations is determined more specifically by market forces than by political decisions of a national or interstate nature.

Finally, there is evidence that these apparently dual processes of class formation are closely linked. Skinner, for example, describes the emergence of "gentlemen farmers" and "civil servant farmers" in Ouagadougou:

[a] small but influential group of fonctionnaires...[who have] had little difficulty obtaining land--even valuable rice land--from periurban and rural chiefs. They either bring rural relatives to settle on these farms as cultivators, or hire youths in Ouagadougou to go work the farms (1974:51).

Donor investments make possible such agro-parastatals as the AVV, thereby creating the basis for the flow of surplus from tenants on the schemes to members of the government bureaucracy who experience it in the form of salaries. In many cases, some part of this income is then converted into gifts or payments to individuals or groups who control access to land; another fraction is invested in land and/or labor, thus providing for the articulation of private class relations.

The articulation of domestic production relations with emergent class structures occurs by virtue of the labor they supply. The internal dynamic that pushes the domestic economy to supply labor power under these conditions differs from that which arose during the transition from feudalism to capitalism in Europe. In the latter case, the flow of labor to a nascent capitalist class was the result of the forcible expulsion of peasants from aristocratic domains; the result was the expanded reproduction of both classes (Rey 1973). In Burkina Faso, there is no landed aristocracy whose dynamic of reproduction requires the forced eviction of farmers from the land. The squeeze on simple reproduction described above is quite effective in this regard.

The result of this articulation is increased control over land by the state bureaucracy, accompanied by a loss of control over land by Burkinabè farmers. The strategies for expanded reproduction in the core states having considerable influence on the pattern of development investment in Burkina Faso, and the resultant articulation of domestic, private, and state production relations, effectively remove land from the domestic sphere through appropriation and purchase. At the same time, the squeeze on simple reproduction also acts to restrict the access of farmers in the domestic sphere to arable land. There emerge as a consequence, social relations of production dominated by members of a bureaucratic gentry who control land, either by virtue of their position as managers within parastatal structures or by virtue of their position as landowners, thanks to their privileged access to sources of land.

CONCLUSION

The use of concepts that allow us to impute a sense of directionality is important to the development of any paradigm that seeks to explain social and economic change. One approach to a satisfactory conceptualization involves an examination of the sets of opportunities that are offered to individuals as their situations undergo change, under the impact of the development process. So conceived, change may be looked at as moving in two fundamentally opposed directions, directions which may be characterized as existential or nonexistential.

By existential change I mean change that confronts individuals with sets of opportunities all of whose utilities are negative. For those familiar with the peculiar relation between Salamano and his dog in Camus' *The Stranger*, my point may be a bit clearer. For Salamano, life with his dog (which he hates) is miserable; yet life without his "cur" is also miserable (1954:48-50).

Development that offers choices among negative utilities may be characterized as existential development. In contrast, non-existential development offers the possibility of movement in a positive direction, for the structures of opportunity it promotes and makes accessible to individuals through time are positive.

The current direction of development in Burkina Faso can justifiably be characterized as existential. Donor investments promote a process of dual class formation, which in turn creates four social categories of opportunity. First, there are the farmers who remain in the domestic economy, and whose income levels are very low by any standards (Reyna, n.d.). Second there are farmers who labor as tenants on state agro-parastatal schemes. What evidence we have suggests that the productive capacity of farming systems of the kind introduced by the AVV, in which farmers work as state tenants, offers no great potential for levels of real income higher than earnings of farmers who work their own land, off the schemes (Fuerste 1979:45; Ouedraogo 1976:115; Sprey and DeJong 1977). Emerging, though still by no means common, is a third category: wage laborers who work land in Burkina Faso owned by individuals. Far more frequent in Burkina Faso are people in a fourth category: migrants who have been squeezed from their land and who work in the forest zones of the coast as agricultural wage laborers or sharecroppers. Estimates of earnings by agricultural wage workers during the 1970s were at best only slightly greater than those of smallholders who worked plots in the interior areas of Burkina Faso. Earnings of sharecroppers would be two to three times higher than those of traditional farmers. The tactics employed by the core states to promote the expanded reproduction of capital, as manifested in the patterns of donor investments, have facilitated the creation of this agrarian opportunity structure in which choices are few for the vast majority of Burkinabès. One can be a traditional farmer, a tenant on a state scheme, or a tenant on privately owned land; finally, one can migrate and work land elsewhere. The utilities associated with these choices, considered operationally for purposes of this paper in terms of income levels, are negative. The alternatives amount to a selection among varieties of impoverishment. The choice between being a farmer on land whose quality continues to deteriorate, and being a tenant on state or privately owned land, in the words of one informant, is a choice between *"la merde, la merde, la merde, ou la merde."*

On the basis of increasing experience with the study of rural development, two perspectives on the nature of decision making in relation to the development process appear to be emerging within anthropology. One of these emphasizes processes and structures of decision making by producers (e.g., Barlett 1980); the other, of which this chapter may be considered an example, stresses the need to examine the political economy of decision making. The emerging debate and dialogue among proponents of these perspectives could well capture the anthropological imagination during the 1980s, just as the formalist-substantivist debate did during an earlier period in the theoretical development of the discipline. One difference between those who examine processes of decision making and those who emphasize political economy is

the scope of observation and analysis. The former seek to formulate models of individual choice. The latter place greater
stress on the structure and dynamics of society. The approach
of the former is more concerned with exploring choices that are
made in relation to a particular structure of opportunity; the latter seeks to explain the development of the opportunity structure
itself, in relation to which the choices are made. The difference,
from the viewpoint of a farmer in Burkina Faso, is between knowing which rotten choice will be taken, and why the world is full
of rotten choices. The ability to grapple with the latter question
appears to be of particular importance to Burkinabès and to social
science.

Editors' Note to Chapter 10

What is wrong with livestock development projects in Africa? Michael Horowitz argues that the planners of these projects have a poor understanding of pastoral production systems, and on the basis of this poor understanding, design projects whose impacts have been negligible if not negative on the livelihoods of pastoral peoples. He argues that this persistence of shared misunderstanding among state and international development planners results from an anti-pastoralist ideology with its myths about pastoralists and their management of resources. Because these are rarely if ever critically examined by those with the power to plan and implement projects, one unsuccessful project after another is delivered by bilateral aid. If irrationality is at issue, as planners often suggest, the problem may be more theirs, than the herders'. Rather than scapegoat herders for mismanagement of range and animal resources, Horowitz, like Grayzel, suggests that we must examine the dynamics of pastoral systems and the constraints within which they function. The state, and an anti-pastoral ideology, are often the sources of these constraints. Horowitz draws from his own work with the appraisal of a livestock development project in southeastern Niger, and his struggle with prevailing ideas of planners who insisted that the introduction of pastoral associations and delimited pastoral units was the best way to organize more effective range management. This strategy was based on unexamined ideas about "typical" herders throughout a very large zone in which the real variation in range management practices was considerable.

10
Ideology, Policy, and Praxis in Pastoral Livestock Development

MICHAEL M HOROWITZ
State University of New York at Binghamton

During the early 1970s, a critical review of the main assumptions underlying United States foreign aid challenged the idea that economic growth through capital intensive industrialization and urbanization materially improves living standards of rural poor majorities in the Third World. Despite large sums of money and technical assistance received by poor countries over the preceding decade, the income gap between them and the developed countries was wider than ever; within the poorer countries, the gap between agrarian populations and urban elites had also widened. The 1973 amendments to the Foreign Assistance Act of 1961 provided that henceforth U.S. economic assistance would be directed *in the first instance* to the rural poor (OTA 1984:3), a formal modification of the earlier paradigm that held that savings generated through investments in urban industrial sectors of the economy would ultimately "trickle down" to the poor in the form of new employment opportunities (Rostow 1960). A concurrent review of development assumptions at the World Bank, known as the "McNamara Doctrine," led to increased investments in projects supposed to benefit smallholder peasant producers.

The McNamara Doctrine and the Congressional "New Directions" engendered a new rhetoric and vocabulary of development. Project documents now spoke of "beneficiary populations" and the "poorest of the poor"; technology to be transferred had to be "appropriate" and "capital saving"; those whose lives were affected by interventions were called on to "participate" in the projects. To the conventional technical, economic, and financial analyses of AID project papers and World Bank appraisal reports was added the requirement of a *social* analysis, an exploration of how

*The author gratefully acknowledges David Brokensha, Curt Grimm, Peter Little, Endre Nyerges, Thomas Painter, Irving Rosenthal, Muneera Salem-Murdock, Thayer Scudder, Albert Sollod, and Cynthia White for their many thoughtful comments and perceptive criticisms.

the proposed interventions might affect the local people. According to Morgan, who employs an unfortunate military jargon in an otherwise excellent article, these analyses have the following components:

> Socio-cultural feasibility requires an examination of local values, beliefs, social structure and organization in order to determine the compatibility of the project with perceptions and practices of the target population. Spread effect refers to the likelihood that new practices introduced among a target population will be diffused among other groups. Social impact assessment requires the identification of groups which would be positively affected by a project, those adversely affected, and in what ways. Participation of the target population in all phases of the project--from identification through implementation--is also to be specified (1983:63; see also Cernea 1984).

The benefits of an intervention--a new road, an improved seed, a rural dispensary--were made problematic, and new questions were asked: Who would benefit from the proposed actions and who would lose? To what extent does the project draw on local capacities, needs, aspirations? Are the assumptions underlying the technical and economic analyses of a particular project in any way discrepant from social (and, as was subsequently asked, environmental) realities?

Systematic social analysis contributed to the exposure and falsification of a number of hoary myths about rural life in the Third World. For example, development project documents in the 1960s and 1970s often saw African farmers as "underemployed"; the costs of such additional labor as might be required by an intervention were dismissed therefore as trivial or even nonexistent. Robert Chambers (1983) demonstrates that some of the assumed underemployment is a consequence of the scheduling of project appraisals during the agriculturally less productive dry season, when travel in rural areas is least demanding for visiting experts, resulting in underestimations of labor required on farms during the rains.[1] Land availability was also often held to be

---

[1] I don't mean to exaggerate this point. The capacity of rural production systems to absorb all available labor is limited by its placement in the larger economic system, which forces some of that labor into redundancy and therefore in the migrant wage labor market (see Painter forthcoming). The rural underemployment thesis has recently been resurrected by Critchfield (1982: 29-30), who claims that African men actually disdain farming, preferring to pass their time in beerhalls while dreaming of former glories as herders and hunters. Chambers aptly terms the typical brief dry season guided design or evaluation mission by foreigners who have little understanding of the local scene as "rural development tourism" (1983:10-12).

nonproblematic in many rural development documents, and social analysis had to illuminate the saliency for project design of clear understandings of the realities of land use and tenure.

The most recurrent and, in many ways, the most pernicious myth pervading rural development thinking among both donors and host governments, is the claimed homogeneity of the country-side. The equity concerns of the 1973 amendments to the Foreign Assistance Act notwithstanding, if everyone in rural areas is equally poor, equity considerations are irrelevant.[2]

Despite the rhetoric of the New Directions and despite the many social soundness analyses attached to project design documents, it is sadly clear that development activities during the 1970s and early 1980s reveal little predication of interventions on effective participation by the rural poor. One is left with the impression that donors and host governments rarely demanded more than an appropriate vocabulary of social soundness, participation, and equity, and that they were not genuinely committed to the partnership with the poor that was implied in legislation and doctrine. In the remainder of this paper, I explore this conclusion based on a review of some ten years of pastoral livestock development projects funded by AID or the World Bank in West Africa and the Sahel (Horowitz 1979). Not a single one of these projects was identified, appraised, or implemented with more than a cosmetic veneer of participation on the part of the supposed

---

[2]Examples of assumed socioeconomic homogeneity are found in AID documents that were supposed to serve as descriptions and analyses of rural poverty: "Given the very low level of national income, the question of equity has little relevance for the Niger scene at this point. While there are a few pockets of amassed wealth within Niger, those that do exist are in commercial areas which are relatively unlinked to the rural population. That is: neither exploitation of the rural people nor accumulation of individual wealth at their expense are problems in Niger" (USAID/Niger 1978:5). According to this analysis, the true causes of poverty are poor education, poor health, poor resources, and "tradition," rather than disenfranchisement and inequitable distribution. Curiously, the document claims that rural Nigeriens don't even know that they are poor, "...or feel that they are living in poverty" (ibid. 57).

A similar presentation of poverty in Senegal acknowledges a modest degree of differentiation in rural areas--"all farms in Senegal are small and it is therefore a question of relative poverty rather than relative wealth"--but attributes this differentiation to the fact that farmers with larger holdings are "better educated, more industrious," and therefore are better targets for development (USAID/Senegal 1978:11, 12).

beneficiary herders.[3] Interventions were informed by an ideology fundamentally hostile to pastoralism.

Pastoral Production Systems and the Objectives of Development Interventions

Pastoral production systems are based on the husbandry of ruminant livestock in arid and semi-arid rangelands[4], where the bulk of forage is natural rather than specifically grown for fodder and where animals generally move to their feed rather than have the feed brought to them. The specific pastoral producers that are the foci of development interventions in sahelian and Eastern Africa, in the Near East, and in parts of Asia are further distinguished from ranchers in the developed world by deriving a substantial portion of their subsistence directly from the herds (in the form of dairy produce, meat, and occasionally blood). None of them subsists entirely on the produce of the herd, however, and the agricultural produce consumed is either grown by the herders themselves (in which case the term "agro-pastoralist" is often used), or obtained via market purchase, trade, or, rarely today, tribute and pillage from sedentary peoples. Today an increasing fraction of the income of pastoralists comes from their participation in the market and in the wage labor economies of their regions.

African countries in which pastoralism forms a prominent component of the economy are poor and often landlocked.[5] It is little wonder that governments view the vast herds of cattle and sheep (if not camels and goats) as prime commodities to be offered on regional and world markets. Hence the principal objective of interventions from the perspective of host country

---

[3]As I shall discuss below, AID's Niger Range and Livestock Project enjoyed a first phase in which a good deal of attention was paid to both the socioeconomics and the human ecology of the region, with the objective of designing an action phase consistent with these realities. The actual implementation of the second phase, renamed "Integrated Livestock Production," appears to have rejected, or at best ignored, many of the findings (Swift 1984).

[4]There is no standard definition of dry rangelands; estimates of the upper limit of annual rainfall vary between 400mm and 800mm. According to Sandford (1983:2), some 50 million km^2 or 35 percent of the earth's land area is dry. Within these areas, livestock husbanders may number 40 million persons.

[5]In Sub-Saharan Africa, pastoralists are most numerous in the Sudan, Somalia, Chad, Ethiopia, Kenya, Mali, Mauritania, Niger, Senegal, Burkina Faso, Uganda, and Tanzania, in that order.

governments is increased production, especially of beef. Some of
that increase is destined for the export market to improve trade
and fiscal balances: Sudan, Ethiopia, and Somalia send animals to
the Gulf states, while Chad, Niger, Mali, and Burkina Faso
export to coastal West Africa. The remainder is sent to domestic
urban markets and sold, sometimes at politically depressed prices,
to satisfy governments' need to provide cheap food to civil
service and private sector urban consumers.

In addition to increasing herd productivity, there are often
subsidiary objectives attached to interventions in pastoral production systems (often by donor organizations rather than by host
governments). These objectives are:

- to retard or reverse environmental degradation while
  improving forage quality of the range;
- to improve producer income and the quality of pastoral
  life; and
- to provide a favorable economic rate of return (especially for projects appraised and funded by the World
  Bank).

It is not easy to increase production while improving rangeland conditions, and to keep consumer prices low while improving
producer income--all the while assuring an adequate return on
investment. The concurrent satisfaction of all these objectives
never occurs.

With the exception of purely veterinary measures, livestock
development interventions have exceptionally poor performance
records (Horowitz 1983). Because of this, donor attitudes toward
efforts in the sector oscillate wildly. At one extreme donors are
manic with enthusiasm for some new approach (e.g., group or
individual ranching, genetic improvement of stock, health measures, improved watering points, supplemental feeding, range
"management," feedlots, abattoirs, pastoral associations, and
herders' cooperatives). At the other they are depressed from the
evidence of evaluation after evaluation demonstrating poor or negative returns on investment and failures to achieve project objectives. The extraordinary attention and huge sums (Eicher 1985)
devoted to an almost unbroken string of failed projects doubtless
derives from the paucity of even slightly more potentially productive alternative arenas to compete for donor attention in poor pastoral countries.

What is wrong with livestock development? Why have planners and technicians been unable to design and implement interventions that would achieve their objectives? *The first inescap-
able conclusion is that fundamental errors about the nature of
pastoral production systems are maintained by planners and technicians, and these errors lead inevitably to flawed projects.*
Planners often maintain a portrait of pastoralists which, however
persuasive it might appear, in fact caricatures rather than describes the pastoral enterprise. The portrait substitutes untested
assumption for verifiable fact, rhetoric for analysis, and it impos-
es ethnocentric models that project motives drawn from alien environments. Ignoring or misunderstanding much of what *is* known
about pastoral production systems, the caricature serves to
justify a development posture that has both a disappointing

performance record and disastrous unintended consequences (Darling and Farvar 1972, Talbot 1972). *The second conclusion is that even where planners have access to sound information and analysis, political considerations may lead to their being ignored in implementation.*

Anti-nomadism and the Myth of the Pastoralist

It would be comforting to exempt anthropologists from any responsibility for the flawed perceptions with which herders are viewed by planners and technicians, but that comfort must be denied. Despite the fact that "the relationship between anthropologists and development planners and administrators has frequently been characterized by mutual incomprehension as well as a certain degree of tension" (Haaland 1977:3), the latter have often cited anthropologists in support of their positions. The characterization of herders as manifesting an irrational "cattle complex," in which animals are kept for their "symbolic" rather than economic value (Herskovits 1926), reinforced stereotypes as old as Ibn Khaldun (1967:304-5), that herders are more concerned with the number than the quality of their livestock, and that their pastoralism is a threat to the environment and civilization itself. The great synthesizer of ethnography, George Peter Murdock, wrote of the Bedouin movement into North Africa in the 11th century:

> Illiterate nomads, intolerant alike of agricultural and urban civilization, they preempted all land suitable for grazing, upsetting everywhere the fine balance which the Berbers had achieved between cultivation and animal husbandry. They converted fertile fields to pastures by destroying or neglecting the waterworks constructed by the labor of centuries. Their flocks devoured the natural cover of vegetation, ultimately ruining the forests...and by overgrazing induced erosion which converted even pasture lands to barren semi-desert (1959:393; see also Lomax and Arensberg 1977:676).

Of course, not all anthropologists share the morality of anti-nomadism (cf. Asad 1973), but anthropological writings are selectively cited in its support, and it is only in the last two decades that field studies have seriously begun to provide contrary evidence.

Anti-nomadism finds its main support at prominent levels of development administration. It is perhaps easy to dismiss the proposal of E. H. Palmer, who, some 110 years ago, said of the Bedouin:

> wherever he goes, he brings with him ruin, violence, and neglect. To call him a "son of the desert" is a misnomer; half the desert owes its existence to him....The soil he owns deteriorates, and his neighbors are either driven away or reduced to beggary by his raids and depredations. If the military authorities were to make systematic expeditions

against these tribes, and take from them every camel and sheep which they possess, they would no longer be able to roam over the deserts, but would be compelled to settle down to agricultural pursuits or starve...They might thus be tamed and turned into useful members of the community (1977:297, 299-300).

With a rhetoric less bellicose than Palmer's, but with a similar commitment to sedentarization--whether voluntary or involuntary --the United Nations Food and Agricultural Organization (1962:363) in its early forays in arid zone livestock actions sought fundamental changes in pastoral practice, by "actions which will make it possible if not essential for the free-ranger grazier and their livestock gradually to rely less and less on the semi-arid grazing resource, and to become more sedentary than they were before. This trend is desirable from a social, medical, and educational point of view." During the sahelian drought some ten years later, FAO (1973:14) escalated their attack, accusing pastoralists of "caring for nothing, disdaining manual labor, balking at paying taxes, and being unwilling to sell their animals...; they do not make the economic contribution to their countries that is rightfully expected of them."

The anti-nomad stereotypes of some historians and early an-thropologists, respectably cloaked in the language of science, continues to inform thinking of development planners, for whom livestock sector actions moved center stage with the sahelian drought of the 1970s. The central thesis of this view is that the objective of each traditional pastoralist is to own the largest num-ber of animals, irrespective of their quality or the available for-age (Montsi 1985:24). This objective is seen not as part of an investment strategy that seeks to convert the income or increase of the herd into other values, but is uniquely a matter of pres-tige: the larger the herd, the more important is the herder (Nestel et al. 1973:14). As evidence for the essential irrationality of this practice, development planners claim to have discovered perverse or "backward bending" supply curves, in which the number of animals sold varies inversely with market prices (cf. Swift 1974:451). Further, it is claimed that African stockmen regularly retain post-adolescent male animals substantially in excess of reproductive needs (World Bank 1976: Annex 3:9-10), additional evidence that herds function as symbols of status and not as capital. Facilitated by new watering points and by modern veterinary medicine, the inherently irrational objective of owning the largest number of animals leads to rapid increases in herd size, and a dangerous exceeding of the carrying capacity of fragile semi-arid environments.

To compound the situation, individual herd owners are seen by development planners as having no responsibility for maintain-ing environmental productivity. While animals are individually owned, we are told, pasture is a communal resource, and there-fore treated as if it had no value. Each herder seeks to maximize pasture consumption by his own animals, since the costs of the resultant degradation are borne by all users, while the benefits accrue exclusively to the individual herd owner: the situation is known as the "tragedy of the commons" (Helman 1972:5; UNCD 1977:13; Hopcraft 1981:225). Once all possible benefit from a particular place is derived, the herder moves on to find fresh graze, and leaves barren sterile ground in his tracks. This mobility precludes not only the accumulation of useful material goods, but also access to health and educational facilities. Unschooled, in ill health, and without the implements of modern life, pastoral existence has been qualified by development planners as miserable, and its "quality" in dire need of improvement.

Since herd expansion, open access to range, and nomadism in a fragile ecosystem are often considered by planners to be prime causes of desertification, that is, the permanent decline in the capacity of the environment to produce useful crops (SOLAR 1976:1; Lamprey 1983:656), pressure mounts to change traditional pastoral practice. As the animal charge on the range increases, and the land which does not belong to the herder and in which, therefore, he has no conservationist interest, is overgrazed, palatable perennial species of grass are replaced by less palatable annuals, soil is lost through wind erosion, and an ever increasing number of animals is compacted on land whose productivity is rapidly declining (Picardi 1977:164-5). In the past, it is claimed, periodic droughts and epidemics reduced herd numbers and gave the land an opportunity to recover. But the advent of new watering points and large-scale vaccination against epizootics frustrate the equilibrium mechanism, and lands no longer benefit from periodic massive reductions in charge. Making matters worse, we are told, in the false belief that such action is beneficial, herders set fire to the range, reducing the amount of graze, sterilizing soil by killing nitrogen-fixing bacteria, driving out moisture, and contributing to more severe drought.

Development planners and technicians wonder how so non-adaptive an economy, so destructive of its own resource base (Lamprey 1983:656), could survive, for herders seem to hew to ancestral traditions that are hundreds if not thousands of years old (Picardi and Seifert 1976:9). Even planners who confess some sympathy or admiration for the freedom of pastoral life find it incredible that a system dysfunctional to the individual, the animal, the habitat, and the larger political entity in which it occurs could maintain itself essentially unchanged for so long.

The Myth of Pastoralism and Development

What is really incredible is the tenacity with which intelligent people maintain this calumnious stereotype and rely on it to influence development programs despite their poor results. Rather than puzzling over the behavior of pastoralists, one wonders why planners remain wedded to such irrationality in the face of decades of contrary evidence. Sandford makes a stab at understanding:

Unfortunately, as regards the assessment of both desertification and growth in livestock numbers, the wide extent of the agreement about what is happening has now begun to affect the evidence itself, so that the two are mutually reinforcing. When the initial evidence in a particular situation does not support the conventional view it is regarded with suspicion and, in the best of faith, the evidence is then adjusted so as not to give a misleading impression, i.e., it is altered to come in line with the expected conclusions. The fact of this adjustment is then lost sight of, and the adjusted evidence is treated as independent support for the Mainstream view (1983:15).

Sandford cites several instances of data being cooked to support the stereotype portrait of pastoralism. Information on herd size in Botswana from field censuses was changed to correspond with preconceived notions. A country case study for the 1977 United Nations Conference on Desertification was officially rewritten to argue that desertification *had* occurred despite the author's statement that evidence *did not* support the claim.

General acceptance of the tragedy of the commons notion leads to attempts to assign responsibility for environmental conservation to identifiable individuals or groups of individuals under the assumption that *private* ownership of the range results in better management. After an exhaustive review of the literature and examinations *in situ* of a large number of development efforts, Sandford concludes to the contrary that

there is extremely little evidence to suggest that the stocking rates, rests, and rotations recommended for African rangelands on the basis of experience elsewhere [mainly in the United States and Australia] enable any more productive or environmentally benign use of Africa's rangelands to be made than do traditional systems (1983:16).

Instances of projects that sought to improve productivity and/or range conditions by restricting access or by outright privatization of pasture are widespread throughout sahelian, eastern, and southern Africa, including World Bank-funded activities in Senegal, Burkina Faso, and Niger, the Botswana Tribal Grazing Lands, group ranches in Kenya and Tanzania, and various AID-funded interventions in Somalia and Lesotho.

In 1978, the World Bank appraised a livestock project in Niger that included, as one of its elements, the establishment of pastoral associations that were to be assigned responsibility for specific tracts of rangeland or "pastoral units," based on traditional land use patterns. The idea was to define geographically an area of exclusive use by a pastoral association, itself based on some preexisting social grouping. In exchange for various services--including animal health and new or improved watering points--members of the association would agree to follow prescribed range management practices, such as holding animal numbers below the area's estimated carrying capacity and obeying directives on pasture rotation. The model had been developed for the World Bank's Second Livestock Project in Chad (Dulieu et al.

1977; World Bank 1978a), although that project had not been
evaluated at the time of the Niger appraisal.[6]

The new project was appraised in southeastern Niger where,
in the late 1960s, I had carried out field research among Ful-
fulde-speaking herders and agropastoralists and Kanuric-speaking
farmers (Horowitz 1972a, 1972b, 1974, 1975). As social analyst
on the appraisal team, drawing on several years of intimacy with
the area, I concluded that the sociological conditions claimed for
Chad did not obtain in the proposed project region, and that neither pastoral associations nor pastoral units were likely to be
successfully introduced. In the first place, among the WoDaaBe,
the main herding people of the area, there were no "traditional"
social groups with herd management responsibilities larger than
the family or small group of agnatically-related families that constituted a herding camp. On the contrary, the tremendous complexity of the region favored maximum decentralization of herd
management decision-making.

> The herd manager--who may be a single adult male--decides
> where the animals pasture, how long they remain there, how
> they are watered, which animals are castrated, which are
> culled, etc. These decisions are made on the basis of locally
> available and processed information. The herd manager mon-
> itors the quality of pasture, largely through milk produc-
> tion, and moves his animals when he decides that a better
> quality pasture is available elsewhere. Rainfall is highly
> variable in time and place. Given the great disparity of
> pasture quality within what appears to be very close areas,
> it would clearly be dysfunctional to have herd management
> decisions made by persons who are not privy to local
> microecological data. Fragmentation of lineages keeps

---

[6]The Bank's Chad appraisal report claimed that traditionally
Arabic-speaking cattle herders had organized groups that could
readily be transformed into pastoral associations: "The typical
extended family has about 12 members, owning 30-40 cattle and
20-30 smallstock...; the family head is the key decision-maker in
matters of livestock management. A few hundred extended
families constitute a *tightly structured pastoral group* which,
traditionally, was the only entity able to undertake the
construction of watering points; this function re-inforced the
group's role as the controller of land-use patterns" (Horowitz
1978:3, my emphasis). It was intended that "...through the
delineation of pastoral units and recognition of associations of
pastoralists, it will be possible (a) to improve management of
communally-owned pastures and to emphasize improved animal
husbandry rather than allowing for unrestrained herd growth as a
means to increase output, and (b) to allocate stock watering
points to specific associations of pastoralists, thus giving them
the incentive necessary to participate in maintenance and ease the
pressure on the Government budget" (ibid.:6).

authority very close to the physical and sociopolitical conditions to which the herd must react (Horowitz 1978).

There are no social groups among the WoDaaBe of eastern Niger
in which political leaders have the authority to command the behavior of persons not members of their immediate households.
The WoDaaBe have elaborated no system of chieftainship in which
persons other than the herd manager stand in privileged relationships to decisions regarding the nature, movement, and well-
being of animals. The search for large social groups to manage
range use would, I felt, be chimerical, despite the Bank's convic-
tion that such groups existed east of Lake Chad and therefore
should exist equally to the west.

My second objection was that specific social groups do not
have exclusive access to tracts of land large enough to constitute
pastoral units, again regardless of what had been claimed for
Chad. The unpredictability of rainfall—hence of pasture—requires that herds move opportunistically, and that exclusive and
total restriction to some defined tract of land would necessarily be
maladaptive (unless that tract were so large as to contain
adequate pasture in all years—in which case a single group would
have to claim exclusive occupancy of parts of Niger, Nigeria,
Cameroon, and perhaps Chad as well!). My summary recommendations suggested that while pastoral associations and pastoral
units were probably inappropriate, the project could introduce
pastoral *centers*,

> located at strategic points of assemblage..., bringing a vari-
> ety of services to the herders which they can use on a vol-
> untary basis: advice (but not direction) about the quality
> and location of pasture; veterinary programs; productivity
> advice (castration, breeding, culling); marketing services
> which do not interfere with the traditional arrangements; a
> store, perhaps a buyers' cooperative, with reasonable prices
> and honest quantities; a grain distribution center; educa-
> tional and health services...

> It is critical [the appraisal report went on to say] that field
> studies prior to the introduction of pastoral centers (let
> alone pastoral units and pastoral associations) be competently
> done [and] account for the movements of peoples and animals
> over a long enough period of time so that the range of alter-
> native strategies and responses in years with plentiful rain-
> fall and in deficit and extreme deficit years be revealed.

The World Bank found the notion of pastoral units and pastoral associations so persuasive, however, that despite the appraisal recommendation, a second consultancy was employed, focusing now several hundred kilometers west of the appraisal area.
Among the preparation documents for the Niger livestock project
was a clear commitment to spatially demarcated pastoral units:

> The zone will be organized by geographically carving out
> pastoral units. A pastoral unit is conceived of as a portion

of the territory where, in a normal year, elementary groups of herders can undertake a full transhumant cycle. In that context, each elementary group will be accorded priority rights of access to a dry season watering point and to the pasture on which it depends....Over time, a pastoral unit will correspond to a cooperative. The size of these units tentatively proposed are: 50-60 households and 800 to 1,000 TLU [Tropical Livestock Units of 250 kg animal liveweight each] per group; six or seven of these groups will form a sector, and three to five sectors will constitute a pastoral unit, representing 7,000 to 10,000 persons and 25,000 to 30,000 TLU. The first goal will be to create 12 pastoral units in the zone (République du Niger 1977:14-15).

Within the geographically defined zone, *exclusive* use rights would be officially accorded to a specified pastoral association. Concentrating on an area several hundred kilometers west of the appraisal zone, in which highly stratified Tamasheq- and somewhat less stratified Tubu-speaking peoples are most prominent among herding groups, attempts were made to define the perimeters of pastoral units in terms of pre-existing utilization by "tribes" (Dulieu et al. 1978). Curiously, the new study agreed that exclusive use rights do not exist in this region, other than in regard to watering from personally owned wells. The authors nonetheless concluded that the pastoralists would not object to their imposition since they appreciate the technical advantages that would thereby accrue to them (ibid.: 123). It is to the Bank's credit that once the project got under way, and despite the assurances from the second study that pastoral units were viable, the socioeconomic and environmental realities of the region led to a return to the original appraisal recommendations. A recent (1985) internal World Bank memorandum states:

The appraised design of [Niger] Livestock I provided for a sequence of interventions in the pastoral zone: (a) spatial delimitation of pastoral units, i.e., areas customarily grazed by clearly identified groups of pastoralists; (b) constitution of associations of pastoralists, i.e., formal recognition of groups of pastoralists and of their grazing rights in their pastoral units; (c) construction and operation of pastoral service centers; and (d) provision of water points and credit as well as services....[But] after only six months' sociological field work, the extent and direction of pastoralists' movements was far greater than had been understood. This problem had been spotted by the appraisal sociologist...

Thus the establishment of pastoral units, initially the first item in the sequence of interventions, was deferred to last. Subsequently introduction of pastoral associations themselves was deferred, and, in fact, by 1984 the only initially anticipated intervention that had been installed were four pastoral centers. Rather than the Chad-like associations of hundreds of families each that the World Bank and Niger Government wished initially to establish, small lineage fractions were recognized as Groupements Mutualistes

Pastoraux, and given access to credit.   These groups "are too small, however, to provide the basis for delimiting pastoral units or to be given the authority, that had been envisaged for pastoralists' associations, for controlling access to water and grazing" (ibid.:8).

The Realities of Pastoralism

The ancient accusation that pastoral herding inevitably leads to overgrazing and to secular environmental degradation finds a receptive audience today among those sensitized to the fragility of the world ecosystem.   If modern man with all the technology at his disposal is unique among animals for fouling his nest with chemical and biological pollutants, can "primitive" man, whose sense of history and historical responsibility may be even more truncated, be exempted from the charge?   It is curious, however, that for all the repeated assertions of herder responsibility for environmental degradation, precious little supportive hard evidence has been marshalled. In place of data and analysis, one author quotes another, invoking "common knowledge" or "general agreement."[7]   Lamprey states categorically that the evidence pointing to over-grazing as the cause of "widespread damage to semi-arid   and   arid   zone   grasslands...[is]   overwhelming" (1983:656), but neglects to share that overwhelming evidence with the reader.   Since the claim has caused governments to restrict access to the range and to lower stocking rates[8], actions that are resisted by the majority of pastoral producers, and since these actions rarely increase productivity, improve income, or enhance rangeland capacity to sustain useful crops, it is important that its evidence be persuasive.   The accusation can be segmented into three components, each of which requires demonstration:

     (1) it must be shown that the rangelands are being
          degraded;

---

[7]"It is *generally agreed* that overstocking and the lack of managed grazing patterns in the Sahel are the most important causes of desertification in the region and that desertification is a symptom of more fundamental problems of rapid population growth and the inability of individuals and communities to adopt *known land management and conservation technologies*" (Ferguson 1977:7, emphasis added).

[8]It may happen that the project benefits the larger herd owners at the expense of the majority of pastoralists, as in the Botswana Tribal Grazing Lands project, where only elite herders were able to obtain ranches.   In such cases, development projects serve to strengthen the socioeconomic differentials that exist within the society, and accelerate the transformation from domestic to capitalist modes of production.

(2)   it must be shown that overgrazing is the cause of degradation; and
(3)   it must be shown that overgrazing results from (a)
common access to pasture; (b) an unwillingness to limit
stock numbers; and (c) lack of constraints on pastoral
mobility.

I have argued elsewhere that the "evidence" thus far marshalled in support of these claims is fragmentary, often misleading, and often subject to more persuasive alternative explanations
(Horowitz 1979, 1981, 1983). Similar observations have been made
by Fouad Ibrahim (1978), who demonstrates that biological declines in Darfur (Sudan) rangelands are caused by extending
crop cultivation where it is ecologically inappropriate given existing technology, and *not* by pastoralism. He proposes that one of
the most effective measures that states can undertake to maintain
rangeland productivity is to define and enforce an "agronomic dry
boundary," beyond which cultivation should not be permitted.
(Ibrahim recognizes, of course, that the northward migration of
cultivation in the Sudan is a consequence of rainfed farmers' inability to increase or even maintain levels of grain production
except by lateral expansion. Labor is already stretched to its
limit, and additional capital is unavailable to small producers.)
Sandford (1983:79-80) says that pastoral land brought into cultivation may over the short run show an increase in productivity,
but over the long term productivity declines rapidly due to nutrient depletion and soil erosion. He further notes that even pastoralists may cultivate rangelands in the attempt to guarantee title to
land, "because only the rights of cultivators to land are recognized by government and protected by law."

Social scientists--who are sometimes accused of suffering
from "bleeding heart syndrome"--are not the only ones skeptical
of claims about pastoral responsibility for desertification. Some
ecologists and agrostologists argue that the very identification of
desertification is not simple. The task of distinguishing true
desertification from temporary declines in production and changes
in species composition due primarily to poor precipitation, requires the accumulation of evidence over a substantial period of
time (Warren and Maizels 1977:1). "Climate," says a recent
UNESCO review of desertification in Niger, "is the prime cause of
the observed changes" in vegetation (Bernus et al. 1983:37).
Furthermore, the composition, mass, and quality of vegetative
cover may change due to herding, but it is not inevitable that
these changes are, in the aggregate, negative. A study of graze
and browse in the Senegalese Ferlo sylvo-pastoral region concludes that during the twenty years since deep wells were introduced, changes in the natural pasture have been only slightly
greater than those attributable just to shifts in rainfall (Valenza
1975). Perhaps nothing so "demonstrates" to planners the de-
structiveness of pastoral practice as the recurrent burning of
rangelands, and country after country has issued regulations
forbidding it. It is not at all clear, however, that such burnings
are, on balance, detrimental. A long-term biological study of
Malian pastoralism concludes that current practices of burning
have beneficial impacts on the nutrient quality of graze in

nitrogen-poor rangelands (Breman, et al. 1978:8; Penning de Vries and Djiteye 1982).

While clearly there is a good deal that we do not know about pastoral peoples and pastoral production systems, we do know that the characteristics of these systems have profound relevance for a development consisting of economic growth, socioeconomic equity, and political participation. Among these characteristics are:

- mobility;
- constraints on access to pasture and water;
- decentralization of authority regarding the movement and welfare of animals[9];
- social organizations of sufficient flexibility to allow for the simultaneous exploitation of a range of ecological opportunities;
- species and demographically complex herd structures;

---

[9]Haaland sees in the decentralization of herd and range management the homeostatic mechanism that provides for continuing adaptation among fluctuating pastoral resources, population growth, and the environment:

Since collective economic responsibility has implications which make it extremely difficult to maintain a stable pastoral adaptation,...in most pastoral groups it is not the whole group which is responsible for members' livelihood, but the individual households. This has implications which serve to maintain a stable adaptation. Population growth and increased pressure on the pastoral niche lead to decreased income per animal, which means that the minimal size of the herd required to maintain the viability of the household increases. With individual responsibility this leads the households who fall under this minimal level to invade on their livestock individually. Pressure on the niche does thus not lead the whole group to lose viability, but leads to a selective exclusion of individual households from the pastoral adaptation...before starvation for the pastoral group as a whole occurs. In an adaptation of specialized pastoralists with individual responsibility, there are thus automatic controls which regulate the pressure on pasture. When pressure and overgrazing increases, the exclusion process from the nomadic population increases, and the pressure is relieved. It is thus possible to maintain a long-term stability in the pastoral adaptation. A pure nomadic adaptation is self-regulatory with reference to overgrazing (1977:184).

While Haaland's purely ecological explanation ignores the variety of positions that pastoral groups occupy in larger political economies, it nonetheless provides an interesting alternative to the inexorable logic of the tragedy of the commons.

- complex patterns of animal exchange and circulation;
- complex relationships with sedentary farmers, townspeople and traders.

The various characteristics of pastoral production systems are functionally interrelated, such that modifications in any one of them may involve changes, often unanticipated by development planners, throughout the system, which can lead to the defeat of seemingly well designed interventions. It is important to note that these interrelationships exist in a wide variety of political economic settings of pastoralism. That is, they do not invariably generate a specific social system, or a specifically *pastoral* mode of production (see Asad 1979; Barth 1964; Khazanov 1984); rather, they reflect adaptations by herding societies, whether egalitarian or stratified, to provide a set of technical constraints for ruminant grazing in semi-arid environments. The most developmentally salient of these propositions are the following (discussed in detail in Horowitz 1979):

1.   Under conditions of semi-arid grazing of large and small ruminants, in which the quality of pasture and the availability of water are highly variable in time and space, mobility conveys greater survival value than sedentarization.
2.   The quality of pasture is closely monitored by pastoralists (through visual inspection of herbage, through milk yields, and through assessments of nutritionally-related animal health), and if possible herds are moved when that monitoring indicates better pasture is available elsewhere.
3.   Agreements among social groups allowing broad access to the range facilitates these necessary movements. Nevertheless, there are often priorities over land use that limit unrestricted access. Ownership of wells, for example, may effectively constrain land use for those without water rights.
4.   Under non-capitalist modes of production, a prime function of the herd is direct maintenance of the herding population; that is, the pastoralists are the prime consumers of herd produce.
5.   Secondary herd functions are to provide cash through sale of pastoral produce, to provide meat for domestic consumption, and, frequently, to provide manure for agricultural fields in exchange for dry season pasture on stubble and crop residues.
6.   To provide for all these functions, a large number of animals is kept, often, where habitat permits, of different species.
7.   Herders seek therefore to increase herd size, sometimes cloaking their quite practical goals with symbols that may lead outsiders mistakenly to think that the desired increase is a consequence of irrational or prestige mechanisms alone (see Harris 1975).
8.   Despite the desire to have a large number of animals, there are managerial and labor constraints on herd size. Herd expansion beyond that point leads to diminishing returns, reflected in the losses from disease, predation, theft, runaways, or in increased labor costs.
9.   Traditionally herd size was often maintained within manageable limits through institutionalized exchanges in egalitarian societies and by attempts to control additional sources of labor--

owners who sold no animals. Among others, especially the FulBe who are stereotyped as cattle-hoarders par excellence, animal sales amounted to 26 percent of herd size per year, an annual rate that would totally deplete their herds if continued. Similarly, concerning herd movements in the area, about half of the FulBe herds with fewer than 100 animals went on transhumance while none of the Bamana herds with fewer than 100 cattle did so. An explanation of these differences was made more difficult by the observation that even though transhumance to distant seasonal pasture was necessary to sustain the production system as a whole, it did not appear to be necessary for any particular herder to make the arduous trek. While my sample was limited and very site specific, at least for the period and the herds I studied, animals that went on transhumance did not appear to be significantly more productive than those that remained in the area, in terms of lower calf-mortality, higher survival rates, or greater weight gains.

Qualitative Findings: A New Dimension

These variations in practices could not be explained by any of the macro generalizations already noted for the pastoral system. Their understanding required attention to micro-level consideration, to individual desires. Such data are not easily retrieved either from general surveys or direct questioning, but were obtained from observations made while I was living with the FulBe of the Doukoloma Forest.

To begin with, not all FulBe had animals, even though cattle were the mainstay of FulBe life. In fact, many of them had sold all their cattle, and for reasons other than hardship, as we will see. What all the FulBe did possess was a code of behavior and values, *pulaade*, which they guarded more fiercely than their animals. Of the complex of values that composed *pulaade*, four stood out: intelligence, beauty, wealth, and independence.[8]

The FulBe admired any demonstration of intelligence, and believed that they, as a group, were particularly well-endowed with this trait. An intelligent person was at once curious, observant, analytical, probing, cunning, and calculating. The FulBe were fond of distinguishing themselves from the Bamana by saying, "we think with our heads, while the Bamana think with their hearts."

The FulBe attitude about physical beauty was similar; they considered themselves to be better looking and more intelligent than their neighbors. This attitude was true for men and women.

---

[8]The most complete discussion of FulBe values can be found in P. Riesman's sensitive book, *Freedom in Fulani Life: An Introspective Ethnography* (1979). Riesman's work is not only an excellent portrayal of FulBe life, but a daring example of the researcher using his own emotional capabilities as a research tool.

To be beautiful was to have a clear, light complexion, a long, lean body and face, thin lips, and a thin straight nose. (These traits, particularly skin complexion, were considered to be related to a high milk diet.) Songs about attractive youth in the area, both male and female, were far more common than songs about cattle, and even an elderly person's reputation for beauty was remembered and praised.

The fundamental value of beauty was in the pleasure it gave the beholder. If the possessor was a woman, beauty was also an avenue toward achieving the third most important FulBe value, wealth. For women, the most common form of wealth was jewelry (gold, silver, and amber), often received as gifts. For men, the most obvious and coveted form of wealth was cattle. The owner of a large herd was both envied and admired. Men paraded their herds; women displayed their collections of earrings, bracelets, and necklaces on the appropriate occasions. The prestige given to owners of cattle and jewelry, however, was not only due to a special value placed on these possessions per se, but because they were a form of capital savings. They were easily convertible into cash for the purchase of desired goods and services, such as a life of leisure; security in old age. That self-satisfaction is the ultimate purpose of wealth was an idea echoed in their proverbs: "If it was not for the stomach (one's appetites), riches would be worthless," and "A poorly dressed elder is disdained; a rich man is admired."

Finally, freedom and independence were perhaps the most complex as well as the most important of all their values, and in a sense they incorporated all the others. To understand this it is necessary to know that the western Sudan is characterized by a hierarchical social structure that ranks people from free nobles, warriors, or religious leaders, to free peasants, casted workers (entertainers, artisans) traditionally freed slaves, and finally, former slaves. The system reflects a history of warfare that resulted in tremendous movements and rearrangements of groups and individuals both socially and geographically.

For the FulBe, the very definition of a *pullo* (the singular of FulBe) was a "free cattle oriented person." This meant several things. Socially, it meant being legally free now, but also, being descended from historically free people. The physical traits seen as beautiful were perceived as an indication that the person did not have non-FulBe, especially slave, ancestors. In daily activities, to be independent as well as free meant not to be commanded by someone else; but rather to be autonomous; to be able to make one's own decisions; and certainly not to have to work for another. To be truly independent in this manner required economic freedom, which was of course directly related to one's wealth. Conversely, to be wealthy in the FulBe perspective, and given the challenges that faced them (including both governmental and private parties occasionally seeking to expropriate their riches) required that the FulBe be cunning and worldly wise. In the end, the ideal of freedom was the single most important value of all, and for the individual FulBe (*pullo*) the joy of being free and the shame of not being free were major motivating factors throughout life. Though there could be unattractive and unintelligent FulBe, it was considered inherently contradictory and therefore impossible for there to be nonfree FulBe.

The Emotional Side of Pastoral Life

It may be asked quite legitimately whether this analysis helps to explain the individual variations in livestock production behavior described above, and, even if it does, how useful is it for the design and implementation of a livestock project? To answer these questions, we can begin by focusing on data concerning specific sales by individual owners.

As already noted, overselling sometimes occurred to such an extent that the reproductive potential of individual herds was threatened. These sales were motivated by the desire for wealth and beauty. Concerning wealth, expenditures were for clothes, jewelry, and such modern desirables as cassette recorders and expensive watches. For beauty, the major expense (in fact the greatest expense of all) was the extramarital pursuit of beautiful women. Because of this, some herders virtually liquidated their assets. Often these were youth who had just come into an inheritance, or old men out for a last fling. Of course some may claim these are desires common to males in many societies. The fact was, however, that whether or not Bamana men shared the same desire, it was not a major motivation behind their decisions on how to allocate their resources. The question is one of intensity as well as existence. For the FulBe the pursuit of beauty was not only a desire but a driving obsession that often overrode economic benefit or family solidarity.

In terms of deciding to go on the transhumance, the pursuit of physical beauty actually explained certain migration choices. In several cases the only reason for certain herds straying from the normal course was that the herder was actually more interested in a specific amorous liaison than greener pastures for his animals. In the majority of cases, however, it was the desire for independence from family and community, from social constraints, and from governmental authorities, that guided the herder's decision. No doubt engendered by generations of practical experience, continuous migration itself, as well as a psychological readiness to move, were seen and felt as necessary[9] preparation for the future, even if unnecessary at the moment. This situation was reinforced by an appreciation of the arts of cunning, calculation, situational analysis, and flexibility, plus the particular knowledge of new areas gained through experience on the trek. The FulBe were as culturally and emotionally predisposed towards

---

[9]"...it is important to understand that both Fulani political organization and their love of independence contribute significantly to the Fulani ability to take advantage of the economic resources of the Sahel" (Riesman 1980).

going on transhumance as the neighboring Bamana agriculturalists were predisposed to maintaining the solidarity of their large established families and settled community.

Thus the adaptive strategy, for the people I knew, was more than simply a way of life. It was a source of pride, and in many ways a thing of beauty. Their emotional tie to the FulBe way, what they called *pulaade*, did not override economic and environmental realities, but it certainly conditioned the nature of their response to them.

One might ask whether these values and emotions are not commensurate with basic economic and environmental circumstances, and, therefore, are really reflections of surrounding material reality. In truth, the answer is not clear cut. In some instances one can fairly easily extrapolate one from the other. Regardless of their mutually reinforcing or conflicting appearances, however, at the moment when an individual must act, the desire to achieve valued objectives, not the macro generalizations of the pastoral production system or its environment, are the immediate causal agents of that individual's behavior. What really motivates people to act is the emotional satisfaction, the physical or psychological pleasure (or avoidance of pain) they derive, or expect to derive, from the particular conduct in question.[10]

New Implications for Project Design

In the case we have considered here, the analysis of production problems from a macro-perspective, and the consideration of marketing, transportation, and managerial constraints led to several recommendations for possible interventions. These included suggestions to remove government-imposed disincentives, such as excessively low prices and a rigid system of taxation, and to concentrate on improving the few poor range areas as a means of promoting more effective use of the entire resource base. All of these recommendations included the possibility of largely unilateral government actions. They contained little potential, however, for instituting changes in the basic managerial practices of herders in the areas of actual grazing or marketing. Changes of this kind would require active herder participation, and the extent of their participation would be largely determined by their appeal to the already identified emotive considerations. Regrettably, the emotive factor was not only neglected, it was to a large extent being directly contested.

The project called for development of a single grazing area for year-round use. This strategy implied government intrusions in those areas of decision-making most prized by FulBe herders. The delimitation of a single grazing area, accessible to clearly

---

[10]The basic statement of economics, "needs are met by goods," can be translated into psychoanalytical language by "drives are satisfied by objects" (Gintzburger 1973:227).

identified owners and animals, constituted a real threat to the
FulBe's desire to remain as independent from outside authority as
possible. The system of regulated grazing proposed by the project, in which herders would follow the advice of technicians, provided no possibilities for the exercise of judgement by the FulBe,
let alone cunning, and thus nearly negated these important skills
as critical elements in successful management. Lastly, the economic strategy of the proposed grazing area and the associated
fattening operations (in which each participant would fatten one
or two animals for sale when larger animals were at a premium)
focused on maximizing returns on a small number of animals.
This too was inconsistent with FulBe aspirations toward wealth
based on continuous growth of readily convertible capital (animals) rather than a fixed but secure income. The project was
not likely ever to generate the voluntary participation, let alone
the enthusiasm, of the FulBe in the area.

The situation, as described, promised to end, as is so often
the case, in a stalemate between the desires of the project planners and those of the would-be beneficiaries. Such outcomes
could be avoided, however, and might even take on a positive
character if development planners could become more responsive
to the emotional needs and desires of the beneficiary population.
Neither good plans nor insightful analysis can generate efffective
development if implementation does not deal with people as people.
To do so requires that planners take into account those unquanti-
fiable, possibly irrational, emotions that influence decision making.

The importance of the FulBe's search for pleasure and emotional satisfaction as a major factor in their behavior as producers
presents a thorny problem for those who tend to view life largely
as a series of economic or production coefficients. It is this gap
in the perception of human motivation that so often serves to distinguish the perspectives of successful community organizers from
those of most development planners and administrators. It has
been my experience that when people have refused to cooperate
with apparently profitable but arduous development programs, it
was not necessarily because they did not *see* the economic benefits. Rather, it was because they objected to demands for markedly increasing labor inputs, or because they feared the attendant attack on community values. Such reactions are often more
emotional than calculating. To the would-be participant there is a
perceived threshold beyond which pernicious labor becomes more
painful than indolent poverty. Similarly, adults in many traditional societies feel painfully ashamed when they must submit to
the dictates of others, especially those younger than they.

Trade-offs of this kind need not occur. When some of the
FulBe learned that free veterinary services were being proposed
as an incentive for people to participate in the project, they opposed the idea. They preferred to continue their sub-rosa practice of privately paying government veterinarians, because doing
so allowed them to control the selection of service providers and
to punish those who failed to give what they felt was satisfactory
performance. The actual degree of satisfaction was determined
partially by the success of the treatment and partially by the

attitude of the veterinarian in terms of politeness and accommodation.

Implications for Development

It is precisely because of negative emotional reactions, such as those noted, that many livestock development projects have failed and will continue to fail. Such projects, regardless of their technical appropriateness, constitute a threat to the herders' freedom of movement, and in addition, threaten their basic role as free decision makers in the production process[11]. The FulBe value this freedom as among the most emotionally satisfying aspects of their way of life, and consider it an end in itself.

For other groups, such individual freedom is not so cherished, and, moreover, may be actively discouraged. Such was the case among the surrounding Bamana agriculturalists, whose production system was based on cooperative work groups. The Bamana resisted activities that promoted individual decision-making, e.g., the use of privately-owned plow oxen as a substitute for field preparation by communal youth groups. They perceived this individuality as a threat to group solidarity. Individuals within such groups, however, maintain their own agenda of priorities and desires that motivate the degree and nature of their adaptation to their cultural milieux.

Whatever the shared attitude of group members toward individual freedom or initiative, or any other group value, individual members routinely use what powers they possess to manipulate circumstances to satisfy their wants. This phenomenon is repeatedly seen among all levels of personnel and participants in development projects. Many readers will have seen instances of this: paramedics who remove vaccines from dispensary refrigerators to make room for bottles of Coca-Cola; development project personnel who use project vehicles and fuel to visit a distant festival; farmers who use agricultural credit for everything from purchasing radios to opening stores; and the continuing exodus of youth from rural villages to urban centers. In all of these decisions the preferred course of action promises to provide some emotional satisfaction, while the non-preferred--albeit recommended--activity is perceived as meaningless and boring, perhaps even as painful.

---

[11]Horowitz notes, "The power of the state is involved to prevent incursions on the land from persons and animals not included in the scheme, and to control the movements and numbers of animals of those who are. In other words, in order to participate --and this participation is not invariably voluntary--the herder gives up control over his major adaptive strategy, mobility.... Previous experience with similar projects in East Africa leads one to doubt that herdsmen will enthusiastically delegate authority over herd movements and structures to persons not directly responsible for animals" (1979:17).

CONCLUSIONS

Development's Blind Eye to Emotions

In this chapter we have argued for the importance of taking into account the feelings of people who are affected by development programs. This position may be criticized as overly indulgent and insufficiently rigorous, given the crisis of survival that faces much of the world's populations. There are doubtless many well-intentioned development workers who claim that the pastoralists' attachment to their herds, of traditional farmers to their customs, or of many people to the psychological importance of having many children, are all examples of irrational values that obstruct the formulation of rational development policies. The contradiction arises when these emotional factors, often stressed in explanations of why beneficiary populations do not respond to development programs, are then given so little emphasis as valuable tools to encourage people to alter their ways.

From the individual's perspective, many positive long-term social policies are irrational because they require people to make sacrifices during the short-term for benefits that will accrue to later generations. Concomitantly, if a society encourages herders to derive immense satisfaction and esteem from the possession of a large herd, what, in one sense, has been achieved is that human emotions have been harnessed and channeled toward the protection of the next generation's inheritance against the more predatory, immediate emotional desire of the individual to convert holdings into consumable goods and services. In such cases we are dealing with cultural mechanisms to control and redirect feelings of satisfaction rather than dispassionate considerations of economic profitability or rational strategies.

While certainly cognizant of their own needs for pleasure and comfort, in general development planners fail to include this sphere of human activities in their plans for others. On the contrary, they often attempt to subvert or destroy indigenous emotion satisfying institutions. Expenditures on folk festivals or religious structures are often labeled by planners as non-productive, and efforts are sometimes made to redirect these investments into shovels and fertilizer. My intention is not to suggest that shovels and fertilizer may not be necessary, but to propose that it is also destructive of a society and its production systems to drain it of its human vitality.

The Need for Programs that Satisfy Emotions

A measles vaccination team once came by my village with a movie projector that was used to show two short health films and a full length version of "The Three Musketeers." It was a major event in the area. People who would not pay for vaccinations did pay the admission price to the film (proceeds of which were used to pay for the vaccination). In like manner, rather than discouraging annual folk festivals because they are too costly, project planners could provide support for festivals in connection with development actions. In West Africa, the harvest is often followed by a community celebration. In contrast, the harvests on most modern irrigation projects are followed by a billing of participants for expensive administrative and technical inputs. One needn't be a behavioral psychologist to discern the positive and negative reinforcements in these cases.

When we speak of development, we should not forget that we are concerned, ultimately, with life, and not with economic parameters or production per se. If a doctor takes a person's pulse, it is done in order better to understand and to restore health; not as an end in itself. Why then are developers so often reluctant to acknowledge that emotional enjoyment and satisfaction are as important to human existence as calories and labor capacity? Is it really inappropriate for development planning to promote activities that are humanly satisfying, and, more specifically, programs that, while increasing the productivity of cultivators and herders, also address, even satisfy, their emotional needs? For example, why can't regional service centers be planned to include focal points for community activities--for conviviality--as well as produce markets, warehouses, and feeder roads? Why can't development research on local "needs" include the study of what local people feel and desire, socially and spiritually, as well as economically; and insofar as possible, why can't development programs take account of these factors?

Ideally, the daily experience of those engaged in development work should contribute to a growing understanding and sympathy for those they are purportedly helping. In reality, the opposite is often the case. Of course the situation is not unique. A similar malaise is encountered among politicians who become estranged from the daily realities of their constituents; among doctors who are more concerned about laboratory techniques than their patients; and among academics who are pressured to publish papers for their colleagues instead of encouraged to impart knowledge to their students. In many professions, career advancement seems to be accompanied by an increasing distance from the human experiences of daily life. Far too many field and academic development professionals are, in like manner, allowing problem-solving through person-to-person contact to give way to highly abstract criteria for decision-making.

Once again, I should like to draw from my experience. I began my career in development abroad as a Peace Corps volunteer. I ate, laughed, fought, worked, and became emotionally involved with the people I was supposedly there to help. With very modest means, I obtained some very slight successes. As an anthropological researcher working among pastoralists in Mali, my involvement was somewhat less emotional. At that point I was more objective and perceptive, and learned more about the people around me in two weeks than I learned in two years as a volunteer. I made relevant observations, but accomplished nothing of immediate importance in practical development terms. I did, however, gain insights of inestimable value to my present work. Today, as a bureaucrat in a development agency, I find that I am now contributing at enormous expense to some significant successes, but also to some very great failures. I occasionally learn, in a helter-skelter fashion, about the people I deal with, but such knowledge is now acquired largely incidentally to my official responsibilities, and is often considered irrelevant, or at best superfluous, by many of my associates. As with so many of my colleagues, I am living off the rapidly thinning fat of past experience.

To engender meaningful human involvement, research and development need a continuously renewed emotional dimension. I experienced this dimension as a volunteer in the Peace Corps, and later as an anthropologist doing field research, but have begun to lose it as a development bureaucrat. Also many of my colleagues in development work—of all nationalities—are aware of a growing emotional chasm between them and the people they seek to assist. This affects us as individuals and it affects both of the professions in which I work. Anthropology itself is changing as it seeks to become less individualistic and more "scientific." Development work is becoming more impersonal as it strives to become less ideological and missionary-like, and more professional.

The Development Agent: A Fragmented Personality

The difficulties that face persons in development work are several. First, there is a need to rediscover the validity of emotions as operative factors worthy of analytical consideration. Second, we must accept that the principal means still available for the study of human emotions is the most primitive: human empathy. Regrettably, the structure of development work is such that it often dehumanizes both those who practice it and those who should benefit. This may not be an intentional outcome, but it happens just the same when efforts are made to reduce complex human phenomena to easily manipulable figures; when a caste of development agents emerges with few if any links to a separate caste of "beneficiaries"; and, finally, when encouragement is given to the institutionalization of a cross-national bureaucratic and academic logic and rhetoric that interferes with rather than facilitates true representations of daily life.

The question is how to achieve some modest amalgamation between the emotional involvement of the grassroots community development worker and the analytical discipline of the trained researcher, and to incarnate these in the form of a caring development bureaucrat. A beginning might be made by combining in the same job the three fundamental human experiences in question: regular participatory contact between project participants and implementers; systematic study and application of developed methodologies for the retrieval of qualitative as well as quantitative information; and responsibility for policy decisions.

Organizational Reform: the Place to Begin

In general, the present social structure of development work tends to do just the opposite of what is needed. For example, under the American system, implementation is mostly done by Peace Corps volunteers, private voluntary agencies, or private contractors, all of whom are kept at arms length from any policy decision role. Most analysis is done in the form of short-term consultancies or by specialized researchers, both of whom generally leave behind their recommendations without having to live with them. Decisions, especially those regarding funding, come from administrative officials who are responsible to yet higher echelon administrators until, ultimately, the power of approval comes to rest on the highest and most emotionally remote point possible in relation to the activity in question. Since promotion to authority is normally unidirectional, from field worker, to analyzer, to administrator, even those who start out with some personal knowledge, emotional involvement, and understanding of specific circumstances, eventually use up their experiential capital and revert to decision making by formulae.

The situation, of course, is somewhat inherent in any bureaucratic structure, but this does not make reform or moderation impossible. Recently AID began an experimental program of rotating selective academic professionals between their universities and longterm (two years) overseas assignments to USAID missions. Such innovations are promising, but still insufficient, since what is called for is a mixing of roles as well as institutional positions. What is needed is a crisscrossing of jobs in all directions: development workers who return to academic or policy research positions; academics who become temporary agency implementers; administrators who are rotated back into implementation and analytic tasks; and implementers who are given policy decision-making roles. This rotation of tasks would promote the development of cultural expertise. For example, instead of the present policy among development assistance organizations of rotating people out of geographic areas after periods of four to eight years, professionals should become personally experienced in one or two culture areas for their entire careers.

No doubt numerous other mechanisms could be evolved to further this cause. Serious in-depth crosscultural training for development personnel is still almost nonexistent. "Community participation" could be given added meaning by requiring more frequent encounters between participants and development agency personnel, and by insisting on the right of a "community veto." This would force planners, implementers, and policy strategists to take honest account of people's desires. The very writing of this chapter gave me a unique opportunity to reflect back on past moments of intense human contact with the FulBe pastoralists among whom I lived. It required me to reappraise the meaning of that experience for my present professional activities that are concerned with helping determine the future of similar groups who fate has ordained would become "targets" of development.

Development personnel should be placed in direct contact with the realities of the people whose lives their projects are changing. They must understand--emotionally as well as intellectually--how their proposals translate into actual human experience.

Ultimately, it is our common humanity that should be the universal coefficient of development work.   This requires a recognition of our common needs, be they intellectual, material, spiritual, or emotional.   It also requires a continuous renewal and reaffirmation of this truth in the policies and practices of development agencies.   There is no reason it cannot be done, for another common heritage of humanity is free will, that freedom to decide and determine that is so cherished by the FulBe.   We need only have the same desire and courage to exercise it as they.

Editors' Note to Chapter 7

Marginal populations have long been the bane of govern-ments, and for almost twenty years for development planners too. They leave the country or province without notice, are notorious for fleeing from government tax collectors, and are generally disorderly. They are accused also of ruining the environment with their maladaptive techniques of animal husbandry and culti-vation. Allan Hoben describes his work with the evaluation of a USAID project designed to resettle inhabitants of the Mandara mountains in Northern Cameroon in the Benoué Plateau region to the south. The kirdi (pagans), as they are often called by lowland peoples, are accused by the government and USAID of spoiling their mountain habitat. Hoben investigated, and discov-ered what many social scientists have doubtless found in similar circumstances. The mountain dwellers, in fact, had been pre-serving, not degrading, their environment. He also discovered that the real issue was not mountain ecology, but power. The question was how could the state exercise greater control over the kirdi, and at the same time promote accumulation on the underpopulated Benoué plateau? The answer was to move them to the plateau and transform them into cotton growers. Hoben concluded that the original project idea was not sound, and proposed instead to assist mountain dwellers without having to relocate them. In his conclusion, Hoben also touches on issues familiar to many social scientists who have watched local initiatives and good but modest ideas for local improvements become incorpo-rated by large, expensive development projects.

7
Assessing the Social Feasibility
of a Settlement Project
in North Cameroon

ALLAN HOBEN
Boston University

INTRODUCTION

During 1976 I conducted a study of the social feasibility of a
proposed rural development and resettlement project in the
Mandara Mountain region of North Cameroon for the United States
Agency for International Development (AID). Partly as a result
of this study, the director of USAID in Cameroon decided not to
move ahead with the design of the project, and instead, initiated
several other small-scale projects dealing with problems faced by
mountain peoples in their home areas.

This chapter seeks to answer three questions repeatedly
asked by academic colleagues and students: (1) Do development
agencies ever follow the advice of anthropologists? That is, can
anthropologists really influence decisions made by these agencies?
(2) Can anthropologists conduct a useful study in a few weeks or
months rather than requiring longer periods (12-18 months),
especially in regions where they have no previous fieldwork
experience? (3) Can applications of anthropology to development
be intellectually challenging, particularly in short-term studies?
My answer to each of these questions is an emphatic but qualified
yes. In some situations it is worthwhile to bring an anthropological perspective to bear on the process of decision-making for
development, but it is necessary to appreciate that the process is
complex and that the anthropologist's contribution has limits.

The present discussion sketches the course of my involvement in the Cameroon project, describes the way I conceptualized
the task, and outlines the research strategy I adopted to carry it
out. It also presents a shortened version of the report I submitted to USAID in Yaoundé in April 1976, and provides a brief
epilogue concerning subsequent USAID activities in the Mandara
Mountain region. In the conclusion, I attempt to draw lessons
from this and my subsequent three years of experience as Senior
Anthropologist for Policy with AID in Washington, D.C.

169

Initial Contact with the West Bénoué Rural Development Project:
Preparations for a Social Prefeasibility Study

During March 1976 I was contacted by the AID-Cameroon
Desk Officer in Washington, D.C. He had read a report I had
prepared for AID several months earlier, on the impact of agrarian reform in Ethiopia, and asked if I could travel to North
Cameroon the following week to participate in a feasibility study
of a proposed rural development project there.

I objected that it was the middle of Boston University's
spring term and that I had never done fieldwork in French West
Africa. He countered that the assignment was for only three
weeks, that the other member of the study team--an economist
--was familiar with Cameroon, and that anthropologists with West
African experience whom I had previously recommended for the
job were not available. Moreover, he added, our team would be
briefed in Washington and would stop in Paris to meet with the
leading French experts from the Office de la Recherche Scientifique et Technique Outre-Mer (ORSTOM) on North Cameroon.

After contacting a history graduate student who had just
returned from North Cameroon, obtaining approval from my university, and arranging for someone to teach my classes, I agreed
to go. In addition to the dubious benefit of basking in
Cameroon's 110-degree April heat and my unquenchable desire to
see yet another African state, I was very interested in the possibility of making a useful contribution to development planning in
a country where I did not have extensive field experience.

With the help of the Boston University African Studies
librarian and the history graduate student, I hastily initiated a
literature search on Cameroon, and on AID's program there and
the peoples of the Mandara Mountains and other parts of North
Cameroon. Fortunately, the trip was postponed for three weeks,
giving me time more thoroughly to review AID documents and
much of the relevant French and English material I was able to
locate, and to formulate specific questions that helped me focus
my reading.

I learned that the USAID mission in Cameroon was initiating
several projects in Northern Province, which is the most remote,
hence from USAID's perspective, the country's most underdevel-
oped region. This largely sahelian province had been selected
for special attention, in keeping with AID's Congressionally
mandated emphasis on alleviating rural poverty.

In addition, development of the north ranked low among the
Cameroon government's economic planning priorities, which emphasized infrastructure, cash crop production, and industry in
the country's southern region. USAID's project proposals and its
focus on rural development in the north was acceptable to the
central government in Yaoundé, however, because of the region's
particular historic, cultural, and political position within the
nation. Prior to colonial rule and the resultant reorientation of
the economy toward the export of cash crops through the southern port city of Douala, it was the Fulani-dominated emirates of
the north, with their cultural, economic, and political ties to
other Islamic polities in the region, that were considered

'civilized'.   Conversely, the southern forests and savannah lands were regarded as tribal backwaters.   Indeed, the president and a number of other high officials in the national government at the time of my work were from the north, and the province still enjoys a considerable degree of autonomy compared with other regions.

The project proposed by USAID for the northern region was called the West Bénoué Integrated Rural Development Project (henceforth the West Bénoué Project).   Its purpose was to encourage the resettlement of 20,000 farm families (approximately 80,000 people), from the heavily populated Mandara Mountains in the north to a much more sparsely inhabited region, the Bénoué Plateau, to the south (see Map, page 172).   USAID anticipated that the project would result in an improvement in the living conditions of poor rural populations in the north, and afford greater protection of the area's fragile soils.   This was to be done by bringing the fertile alluvial soils of the West Bénoué region into cultivation, thereby reducing pressure on the poorer soils of the Mandara Mountains.   Through the withdrawal of some   poorer areas from cultivation, the project's designers expected that natural   vegetation   would   return,   and   soil   fertility   would eventually increase.

At the time I was contacted, the project was little more than a short descriptive document (an AID Project Identification Document, or PID), based on a very preliminary World Bank report, and it had been included in USAID Cameroon's annual budget submission for possible elaboration.   Little staff time had been invested in the project design, and USAID had no previous commitments regarding it to Cameroonian leaders or government ministries.   Moreover, the USAID mission was aware that social and economic information vital to the elaboration of a project was lacking.   All these circumstances had an important bearing on my role, although I did not fully appreciate them at the time.   In fact, the USAID mission director and his staff had *not yet made a decision* on the project and were seeking help in determining whether to move ahead with the time consuming, complex, and expensive process of project design.

On the basis of the 1977 West Bénoué Project Identification Document and my brief telephone conversations with the Cameroon Desk Officer in Washington, I formulated some preliminary questions even before obtaining the literature on the area:

1.   Who are the people to be resettled and what was the schedule for resettlement?
2.   Which other ethnic groups are to be affected by the project?
3.   How are those to be resettled selected?
4.   What are the attitudes toward the resettlement, of those selected to move and of those not selected?   Do these attitudes vary by group characteristics?   By class?
5.   To what extent are choices given to those involved in the resettlement?   Once having moved, can they return home?   If a return is permitted, is it realistic to believe that it will be possible?

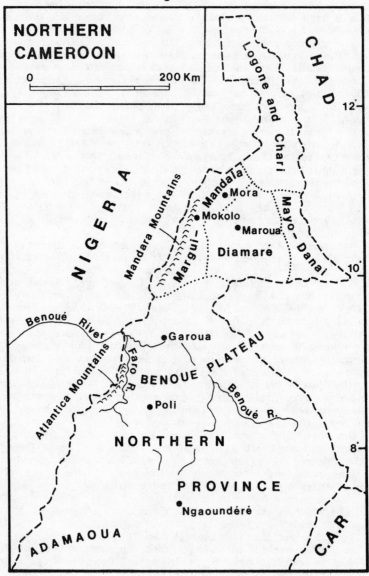

Figure 2.

6.   What knowledge is there about previous attempts to resettle people from the Mandara Mountains to the plains areas in the south? What social and political problems, if any, have arisen?

7.   What are the class structures and occupational characteristics of the populations to be resettled? Are there systematic relations between factors such as lineage, age, sex, and household composition, and people's perception of migration to the plains? If so, what?

8.   Historically, what has been the nature of the relationship between the mountain people and the plains dwellers, in political terms, economic terms, ecological differentiation, religious, and class terms?

9.   What are the ecological and agronomic constraints on agricultural productivity in the mountains? Would the outmigration of 10, 20, or even 30 percent of the population significantly affect these constraints?

10. What is the system of land tenure in the mountains? What are its demographic consequences? What happens to the land claims of farmers who leave the area? Can those who have left return and claim their land? Does this create conflict? Between whom? Are there relations of inequality based on differential access to land, water, or other scarce productive assets?

11. What is the religious significance of land, homesites, and geography? How do they affect patterns of outmigration?

12. Are there good demographic studies of population dynamics in the region, including short- and long-term migration? What principal causal factors are revealed by the studies? Whom do they affect, and why?

While tentative, the above questions indicate how I was intuitively drawing upon a considerable body of theory and data from anthropology, land-tenure studies, and other related disciplines. At the same time, I was attempting rapidly to formulate lines of inquiry for my study.

The literature search at the University eventually produced more than 500 items dealing with peoples of North Cameroon, but very few of them concerned the ethnic groups to be affected by the resettlement scheme. The most promising materials were a few monographs and articles by French geographers and a social anthropologist, and several were directly relevant to my preliminary questions. There was, for example, an excellent study by Hallaire (1971) of the forced relocation of hill people on the plains.

Using some of these materials, I was able to place my specific questions about institutional and ecological features of Mandara Mountain populations in a larger context. In some cases I was able to provide answers; in others I was better able to clarify the original questions. This led to an iterative process that continued throughout my work.

I was also able to draw parallels between cultural patterns, institutions, problems, and processes in the Mandara Mountains and those in parts of West Africa I knew better. The social organization and religion of the largest ethnic group in the Mandara Mountains, the Mafa, resembled those of the Talensi, analyzed by Fortes (1945). Also similar was their status as a non-Islamic refugee group in a hilly area surrounded by more powerful kingdoms. The labor-intensive, terraced farming system of the Mafa and their neighbors was similar to that of the Kofiar of Nigeria (Netting 1968). The Mafa also resembled the Kofiar in their change to more extensive, shifting cultivation once more land was available in plains areas. Conversely, the Mafa land tenure system contrasted with many others in Africa, due to its degree of privatization and the tendency to exclude some sons entirely from inheritance. These characteristics were, however, consistent with the high labor cost of terrace construction and maintenance, and the intensive land-use pattern. The forms of colonial domination, and the attitudes of European officials and the Fulani elites toward the naked pagan hill people were also familiar to me from my previous reading on West Africa.

By drawing upon theory and comparative findings in a variety of subfields in anthropology, and through familiarity with the general ethnography and history of the region, I was able to select and interpret relevant material in ways not possible for AID officials, technicians, and many other nonanthropologist social scientists.

Departure for Cameroon

By the time I left for Cameroon in April, I had gained a preliminary understanding of the project setting, the people to be affected by the project, and key issues requiring clarification. During the three weeks in Cameroon that followed, I learned a great deal, but did not find it necessary to alter the conceptual orientation developed during my earlier reading. The briefing provided at AID headquarters in Washington was disorganized and not very informative. Once in Paris, I was able to spend several useful hours in the company of the economist team leader and with a leading French geographer, Jean Boulet, who had done extensive work in North Cameroon. Finally, I was able to purchase a number of monographs not available in Boston. Following our arrival, we spent the first four days in Cameroon's capital, Yaoundé. There followed a series of protocol visits with ministry officials and representatives of other international development agencies. Next, I sought out and interviewed individuals from diverse national, regional and ethnic groups, academic disciplines, and political orientations. This enabled me to compare their views on the project's assumptions concerning problems faced by people in the Mandara Mountains and the proposed solutions for them.

My strategy during these interviews was similar to that of African historians using oral traditions as source material. It was to seek out and to give greatest credence to information on which there was high consensus or that seemed to contradict the expected class, ethnic, occupational, or situational biases of a particular informant. This enabled me quickly to resolve some issues and concentrate my effort on investigating more problematic points.

On April 26 I flew to Garoua (see Map, page 172), the capital of Northern Cameroon, with the team leader and a USAID official from Yaoundé, to begin another round of protocol visits and a five-day field trip. We flew low over the West Bénoué plain, the better to see the terrain, and landed briefly at Poli for interviews with officials and a missionary. We also visited the eastern section of the area by car as far as Tcheboa.

I spent most of the remaining time driving in a circuit from Garoua through Maroua to Mora in the north and then back through Mokolo and down the length of the Mandara mountains to Garoua, accompanied by a Cameroonian historian from the region. We stopped frequently during the trip to visit with local officials and their followers. Despite their obvious bias as members of the local elite, these people were generally helpful and informative, particularly on topics I had learned about prior to the trip.

Early in May I returned to Yaoundé, where I verified and analyzed my material, drafted the conclusions and recommendations for my report, and presented them to the USAID mission director for discussion. In sum, I concluded that from a social and ecological soundness point of view, the proposed project faced serious problems, that it was based on incorrect assumptions, that it would not achieve its goals of resettlement and would not raise the real income of the vast majority of the rural poor in Margui-Wandala region. This was supported by a list of reasons and followed by recommendations for alternative activities to be considered among the inhabitants of the Mandara Mountains. The mission director consequently asked me to extend my stay in Yaoundé by ten days and to write up my findings in greater detail. The remarks to follow are based on that final report of the social feasibility study.

TOWARD A SOCIAL FEASIBILITY STUDY
OF THE WEST BENOUE RURAL DEVELOPMENT PROJECT

Objective and Perspective of the Feasibility Study

The social feasibility study sought to identify the groups and individuals that would be affected by the West Bénoué Project, to examine their perceptions of the project's effects on their interests, and to assess how their interests might be affected by the project. An underlying assumption of the analysis was that the project (or alternative projects) would not succeed unless it engaged the interest of the low-income farmers to be affected; persons who exercised political influence; and finally, of authorities who would be responsible for implementation of the project.

While any development project may be considered a strategic resource whose use may affect the interests of many groups, a resettlement scheme such as the West Bénoué Project may have an unusually great impact because of the radical changes it introduces in the lives of the settlers, those who are left behind, and those already in the area of new settlement.

As proposed in the original Project Identification Document, the West Bénoué Project would affect the interests of eight categories of people:

1.   families to be resettled at a great distance from the kinsmen on whom they depended for sociability, mutual aid and risk aversion;

2.   aging parents of young migrants who depended on their children for labor, honor, and support in their declining years;

3.   village headmen and local district officials in home areas whose prestige and revenues were proportional to the number of tax paying households under their authority;

4.   traditional local authorities in plain areas who stood to gain tax paying subjects, but who have long tended to view mountain peoples as culturally inferior serfs;

5.   pastoralists and farming peoples who were already using some of the resources in the West Bénoué plain to be put at the disposal of settlers;

6.   Cameroon and expatriate personnel who might have been employed by the project;

7.   regional administrative officials who sought to curry favor with their superiors but who under existing conditions were not responsive to the needs or demands of those they administered;

8.   parastatals and their constituents having a vested interest in maximizing the production of cash crops with little regard for the effects on food production or the environment.

The emphasis placed upon interests and decision making processes in this analysis led to consideration of micro-studies that revealed the institutional context of decision making as well as aggregate statistics. The ultimate goal of the analysis was to clarify the relationship between the decisions of individual farmers and their consequences for longer-term ecological, economic and demographic trends.

Overview of the Project and the Peoples of the Mandara Mountains

The proposed West Bénoué Project sought to facilitate the movement of poor farm families from the overpopulated Mandara Mountains to the underpopulated and more fertile West Bénoué River plain region. The proposed resettlement area covered about 13,000 square kilometers of the Bénoué Department (including all of the Poli Arrondissement and most of the Garoua Arrondissement). It was therefore necessary to identify the peoples and the problems of the Mandara Mountains.

The Mandara Mountains extend along the Nigerian border of Northern Province some 150 kilometers from the Bénoué Basin in the Mandara Plains in the north. For the most part they fall within Margui-Wandala, one of five departments that together make up Northern Province (see Map, page 172). The mountains

consist of a central plateau averaging 800 meters in altitude,
bordered by an eroded mountain zone that drops away to the
piedmont and the plains beyond.   Average annual rainfall in
mountains is 900 millimeters (IRSC n.d.) concentrated during the
rainy season between May and September.   There are, however,
sub-regional and annual variations in the duration and
distribution of rainfall, and these are critical for agriculture and
population movements to be discussed below.

The total population of Margui-Wandala Department is estimated to be 446,234, with an average density of 63 persons per
square kilometer (see Table 1). The greatest part of the population, however, is concentrated on the northern and northeastern
mountain slopes, where densities may exceed 300 persons per
square kilometer.

Table 1

Population of North Cameroon

Department	Area	Population	Density
Logone and Chari	12,133	117,574	10
Margui-Wandala	7,129	446,234	63
Diamare	9,698	460,844	48
Mayo-Danai	5,303	219,542	41
Bénoué	66,090	372,902	6

Note: The population totals shown in this table are based on
preliminary estimates from the 1976 census; they are considerably
higher than those used in Boulet 1975a.

Ethnographers distinguish among as many as 27 ethnic
groups in the Mandara Mountain area.   To facilitate this discussion, however, I have adopted Boulet's (1970) convention of
grouping the population in two clusters.   The first cluster
includes the peoples who inhabit the high plateau to the south of
Mokolo.   This southern ethnic cluster includes the Kola, Hina,
Daba, Guider, Falai Kangou, Kapsiki, Bana, Djimi, Goude, and
Njegn, and accounts for about 16 percent of the population in
Northern Cameroon (see Table 2).   The second cluster is composed of the peoples who dwell in the rugged mountains and detached massifs to the north and east of Mokolo, and accounts for
nearly twenty percent of the northern population (Table 2).
These include the Mafa, Hide, Mineo, Mabass, Mouktele, Podoko,

Table 2

Size of Major Ethnic Groupings in North Cameroon[a]

Major groupings as percentage of total (total = 1,617,096)

	Percent
Islamic	34.5
Southern-Highland[b]	0.5
Northern Mountain[c]	0.6
Plains (non-Islamic)	3.6
South Bénoué	7.0

Ethnic Groups Within the Northern Mountain Grouping

Mafa groups	46.1
Mora groups	33.0
Mofou groups	20.9

---

[a]After Boulet 1975a

[b]This grouping includes the "southern ethnic cluster" and some highlands peoples, such as the Fali, who now live outside the Margui-Wandala Department. Some of the Fali have moved into the plains in recent times.

[c]This is the "northern ethnic cluster."

Maora, Vame-Mbreme Mada Ouldeme, Zoulgo-Guenejek Ourza Mouyengue, MokyoMolkoa, Mbokou, Guelebda and Mofou.

Most of the southern cluster populations are thought to have arrived on the Mandara Mountain plateau during the last two centuries, taking refuge from warlike and more politically centralized groups which invaded their former lowland territories. Since the cessation of intergroup warfare, most of them have begun to move back onto the plains. Agricultural techniques are not as intensive among southern cluster populations as among the northerners, and population densities range from only 10 to 40 persons per square kilometer. The agricultural techniques of the northern cluster peoples are intensive. They are well adapted to mountain conditions, and support high population densities. While population and administrative pressure have forced many of the northern farmers to move into the piedmont in the past few decades, there has been no massive voluntary exodus to the plains comparable to what has occurred in the south.

Because of their larger numbers, higher population densities, high fertility, and rapid rate of population increase, the northern peoples are considered to present a greater problem than the southerners. Because of this they have been subject to the greatest pressure to move from their mountain homes, thus they will be given greater consideration here than peoples of the southern cluster.

Basic patterns of settlement and social and political organization are similar among the northern mountain peoples. The basic social unit of production, consumption, and resource control is the household centered on a man, his wives, and their unmarried children.

Geographically, individual households are scattered over the cultivated, terraced lands. With the exception of modern administrative and market centers, there are virtually no nucleated villages. Social ties and patterns of interaction group the scattered households into sprawling, traditional hamlets, containing from 25 to 50 households. The hamlets, in turn, are grouped into named political communities of from 100 to more than 1,000 households, often referred to as villages. Political communities are normally separated from one another by such natural features as ravines and, in the past, stretches of uncleared bush.

The institutional framework of hamlet and village is a system of patrilineal descent groupings so arranged that each "village" community is made up of several discrete but intermarrying clans, each with a membership of 40 to 1,000 households. Membership in clans crosscuts membership in hamlets.

Each clan is considered by its members to be made up of the descendants *in the male line only* of a common ancestor who, according to local belief, first cleared a portion of the village lands by virtue of first occupancy or through securing the permission of the older village inhabitants. Common descent gives members of each clan a sense of political solidarity against all others, unites them through the sharing of a complex set of ancestral beliefs and practices, and is the basis for sharing reversionary rights to clan lands. Members of the same clan are forbidden to intermarry. Each clan has a senior elder or head; one of these clan leaders is selected to be the village leader, although he exercises little direct authority and is considered as first among equals.

Political relations between the clans that make up a village and between clans in different villages are structured in large part by marriage alliances through which one clan takes its wives from other specific groups. Over time, this creates close-knit kinship ties between clans through the female members.[1]

Detailed case studies by Martin (1970) indicate that, far from being a static system in which clan size and location were determined by chance or birth alone, demographic pressures, political motives, and above all the desire for land led to manipulations of the kinship and descent ideology by politically powerful factions.

---

[1] Every man's mother must come from another clan, and every man's sister and daughter must eventually marry into a different clan.

For purposes of day-to-day sociability and cooperation, geographical proximity and friendship determine interhousehold relations. In a ritual context and on less frequent but critical occasions when disputes arise over rights to land and office, the
system of clans and their constituent lineages is most important to
the mountain farmers in defending their security and interests.
When interpreting patterns of migration it is essential to bear in
mind that ties with kinsmen and clansmen are the basis for the
mountain farmers' social, economic, and political security.

Between villages, and even more so between ethnic groups,
there was little sense of common identity or interest in the past.
There was little trade, and in most instances virtually no supra-
village political authority. Even today, the various ethnic groups
of the northern cluster do not appear to conceive of themselves
as having common goals or sharing a common predicament.

Stereotypes of Mandara Mountain Peoples and their Historical Consequences: The "Kirdi Problem" and its Solutions in Administrative Perspective

If the Mandara Mountain dwellers lack a shared sense of
identity in their own eyes, they have been assigned to a single
conceptual category, the *Kirdi,* by Islamic and more centralized
peoples of the plains.[2] Inherent in the concept of Kirdi is a
stereotype of what mountain people are like and how they should
be treated. This view of the mountain people's character has
changed very little during the past century, but ideas about how
they should be treated, and how to solve the "Kirdi problem,"
have changed with the evolution of colonial and post-colonial
administrative policy.

According to the stereotype, the Kirdi are above all pagan,
naked, poor, backward, and lack government. A Kirdi who
breaks away from the stereotype, who, e.g., moves to a Muslim
town on the plains, converts to Islam, and adopts Fulani dress
and lifestyle, is no longer considered a Kirdi. This continual
process of conversion and assimilation has drawn off members of
the Mandara Mountain population and has produced a situation
where "former Kirdi" outnumber Muslims two to one.

During the pre-colonial period, the Mandara Mountains were
on the marchlands of a series of Sudanic kingdoms and empires.
For the most part, contacts between the inhabitants of the Mandara Mountains and their neighbors were limited to sporadic fighting and limited trade. Only after the rise of the Adamaoua Emir-
ate were largely unsuccessful attempts made to reduce the northern mountaineers to tributary status (Martin 1970:38).

-----

[2]The term *Kirdi* derives from Choa Arabic and signifies
'infidel', i.e., non-Islamic pagan. The term is also applied to
other non-Islamic groups of North Cameroon who live in the
(Footnote Continued)

German colonial administration did little to change the relationship between the Islamic plains powers and the pagan mountain people, or to alter the Kirdi stereotype. Likewise, the replacement of German by French administration after World War I did not initially change the relationship between the Fulani and Mandara chiefs and their mountain vassals. The primary objective of the French administration, which, in Mokolo, was a military administration until 1940, was to pacify the unruly mountain dwellers; to establish more effective control over them. At first, the French gave a free hand to the Muslim chiefs, who exacted what tribute they could from the Kirdi and occasionally raided mountain villages for booty and slaves (Martin 1970:40-42).

By 1931, the northern Mandara Mountain peoples had been pacified and placed more firmly under the control of government-appointed Muslim Mandara and Fulani chiefs. In the same year, a plague of locusts brought famine to the region and forced many mountain dwellers to take temporary refuge as paid laborer-dependents with Muslim groups in the adjacent lowlands. The following year, most of the mountain people returned to their former lands, but the idea that their resettlement in the plains was a solution to the "Kirdi problem" had been planted in the minds of French administrators (Martin 1970:42). Once settled in the plains, the Kirdi might live better, but more importantly, they would be easy to rule. This desire on the part of the administration to resettle the Kirdi in order better to integrate them economically and better to control them, would not end with Cameroon's independence from French colonial rule in 1960.

One of the first acts of the new Cameroon administration was to force the Kirdi to clothe themselves with whatever cloth they could afford to buy. At the same time the mountain peoples were pressured to abandon the homes and terraced fields they and their ancestors had toiled to build. These pressures reached a climax in 1963, when more than 39,000 mountain people were forced to leave for the lowlands (Boutrais 1973:59). Attempts to resettle the Kirdi in the plains continued during subsequent years. The proposed West Bénoué Project was thus not without precedent. Much could be learned from past experience. In order to understand the human, economic, and environmental effects of this massive displacement from one ecological zone to another, it was necessary to examine the situation from the perspective of the Kirdi themselves.

Since the early 1960's the North Cameroon administration has continued its efforts to resettle the Mandara Mountain peoples in the plains by means of several development projects. In all cases these projects aimed to bring mountain dwellers under more direct government control, promote the assimilation of Islamic culture by the mountain ethnic groups, and increase the production of cash crops in the plains. These resettlement efforts have frequently

---

(Footnote Continued)
plains, including the Moundang, Toupouri, Massa, Mousey, and Mousgoum.

been coercive in nature, due to policy or excessive administrative zeal, and have suffered numerous difficulties. Among these are the following:

1.   a near total disregard for the knowledge of small-scale producers who use traditional agricultural practices concerning soil conservation and crop management;
2.   excessive reliance on the introduction of technology as a means of removing the production constraints faced by small-scale farmers;
3.   an emphasis on increasing the production of cash crops at the expense of food production and soil conservation practices;
4.   no allowance for the participation of settlers in the planning and implementation of projects;
5.   large investment in costly infrastructure in short-term projects;
6.   poor coordination and conflict among the agencies involved in planning and implementation;
7.   monopolization of the best soils by regional elites.

Aspects of Organization for Agricultural Production, Land Tenure, and Population Dynamics among Mandara Mountain Dwellers[3]

In 1976, an AID-sponsored survey concluded that terraced farming in the northern Mandara Mountains has little productive potential and that the optimum use of terraced sites would be managed grazing at a low level of production (USAID/FAC:1976: 165-6). In light of this negative assessment it is puzzling that the area has the highest population densities found in North Cameroon (IRSC n.d.), among the highest per hectare wet-season crop yields in North Cameroon (1,000 kg/ha.), adequate nutrition (in regional comparative terms [Boulet 1970:210]), and as high a rate of population increase as any group in the North (Podlewski 1966:181).

A closer examination of the data indicates that although population pressure creates problems for individual mountain farmers, there is no evidence that it is leading to a deterioration of the environment or a decreasing standard of living. Detailed research on Mafa agriculture by Jean Boulet (1970, 1975b) reveals a labor-intensive, land-efficient, and environmentally conservationist farming system. This system employs anti-erosion techniques that include the construction of stone-walled terraces that follow mountain contours and vary in width according to the slope, banking

---

[3]The material in this section is based in large part on studies of the Mafa, the largest and most dynamic ethnic group in the northern cluster of "true mountain farmers." Other ethnic groups in this cluster are similar to the Mafa.

of earth and grass to form a network of miniature dikes around each millet or sorghum plant to prevent run-off and form a moisture-retentive compost; and drainage control. Rather than depleting the soils, as the above-cited report claims, the terracing techniques may *improve* soil quality (Boulet 1970:209). The maintenance of fertility in a system of continual land use is further promoted by crop rotation, the burning of refuse left in fields from the previous growing season, the application of animal manure, and the maintenance of an arboreal cover.

The basic social unit of production, consumption, and land-ownership among the Mafa and related groups is the household. It is of particular interest in the Mandara Mountain region because it is remarkably autonomous from larger management units based on kinship, vicinage, or chiefship. The Mafa household, composed of a man, his wife or wives, and his unmarried children, has an average number of six members. Only the youngest son may remain in the household after he marries. Except for the youngest, married sons do not remain under the authority of their fathers with regard to the control of land resources or the organization of work.

Within the household some tasks are assigned on the basis of age and sex, but all able members work on the all-important millet and sorghum crops during periods of heavy labor needs. There are two peak periods. The cultivation season lasts from late June to early September. Weeding and diking must be done, and fodder must be carried to the livestock. The second period of heavy labor is the harvest season, which occurs in October and November.

Dry-season labor requirements are considerably lower, and increasing numbers of young men have begun to migrate seasonally to the plains. They work for Fulani and Mandara landlords as wage laborers in the recession cultivation of sorghum. Seasonal migration may increase due to population pressure and the need to obtain cash for tax payments. From the point of view of the young migrant, however, the principal goal is money that will help pay a brideprice, enabling him to establish an independent household. A growing number of young men also migrate during the rainy season, seeking employment on cotton and peanut schemes, and in the towns and cities. Despite increasing participation in wage-earning activities, the average Mafa household continues to operate within a predominantly subsistence economy.

Mafa land-tenure recognizes individual land rights to a much greater degree than many other African systems of land tenure. A household head can dispose of his fields as he wishes, leave them unused, rent or loan them to whom he pleases, give them to his sons, and even sell them. The only limitation is that the recipient must be a clan member.

In contrast to most African land-tenure systems, the Mafa system does not require a father or his "successor" to provide land for all his sons. Instead, the head of a household gives land to his eldest son at the time he marries, only if he is able to do so without jeopardizing the parental household's land needs. If there is sufficient land when the second son marries, he also may receive some, and so it goes for subsequent sons, until a critical threshold for household land holding size has been reached (about two hectares, Boulet 1975a). Only the youngest son is sure to acquire land, for he remains in his father's household even after marriage, and eventually inherits the household, its lands, and the largest share of moveable property. Daughters do not receive land by gift *inter vivos* or through inheritance.

Sons who are unable to secure land from their fathers may attempt to borrow it from clansmen or others within their natal community. If land cannot be had in the natal community, young men may settle in another community where land is available. Doing so places them at a social and political disadvantage, for unless they are resident in a community where their clan owns land, they have no rights of citizenship; thus they cannot take part in clan councils and rituals or expect the natural and supernatural protection accorded clan members. Most important, if they cannot acquire land rights through outright gift or purchase, they are subject to eventual eviction. A disproportionate number of those who permanently leave the Mafa region are from this partially dispossessed class of non-inheriting sons. Their numbers have increased during recent decades because of greater population pressure and increasing land values, caused by the incipient commercialization of agriculture (Martin 1970:77).

We have seen that the highest population densities, fertility, and population growth rates are found among the northern mountain peoples, who are farthest from the West Bénoué area, and who have been the least inclined to resettle in the plains.[4]

These high rates of growth may be related to the labor-intensive mode of agriculture, patterns of household organization, and health factors, including adequate nutrition and low rates of venereal disease and debilitating diseases like schistosomiasis, associated with life on the plains.

Whatever the causes of this growth rate, it is useful to evaluate available materials in order to consider the effects it has had on population dynamics from the pre-colonial period to the present. High population densities were necessary for the northern Mandara peoples to maintain their intensive terraced system of agriculture. The labor requirements of agriculture would thus establish minimum population levels. Formerly, the upper threshold of population densities was probably set by the carrying

---

[4]Podlewski (1966:175, 181) found that, with the exception of the Daba, all the plateau groups of the southern cluster of Mandara peoples have stationary or decreasing populations, while the Mafa have a crude natality rate of 284, a fertility rate of over 8 live births per woman, and a population growth of 2.5 percent/year. The Mofou groups are also increasing. Unfortunately, I have not been able to find data on the Mora mountain groups. Data on fertility and population growth are summarized in map form in Podlewski (1966:175, 181). Boutrais (1973), Martin (1970), and Hallaire (1971) are helpful sources on this issue.

capacity of the agricultural system during periods of scarcity, when rainfall was inadequate or inadequately spaced. During these periods there were famines, emigration, and some individuals were sold into slavery. Warfare also served to limit population to some extent and led to clans displacing one another as they competed for land resources. The same factors that have encouraged high population growth rates historically are at work today, but the demographic responses of the people have changed. There has been increasing population movement into formerly forested and unoccupied piedmont zones immediately adjacent to the mountains. The cessation of warfare with plains dwellers has enabled large numbers of mountain people to seek temporary refuge among the plainsmen during times of famine, such as occurred in 1931 and 1966.

Family budget data indicate that increasing opportunities for seasonal and long-term labor migration may be resulting in the importation of millet into the mountains.

The Social Feasibility of the West Bénoué Project

A review of available evidence suggested that from the view-point of demography and agriculture, the proposed project area on the Bénoué plain had considerable potential for resettlement.

Additional Questions. From the perspective of social fea-sibility, however, several questions remained to be answered. Among them were the following which will be addressed below.
--   Who lived in the proposed resettlement area?
--   Why weren't more people living in the area?
--   Might there be problems between the settlers and mem-
       bers of ethnic groups already in the area?
--   Which peoples were most likely to settle in the project
       area?
--   Would settler recruitment be voluntary?
--   How would the project affect the environment?

Since a number of reports on the project area and the proj-ect are available (Boulet 1972; 1975a; 1975b; Brabant 1976; Bra-bant and Humbel 1974; Humbel and Barbery 1974; Marticou and Audebert n.d.; Morris 1976; IBRD 1974; USAID 1975), I will raise a number of issues pertaining to the social and institutional soundness of undertaking a resettlement scheme at the present time. I am primarily concerned with the social and political en-vironment of the West Bénoué region and with whether the prob-lems that have plagued resettlement in the north can be overcome more easily in this environment. By raising these issues, I do not mean to imply that resettlement in the West Bénoué region is impossible or undesirable. Rather, I am trying to identify diffi-culties that would have to be overcome before it could occur on a significant scale.

1.   Inhabitants of the resettlement area. At the time of my visit to North Cameroon, the proposed resettlement zone was in-habited by approximately 70,000 people belonging to at least ten ethnic groups. The largest of these was the Fulani, accounting for slightly more than half of the total. The Fulani were located

principally in the northern part of the region and in the west along the Faro River. Descendants of cattle-herding nomads, they continued to place a high value on cattle and maintained large herds even though crop production formed their subsistence basis. Although most Fulani were neither wealthy nor powerful, theirs was the dominant ethnic group in West Bénoué (Martin 1976). Their leaders still enjoyed considerable authority and autonomy in much of the project area, thus the rights of Fulani herdsmen could not be disregarded.

The second largest ethnic group was the Doayo, who made up about 20 percent of the population. The Doayo farmed and kept small trypano-tolerant cattle on the lower slopes of the Poli Mountains in the southern part of the proposed project area. Less numerous groups included the Koma and Tchamba, who lived on the piedmont between the Faro River and the Atlantica Mountains. Together they accounted for 16 percent of the population. Other groups included the Doupa and the Fali.

2. Reasons for low population densities. Given the seemingly high agricultural potential of the area it was difficult to explain why such a large expanse contained so few people. Oral tradition, travel reports, and surface-site archaeological evidence all suggested that at least some of the area had been more densely settled in the past.

For hundreds of years the Bénoué region was an area for invasion and conflict. Bata, followed by Fulani invasion and oppression early in the 19th century, drove the Nyam Nyam toward Ngaoundéré and may have forced the Fali and Doayo into northern and southern highlands. Further exodus was caused early in the 1900's by German suppression of a Mahdist rebellion among the *lamidos* southeast of Garoua. The emptying of Bénoué populations continued, spurred on by colonial forced labor recruitment.

Disease is often cited as another cause of depopulation, but the evidence is less than convincing.

Finally, gradual soil depletion may have played a major role in the depopulation of the Bénoué region. No doubt each of these factors accounts in part for the anomaly of sparse populations in the Bénoué area, but available evidence does not allow a satisfactory evaluation.

Local officials can be expected to show ambivalence toward the project. On the positive side, the addition of new tax paying subjects is welcome, since local revenues, legitimate and otherwise, will increase with the influx of migrants. On the negative side, the newcomers may come into conflict with the local leader's supporters and encroach on their resources through cultivation, grazing, or fishing. At the higher level there can be little doubt that government officials are positive towards development projects in their areas of jurisdiction.

3. Potential for conflict between settlers and inhabitants. In addition to competition for resources between cultivators and more or less transhumant herdsmen, little love was lost between the mountain peoples and the Muslim plainsmen, who still tended to regard them as serfs. The Kirdi stereotype would probably be slow to change; thus, the possibilities for conflict were real as settlers moved into the plains.

4.   Most likely settlers.   Evidence drawn from several studies of settlement schemes in North Cameroon suggested that if the West Bénoué Project were to be successful, it would most likely attract settlers from the non-Islamic peoples of the nearby plains such as the Moundang and the Toupouri, rather than the people "planned for," i.e., those from the more distant and ecologically different Mandara Mountains. Indeed, it was likely that a substantial number of settlers would come from Chad and Nigeria rather than Cameroon. Thus, the people whose resettlement in the Bénoué region was the most desired seemed to be the least likely to settle there.

5.   Voluntary nature of resettlement.   Given all previous experiences with resettlement programs in the region, it seemed probable that in at least some cases zealous administrators would pressure some of their subjects to volunteer for resettlement. Thus, the "voluntary" character of the resettlement process was less than certain and merited careful attention.

6.   Environmental impact.   It was not possible to predict the environmental effects of the project without knowing exactly how it was to be implemented. From past experience we knew that the promotion of extensive farming and cash crops could lead to the exhaustion and/or erosion of the fragile soils. Also, since the best soils were already being used, it was likely that poor-quality soils would be brought under cultivation in some instances.   If this occurred, settlers were likely to cut the trees, kill the game, and leave.

Summary of Points Concerning the Project's Feasibility. Given the likely answers to these questions and what we have already seen in the preceding sections, the social feasibility of the West Bénoué Project under consideration by USAID/Cameroon seemed very poor. By way of summary, these points are presented below.

We have seen that the high population densities of the northern Mandara Mountain region were based on an ecologically sound, labor-intensive system of agriculture. The combined practices of terracing, manuring, crop rotation, and maintenance of selected shade trees increased rather than decreased the agricultural potential of the area, despite high population densities. Failure to cultivate terraced land rapidly led to erosion, depletion of the soil's organic content, and finally to a gradual loss of agricultural potential. Once population densities dropped below a minimum threshold it was no longer possible for the remaining population to maintain the intensive terraced farming complex. This in turn, could lead to the collapse and abandonment of entire mountainsides. Finally, past experience indicated that farmers from the most intensively farmed and densely settled mountain groups were least likely to voluntarily settle on the plains, except in the piedmont areas adjacent to their natal villages.

Evidence from previous attempts to settle Mandara Mountain farmers in the plains revealed that the programs were viewed by some administrators as a means of controlling mountain dwellers. The objectives were often those of moving the unruly pagans down to the plains where they could be more easily administered, more effectively taxed, encouraged to raise cash crops, and brought into contact with the unifying influence of Islamic civilization. The programs were designed with little regard for local social organization and were often authoritarian if not coercive in their implementation. Often-times this was a reflection of continuity in administrative perceptions of the "Kirdi problem" and its solutions.

A heavy emphasis on cash-crop (e.g., cotton) production in resettlement areas, and the methods used by project personnel have acted together to cause some soil degradation and erosion problems. As for the "beneficial" effects on sending areas, large-scale displacement of mountain populations resulted in the degradation and abandonment of terraced farming eco-systems, hence reduced rather than increased the total carrying capacity of North Cameroon agriculture.

With the exception of a recent resettlement project financed by the Fonds Européen de Développement (FED), in the N.E. Bénoué, services provided by development projects seriously deteriorated in all earlier settlements. Despite high capita infrastructure investments, there was little evidence that resettled farmers enjoyed higher real incomes than farmers who did not resettle. In addition, taxes often amounted to from between 10 and 20 percent of total estimated cash income.

In spite of change in the authoritarian policies of SODECOTON (La Société de Développement du Coton), many farmers in piedmont and plains settlement schemes are being forced by the administration to plant one-half hectare of cotton.

On the basis of my observations and information available in existing literature, I concluded that USAID should not undertake a further feasibility study of the West Bénoué Integrated Rural Development Project, although I did suggest that such a study be reconsidered several years later (in 1979 or 1980). By then, I reasoned, the results of the latest in a long series of resettlement programs in the region, financed by FED in the North East Bénoué, should be clearer.

In the meantime, however, I made several recommendations to the USAID mission in order to pursue a variety of objectives in the shorter term. Briefly, these objectives included: improvements in levels of rural income, health, and nutrition; the creation of local employment during the long dry season; and increased agricultural production, hence an alleviation of food crisis situations.

I recommended that USAID consider the following activities in the mountain regions, rather than the plains, in order that Mandara Mountain peoples benefit from development programs without being uprooted from their habitats:

--the development of cisterns or dams which would improve household water supply and make possible the labor-intensive small-scale production of irrigated crops during the dry season;

--more effective selection and cleaning of seeds for varieties of millet and sorghum presently grown in terraced farming;

--chemical protection of stored food against insect damage;

--improvement of health-care delivery and family planning services.

--I also suggested that USAID should call in a French speaking development economist with extensive experience in agricultural price policy in order to study the price structure of cotton and peanuts and, if warranted, to discuss the results of this analysis frankly on an informal basis with high level Cameroon officials in the Ministries of Planning and Agriculture. The object of such discussions would have been to persuade Cameroon officials that on the basis of comparative evidence it would be in the interests of the government and producers to raise producer prices. It was essential that these discussions be seen as an exchange of views and not as an attempt by the American government to dictate Cameroon policy.

--Finally I proposed that USAID provide the fiscal and human resources needed to systematically study changes in patterns of land use, land tenure, migrant labor, and population distribution in the more densely settled plains of the northern province, and the potential for the creation of employment in the region's towns.

EPILOGUE

The USAID director was convinced by my report that previous resettlement efforts had not worked well, and he accepted my recommendation that development efforts should be directed toward improving conditions in the Mandara Mountain region itself rather than resettlement on the plains followed by efforts to improve the situation there.[5] He subsequently decided to fund the construction of several small dams intended to reduce the time and effort women devoted to obtaining water for domestic use and thereby to increase time available for other more productive activities. In addition, he planned several small-scale follow-on activities, including garden irrigation, agriculture improvement, education, and health.

The dams were to be constructed with local labor, using a contracting instrument that enables AID to avoid dependence on major firms employing sophisticated engineering and capital-intensive techniques. The other activities were to be initiated individually, rather than under a single large integrated rural development project.

As often happens in foreign-assistance programs, the planned emphasis on rapid, small-scale, technically simple, labor-intensive activities proved to be difficult to realize. The water project required, as do all AID development projects, the completion of extensive social, environmental, health, financial, and engineering feasibility studies. There were inevitable delays in carrying these out, and controversies in USAID and/or Washington about the implications of their findings. A project

---

[5]Personal communication from John Kochring, former AID director in Cameroon, June 1981.

implementation agreement was signed in August, 1980, after three years of design work. By this time the mission director had been transferred to Washington and the project's character had changed considerably. The dams were to be built by a large American firm, using heavy machinery rather than local labor. As a result, the original estimated price of $5 million for the construction of 35 dams increased to nearly seven million, but the number of dams to be built decreased by almost two-thirds--to twelve. Moreover it is reported that in some sites unsuitable subsoils made the retention of water impracticable.

The small-scale activities planned for a follow-up to the dams were combined into a single Mandara Mountain Area Development Project, which was to be designed by a U.S. university under an applied research contract established by another branch of AID in Washington. In November, 1979, the USAID mission in Cameroon submitted a preliminary $10 million proposal to build a research center in Mokolo, to sponsor four studies, set up a rural credit system, build rural roads, and support educational programs in the area. In January, 1980, the proposal was turned down in Washington on the grounds that it was too vaguely formulated. The Washington reviewers did, however, authorize $200,000 for further design work by a university team. Nearly a year later, the university contractor proposed an even larger project, including $10 million for the research center in Mokolo alone. By this time, however, there had been another change in the USAID-Yaoundé mission director. The new USAID director, seeking to satisfy the Reagan administration's policy emphasis, decided to focus all new programs on the more productive southern region of the country which in his judgment was of greater interest to the Cameroonian government. Thus, according to an AID official in Washington, the Mandara Mountain Area Development Project "died a quiet death."

The Challenge of Rapid Social Analysis

Having presented this case study material, and on the basis of experience in many other similar situations, I would like to address the three questions asked at the beginning of this Chapter. To the first question, "Do development agencies ever take the advice of consulting anthropologists?" the answer is a resounding "sometimes." It is therefore very important for anthropologists to use their skills to understand and "diagnose" the decision-making context in which they are working. All too many anthropologists, who are sensitive field-workers in other situations, fail to do this.

The general goal of analyzing the decision-making context is to discern (I) what range of options remains open with regard to funding levels, choice of technology, staff size and composition, long- and short-term participant training, project location, site selection criteria, and timing; (2) how the choices between options are conceptualized, including trade-offs between growth and equity, the assumptions that are being made about the productivity, health, income strategies, or risk-aversion techniques of local people; (3) the assumptions being made about ethnic, social, economic, or political differentiation within the beneficiary population; and (4) the kinds of information that will influence options considered and choices made.

It is more difficult to answer these questions than to ask them. Answering these questions in a bureaucratic setting involving a geographically dispersed donor organization, host country officials at various levels, and a variety of contractors, technicians, and scientists from many disciplines can be very challenging. It is useful to try to learn about the organization you are working for:

1. What are the major economic and political functions of the donor agency, and how are they shaped by its institutional environment? How do these affect its institutional and individual incentives? For example, bilateral donors must obligate appropriated funds obtained from legislative bodies within a fixed time frame, often leading to pressure to spend large sums without adequate information. They must support national policy, yet please host country officials and/or politicians.

2. What is the current agency policy in general terms and in regard to your specific task?

3. Are the functions, and hence the incentives, of the donor's field office different from those of the organization as a whole? How do its relations with host country officials affect these functions and incentives, particularly in relation to the work you are doing?

4. Who are the key decision-makers who will judge and use your work, and what are their backgrounds?

5. What disciplinary frameworks and/or intellectual paradigms are key decision-makers using? Within their framework, what are their main assumptions concerning the project on which your advice is being sought?

6. What is the decision-making process with regard to project identification and design within the donor agency? Inevitably this process is closely tied to the organization's annual budgetary cycle of obtaining, obligating, and disbursing funds.

7. At what stage in this decision-making process is the project on which you are consulting? Most important, what has already been decided, and what is the level of commitment to these decisions?

8. Are there key officials in the decision-making process who share your values, objectives, and disciplinary orientation, or for any other reason are likely to promote or defend your position on controversial issues?

While some of these questions must be answered on a case by case basis, it is very helpful to obtain a general understanding of development agencies (Tendler 1975, Hoben 1980), the stages of project identification, design, implementation, and education , and anthropologists' roles in each (Partridge 1984) before undertaking development work. Understanding the organizational setting on which you are working also enables you to make a more effective presentation of your findings and recommendations. You should consider the following points in preparing your presentation to the donor agency:

1. Discuss your findings with other members of your team and with key agency decision-makers as often as possible. Do not wait until you have finished your report.

2. In discussion and in your report, focus on key assumptions others are making about the nature of the problem to be addressed and the linkages between the proposed project and expected results, and examine the validity of these assumptions in terms of what you can learn about the organization, interests, beliefs, and attitudes of local groups.

3. Try to base your argument about what should or should not be done on past experience both within the area you are studying and elsewhere under similar conditions. Development administrators tend to be pragmatists, and rely heavily on common-sense reasoning. In some cases, they may give little credence to unsupported theoretical arguments. Moreover, their career incentives reward them more for avoiding than for taking risks in innovation. Indeed, it is because of the real and tactical significance of case studies and precedent that it is often better to employ an anthropologist with extensive comparative experience on the relevant development problem, rather than one who knows the area intimately but is unfamiliar with developmental experience on the topic gained elsewhere.

4. If you identify a problem, try to recommend a specific and realistic solution. If this is not possible, then consider a number of possibilities. Anthropologists have a reputation for being insightful, negativistic, and not very helpful.

5. Clearly summarize your findings and recommendations at the beginning of your report. The body of the report should be clearly written with a minimum of academic (and development bureaucrat) jargon. Never lose sight of your potential readers who will be AID planners in search of guidance in decision-making, not abstract discourse or endless detail taken from local or comparative ethnographic material. All material in the report should be demonstrably relevant to your arguments and eventual conclusions which should be clearly presented at the end as well as at the beginning.

The second question, concerning the usefulness of short-term consultancies, is rather simplistic. It assumes that no previous relevant in-depth field research has been carried out or that anthropology is so subjective that we cannot depend on the work of other anthropologists. It also overlooks the fact that the extra information and added precision yielded by a long-term in-depth study is often not needed, once basic relationships have been understood with sufficient clarity, to make a decision. In my Cameroon study, for example, a longer study could have established the social, economic, and environmental costs of resettlement schemes more precisely, but it would not have affected AID's decision to reject the project. Indeed, an unnecessary long-term study runs the double risk of producing results only after a decision has been made and of creating the expectation that there will be a project. There are, however, situations where longer-term, intensive research is needed. One of the anthropologist's most important tasks is to help identify these situations, and to develop sound arguments as well as guidelines for studies of this kind.

Short-term studies of the kind frequently done by consulting anthropologists can be extremely challenging and often exhausting. While there is no special methodology for short-term studies, the approach described in this chapter is similar to that used with success by other anthropologists working in development.[6] Key elements in this approach include:

1. Take time at the beginning to develop a clear idea of what you want to learn and why.
2. Make full use of available written material, even if this requires visits to libraries and documentation centers not on your proposed itinerary.
3. Identify a short list of experts, contact them, and discuss the issues of interest to you. If possible pursue these contacts before *and* after you have done the bulk of your reading. Do *not*, however, become a burden to them!
4. Consult anthropologists and other social scientists carrying out fieldwork in the area. You may obtain useful insights long before the formal publication of their results, and doubtless they will be able to offer a rich fund of information about local conditions and trends on many topics in addition to the topic with which they are formally concerned. If you can visit their research sites, you may be able to discuss your topic with their informants. Once again, be especially aware of imposing on these people, clearly establish which details may be used in your report, secure permission to cite if necessary, and show your appreciation for their help.
5. Identify as many different interest groups as possible, and learn the views of each.
6. Focus your efforts at information-gathering issues where there is strong disagreement between members of different interest groups.
7. Locate studies using differing techniques of data collection and analysis.

The third question, concerning the intellectual challenge of work in development again seems to reflect an academic bias

---

[6]A useful overview of these approaches can be found in "Shortcut Methods in Information Gathering for Rural Development Projects," a paper by Robert Chambers prepared for the World Bank Agricultural Sector Symposium, Brighton, Institute for Development Studies, University of Sussex, January 1980.

against applied work. In my view, development anthropology is not a distinctive subdiscipline having a special body of theory and method. Rather, it is an attempt to apply an anthropological perspective and comparative anthropological findings in order to clarify and anticipate the consequences of important decisions concerning the allocation of resources both for policy-makers and for those affected by the policies. Consequently there can be no good development anthropology unless it is good anthropology. But in addition, and here is an important part of the intellectual challenge, the complexity of the situations involved often forces the anthropologist in development to draw upon intellectual and theoretical resources from other fields as well as her/his own.

There are, to be sure, characteristic differences in the way theory is used and in the intellectual styles of development work and academic research. In development, the anthropologist is called upon to illuminate a particular empirical situation (perceived by development bureaucrats as "practical") as fully as possible and therefore to be theoretically eclectic. In his academic re-search, by contrast, he is rewarded for finely focused theoretical and methodological contributions and has incentives for dismissing many aspects of the situation he studies with a *ceteris paribus* argument.

A second difference is that in development work it is usually more fruitful to focus on a process, such as risk aversion, acqui-sition of credit, or treatment of illness, that may be associated with specific aspects of social structure (such as household, kin group, or voluntary association), than to focus on a particular structure and investigate its range of processes or functions. This is because a focus on process provides criteria for deciding which of a vast array of socio-cultural forms in a particular set-ting are relevant to the developmental-planning issue, and hence to the consultant's study. It also helps to gain the attention of other experts and planners who have little patience for lengthy ethnographic descriptions of a lineage, voluntary association, or ritual kinship, unless the purpose of the discussion is clear at the outset.

Editors' Note to Chapter 8

The history of cooperative organization in West Africa is a spotty one at best. Countless development projects have attempted to organize local cooperatives as a means of making credit available to smallholders, of increasing state capture of marketed crops, or for the rationalization of peasant production. Occasionally, as in the case described by Tom Painter, planners attempt to construct cooperatives on what they assume to be viable local social structures. The hope is that the resultant "fit" and function will be successful. Painter describes possible bases for cooperative organization in southwestern Niger where an agricultural development project was being planned, but argues that their promise was outweighed by an even larger obstacle to success. This is the combination of high risks and low returns in rainfed agricultural production, precisely the area of activity being promoted by the project. He argues, like Horowitz, that we must better understand local forms of cooperative action and the forces that affect and weaken them if they are to serve as foundations for cooperatives that will benefit local populations.

8

In Search of the Peasant Connection: Spontaneous Cooperation, Introduced Cooperatives, and Agricultural Development in Southwestern Niger

THOMAS M. PAINTER
Institute for Development Anthropology

During the fall of 1978, I was engaged briefly as a consulting sociologist with a World Bank appraisal mission in the Niger Republic. The Bank and the Government of Niger were in the final stages of preparing an agricultural development project, the Projet de Développement Rural du Département de Dosso (henceforth, the Dosso Project or simply, the Project), in the Dosso region of southwestern Niger (see Map, page 9), a project that was to be cofinanced by the Bank and the government for a period of five years beginning in 1979–1980. As the mission sociologist, I was asked to examine several issues, one of which was the potential for peasant participation in the Project's cooperative organizations.[1]

---

*Several people kindly agreed to read an earlier version of this paper and made many helpful suggestions for improvements. I wish to thank Dan Aronson, Stephen Baier, David Brokensha, Peter Easton, Michael Horowitz, Louise Lennihan, Thayer Scudder, Louise Sperling, and, in particular, John Collins, who made extensive comments. Finally, my thanks to Michael Painter for numerous editorial suggestions, and to Vera Beers for typing the many revisions this paper has undergone.

[1]Insofar as they might affect or be affected by the Dosso Project, the following points were examined: (a) the distribution of tasks between male and female members of the area's peasant households; (b) land ownership; (c) the sharing of land between herders and sedentary cultivators in the area; (d) differences in social structures between Hausa and Zarma villages; (e) participation by the area's producers in cooperative organizations; and (f) the impact of seasonal and permanent migrations out of the area. Only three weeks of field time in Niger were allotted for the investigation of these issues. Elaboration of the last point eventually led to an independently financed research project, currently under way (Painter 1980a).

The Dosso Project's program called for the gradual extension of agricultural credit to peasant producers in the project zone, through rural cooperatives. The organization of rural credit cooperatives was not new in the region: they had been promoted for some time, most recently by the Dosso Project's predecessor, the Dosso Productivity Project, which began in 1974.[2] Moreover, rural marketing and credit cooperatives had been promoted in Niger since the early 1960s by the government's credit and cooperative agency, the Union Nigérien de Crédit et de Coopération (UNCC).[3]

The Bank was particularly concerned that the region's peasant producers actively participate in the Project's credit cooperatives. Failure to participate would hinder diffusion of the improved production techniques being promoted by the Project. This, in turn, would jeopardize the Project's principal objective--widespread increases in levels of rain-fed agricultural production of millet, sorghum, and cowpeas. I became intrigued, therefore, by the possibilities of identifying spontaneous forms of cooperation among the peasantries of the Dosso region that offered promise as eventual links for the Project's desired cooperative forms. Implicit were the assumptions that such links would be conducive to a better sociocultural fit between spontaneous[4] (or traditional) and introduced (or modern) cooperative structures, and that they would encourage receptivity to the Project's efforts among the region's populations. In a sense, I was engaged in a hurried search for a "peasant connection."[5] Thus, I

----

[2] Cofinanced by the Government of Niger and the French *Fonds d'Aide et de Coopération* (FAC).

[3] Cooperatives initially were concentrated in the Maradi and Zinder departments in the south central part of Niger (Charlick 1974; Collins n.d., 1974, 1976), the most important groundnut producing area, and in places where cotton production was being promoted, such as in the Majya Valley (Raulin 1969). As late as 1977, some areas of the Dosso department remained without cooperative coverage of primary agricultural marketing activities (République du Niger/Banque Mondiale 1978 II:29). Niger's cooperatives, like those throughout francophone West Africa, were predated by the Sociétés de Prévoyance, introduced by the French colonial administration.

[4] This is Raulin's (1976) term. Of all the students of agrarian society in Niger, Raulin (1963; 1969; 1971; 1976) and Olivier de Sardan (1969; 1974; 1982) have given the greatest attention to indigenous forms of cooperation. Raulin (1969) has made the most detailed exploration of the links between indigenous and introduced forms of cooperation.

[5] Neither the term nor the idea is original, although they
(Footnote Continued)

set out to describe the nature of spontaneous (indigenous) forms
of cooperation, the character of the links--if any--already existing between spontaneous and introduced cooperatives in the
region, and to consider the potential for further linkages over
the course of the Project's first five-year phase.

SPONTANEOUS COOPERATION IN THE DOSSO REGION

Kin-Based Forms of Cooperation

Introduction. Kin ties provide one important basis for indigenous cooperation and mutual assistance in rural Niger. The
focal point of these cooperative relations is the peasant household, a term that will be used throughout this paper and will
subsume the more specific local forms found in southwestern
Niger, known among the region's hausaphone peoples as *gida* and
as *windi* among Zarma speakers. [6]
Intermediate to the more restricted household form and the
more encompassing lineage, there occurs a second kin-based frame
for cooperation. Among hausaphone peoples this is referred to as
gandu. Led by an elder male, a father or the eldest of several
brothers, *gandu* incorporates the heads of several conjugal units
linked to the leader by blood ties as sons or younger brothers.
These men and their immediate families, if they are married,
cooperate in relations of production and consumption vis-à-vis
land, which is inherited through the patrilineage and managed by
the elder member. Some of this land is cultivated by all active
household members, while some is allocated annually to individual
members of the families making up the larger unit. These individual fields are known as *gamana*. *Gandu* refers at once to a
social unit of residence, production, and consumption, and to the
communal fields that are the basis for the subsistence of its
constituent members. [7] In *gandu*, all active members work on

---

(Footnote Continued)
have been modified from their initial application (Agbonifo and
Cohen 1976).

[6]Very schematically, the term *gida* and its rough equivalent
among zarmaphone peoples, *windi*, refer both to a physically
delimited residential entity--a compound or concession--and to the
social unit comprising those who reside therein. In its simplest
form, the *gida* or *windi* is headed by a married male and occupied
by him, his wife or wives, and the children of his one or more
conjugal families (Hill 1972:243; Lateef 1975:408-409; Mainet and
Nicolas 1964:44-45; Raynaut 1972:34-36).

[7]See Wallace (1978) and Buntjer (1970), and the work of Hill
(1972), Nicolas (1971; 1974), and Raynaut (1972; 1976; 1977a)
concerning the diversity of productive relations to be found
within *gandu*.

communal fields a prescribed number of days each week during the growing season. Part of the production is consumed by the *gandu* head and his wife (or wives), their dependent children, and other members. Another portion is set aside in granaries belonging to the head for use as seed the following year, and as a hedge against the "hungry season" months immediately preceding the next harvest, when supplies are likely to be low. Finally, as the recipients of members' labor in *gandu*, the *gandu* head is responsible for paying taxes for all active members[8] and assisting with expenses when unmarried sons wed.

After completion of labor in *gandu* fields, household members work their individual (*gamana*) fields. Unlike *gandu* production, produce from *gamana* fields belongs to the individuals who work them. *Gamana* produce may be sold, and the resultant cash used for personal needs. *Gamana* production affords dependent members of joint family households a degree of economic independence they would not otherwise have, and provides the basis for further investment. Cash from the sale of *gamana* crops is an important factor in the acquisition of small livestock by women. For younger men, who may travel to the Guinea Coast countries for several months following the harvest season in Niger, proceeds from sales of *gamana* production may be used to pay for transportation or may constitute a source of capital for launching petty commerce.

In contrast to the organization of production among hausaphone people to the east, relatively less attention has been given to these features among zarmaphone peoples.[9] Nonetheless, a collective/individual distinction also occurs along the lines described above. Thus *windi koy fari* refers to fields managed by the household head and worked by all male members. The term *kourba* is applied to individual plots allocated to junior members of the household and dependents. However, the terminological parallel breaks down beyond the household level (*windi*), for there appears to be no specific Zarma term corresponding to the

---

[8]Niger's head tax (*impôt de capitation*), a continuation of taxes introduced early this century by the French colonial administration, was considerably reduced in 1977-1978. The remaining *"taxe d'arrondissement"* is also collected on a *per capita* basis.

[9]Until recently, very little research done in the area has accorded much importance to the basic features of the social organization of production. See, for example, Beauvilain (1977) and Diarra (1971:101-102). Literature based on research among zarmaphone groups elsewhere in western Niger shares this lack of attention to important details concerning the production and reproduction of local social structures. See Goldmark (1977)--a paper having Zarma land tenure as its central focus--Guillaume (1974), Lateef (1975), and Sidikou (1974:103-104, 115-120, 139-140). Cf. Painter (forthcoming:Chapter II) and Stier (1980).

Hausa *gandu* (Olivier de Sardan: personal communication). Organizationally, the distinction does occur and is of some significance, for produce from individual or *kourba* fields belongs to the individuals who work them.

Anthropologists who have done research among the Hausa and Zarma peoples of Niger describe a breakdown over time of these kin-based forms of organization. There has been described a concomitant gradual shift toward more restricted family forms, in which younger household heads enjoy greater decision-making autonomy and greater control over the allocation of the product than they would if they remained dependent members within a *gandu*-like framework (Arnould 1982:604; Olivier de Sardan 1984:249-253; Raynaut 1980:37-45). Finally, it is possible that the dissolution process is considerably more advanced among the Zarma than among the Hausa to the east, where kin structures[10] may have proven themselves to be more resilient.

Members of lineages and lineage segments frequently cooperate during times of need for a variety of purposes, the most important of which revolve around agricultural production. Within the lineage, kin loyalties may be invoked as a means of mobilizing assistance and labor; but the sense of obligation to respond to these requests is less than in the forms considered above. In many cases, lineage members reside in the same section of a village community. In smaller cultivation hamlets that have split from parent villages, what applies to a section of a larger village may hold true for the smaller community as a whole. These residential areas, occupied by members of a lineage plus their respective conjugal families, are referred to variously in the literature as "quarters" or "wards." Nigerien civil servants in the Dosso region refer to them as "traditional quarters."

These kin ties facilitate mutual assistance when, for example, the labor supplies of the immediate household prove inadequate. Such "labor bottleneck" periods occur when new fields are being cleared and prepared for cultivation, and particularly during crucial weeding operations that follow planting. In addition, mutual assistance from lineage members takes the form of help with house construction and repair, the preparation of irrigated gardens, and, where the conditions permit, cash loans (cf. De Latour Dejean 1980:118).

---

[10]This possibility has been suggested by Olivier de Sardan (personal communication), and may be amplified somewhat by further consideration of the relative historical consequences for Hausa and zarmaphone peoples of colonial conquest, education, and their participation in the developing Guinea Coast/hinterland regional economy. Whereas zarmaphone peoples have long been involved in patterns of seasonal migrations to the Guinea Coast, the economy of hausaphone peoples to the east was marked less by migrations than by the production of agricultural cash crops (groundnuts) for export. See Fuglestad (1974:21-24), and Higgott and Fuglestad (1975:384-385).

Infrequently a village-wide phenomenon, these forms of intravillage cooperation are based on claims of mutual assistance having considerable strength. Thus, they are likely to be singled out by planners and sociologists as a possible basis for the introduction of new cooperative structures.

Observations in Dosso. During the course of early discussions and interviews with government staff involved in the Dosso Productivity Project, I was told of a widespread coincidence within the Productivity Project zone between membership in village quarter-based lineages and voluntary membership in local production groups (Groupes Mutualistes de Production, or GMPs) introduced by the Productivity Project during the period 1974-1978. The production groups were introduced to facilitate the systematic application and evaluation of the Productivity Project's extension themes as they were used by persons in the Project zone.[11]   We were assured by a member of the Dosso UNCC staff that the Productivity Project's GMPs invariably consisted of males sharing lineage ties and living in the same village quarter. The claim was significant because it held out the possibility that cooperative structures promoted by the government were linked to indigenous forms of cooperation in a manner without parallel in the history of cooperative promotion in Niger.

My reaction was mixed. I was initially encouraged by the imputed linkage, but was also skeptical of the claim. My skepticism was based on several years of personal experience with marketing and credit cooperatives in the south central (Maradi) region of Niger as well as on my familiarity with the available literature. There appeared to be no particular method behind the connection described by the UNCC representative, nor was there any apparent assurance that the connection could be reproduced in the future. My misgivings were reinforced by the impression during subsequent interviews that, although the connection was abundantly clear to UNCC personnel, it was considerably less apparent to other government staff concerned with the Productivity Project's operations. My subsequent efforts to clarify the

---

[11]These were not cooperative production groups per se, but loose conglomerations of peasants who volunteered to try out the Productivity Project's extension themes on borrowed plots, whose dimensions were predetermined by Project requirements of ease of application. For example, recommendations for fertilizer use were expressed in kilograms per surface area measured in square meters or portions of a hectare. Given the irregular size of most peasant fields, calculations would have been rather complicated; hence, "rationalized" i.e., rectangular, fields were introduced. Despite the use of signed "contracts" to insure access of land users to borrowed land during the two-year participation cycle required by the program, there were several cases of owners reclaiming their well-fertilized land after the first year. Similar problems occurred in the Dosso region during the Dallol Maouri Project, almost a decade earlier (FAO/UNDP 1968:iii).

issue during visits to two villages did little to help.   In one village, GMP members were also members of residentially proximate patrilineages.   In the other, no relation between the two networks was apparent.

The available evidence did not permit any firm conclusions or recommendations about the predominance or strength of the kinship connections described by UNCC, and further investigation was needed.   However, no local inclination to study the problem was evident, and consideration by the World Bank for pertinent research was limited to plans (eventually scrapped) to provide for sociological follow-up once the Project was under way.   The kind of information that would have been extremely useful as a point of departure for further study during the appraisal mission would not be available until sometime after the beginning of the Dosso Project, if at all.

The early implementation stages of the Dosso Project were destined to suffer from several sociological blind spots of the sort that characterize many rural development projects in West Africa (cf. World Bank 1978b).   The low priority accorded to sociological issues during the early phases of Dosso Project planning was reflected in preliminary documentation prepared by the World Bank and the Niger government prior to our visit to the Dosso region (République du Niger/Banque Mondiale 1978).   Despite its lengthy, two-volume format, the report on the Dosso region prepared by an earlier World Bank mission limited its consideration of the issues discussed above to a few lines.

Discussion.   Numerous questions persisted concerning the nature and incidence of the connections between spontaneous and introduced forms of cooperation.   Without further and more closely focused investigation, the potential for forming viable linkages between spontaneous forms of cooperation and cooperatives for the diffusion and use of credit and innovative production techniques would remain unclear.

A second point is of particular relevance to those who may be inclined to see in kin-based forms of cooperation a convenient basis for the superimposition of cooperative structures for "development."   Descriptions of rural society in Niger repeatedly emphasize the growth of individualism within traditional corporate social structures and at their expense.   For example, the decline of *gandu* among the Hausa has received particular attention, but remarks of this kind are sweeping enough to include forms of productive organization in the zarmaphone areas of the Dosso region as well.[12]   An increasing orientation toward a cash economy figures importantly in explanations for the demise of

---

[12]See, for example, the work of Arnould (1982:350); Nicolas (1969; 1971), Olivier de Sardan (1969; 1974), Raulin (1963:108), and Raynaut (1975; 1976; 1977a; 1977b).   The materials cited here give greatest attention to sedentary peasant cultivators. The considerable literature on Niger's pastoral groups has been omitted.

cooperation in rural Nigerien society. These changes may seem very modest when compared to those one sees, for example, in the cocoa-producing areas of Ghana or the plantation zones of Ivory Coast; but, they are significant nonetheless, and promise to seriously compromise the appropriateness of indigenous structures as foundations for the introduction of development cooperatives. Traditional social structures in rural Niger are not merely "traditional," they are transitional, and must be recognized as such (Bernstein 1977; Goddard 1973; Nicolas 1971; Stavenhagen 1975). Because they are dealing with transitional structures, development project planners need to be somewhat circumspect in their plans to construct "modern" forms of cooperative organization upon indigenous structures, however convenient they may appear.

In retrospect, the potential for difficulties of a state-sponsored development strategy that stresses links between lineage-based and introduced forms of cooperative organization merits careful consideration. The problem resides in the possibility for contradictions arising between goals of enhancing general access to credit and improved production techniques within village communities, and reinforcing highly selective access due to an emphasis on lineages as favored indigenous structures. It may be argued that reliance on lineage structures in this manner contains much the same--if not greater--potential for selective consolidation and accumulation as occurred during earlier phases of agricultural development in Niger, when emphasis was given to equipping handpicked individual ("progressive") farmers. In both cases the possibilities for benefits accruing selectively to some elements within the community at the expense of lineages or lineage segments having more limited resources is considerable. The result of this strategy, with its obvious appeal to those sensitive to considerations of sociocultural fit, may exacerbate rather than diminish processes of economic differentiation in the Dosso region.

Non-Kin-Based Cooperation

Introduction. Indigenous cooperation having no necessary basis in kinship takes a variety of forms in rural and urban areas of West Africa (Ames 1959; Kerr 1978; Little 1957; Moore 1973; Remy 1967; Sénéchal 1973; Wallerstein 1964). They are referred to in the literature variously as mutual assistance, mutual aid, labor exchange, or collective labor groups or associations. They provide an important source of nonwage labor in rural West Africa, most frequently manifesting themselves locally as work parties.[13] They are referred to in the Dosso region of Niger as *bogu* among the Zarma and and *gaya* among hausaphone peoples.

---

[13]For variations within each category see Beauvilain (1977: 138-139), FAO/UNDP (1967:43; 1968:129), Goldmark (1977:7), and
(Footnote Continued)

The historical origins of these mutual assistance associations in Niger are a topic of debate. At least one observer suggests that their contemporary form may be linked to initiation groups that considerably predate the arrival of Islam in the area (Raulin 1963:64, 68; 1971:326-327). These initiation groups, often termed age-classes, were originally cohorts of village youth of roughly similar ages that had a sense of membership and affiliation based on the shared experience of circumcision. The sense of membership was occasionally reinforced among cohort members by sharing a common name, a leader, taboos, and, occasionally, a secret language (Hama 1967:220-222). The extent to which age-grade members identify with peers, the duration of their identification, and their participation in activities based on age-grade membership varies considerably in West Africa.

On the basis of what little we know, we may tentatively suggest that the intensity of a sense of shared membership felt by cohort members in Niger is considerably less than one would expect to find, for example, in the *ton* of the Bambara in Mali (Hama 1967:221; Lewis 1978:41-42; Leynaud 1966). The transition of the individual from the status of youth to that of adult does not appear to be very eventful in the peasant formations in southwestern Niger (Raulin 1971:320-321).

The lack of emphasis on these life passages results in age being much less important as an organizing principle than elsewhere in sudano-sahelian West Africa (cf. Rouch 1954:39). Age may serve as a general organizing principle, but it is most important because it signifies de facto membership in the ascribed status of youth, which is separated from adult status through subservient and deferent behavior that reinforces boundary markers (Raulin 1971:332). Age may have been a more important organizing principle in the past. Raulin (1963:75) argues that the role of the age-grade as a framework for the mobilization of labor in rural Niger has declined historically as the overall importance of mobilizing labor supplies--whatever the basis--has increased.

This is not to suggest that village youth and young men do not constitute a social category that plays an important role in rural social life. Each village has a youth leader (*sarkin samari*) whose task has long been to mobilize the labor resources of local youth for a variety of goals. This amorphous structure has repeatedly been used for state ends since the early 1960s.

Mutual Assistance in the Dosso Region. Extra-kin forms of cooperation occur in the Dosso region and provide a valuable source of labor for those who are able to sponsor them, but little is known concerning their incidence. Once mobilized, labor organized on the basis of non-kin relations is utilized for purposes similar to those we have seen in connection with kin-based

---

(Footnote Continued)
Lateef (1975:403). Of particular merit are the descriptions by Guillaume (1974:65-73), Olivier de Sardan (1969:121-135; 1974:14-17; 1982), and Raulin (1963:69-71).

cooperation: agricultural tasks, house-building, and, less frequently, such communal activities as well-digging.[14] Most non-
kin labor parties are short-lived, rarely lasting more than one
day.

In principle, cash is not the form of remuneration given to
gaya and *bogu* participants, a characteristic that serves to distinguish further these forms from the Bambara *ton*. Food, tobacco,
and cola nuts generally are provided by sponsors. In addition,
among some of the Zarma Songhay-speaking groups of Western
Niger, entertainment and vocal encouragement to spur the workers may be provided by praise singers or young women from the
village. Besides receiving sustenance during the day's labor,
work party participants gain, at least in principle, the right to
claim the sponsor's labor in time of future need. Thus, sponsors
incur the obligation of providing labor when participants organize
work parties of their own; hence the saying, "Today's employer
may be tomorrow's laborer" (Raulin 1971:336).

Hill (1972:251) reports that, in northwestern Nigeria, sponsors may pay participants in cash at a level well below the going
agricultural wage rate. The incidence of this practice in Niger is
not known, although cases have been reported by some observers, and we should not be surprised to discover it in the Dosso
region. More than twenty years ago, in the south central region
of Niger (Maradi), Mainet and Nicolas (1964:112) described a
situation in which groups of villagers worked in individuals' fields
for a fixed sum of 100 CFA francs per day, a practice they interpreted as displacing extra-kin forms of cooperation.[15] If this
tendency continues, it entails more than the replacement of nonwage labor. It involves the fundamental transformation of a
long-standing, normative social relation of production in rural
Niger. On the one hand, the sponsor must now produce cash
payments for field work; on the other, he is finally freed of all
the reciprocal labor demands that constituted this form of mutual
assistance. Tendencies of this kind in the Dosso region are not
known. But there is reason to believe such changes are more
advanced in southwestern Niger than elsewhere, and we may
anticipate that their tempo, specific forms, and consequences will
vary (Beauvilain 1977:138-139).[16] With the exception of studies

---

[14]Once again, there is substantial variation. This reflects
adaptations to geographical and climatic factors as well as the
astuteness of the observers who record the variations (cf. Lateef
1975:403; Olivier de Sardan 1969:124-126, 1982:74-75; Raulin
1969:11).

[15]Currently the daily wage rate for agricultural laborers in
the Dosso region varies from 750 to 1,000 CFA francs ($1 =
approximately 300 CFA francs).

[16]This is particularly likely in low-lying areas (*bas-fonds*),
(Footnote Continued)

by Beauvilain (1977) and Guillaume (1974), agrarian change of this type has received little attention in southwestern Niger.

Schematically, collective labor forms in southwestern Niger may be distinguished on the basis of the degree of obligation involved in the labor exchange and the degree of locally perceived social equality between sponsors and workers (De Latour Dejean 1980:118; Olivier de Sardan 1969:129 ff., passim). Using this distinction, whose basis is found in the concepts used by Niger's peasantries as well as those who study them (Olivier de Sardan 1982; Raulin 1963:68; 1971:335-336), we may briefly inventory dominant forms of mutual assistance that entail the organization of labor.

Where obligation and inequality are important, variations on two themes are common. First, agricultural labor is mobilized among younger members of the village community (males in particular) for the benefit of older members (Olivier de Sardan 1974:15-16). Second, commoners' labor is mobilized for those of higher rank. In both cases, labor is appropriated by those who occupy a higher status in the village.

An example of the first theme entails the mobilization of friends' labor by young fiancés in order to work the fields of prospective or actual fathers-in-law, an obligation that may continue for several years after marriage (FAO/UNDP 1967:44; Guillaume 1974:73; Olivier de Sardan 1969:129; 1974:15-16; 1982). The second, perhaps more widely known, involves the irregular and village-wide mobilization of labor for purposes of completing various tasks for the benefit of the village chiefs, local nobles, and/or the state (Guillaume 1974:65-67; Raulin 1971:335; FAO/UNDP 1968:97).

This second form of labor mobilization has been used to good advantage in the past by those wielding power in West Africa. The extraction of labor prestations was a common occurrence during the precolonial period. Much more severe forms of *corvée* were introduced by the French colonial regime, which used them extensively to promote administrative penetration of rural areas of the colonial territory (Fuglestad 1974; Higgott and Fuglestad 1975:384; Olivier de Sardan 1984:167-172; Painter forthcoming: Chapter XI; Rothiot 1984:298-316; Spittler 1977). Village chiefs and the *chefs de canton*, whose position was created by the colonial administration, were called upon to provide quotas of men for constructing and maintaining buildings, roads, landing strips, telegraph lines, and other public works, and to ensure that villagers cultivated the commandant's field. With Niger's independence, the colonial regime ended, but state mobilization of village labor for infrastructural purposes did not. *Investissement*

(Footnote Continued)
where water tables are shallower, making possible the year-round production of irrigated crops (vegetables, manioc, fruit trees, sugar cane, etc.) for sale as well as local consumption. See De Latour Dejean (1975; 1980) and FAO/UNDP (1968:129).

humaine replaced the labor prestations. The political party's[17] field, which villagers were required to work, replaced the commandant's field. Villagers also were required to construct lodgings for visiting Party and government dignitaries (Raulin 1971:335). In addition, the Party promoted youth organizations for purposes of political socialization and labor mobilization. Thus, with independence came a major attempt to use the traditional youth organization, the *samaria*, for state purposes (Raulin 1971:324, 339-340). Since the 1974 *coup d'état*, the *samaria* has once more been given great attention by the government for similar reasons. This emphasis has continued to increase since the late 1970s with government promotion of the populist Development Society.

Mutual assistance in which obligation plays a relatively minor role and reciprocity among social equals prevails is found in non-kin-based cooperation organized by persons other than chiefs, nobles, elders, or the state. While this distinction is admittedly relative, it is widely recognized among the peasant populations of southwestern Niger, who distinguish between reciprocal help between unequals and mutual assistance between equals (Raulin 1963:68).

Under the conditions of relative peer equality, age-grades may once have figured importantly in the organization of collective labor, but their present significance in Niger is negligible. The suggestion that indigenous forms of cooperation in Niger are in transition, and that the importance of age-grades has declined substantially as a basis for local labor mobilization, comes from Raulin, who stresses that the form, if not the organizing principle, of age-class collective labor has been gradually adopted by heads of households who are increasingly deprived of the domestic labor supplies formerly made available within the extended family household (1963:75-76). This deprivation, in turn, stems from the long-term erosion of the size of *gandu* and the equivalent form among the Zarma, as younger males break away from the larger unit to establish their own independent households.

In principle, household heads are able to compensate for inadequate domestic labor supplies by sponsoring labor parties whose origin may be found in age-class membership. In practice, the capacity of persons in need of labor to mobilize the resources necessary to sponsor labor parties in a timely fashion may vary greatly (Painter forthcoming: Chapter II). Households having the resources to sponsor work parties are in a position to appropriate the labor of other community members when needed. Through the mechanisms of the work party, sponsors are able to retain the nonwage features of kin-based labor, while drawing from labor sources beyond the confines of the household. The issue of relative efficiency and costliness in relation to wage labor for the

---

[17]The *Parti Progressiste Nigérien*, the local branch of the *Rassemblement Démocratique Africain*, or PPN-RDA, defunct since the military coup d'état of April 1974.

completion of comparable tasks is the subject of ongoing debate among the region's peasants and those who study them (Beauvilain 1977:138; FAO/UNDP 1967:43; 1968:129; Raulin 1971:336).

Discussion. What was once a form of labor mobilization whose access was relatively equally distributed among members of age-classes thanks to shared perceptions of membership, attendant obligations, and the value of mutual assistance, has become increasingly selective. It operates disproportionately to benefit only those villagers whose wealth enables them to translate labor needs into labor sponsorship. In principle, any community member may sponsor and benefit from a nonwage labor party. In practice, the capacity of members to benefit varies greatly. While household heads may be able to count on the unremunerated labor of their wives and daughters to prepare and deliver food supplies to their labor party workers, household size and the adequacy of household grain supplies necessary for food preparation differ considerably within rural communities. This factor becomes especially critical during the cultivation season, when the previous year's harvest reserves are likely to be low or exhausted. Household capacities to mobilize the sums of cash needed to buy kola nuts, tobacco, and other items supplied to workers are also at their lowest during the cultivation period. The principle of reciprocal labor exchange persists as ideology and is no doubt highly valued by peasants in the Dosso region, but the realities of incidence and accessibility may be discrepant with values. Closer examination may reveal that more is involved in the activation of these forms of mutual assistance than principles of rural reciprocity and cooperation. It should not surprise us to discover that, however accessible these forms of labor mobilization may appear within the village community, they are not equally available to all.[18]

The preceding remarks are made in retrospect. At the time of my trip to Dosso, I concluded that non-kin-based forms of cooperation might lend themselves to the "construction of cooperative production structures," and that there was "no reason a priori other than considerations of stability for one indigenous structure to be favored over another" (Painter 1979:2).

Further consideration of the issues leads to greater caution. The peasant connection is clearly more complex and less easily amenable to the requirements of agricultural development programs than I initially imagined. It is difficult to disagree with the position that local forms should be buttressed where possible as a means of providing the peasantry with added leverage in relation to the development process and to state and international

---

[18]Aside from casual observation, this issue to my knowledge has not been investigated in the Dosso region. Evidence of unequal access to institutions of mutual assistance is available from the eastern and northeastern regions of Burkina Faso (Remy 1967:62; Sénéchal 1973:262-268). De Latour Dejean (1980:118) mentions the question with regard to Niger.

development planners who mediate and attempt to redirect the process through planning and projects.[19] The task of social scientists who study, and endeavor to grapple with the development process through discrete projects and programs, is to pursue a better understanding of these local forms, the processes of change that affect them, and their responses--be these strategies of adaptation or resistance. Only then will we be minimally equipped to enter areas like the Dosso region of Niger and seek to use peasant social institutions for purposes of development.

PARTICIPATION OF PEASANT PRODUCERS IN COOPERATIVES

Peasant Risk-Taking and Rural Cooperatives

What little systematic evidence we have suggests that peasant participation in cooperatives depends on whether introduced cooperative organizations are objectively beneficial to members as actors within larger domestic units, and on whether members subjectively define them as beneficial.

Objectively speaking, the performance record of rural cooperatives, in Niger and throughout much of Africa, in these respects has generally been disappointing.[20] Minimally, state-sponsored cooperatives should help to reduce risks faced by peasants who are continually encouraged by development planners to innovate in rain-fed agricultural production. In general, we can say that the rural credit and marketing cooperatives that have been introduced in Niger since the early 1960s have not satisfied this minimal requirement.

State-sponsored agricultural development programs that channel peasant access to credit through locally organized cooperatives in Niger have frequently been characterized by a lack of flexibility. State loan reimbursement schedules, arranged on a yearly payment basis, rarely make routine allowances for the likelihood that substantial variations in the conditions of production will affect harvests, resultant rural incomes, and hence, the capacity to reimburse. When allowances are made, they as often as not reflect very serious circumstances, in which reimbursement by

---

[19]This is Belloncle's argument *contra* Meister (1966; 1977). See Belloncle and Gentil (1968:1) and Belloncle (1978; 1979). For a critical response to Belloncle's perspective, see Painter (1981).

[20]For Niger, see Bachard (1976), Charlick (1972; 1974), Nicolas (1971), and Painter (1980c:17-21). For an overview of cooperative programs in several sahelian states, see Derman (1980). For an evaluation of programs elsewhere in Africa, see Apthorpe (1972) and UNRISD (1975:45-51). See also Apthorpe (1977) and Saul (1971), plus relevant essays in Nash, et al., eds. (1976).

through captives, slaves, hired shepherds--in stratified societies. An index of the transition from domestic to capitalist modes of production among herders today is the recurrent discovery of permanent pauperization of those whose herds fall below minimal recovery levels, and the consequent emergence of herding proletarians in what were formerly egalitarian societies (Horowitz et al. 1983; White 1984).

10. On dry rangelands, pastoral production systems converting natural forage into produce suitable for human consumption tend to be more efficient and more environmentally sound than either ranging or rainfed cultivation.

11. While there is considerable agreement that pastoral systems were adaptive in the past, there is concern that their adaptiveness is threatened by a variety of recent changes, in addition to possible secular climatic changes and government controls over cross-frontier movements, including:

11.1 human population growth (although most of the data indicate slower growth rates for pastoral than for neighboring sedentary peoples);

11.2 herd growth, due to veterinary interventions (although because of the recency of reliable censuses for pastoral livestock, it is difficult to document this growth precisely or convincingly);

11.3 new watering points, drilled by governments, for which conventional use agreements do not apply (the Niger government, for example, allows no constraints on access to water from deep bore holes);

11.4 the movement of agriculture--both rainfed and irrigated--into formerly pastoral regions.

From the above characteristics and propositions about pastoral production systems, plus the agreement that pastoral sector interventions, other than purely veterinary (Horowitz 1983), have been singularly unsuccessful, one is led to a conclusion: *interventions that seriously affect mobility and/or threaten the ability of the herd to support optimum numbers of persons will be resisted by pastoralists and will result in failed or at best poor projects.*

Several caveats must be added to the argument outlined above:

(1) I am not claiming that dry rangelands are not degrading nor that herders do not contribute to such degradation as may exist. My position is merely that neither the degradation nor the herders' role in it has been so persuasively demonstrated as to justify interventions that seek radically to modify pastoral practice against the will of the majority of livestock holders.

(2) I make no claim that pastoral production systems as they currently operate maximize the productive potential of dry rangelands, only that the systems that have been proposed or are operating in projects with which I am familiar are either less productive over the long run and more degrading of the environment, or they impose risks on the herders that are incommensurate with the possible gains.

(3) Finally, I am not asserting that pastoralists' interests in their production systems or their habitats must take precedence over all competing claims. I appreciate that states may have priority interests, and rangelands may be transformed into fields for irrigated agriculture or merely to serve as military installations. I object to masking these priorities in a rhetoric that pretends to benefit the pastoral users.

Research Needs

There is universal agreement that development efforts in the pastoral livestock sector have done poorly at best, and there is often a call for "more research." Yet herein lies a dilemma. When the rush is on to do *something*, to respond, for example, to an environmental crisis or to famine, there is plenty of money but little receptivity to investing any serious amount in critically examining the assumptions that inform action. Are rangelands deteriorating? Is pastoral practice responsible for that deterioration (i.e., is the desert the son of the Bedouin)? Are the proposed interventions—such as reducing stocking levels by increasing offtake; improving pasture by substituting private for communal ownership; settling nomads—appropriate?

To suggest during times of crisis that what is needed is intensive, long-term study by persons knowledgeable about pastoralism and comfortable in the local language, almost invariably engenders the response from planners that "We haven't the time," or "These people have been 'studied to death.'" When the crisis ebbs, and donor attention shifts to other sectors and subsectors, it should be possible to undertake serious and longterm research. But the necessary donor interest—and therefore funding—is then no longer present. It is little wonder that the same old—and failed—projects are dusted off with but a veneer of rhetorical updating to respond to the next crisis.

In the unwillingness to examine the realities of pastoral production systems, and to test the effects of alternative interventions, we assure continued project failure. As Sandford says, "I believe that governments should try to discover pastoralists' objectives, not only on moral grounds, but because failure to take such objectives into account in pastoral development programs in the past has led to the failure of those programs also in terms of the government's objectives" (1983:22). Knowing what herders do and, more importantly, why they do it is not easy. The typical "quick and dirty" study (more elegantly but inaccurately labeled "rapid rural appraisal"), carried out in a late design stage of project planning and rarely based on intimate prior knowledge of the area, leads to understandings skewed to the specific time and place in which it was made. This then misrepresents the dynamism and opportunism of the pastoral production system, which, adapted to a fluctuating environment, contains enormous variations in the number of animals that are herded at any one time, their species and demographic composition, the ease, frequency, and location of movement, the number of persons directly sustained on herd produce, and so on. We do have one contrary case demonstrating that sound socio-economic and ecological understandings are necessary but not sufficient conditions for sound development.   Also necessary is the political willingness of governments to share decision-making with the local populations.

Despite an initial reluctance and intermittent impatience while waiting for "action," the Government of Niger showed considerable wisdom in agreeing to a delay of full-scale livestock project implementation in a vast region of the Sahel until an integrated multi-year study of the socioeconomics and ecology of pastoral herding could be undertaken.   The U.S. Agency for International Development supported the study, in a desire to predicate its interventions on a solid base of knowledge.   The reports, which have recently been assembled in complete form (Swift, ed. 1984), provide an excellent set of insights and understandings about this complex region involving two culturally and linguistically distinct pastoral peoples: Twareg and WoDaaBe.   The optic of AID's Niger Range and Livestock Project (AID-NRL) was exactly the reverse of the World Bank's project of the same name.   Rather than attempting to impose an organizational structure on the herders, AID-NRL spent considerable field effort in identifying what the existing structures are and what are their capacities to serve as vehicles for development interventions.   Clearly not identified by the study were traditional units that in any way approximated Pastoral Associations as envisaged by the World Bank.   On the contrary,

> the basic resource-managing unit above the household level is a camp composed of from one or two to 10 or 20 households, rarely more, which makes up a population ranging from approximately 10 to 100 people.   The composition of these camps varies from season to season or according to herding decisions taken individually by each household, so camps are not stable units.   At a higher structural level, migratory groups, lineages and tribes meet a variety of important social organizational requirements, but these structures are unadapted to the needs of modern government and the administration of a development program.   Some aspects of traditional tribal organization, for example the Twareg class structure, retain potentially exploitive elements inappropriate to a modern democratic country concerned with equitable and participatory development (ibid.:703).

The AID-NRL project final report concludes that there are no easy ways of implementing large-scale development in the pastoral zone, especially interventions dealing with animal production and range management.   One can sympathize with the reluctance of a host government or donor agency to accept such conclusions. But AID-NRL did not stop there.   Instead of imposing top-down actions on unwilling herders, project management sought to elaborate actions that emerged from herders' own interests and priorities and that could not be readily captured by local elites.   The herders' concerns proved to be something of a surprise for those who felt they would request new watering points as their greatest need.   Initially, herd reconstitution, reflecting substantial losses from the 1968–1974 drought, was the first priority. Secondly they wanted year-round access to grain at reasonable prices. And thirdly they wanted local people trained as para-medical and para-veterinary workers. (By 1981, according to Albert Sollud, the herders priorities became, first, access to grain, second, access to credit for any purpose, and third, access to good pasture.) "It was agreed that no attempt would be made to define boundaries within which pastoral groups would have exclusive grazing rights, or to place any potential limitation on herder movement" (ibid.:709). Herder associations were established with memberships of from 15 to 30 families, or from 100 to 200 persons, and membership was entirely voluntary; an individual was free to resign at any time after settling his debts with the group.

A major finding of the research was the large number of persons in pastoral communities who did not own sufficient animals to sustain them as independent herders and were forced to find alternative livelihoods, mainly as hired shepherds. The old redistributive mechanisms no longer operated to allow persons who lost their animals to rebuild, because ownership of large herds had shifted to merchants, civil servants, and large farmers with whom herders do not share a moral community, or, among Twareg, to important and powerful persons who increasingly identified their destinies with national elites rather than with their own ethnic groups.

While socioeconomic studies and organizational interventions were the centerpieces of AID-NRL, some important animal production and range management findings were also made. The ecology team discovered that moderate grazing in the early rainy season, which is in fact the practice of Nigerien pastoralists, provides for greater residual moisture, a "soil moisture reserve," than does the lighter grazing pressure often recommended by pasture management specialists. "Increased soil moisture at the end of the rainy season affects the quality of the vegetation by decreasing percent dry matter, extending the 'green feed' period, and by increasing perennial regrowth, thus possibly allowing additional animal gains" (ibid.:758). The ecologists discovered that many pastures are actually *under*utilized, and recommended harvesting those grasses for hay and silage to provide high protein feed supplements in the dry season.

AID-NRL sought to increase producer income and to achieve its more equitable distribution. According to the AID Audit Report of February 1985 the Niger Government did not share USAID's emphasis on focusing the successor project, now called Niger Integrated Livestock Production (ILP), on those herders most severely affected by the earlier drought. "During implementation, the associations were selected on a geographical basis, thereby helping all herders. However, due to lack of data about the Tuareg people, most of the project was designed around the poorer WoDaaBe" (AID 1985:5). The auditor seemed especially to fault the notion of *communal* herds, from which indigent WoDaaBe could borrow stock to reconstitute their individual holdings, although in fact NRL was not inclined toward WoDaaBe. Twareg formed more than half of the project herder associations, and USAID/Niamey vigorously objected to the auditor's implication that the project was biased toward the poorer of the poor.   "The Project most emphatically was not designed around the poorer WoDaaBe," protested the USAID mission (USAID cable to AID Washington 1 April 1985).   The auditor challenged what he felt was an undue attention paid to the poor, rather than to the Twareg, "whose caste system promotes the welfare of the wealthy" (ibid.:6).   In a vein similar to that of the auditor, ILP Animal production advisor Gregory Perrier objects to the provisioning of credit to poor producer families because that delays their departure from pastoralism into the wage sector of the national economy.   Such a transition, Perrier feels, is economically and environmentally desirable (1985:1-5).   How far we have come from the New Directions!

ILP itself ground to a near halt with the massive drought of 1984, as herders and animals fled the region. There is clear indication when the project resumes that it will ignore major findings of AID-NRL, and attempt a more conventional tilt to production per se.   Having shown an initial courage in carrying out the study, the Niger Government appears to be shying away from its implications, that the best way to proceed with livestock sector actions is to vest major decision-making with the herders themselves.   If this project fails to meet its objectives, it will not be for want of data and analysis but for systematically ignoring them.   Despite the trenchant and empirically well-supported conclusions of the AID-NRL project from both social and biological scientists favoring continuation of established patterns of range use, the Government of Niger, in 1983, officially proclaimed a policy "limiting the movements of nomadic peoples," and achieving thereby "the end of nomadism in Niger" (Bernus et al 1983:82). An officially-sponsored conference on livestock development in Tahoua, Niger, in April 1985 called for an end to what it contemptuously termed *"l'élevage contemplatif,"* and called for the shift of mobile herders to a more sedentarized agro-pastoral economy.   If the state enforces this policy, the predictable consequences will be reduced   productivity, increased environmental degradation, and marked declines in the income and well-being of herding peoples.   Ancient ideologies with contemporary updates continue to guide policy and praxis in Niger.

CONCLUSION

It is not easy to assess the influence of social anthropology and sociology on development in West African pastoral production systems.   While the blatant anti-nomad rhetoric characteristic of project documents during the 1960s and 1970s has moderated somewhat in the 1980s, while all major donor organizations employ social science consultants on their design and evaluation teams, and while a handful of African social scientists have entered the development bureaucracies of their own countries, there is still no evidence that "people," in Michael Cernea's terms (1984), "are put first."   That is, in the case of livestock sector projects, implementation continues to exclude genuine participation by pastoralists.   The apparent inability of AID's Niger Range and

Livestock project, which focused squarely on aiding herders in their own terms, to influence the Government of Niger's position in the successor Integrated Livestock Project, is not a good omen. While continuing some of the research program of AID-NRL, and providing modest support to the Livestock Service, ILP has not been able to maintain its predecessor's organizational emphasis or to overcome an official rhetoric hostile to herders. It is perhaps too soon to make any final judgment on these issues, however, because the horrendous drought of 1984 denuded the project zone of both people and animals, and with rains just returning in July-August 1985, full project activities were only then resuming.

It is also perhaps unfair to expect social scientists to compensate for the near total lack of viable technical interventions capable of improving production in semiarid rangelands. "Over the 1965-80 period, it is estimated that donors channeled around $600 million into livestock projects in Africa. It is now clear that foreign aid was far ahead of the basic science and applied research base" (Eicher 1985:31). Apart from veterinary actions, which are often--though not invariably--appreciated by herders, none of the range management, hydrologic, genetic, and marketing (including feedlots, improved cattle trails, creameries, and slaughterhouses) interventions has measurably increased production, enhanced producer income, or retarded environmental degradation. The technical package to produce any of these results at economically feasible levels, let alone all of them, remains elusive. Such measures as could be applied, such as protecting pastoral land rights or providing credit to smallholders, have little support among either donors or host governments.

In addition to the lack of sensible technical interventions and the unwillingness of governments to empower the majority of pastoral herders, we are seeing today a broad retreat from the intent of the McNamara Doctrine and the Congressional New Directions--without legislative authorization--and in their place a reliance on the claimed salutary effects of a "free" market and an unrestrained "private" sector. If by "private sector" was meant pastoral and agricultural smallholders, the new rhetoric would indeed confirm the social science perspective that has emerged over the last decade of work in West Africa and the Sahel: to utilize the power of the state to *assist* smallholders in increasing both their productivity and income. What unfortunately appears to be the case is that the new rhetoric may favor actions with contrary results, rendering smallholders less and less able to pursue satisfactory lives in their own countries and on their own lands.

References Cited

References Cited

Adegboye, Rufus O., Edward Hirabayashi, Wilfred Owen, Jr., Babatunde Thomas, and Dennis M. Warren
1974 A Model for Active Indigenous Involvement in Rural Development and Nonformal Education. Document prepared for Special Roundtable, 14th World Conference, Society for International Development, Abidjan, Ivory Coast, August 13.

Ademuwagun, Z.A., John A.A. Ayoade, Ira E. Harrison, and Dennis M. Warren, eds.
1979 African Therapeutic Systems. Waltham, MA: Crossroads Press.

Agbonifo, Peter and Ronald Cohen
1976 The Peasant Connection: A Case Study of the Bureaucracy of Agri-Industry. Human Organization 35(4): 367-379.

AID   See United States. Agency for International Development and USAID

Almy, Susan
1977 Anthropologists and Development Agencies. American Anthropologist 79(2):280-292.

Althusser, Louis and Etienne Balibar
1970 Reading Capital. London: New Left Books.

Alverson, Hoyt
1977 Peace Corps Volunteers in Rural Botswana. Human Organization 36(3):274-281.

Ames, David W.
1959 Wolof Co-operative Work Groups. In Continuity and Change in African Cultures. William R. Bascom and Melville J. Herskovits, eds. Pp. 224-237. Chicago: University of Chicago Press.

Amin, Samir
1967 Le Développement du capitalisme en Côte d'Ivoire. Paris: Editions de Minuit.

1976 Unequal Development. New York: Monthly Review Press.

Ancey, Gérard
1977   Variation Mossi sur le thème: reproduction de milieux ruraux mis en contact avec le système capitaliste extérieur. *In* Essais sur la reproduction de formations sociales dominées (Cameroun, Côte d'Ivoire, Haute Volta, Sénégal, Madagascar, Polynésie). Travaux et Documents de l'ORSTOM, No. 64. Pp. 1-13. Paris: Office de la Recherche Scientifique et Technique Outre-Mer.

Anthropology Newsletter
1980   Institute for Development Anthropology: Social Equity Must Be Part of Development. Anthropology Newsletter 21:4-5.

Apthorpe, Raymond
1972   Rural Cooperatives and Planned Change in Africa: An Analytical Overview. Geneva: United Nations Research Institute for Social Development.

1977   The Cooperatives' Poor Harvest. The New Internationalist 48:4-6.

Arensberg, Conrad and Arthur Niehoff
1964   Introducing Social Change. Chicago: Aldine.

Arnould, Eric J.
1982   Regional Market System Development and Changes in Relations of Production in Three Communities in Zinder Province, the Niger Republic. Ph.D. dissertation. Department of Anthropology. Tucson: University of Arizona.

Aryee, A.F.
1978   Urbanization and Plural Marriage. *In* Marriage, Fertility, and Parenthood in West Africa. C. Oppong et al., eds. Canberra: Australian National University.

Asad, Talal
1973   The Beduin as a Military Force: Notes on Some Aspects of Power Relations between Nomads and Sedentaries in Historical Perspective. *In* The Desert and the Sown: Nomads in the Wider Society. C. Nelson, ed. Pp. 61-73. Institute of International Studies Research Series No. 21. Berkeley: University of California.

1979   Equality in Nomadic Social Systems? Notes towards the Dissolution of an Anthropological Category. *In* Pastoral Production and Society. L'Equipe écologie et anthropologie des sociétés pastorales, ed. Pp. 419-428. New York: Cambridge University Press.

Asad, Talal, ed.
1973   Anthropology and the Colonial Encounter. London: Ithaca Press.

Ascroft, Joseph
    1974 On the Art and Craft of Collecting Data in Developing
        Countries. Paper presented at the Workshop on Field
        Data Collection in Rural Areas of Africa and the Mid-
        dle-East. Beirut, December 8-14, 1974.

Asiedu-Ntow, K., K. Ayisi-Okyere, William Berg, David Jickling,
Gerald Klonglan, Richard McLaughlin, Kenneth Sherper, and
Jerry Wood
    1976 Economic and Rural Development Management Project
        Paper. Accra: USAID Mission to Ghana.

Atta-Mills, Cadman
    n.d. The Role of the Social Scientist in Development. Dakar:
        Conseil pour le Développement de la Recherche Economi-
        que et Sociale en Afrique (mimeo.).

Bachard, Issoufou
    1976 Problèmes d'intégration des structures modernes de
        développement dans la société traditionnelle (Département
        de Maradi, Niger). Mémoire, Diplôme. Paris: L'Ecole
        des Hautes Etudes en Sciences Sociales.

Barker, Jonathan
    1977 Stability and Stagnation: The State in Senegal. Canadi-
        an Journal of African Studies 11(1):23-42.

Barlett, Peggy, ed.
    1980 Agricultural Decision Making: Anthropological Contribu-
        tions to Rural Development. New York: Academic Press.

Barnett, Tony
    1977 The Gezira Scheme: An Illusion of Development. Lon-
        don: Frank Cass.

Baron, E.
    1976 Note sur les successions des cultures sèches au Mali.
        Colloque sur les Systèmes de Production. Bamako:
        Ministère de Développement Rurale (mimeo.).

Barrès, Victoria, Pierra Brigatti, Annette Correze, Madeleine
Debourg, Marie-Jo Doucet, Véronique Gentil, Sylvia Malachowski,
Franca Pieressa, and Odette Snoy
    1976 The Participation of Rural Women in Development: A
        Project of Rural Women's Animation in Niger, 1966-1975.
        Paris: Institut de Recherches et d'Application des Mé-
        thodes de Développement.

Barth, Fredrik
    1964 Capital, Investment and the Social Structure of a Pastor-
        al Nomadic Group in South Persia. In Capital, Saving
        and Credit in Peasant Societies. R. Firth and B.S.
        Yamey, eds. Pp. 69-81. Chicago: Aldine.

Bauer, P.T.
1982   Dissent on Development. Cambridge, MA: Harvard
       University Press.

Baumgartner, T., Walter Buckley, and Tom R. Burns
1975   Metapower and Relational Control in Social Life. Social
       Science Information 14(6):49-78.

Beauvilain, Alain
1977   Les Peul du Dallol Bosso. Etudes Nigériennes No. 42.
       Niamey: Institut de Recherches en Sciences Humaines.

Bei Agrer
1978   Programme Global d'Etudes et d'Investissements de
       l'Autorité des Aménagements des Vallées de la Volta
       (1978-82). Vol. 1-4. Bruxelles: Bureau Courtoy.

Belloncle, Guy
1978   Coopératives et développement en Afrique noire sahéli-
       enne. Sherbrooke, Quebec: Université de Sherbrooke.

1979   Développement par la participation ou liberalisme sau-
       vage? Réponse à Albert Meister. Esprit 3(29):146-154.

1985   Paysanneries sahéliennes en péril. Carnets de Route
       Vols. 1 and 2. Paris: L'Harmattan.

Belloncle, Guy and Dominique Gentil
1968   Pédagogie de l'implantation du mouvement coopératif au
       Niger. Niamey: Institut de Recherches et d'Application
       des Méthodes de Développement (mimeo.).

Belshaw, Cyril
1974   The Contribution of Anthropology to Development. Cur-
       rent Anthropology 15(4):520-526.

1976   The Sorcerer's Apprentice: An Anthropology of Public
       Policy. Oxford: Pergamon Press.

Berg, Elliott
1975   The Recent Economic Evolution of the Sahel. Ann Ar-
       bor: University of Michigan Center for Research on Eco-
       nomic Development.

1978   Onchocerciasis Control Program: Economic Review Mis-
       sion. (Draft). Ann Arbor: University of Michigan
       Department of Economics.

Bernard, H. Russell and Pertti Pelto
1972   Technology and Social Change. New York: Macmillan.

Bernstein, Henry
1977   Notes on Capital and Peasantry. Review of African
       Political Economy 10:60-73.

Bernus, E., R. Fauck, and B. Peyre de Fabrègues
1983 Mise à jour de l'étude de cas sur la désertification et renforcement de la stratégie nationale en matière de lutte contre la désertification (Niger). Paris: UNESCO-UNSO.

Berreman, Gerald D.
1968 Is Anthropology Alive? Social Responsibility in Social Anthropology. Current Anthropology 9(5):391-396.

Bettelheim, Charles
1972 Theoretical Comments, Appendix I. *In* Unequal Exchange: A Study of Imperialism of Trade. *By* Arghiri Emmanuel. Pp. 271-322. New York: Monthly Review Press.

Binet, J.
1970 Psychologie économique africaine. Paris: Payot.

Blackburn, Robin, ed.
1973 Ideology in Social Science. New York: Pantheon Books.

Blake, Vernon
1927 The Aesthetic of Ashanti. *In* Religion and Art in Ashanti. Robert S. Rattray, ed. Pp. 344-381. London: Oxford University Press.

Bodley, John
1975 Victims of Progress. Menlo Park, CA: Cummings.

Boulet, Jean
1970 Un terroir de montagne en pays mafa: Magoumaz (Cameroun du Nord). Etudes Rurales 37-39:198-212.

1972 Les pays de l'aïre Bénoué. Yaoundé: Office de la Recherche Scientifique et Technique Outre-Mer.

1975a Untitled manuscript prepared for USAID/FAC North Cameroon Resource Inventory. Yaoundé: United States Agency for International Development (typescript).

1975b Magoumaz. Etude d'un terroir en pays mafa. Paris: Mouton.

Boutillier, Jean-Louis
1963 Les rapports du système foncier Toucouleur et de l'organisation sociale et économique traditionelle, leur évolution actuelle. *In* African Agrarian Systems. Daniel P. Biebuyck, ed. Pp. 116-136. London: Oxford University Press for the International African Institute.

1964 Les Structures foncières en Haute Volta. Etudes Voltaïques. Mémoire No. 5. Ouagadougou: Centre Voltaïque de Recherche Scientifique.

Boutillier, Jean-Louis, P. Cantrelle, Jean Cause, C. Aurent, and
Th. N'Doya
    1962 La Moyenne Vallée du Sénégal (Etude Socio-Economique).
          Paris: Presses Universitaires de France.

Boutrais, J.
    1973 La Colonisation des plaines par les montagnards au nord
          du Cameroun (Monts Mandara). Paris: Office de la Re-
          cherche Scientifique et Technique Outre-Mer.

Brabant, P.
    1976 Notice explicative No. 62, carte pédologique de recon-
          naissance feuille Rey-Bouba. Paris: Office de la Re-
          cherche Scientifique et Technique Outre-Mer.

Brabant, P. and Humbel, F.X.
    1974 Notice explicative No. 51, carte pédologique du Cameroun
          poli. Paris: Office de la Recherche Scientifique et
          Technique Outre-Mer.

Bradby, Barbara
    1980 The Destruction of Natural Economy. In The Articula-
          tion of Modes of Production. Harold Wolpe, ed. Pp.
          93-127. London: Routledge and Kegan Paul.

Brain, R.
    1976 Friends and Lovers. New York: Basic Books, Inc.

Brasseur, Jacquetta Hill
    1968 Les établissements humains au Mali. Dakar: Institut
          Fondamental d'Afrique Noire.

Breman, H., A. Diallo, G. Traoré and M.M. Djiteye
    1978 The Ecology of the Annual Migrations of Cattle in the
          Sahel. In Proceedings of the First International Range-
          land Congress. D.N. Hyder, ed. Pp. 592-595. Den-
          ver: Society for Range Management.

Brislin, Richard and Paul Pederson
    1976 Cross Cultural Orientation Programs. New York:
          Gardner.

Brokensha, David
    1966a Applied Anthropology in English-Speaking Africa.
          Monograph 8. Lexington, KY: The Society for Applied
          Anthropology.

    1966b Social Change at Larteh, Ghana. Oxford: Clarendon
          Press.

Brokensha, David and Peter Hodge
    1969 Community Development: An Interpretation. San Fran-
          cisco: Chandler.

Brokensha, David W., Michael M Horowitz, and Thayer Scudder
   1977   The Anthropology of Rural Development in the Sahel:
          Proposals for Research. Binghamton, NY: Institute for
          Development Anthropology.

Brokensha, David W. and M. Pearsall, eds.
   1969   The Anthropology of Development in Sub-Saharan Africa.
          Monograph 10.   Lexington, KY: Society for Applied
          Anthropology/University of Kentucky Press.

Brokensha, David W., D.M. Warren, and Oswald Werner, eds.
   1980   Indigenous Knowledge Systems and Development.   Lan-
          ham, MD: University Press of America.

Buntjer, B.J.
   1970   The Changing Structure of *Gandu*.   *In* Zaria and Its
          Region: A Nigerien Savanna City and Its Environs.
          Department of Geography Occasional Paper No. 4.
          Zaria: Ahmadu Bello University.

Bryant, Coralie
   1980   Organizational Impediments to Making Participation a
          Reality: "Swimming Upstream in AID."   Rural Develop-
          ment Participation Review 1(3):8-10.

Caldwell, John C.
   1975   The Sahelian Drought and its Economic Implications.
          Washington, DC: Overseas Liaison Committee.

Campbell, Bonnie
   1974   Social Change and Class Formation in a French West
          African State.   Canadian Journal of African Studies
          8(2):285-306.

   1978   The Ivory Coast.   *In* West African States: Failure and
          Promise. John Dunn, ed. Pp. 66-116. New York: Cam-
          bridge University Press.

Camus, Albert
   1954   The Stranger. New York: Vintage.

Caplan, Gerald and Vivian Cadden
   1976   Adapting Overseas in the Peace Corps.   ACTION Pam-
          phlet 4200.14 (May).

Cernea, Michael M.
   1984   Putting People First.   The Position of Sociological Knowl-
          edge in Planned Rural Development.   Keynote opening
          address for the VIth World Congress for Rural Sociolo-
          gy, Manila, The Philippines, December 15-21, 1984.

1985   Sociological Knowledge and Rural Development. *In* Putting People First: Sociological Variables in Rural Development. Michael M. Cernea, ed. London: Oxford University Press.

Chambers, Robert
1969   Settlement Schemes in Tropical Africa. New York: Praeger.

1974   Managing Rural Development: Ideas and Experiences from East Africa. Uppsala: The Scandinavian Institute of African Studies.

1980a   Rural Poverty Unperceived: Problems and Remedies. Paper presented at the Institute of Development Studies, University of Sussex, Brighton. March.

1980b   Shortcut Methods in Information Gathering for Rural Development Projects. Paper presented at the World Bank Agricultural Sector Symposium, January. Washington, DC.

1983   Rural Development: Putting the Last First. London and New York: Longman.

1985   Putting <<Last>> Thinking First: A Professional Revolution. Third World Affairs:3. London: Third World Foundation for Social and Economic Studies.

Champaud, Jacques
1970   Mon Caméroun ou le refus de l'agriculture de plantation. Etudes Rurales 37-39:299-311.

Chapple, E.
1970   Culture and Biological Man: Explorations in Behavioral Anthropology. New York: Holt, Rinehart and Winston.

Charlick, Robert B.
1972   Induced Participation in Nigerian Modernization: The Case of Matameye County. Rural Africana 18:5-29.

1974   Power and Participation in the Modernization of Rural Hausa Communities. Ph.D. dissertation. Political Science Department. Los Angeles: University of California at Los Angeles.

Charreau, Claude
1974   Soils of Tropical Dry and Dry-wet Climatic Areas of West Africa and Their Use and Management. Lectures at the Cornell University Department of Agronomy. Ithaca, New York: Cornell University Department of Agronomy.

Ciparisse, Gérard and I. DeGarine
  1978 Anthropological Contributions to the Food and Agricul-
        ture Organization. Current Anthropology 19(1):37-65.

Cissé, Ben-Mady
  1964 *Animation Rurale*: Senegal's Road to Development. Com-
        munity Development Bulletin 15(2):42-47.

Cissé Diango
  1970 Structure des Malinké de Kita.   Bamako: Editions
        Populaires.

  1972 Mandingo Kingdoms of the Senegambia.   Evanston:
        Northwestern University Press.

Cissokho, Cheikh A.K.
  1974 Aménagement et équipement du Delta sur le Fleuve
        Sénégal. Coopération et Développement 49:29-43.

Clarke, William
  1973 The Dilemma of Development. *In* The Pacific in Transi-
        tion.   Harold Brookfield, ed.   Canberra: Australian
        National University Press.

Cleland, David and William King
  1975 Systems Analysis and Project Management. 2nd Edition.
        New York: McGraw-Hill.

Cleveland, David
  1979 Fertility and the Value of Children in Subsistence Agri-
        culture: Savanna West Africa. Paper presented to the
        Annual Meeting of the American Anthropological Associa-
        tion, Cincinnati, OH. November.

Cochrane, Glynn
  1971 Development Anthropology. New York: Oxford Universi-
        ty Press.

  1977 Social Inputs for Project Appraisal. International Devel-
        opment Review/Focus 19(2):9-12.

  1979 The Cultural Appraisal of Development Projects. New
        York: Praeger.

  1980 Policy Studies and Anthropology. Current Anthropology
        21(4):445-458.

Cochrane, Glynn, ed.
  1976 What We Can Do for Each Other: An Interdisciplinary
        Approach to Development Anthropology. Amsterdam:
        B.R. Grüner.

Cohen, Michael A., S.A. Agunbiade, Daniele Antelin, and Anne
de Mautort
   1979   Urban Growth and Economic Development in the Sahel.
        World Bank Staff Working Paper No. 315. Washington,
        DC: World Bank.

Collins, John D.
   n.d.   Groundnut Markets in the Magaria District of Niger: The
        Political and Economic Impact of Government Sponsored
        Cooperatives. Unpublished manuscript.

   1974   Government and Groundnut Marketing in Rural Niger:
        The 1930s to the 1970s in Magaria. Ph.D. dissertation,
        Political Science Department. Baltimore: Johns Hopkins
        University.

   1976   The Clandestine Movement of Groundnuts across the
        Niger-Nigeria Boundary. Canadian Journal of African
        Studies 10(2):259-278.

Comité Information Sahel
   1974   Qui se nourrit de la famine en Afrique? Le dossier
        politique de la faim au sahel. Paris: François Maspero.

Copans, Jean
   1980   From Senegambia to Senegal: The Evolution of Peasant-
        ries. In Peasants in Africa: Historical and Contemporary
        Perspectives. M. Klein, ed. Pp. 77-104. Beverly Hills,
        CA: Sage Publications.

Courel, André and D. Ian Pool
   1973   Haute-Volta. In Croissance démographique et evolution
        socio-economique en Afrique de l'Ouest. John C. Cald-
        well, N.O. Addo, S.K. Gaisie, A. Igun, and P.O.Olu-
        sanya, eds. Pp. 992-1016. New York: The Population
        Council.

Coward, E. Walter, Jr.
   1979   Principles of Social Organization in an Indigenous Irriga-
        tion System. Human Organization 38:28-36.

CRED   [Center for Research on Economic Development]
   1976   Le Secteur agricole de la République du Mali. Vols. 1
        and 2. Ann Arbor, Michigan: University of Michigan,
        Center for Research on Economic Development.

Critchfield, Richard
   1982   Science and the Villager: The Last Sleeper Wakes.
        Foreign Affairs 61(1):14-41.

Cruise O'Brien, Donal
   1971   Cooperators and Bureaucrats: Class Formation in a
        Senegalese Peasant Society. Africa 41(4):263-278.

1975   Saints and Politicians: Essays in the Organization of a Senegalese Peasant Society. New York: Cambridge University Press.

Dahrendorf, Ralph
1959   Class and Class Conflict in Industrial Society. Stanford: Stanford University Press.

Daines, Samuel, Bryant Smith, William Rogers, and Fred Mann
1979   Agribusiness and Rural Enterprise Project Analysis Manual. Washington, DC: Agribusiness Division, Office of Agriculture, Development Support Bureau, Agency for International Development.

Dalton, George
1974   How exactly are peasants "exploited"? American Anthropologist 76:553-561.

Darling, F. Fraser and Mary A. Farvar
1972   Ecological Consequences of Sedentarization of Nomads. In The Careless Technology: Ecology and International Development. M.T. Farvar and J.P. Milton, eds. Pp. 671-682. Garden City, NY: The Natural History Press.

Deere, Carmen
1978   Intra-Familial Labor Deployment and the Formation of Peasant Household Income: A Case Study of the Peruvian Sierra. Unpublished manuscript. Amherst: University of Massachusetts Department of Anthropology.

De Latour Dejean, Eliane
1975   La transformation du régime foncier: appropriation des terres et formation de la classe dirigeante en pays Mawri (Niger). In L'Agriculture africaine et le capitalisme. Samir Amin, ed. Pp. 185-232. Paris: Anthropos/IDEP.

1980   Shadows Nourished by the Sun: Rural Social Differentiation among the Mawri of Niger. In Peasants in Africa: Historical and Contemporary Perspectives. Martin A. Klein, ed. Pp. 105-142. Beverly Hills: Sage.

Delp, Peter, Arne Thesen, Juzar Motiwalla, and Neelakantan Seshandri
1977   Systems Tools for Project Planning. Bloomington: PASITAM, International Development Institute.

Department of State
1980   Guinea. Foreign Economic Trends Series. Washington, DC: United States Department of State.

Derman, William
1973   Serfs, Peasants, and Socialists. Berkeley: University of California Press.

1980   Cooperatives, Initiative, Participation, and Socioeconomic Change. *In* Sahelian Social Development. Stephen P. Reyna, ed. Pp. 605–702. Abidjan: USAID Regional Economic Development Services Office/West Africa.

Derriennic, Hervé
1977   Famines et dominations en Afrique noire: Paysans et éleveurs du Sahel sous le joug. Paris: L'Harmattan.

DeWalt, Billie
1979   Alternative Adaptive Strategies in a Mexican *ejido*: A New Perspective on Modernization and Development. Human Organization 38(2):134–143.

de Wilde, John C.
1967   Experiences with Agricultural Development in Tropical Africa. 2 vols. Baltimore: Johns Hopkins University Press.

Diagne, Papa Syr
1974   Le Delta du Fleuve Sénégal, problèmes de développement. Ph.D. dissertation. Geography Department. Paris: University of Paris.

Diarra, Fatouma-Agnès
1971   Femmes africaines en devenir: Les femmes zarma du Niger. Paris: Editions Anthropos/Centre Nigérien de Recherches en Sciences Humaines.

Diop, Abdoulaye Bara
1965   Société Toucouleur et Migration. Dakar: Institut Fondamental d'Afrique Noire.

Diop, Majhemout
1972   Histoire des classes sociales dans l'Afrique de l'Ouest. Vol. 2. Le Sénégal. Paris: François Maspero.

Dulieu, D. and J. Ch. Clanet, with G. Chapoutot, I. Dare, M. Keita, D. Mignot, and G. Guye
1978   Etude de la factibilité technique du concept d'unités pastorales au Niger: Arrondissements de Tanout et Gouré. Maisons Alfort: Institut d'Elevage et de Médecine Vétérinaire des Pays Tropicaux (for the World Bank).

Dulieu, D., J. C. Clanet, H. Lennuyeux, and J. F. Meyer.
1977   Définition d'unités pastorales au Batha (République du Tchad). Maisons-Alfort: Institut d'Elevage et de Médicine Vétérinaire des Pays Tropicaux.

Dumont, René
1962   L'Afrique noire est mal partie. Paris: Editions du Seuil.

1978   Paysans ecrasés, terres massacrées. Paris: Laffont.

Dunn, John
  1978 African States: Failure and Promise. New York: Cam-
        bridge University Press.

Dupré, Georges and Pierre-Philippe Rey
  1980 Reflections on the Pertinence of a Theory of the History
        of Exchange. *In* Articulation of Modes of Production.
        Harold Wolpe, ed. Pp. 128-160. London: Routledge and
        Kegan Paul.

Duvignaud, Jean
  1972 Change at Shebika. New York: Random House.

ECA   [Economic Commission for Africa]
  1983 ECA and Africa's Development 1983-2008. United Na-
        tions: Economic Commission for Africa. April.

Eicher, Carl K.
  1985 Agricultural Research for African Development: Problems
        and Priorities for 1985-2000. Unpublished paper pre-
        pared for a World Bank conference on Research Priorities
        for Sub-Saharan Africa, Bellagio, Italy, February 25-
        March 1.

Eicher, Carl K. and John M. Staatz, eds.
  1984 Agricultural Development in the Third World. Baltimore:
        The Johns Hopkins University Press.

Elliott, Charles
  1975 Patterns of Poverty in the Third World: A Study of
        Social and Economic Stratification. New York: Praeger.

Ellis, Sir Alfred Burdon
  1966 The Tshi-Speaking Peoples of the Gold Coast of West
        Africa. Oosterhoot, The Netherlands: Anthropological
        Publications. (First published in 1887).

Ernst, Klaus
  1976 Tradition and Progress in the African Village: Non-
        Capitalist Transformation of Rural Communities in Mali.
        New York: St. Martin's Press.

Eskelinen, Riitta K., John Grayzel, John Van Dusen Lewis, and
Hamadoun Sidibé
  1979 Social Anthropological and Rural Economic Studies in
        Mali: The Dukolomba Forest, the Bandiagara Plateau.
        Directed by Michael M Horowitz. Contract No. AID-afr-
        C-1045. Binghamton, NY: Research Foundation of the
        State University of New York. August.

FAO   [Food and Agriculture Organization of the United
Nations]
  1962 Nomadic Pastoralism as a Method of Land Use. Symposi-
        um on the Problems of the Arid Zone. Paris: UNESCO.

1973   Propositions préliminaires pour une approche intégrée du développement à long terme de la zone sahélienne de l'Afrique de l'Ouest. Document de Travail de la FAO WS-D7404.

FAO/UNDP   [Food and Agriculture Organization/United Nations Development Programme]
1967   Projet de mise en valeur du Dallol Maouri. Rapport partiel provisoire 1967: Etudes de sociologie rurale. Mission consultant du 1/7 au 14/8/67. Dosso: Food and Agriculture Organization/United Nations Development Programme.

1968   Projet de mise en valeur du Dallol Maouri. Etude Sociologique. 2 vols. Dosso: Food and Agriculture Organization/United Nations Development Programme.

FAC   [Fonds d'Aide et de Coopération]
1972   Etudes de pré-factibilité: projet d'aménagement et de mise en valeur des Vallées des Volta. Ouagadougou. Ministère du Plan, de l'Industrie et des Mines, Fonds d'Aide et de Coopération.

Faulkingham, Ralph
1977a   Fertility in Tudu: An Analysis of Constraints on Fertility in a Village in Niger. *In* The Persistence of High Fertility. J. C. Caldwell, ed. Pp. 153–188. Canberra: Australian National University Press.

1977b   Ecological Constraints and Subsistence Strategies: The Impact of Drought in a Hausa Village, A Case Study from Niger. *In* Drought in Africa. Vol. 2. David Dalby, R.J. Harrison Church, and Fatima Bezzaz, eds. Pp. 148–158. London: International African Institute/UNEP/IDEP-SIDA.

Ferguson, D.S.
1977   A Conceptual Framework for the Evaluation of Livestock Production Projects and Programs in Sub-Saharan West Africa. Unpublished ms.

Finch, Frederic E., Halsey Jones and Joseph Litterer
1976a   Managing for Organizational Effectiveness: An Experiential Approach. New York: McGraw-Hill.

1976b   Managing for Organizational Effectiveness: An Experiential Approach. Instructor's Manual. New York: McGraw-Hill.

Finnegan, Gregory
1980   Employment Opportunity and Migration Among the Mossi of Upper Volta. Research in Economic Anthropology 3:291–323.

Fleming, Allen
1979a Farm Management in Kita: A Preliminary Report.   First
      Workshop on Sahelian Agriculture.   West Lafayette, IN:
      Purdue University Department of Agricultural Economics.

1979b Progress Report: Kita Area Study.   Report to the Gov-
      ernment of Mali and the United States Agency for Inter-
      national Development, Bamako.

1980 The Use of Labor and Choice of Technology in Agricul-
      tural Production in the Kita Zone, Mali.   Second Work-
      shop on Sahelian Agriculture.   West Lafayette, IN:
      Purdue University Department of Agricultural Economics.

1981 Agricultural Production and the Use of Labor in Alterna-
      tive Enterprises in the Circle of Kita, Mali. M.S. the-
      sis. Department of Agricultural Economics. West Lafay-
      ette, IN: Purdue University.

Fleming, Martha Doerpinghaus
1979 Women's Activities in the Kita Zone, Republic of Mali.
      Unpublished Final Report, West Africa Projects.   West
      Lafayette, IN: Purdue University Department of Agricul-
      tural Economics.

Foltz, William J.
1965 From French West Africa to the Mali Federation.   New
      Haven, CT: Yale University Press.

Fortes, Meyer
1945 The Dynamics of Kinship among the Tallensi.   London:
      Oxford University Press.

Foster, George M.
1969 Applied Anthropology.   Boston: Little, Brown and Co.

1973 Traditional Societies and Technological Change.   New
      York: Harper and Row.

Foster, George M., Thayer Scudder, Elizabeth Colson, and Robert Kemper, eds.
1978 Long-term Field Research in Social Anthropology.   New
      York: Academic Press.

Franco, Marc
1975 La Planification du sous-développement.   In La Planifi-
      cation du sous-développement, critique de l'analyse de
      projets. By Samir Amin, Marc Franco, and Samba Sow.
      Pp. 35-301. Paris: Editions Anthropos-IDEP.

Frank, André Gunder
1975 Anthropology = Ideology; Applied Anthropology = Poli-
      tics.   Race and Class 17(1):57-68.

Franke, Richard W. and Barbara H. Chasin
1980   Seeds of Famine. Totowa, NJ: Allanheld, Osman & Co.

Freilich, Morris, ed.
1977   Marginal Natives at Work: Anthropologists in the Field. Cambridge: Schenkman.

Fuerste, L.J.
1979   Bilan de l'expérimentation d'accompagnement dans le facteur de la Koulipélé 1976 à 1978. Prospectives. Ouagadougou: Ministère du Développement Rural, l'Autorité des Aménagements des Vallées des Volta.

Fuglestad, Finn
1974   La grande famine de 1931 dans l'ouest du Niger. Revue française d'histoire d'outre mer 61(222, 1er trimestre): 18-33.

Gannett, Fleming, Corddry and Carpenter, Inc.
1980   Assessment of Environmental Effects of Proposed Developments in the Senegal River Basin. Dakar: Organisation Pour la Mise en Valeur du Fleuve Sénégal.

Gaud, Michel
1968   The Public and Cooperative Sector in Middle Africa. Annals of Public and Cooperative Economy 39(3):409-434.

Ghana. National Health Planning Unit
1977   Health Planning Data Book for Ghana. Accra: National Health Planning Unit, Ministry of Health.

Giddens, Anthony
1974   The Class Structure of Advanced Societies. New York: Harper.

Gillon, Dominique
1983   The Fire Problem in Tropical Savannas. In Tropical Savannas. F. Boulière, ed. Pp. 617-641. Ecosystems of the World 13. Amsterdam: Elsevier Scientific Publishing Co.

Gintzburger, A.
1973   Psychoanalysis of a Case Study of Stagnation. Economic Development and Cultural Change 21(2):227-246.

Gjessing, Gutorm
1968   The Social Responsibility of the Social Scientist. Current Anthropology 9(5):397-402

Glazer, Myron
1972   The Research Adventure: Promise and Problems of Fieldwork. New York: Random House.

Glick Schiller, Nina
    1981   Reform or Revolution: The Emergence of Two Class
            Views in Anthropology. Council for Marxist Anthropolo-
            gy Newsletter 3(2):3.

Goddard, A.D.
    1973   Changing Family Structures among the Rural Hausa.
            Africa 43(3):207-218.

Goldmark, Susan
    1977   A Brief Analysis of the Impact of Modernization upon the
            Traditional Land Tenure System of the Zarma of Niger.
            Study Paper No. I. Niamey: USAID Niamey Department
            Development Project (mimeo.).

Goodenough, Ward
    1963   Cooperation in Change. New York: Russell Sage Foun-
            dation.

Goodman, Louis and Ralph Love, eds.
    1979   Management of Development Projects: An International
            Case Study Approach. New York: Pergamon Press.

Goody, Jack
    1980   Rice-Burning and the Green Revolution in Northern
            Ghana. Journal of Development Studies 16(2):136-155.

Gosselin, Gabriel
    1978   L'Afrique Désenchantée. Paris: Anthropos.

Gough, Kathleen
    1968   New Proposals for Anthropologists. Current Anthropolo-
            gy 9(5):403-407.

Goussault, Yves
    1973   Stratification Sociales et Coopération Agricole. Revue
            Tiers Monde 14(54):281-294.

    1976   L'Etat et le Développement de l'Agriculture: Le Concept
            d'Intervention. Revue Tiers Monde 17(67):615-633.

Grayzel, John
    1977   The Ecology of Ethnic-Class Identity Among an African
            Pastoral People: The Doukoloma Fulbe. Ph.D. disserta-
            tion. Department of Anthropology. Eugene, OR: Uni-
            versity of Oregon.

Gregory, Joel W.
    1974   Development and In-Migration in Upper Volta. In Mod-
            ern Migrations in Western Africa. Samir Amin, ed. Pp.
            305-320. London: International African Institute/Oxford
            University Press.

1979   Underdevelopment, Dependence, and Migration in Upper Volta. *In* The Politics of Africa: Dependence and Development. Timothy M. Shaw and Kenneth A. Heard, eds. Pp. 73-94. New York: Africana.

Gudschinsky, Sara
1967   How to Learn an Unwritten Language. New York: Holt, Rinehart, and Winston.

Guillaume, Henri
1974   Les nomades interrompus: Introduction à l'étude du canton twareuge de l'Imanan. Etudes Nigériennes No. 35. Niamey: Centre Nigérien de Recherches en Sciences Humaines.

Gumerman, George J.
1973   The Reconciliation of Theory and Method in Archeology. *In* Research and Theory in Current Archeology. Charles L. Redman, ed. Pp. 287-299. New York: Wiley.

Haaland, Gunnar
1977   Pastoral Systems of Production: the Socio-cultural Context and Some Economic and Ecological Implications. *In* Land Use and Development. P. O'Keefe and B. Wisner, eds. Pp. 179-193. African Environment Special Report 5. London: International African Institute.

Hageboeck, Molly
1979   Manager's Guide to Data Collection. AID Program Design and Evaluation Methods Series, No. 1. Washington, DC: Office of Evaluation, Bureau for Program and Policy Coordination, Agency for International Development.

Hall, Edward
1976   Beyond Culture. Garden City, New Jersey: Anchor Books/Doubleday.

Hallaire, A.
1971   Hodogway (Cameroun Nord). Paris: Mouton.

Hama, Boubou
1967   L'Histoire traditionnelle d'une peuple: Les Zarma-Songhay. Paris: Présence Africaine.

Hammond, Peter B.
1959   Economic Change and Mossi Acculturation. *In* Continuity and Change in African Culture. William R. Bascom and Melville J. Herskovits, eds. Pp. 238-256. Chicago: University of Chicago Press.

1960   Management in Economic Transition. *In* Labor Commitment and Change in Developing Areas. Wilbur E. Moore and Arnold S. Feldman, eds. Pp. 109-121. New York: Social Science Research Council.

Handwerker, W. Penn
    1977 Family, Fertility, and Economics. Current Anthropology
          18(2):259-287

Haney, Emil and Wava Haney
    1978 Social and Ecological Contradictions of Community Devel-
          opment and Rural Modernization in a Colombian Peasant
          Community. Human Organization 37(3):225-234.

Hapgood, David
    1964 New Approach to Village Development: Rural Animation in
          Senegal. International Development Review 6(3).

Harris, Marvin
    1975 Cows, Pigs, Wars and Witches: the Riddles of Culture.
          New York: Vintage Books.

Hecht, Robert
    1981 The Long Wait for Guinea's Farmers. West Africa 3:
          578-581.

Helman, Howard
    1972 Cattle Production in West Africa – No Easy Answers for
          the New Enthusiasts. Washington, DC: Agency for
          International Development.

Henry, Frances and Satish Saberwal
    1969 Stress and Response in Fieldwork. New York: Holt,
          Rinehart, and Winston.

Hermann, Eric A.
    1981 Analysis of Selected Agricultural Parastatals in the Ivory
          Coast. Abidjan: United States Agency for International
          Development, Regional Economic Development Services
          Office/West Africa.

Herskovits, Melville J.
    1926 The Cattle Complex in East Africa. American Anthropol-
          ogist 28:230-273, 361-380, 494-528, 633-644.

Hervouet, Jean-Pierre
    1971 Les Eleveurs-riziculteurs au moyen delta du Sénégal,
          (Les Peul et l'aménagement). Master's thesis. Geogra-
          phy Department. Dakar: University of Dakar.

Higgott, Richard and Finn Fuglestad
    1975 The 1974 Coup d'Etat in Niger: Toward an Explanation.
          Journal of Modern African Studies 13(3):383-398.

Hill, Polly
    1963 Migrant Cocoa Farmers of Southern Ghana. New York:
          Cambridge University Press.

1972   Rural Hausa: A Village and a Setting. New York: Cam-
        bridge University Press.

Hill-Burnett, Jacquetta
1978   Developing Anthropological Knowledge through Applica-
        tion. *In* Applied Anthropology in America. E. Eddy
        and W. Partridge, eds. Pp. 112-128. New York: Co-
        lumbia University Press.

Hirabayashi, Edward, Dennis M. Warren and Wilfred Owen, Jr.
1976   That Focus on the "Other 40%": A Myth of Development.
        The Third World Review 2(1):60-67.

Hoben, Allen
1980   Agricultural Decision Making in Foreign Assistance. *In*
        Agricultural Decision Making. Pp. 337-369. Peggy F.
        Barlett, ed. New York: Academic Press.

1982   Anthropologists and Development. *In* Annual Review of
        Anthropology. Volume 11. B.J. Siegel, A.R. Beals,
        and S.A. Tyler, eds. Palo Alto: Annual Reviews Inc.
        Pp. 349-375.

Hodge, Carlton, ed.
1971   Papers on the Manding. Bloomington: Indiana University
        Press.

Holmquist, Frank
1980   Defending Peasant Political Space in Independent Africa.
        Canadian Journal of African Studies 14(1):157-167.

Homans, George Casper
1950   The Human Group. New York: Harcourt, Brace.

1961   Social Behavior, Its Elementary Forms. New York: Har-
        court, Brace, and World.

Honadle, George
1979   Rapid Reconnaissance Approaches to Organizational Anal-
        ysis for Development Administration. Working Paper No.
        1. Washington, DC: Development Alternatives, Inc.

Hopcraft, Peter N.
1981   Economic Institutions and Pastoral Resources Manage-
        ment: Considerations for a Development Strategy. *In*
        The Future of Pastoral Peoples. John G. Galaty, Dan
        Aronson, and Philip Carl Salzman, eds. Ottawa, Can-
        ada: International Development Research Center.

Horowitz, Michael M
1972a   Manga of Niger. New Haven: HRAFlex Books. Three
        Volumes.

1972b Ethnic Boundary Maintenance Among Pastoralists and Farmers in the Western Sudan (Niger). Journal of Asian and African Studies 7(1,2):105-114. *Reprinted in* Perspectives on Nomadism. W.G. Irons and N. Dyson-Hudson, eds. Pp. 105-114. Leiden: Brill.

1974 Barbers and Bearers: Ecology and Ethnicity in an Islamic Society. Africa 44(4):371-382.

1975 Herdsman and Husbandman in Niger: Values and Strategies. *In* Pastoralism in Tropical Africa. T. Monod, ed. Pp. 387-405. London: Oxford University Press for International African Institute.

1978 Social Analysis Working Paper, World Bank Niger Livestock Appraisal Mission. Binghamton, NY: Institute for Development Anthropology.

1979 The Sociology of Pastoralism and African Livestock Projects. AID Program Evaluation Discussion Paper No. 6. Washington, DC: Agency for International Development.

1981 Research Priorities in Pastoral Studies: An Agenda for the 1980s. *In* The Future of Pastoral Peoples. J.G. Galaty, D. Aronson, and P.C. Salzman, eds. Pp. 61-88. Ottawa: International Development Research Centre.

1983a Pastoral Nomadism and Desertification: Myths, Realities, and Development. Paper presented at the 6th World Congress of Engineers and Architects, Tel Aviv, and forthcoming in the Proceedings of the Congress.

1983b On Listening to Herders: An Essay on Pastoral Demystification. *In* Proceedings of the 3rd International Symposium on Veterinary Epidemiology and Economics. Pp. 416-425. Edwardsville, KS: Veterinary Medicine Publishing Company.

Horowitz, Michael M, ed.
1976 Colloquium on the Effects of Drought on the Productive Strategies of Sudano-Sahelian Herdsmen and Farmers. Binghamton, NY: Institute for Development Anthropology.

Horowitz, Michael M, with E.J. Arnould, R.B. Charlick, J.H. Eriksen, R.H. Faulkingham, C.D. Grimm, P.D. Little, M.D. Painter, T.M. Painter, C. Saenz, M. Salem-Murdock, and M.O. Saunders
1983 Niger: A Social and Institutional Profile. Binghamton, NY: Institute for Development Anthropology.

Huizer, Gerrit
    1970   "Resistance to Change" and Radical Peasant Mobilization:
            Foster and Erasmus Reconsidered. Human Organization
            28(4):303-322.

Humbel, F.X. and J. Barbery
    1974   Notice Explicative No. 53, Carte Pédologique de Recon-
            naissance Feuille Garoua. Paris: Office de la Recherche
            Scientifique et Technique Outre-Mer.

Hutton, Caroline and Robin Cohen
    1975   African Peasants and Resistance to Change: A Reconsid-
            eration of Sociological Approaches. *In* Beyond the
            Sociology of Development: Economy and Society in Latin
            America and Africa. Ivar Oxaal, Tony Barnett, and
            David Booth, eds. Pp. 105-130. London: Routledge and
            Kegan Paul.

Ibn Khaldun
    1967   The Maquaddimah. Vol. 1. F. Rosenthal, trans.
            Princeton: Princeton University Press.

Ibrahim, Fouad N.
    1978   The Problem of Desertification in the Republic of the
            Sudan with Special Reference to Northern Darfur Prov-
            ince. Development Studies and Research Centre Mono-
            graph Series No. 8. Khartoum: Khartoum University
            Press.

Institute of Development Studies
    1979   The Continuing Subordination of Women in the Develop-
            ment Process. *Special Issue* Bulletin of the Institute of
            Development Studies 10(3).

IRSC   [Institut de Recherche Scientifique du Cameroun]
    n.d.   Atlas du Cameroun. Yaoundé: Institut de Recherche
            Scientifique du Cameroun.

Jackson, R.H.
    1973   Political Stratification in Tropical Africa. Canadian
            Journal of African Studies 7(3):381-400.

Javillonar, G., et al.
    1979   Rural Development, Women's Roles, and Fertility in
            Developing Countries. Review of the Literature. Chapel
            Hill, North Carolina: Research Triangle Institute.

Jones, Richard and Roger Popper
    1972   Characteristics of Peace Corps Host Countries and the
            Behavior of Volunteers. Journal of Cross Cultural
            Psychology 3(3):233-245.

Jones, William I.
1976   Planning and Economic Policy: Socialist Mali and Her Neighbors. Washington, DC: Three Continents Press.

Kattenberg, D.
1979   Quelques aspects de la culture Mossi. Ouagadougou: Ministère du Développement Rural, Aménagements des Vallées de Volta.

Katz, Stephen
1980   Marxism, Africa, and Social Class: A Critique of Relevant Theories. Occasional Monograph Series No. 14. Montreal: McGill University Center for Developing Area Studies.

Kayongo-Male, Diane and Philista Onyango
1984   The Sociology of the African Family. London: Longman.

Kerr, Graham B.
1978   Voluntary Associations in West Africa: "Hidden" Agents of Social Change. African Studies Review 2(3):87–100.

Khazanov, A.M.
1984   Nomads and the Outside World. New York: Cambridge University Press.

Kimball, Solon and James Watson
1972   Crossing Cultural Boundaries: The Anthropological Experience. San Francisco: Chandler.

Kimble, George H.T.
1962   Tropical Africa. Garden City, NY: Doubleday.

Klonglan, Gerald E.
1976   Social Implications of Decentralized Development: The Ghanaian Case, 1976 – An Application of Social Soundness Analysis. Unpublished paper presented at the Development Studies Program, AID, Washington, DC, June 7.

Koenig, Dolores
1979a Socio-economic Study in the Kita Region. First Workshop on Sahelian Agriculture. West Lafayette, IN: Purdue University Department of Agricultural Economics.

1979b Constraints on the Adoption of Agricultural Equipment in the Region of Kita, Mali. Paper presented at the Annual Meeting of the Society for Applied Anthropology, Philadelphia, PA.

1980   Household Behavior in the Region of Kita and Its Relationship to Agricultural Change. Second Workshop on Sahelian Agriculture. West Lafayette, IN: Purdue University Department of Agricultural Economics.

1982   Social Stratification and Women's Work in the Rural Malian Household. Paper presented at the Annual Meeting of the American Anthropological Association, Washington, DC.

Kohler, Jean Marie
1971   Activités agricoles et changements sociaux dans l'ouest Mossi. Paris: Mémoires, Office de la Recherche Scientifique et Technique Outre-Mer.

1972   Les migrations des Mossi de l'ouest. Travaux et Documents de l'ORSTOM, No 18. Paris: Office de la Recherche Scientifique et Technique Outre-Mer.

Lamprey, H.F.
1983   Pastoralism Yesterday and Today: The Over-grazing Problem. In Tropical Savannas. Ecosystems of the World 13. F. Bourlière, ed. Pp. 643-666. Amsterdam: Elsevier Scientific Publishing Company.

Larson, Donald, and William Smalley
1972   Becoming Bilingual: A Guide to Language Learning. New Canaan, CT: Practical Anthropology.

Lateef, Noel V.
1975   A Techno-Environmental Analysis of Zarma Cultural Organization. Bulletin de l'IFAN [Institut fondamental d'Afrique Noir] 37. Ser. B. 2:388-411.

Lavroff, Dimitri M.
1979   Les Entreprises publiques en Afrique Noire. Vol. 1. Série Afrique Noire No. 9. Paris: Editions A. Pédone.

Lele, Uma
1984   Rural Africa: Modernization, Equity, and Long-Term Development. In Agricultural Development in the Third World. Carl K. Eicher and John M. Staatz, eds. Pp. 436-453. Baltimore: The Johns Hopkins University Press.

Levtzion, Nehemia
1973   Ancient Ghana and Mali. London: Methuen.

Lewis, Diane
1973   Anthropology and Colonialism. Current Anthropology 14(5):581-602.

Lewis, John Van Dusen
1978   Small Farmer Credit and the Village Production Unit in Rural Mali. African Studies Review 2(3):29-48.

1979   Descendents and Crops: Two Poles of Production in a Malian Peasant Village. Ph.D. dissertation. Anthropology Department. New Haven, CT: Yale University.

Lewis, W. Arthur
    1965   Politics   in   West   Africa.   London: Oxford   University
           Press.

Leynaud, Emile
    1966   Fraternités d'age et sociétés de culture dans la Haute
           Vallée du Niger.   Cahiers d'études africaines 6(21):
           41-68.

Leys, Collin
    1975   Underdevelopment in Kenya. London: Heinemann.

Little, Kenneth
    1957   The Role of Voluntary Associations in West African
           Urbanization. American Anthropologist 59(4):579-594.

Little, Peter D. and Michael M Horowitz
    Forthcoming. Subsistence Crops Are Cash Crops. Human
           Organization.

Lloyd, Peter
    1966   The New Elites of Tropical Africa.   London: Oxford
           University Press.

Lomax, Alan and Conrad M. Arensberg
    1977   A Worldwide Evolutionary Classification of Culture by
           Subsistence Systems.   Current Anthropology 18(4):
           659-701.

Londres, Albert
    1929   Terre d'Ebène. Paris: Presses Universitaires de France.

Long, Norman
    1977   An Introduction to the Sociology of Rural Development.
           Boulder, CO: Westview Press.

Ly, Abdoulaye
    1958   L'état et la production paysanne.   Paris: Présence
           Africaine

McCelland, Stephen
    1979   Political Economy and Dependence in Africa: An Annotat-
           ed Bibliography. In The Political Economy of Under-
           development. R. Cruise O'Brien, ed. Pp. 228-272.
           Beverly Hills, CA: Sage Publications.

McFarland, Daniel Miles
    1978   Historical Dictionary of Upper Volta. Metuchen, NJ: The
           Scarecrow Press.

McGregor, Douglas
    1960   The Human Side of Enterprise. New York: McGraw-Hill.

McPherson, Laura, ed.
   1978   The Role of Anthropology in the Agency for International Development. Report on a workshop held May 27, 1977. Binghamton, NY: Institute for Development Anthropology.

Magubane, Bernard
   1971   A Critical Look at Indices Used in the Study of Social Change in Colonial Africa. Current Anthropology 12(4/5): 419-445.

   1976   The Evolution of Class Structure in Africa. *In* The Political Economy of Contemporary Africa. P. Gutkind and I. Wallerstein, eds. Pp. 169-197. Beverly Hills, CA: Sage Publications.

Mainet, Guy and Guy Nicolas
   1964   La Vallée du Gulbi de Maradi: Enquête socio-économique. Documents et Etudes Nigériennes No. 16. Niamey: Institut fondamental d'Afrique Noire - Centre Nigérien de Recherches en Sciences Humaines.

Mali, Paul
   1972   Managing by Objectives. New York: Wiley-Interscience.

Marchal, Jean Yves
   1977   The Evolution of Agrarian Systems in Yatanga. African Environment. 2(4) and 3(1):73-85.

Markowitz, Irving
   1977   Power and Class in Africa. Englewood Cliffs, NJ: Prentice-Hall.

Marticou, H. and Audebert, B.
   n.d.   Les Structures agricoles du Nord Cameroun et de l'Adamao. Yaoundé: Secrétariat d'Etat au Développement Rural, Direction de l'Agriculture, Service des Etudes et des Programmes (mimeo.).

Martin, Jean-Yves
   1970   Les Matakam du Cameroun. Paris: Office de la Recherche Scientifique et Technique Outre-Mer.

   1976   Untitled social soundness analysis. Yaoundé: United States Agency for International Development.

Marx, Karl
   1970   Capital. Vol. 1. Moscow: Foreign Languages Publishing House.

Meillassoux, Claude
   1970   A Class Analysis of the Bureaucratic Process in Mali. Journal of Development Studies 6:97-110.

1972   From Reproduction to Production: A Marxist Approach to Economic Anthropology. Economy and Society. 1:93–105.

1975   Femmes, greniers et capitaux. Paris: François Maspero.

Meister, Albert
1966   Développement économique des pays de l'est africain. Paris: Presses Universitaires de France.

1977   La Participation pour le développement. Paris: Les Editions Ouvriers.

Mencher, Joan
1977   Conflicts and Contradictions in the "Green Revolution." *In* Anthropology in the Development Process. H.M. Mathur, ed. Pp. 370–393. New Delhi: Vikas.

Mickelwait, Donald R., Charles F. Sweet, and Elliott R. Morss
1979   New Directions in Development: A Study of USAID. Boulder, CO: Westview Press.

Mills, C. Wright
1943   The Professional Ideology of Social Pathologists. American Journal of Sociology 49(2):165–180.

Mills, Theodore
1967   The Sociology of Small Groups. Englewood Cliffs, NJ: Prentice-Hall.

Miner, Horace
1956   Body Ritual among the Nacirema. American Anthropologist 58(3):503–507.

Montsi, Sam
1985   Context. *In* Between Tradition and Modernity: Development Management in Lesotho. M. Warren et al. Draft project evaluation prepared for AID Synthesis Workshop on Development Management in Africa. Washington DC, April 29 – May 2.

Morgan, E. Philip
1983   Social Analysis, Project Development and Advocacy in U.S. Foreign Assistance. Public Administration and Development 3(1):61–71.

Moore, M.P.
1973   Cooperative Labor in Peasant Agriculture. Journal of Peasant Studies 2(3):270–291.

Morris, W.H.
1976   Consultant's Report on the North West Benoué Development Proposal. Yaoundé: United States Agency for International Development (typescript).

Murdock, George Peter
   1959 Africa: Its People and Their Culture History. New York: McGraw-Hill.

Murphy, Josette and Leendert H. Sprey
   1980a Farmers' Response to an Intensive Extension Program in Upper Volta. Second Workshop on Sahelian Agriculture. West Lafayette, IN: Purdue University Department of Agricultural Economics.

   1980b Monitoring of a Development Program. Second Workshop on Sahelian Agriculture. West Lafayette, IN: Purdue University Department of Agricultural Economics.

   1980c The Volta Valley Authority: Socio-Economic Evaluation of a Resettlement Program in Upper Volta. West Lafayette, IN: Purdue University Department of Agricultural Economics.

Nash, June, Jorge Dandler, and Nicholas S. Hopkins, eds.
   1976 Popular Participation in Social Change. The Hague: Mouton.

Ndiaye, Etienne
   1968 Rapport sur le peuplement du delta. Dakar: Republic of Senegal, Ministry of Rural Development, Société d'Aménagement et d'Exploitation des Terres du Delta (mimeo.).

Nestel, Barry, D.J. Pratt, M. Thomé, and Derek Tribe
   1973 Animal Production and Research in Tropical Africa. Report of the Task Force Commissioned by the African Livestock Sub-Committee of the Consultative Group on International Agricultural Research. Washington, DC. March.

Netting, Robert
   1968 Hill Farmers of Nigeria. Seattle: University of Washington Press.

Nicolas, Guy
   1969 Développement rural et comportement traditionnel au sein d'une société africaine. Genève-Afrique Acta Africana 8(2):18-35.

   1971 Processus de résistance au "développement" au sein d'une société africaine. Civilisations 21(1):45-62.

   1974 La pratique traditionelle du crédit au sein d'un société subsaharienne (Vallée de Maradi, Niger). Cultures et Développement 6(4):737-773.

Norman, David W.
1972 An Economic Survey of Three Villages in Zaria Province. 2 vols. Zaria, Nigeria: Institute for Agricultural Research, Ahmadu Bello University.

1974a Inter-Disciplinary Research in Rural Development: The Experience of the Rural Economic Research Unit in Northern Nigeria. Paper No. 6. Washington, DC: Overseas Liaison Committee, American Council on Education.

1974b Rationalizing Mixed Cropping under Indigenous Conditions. The Journal of Development Studies 11:3-21.

Olivier de Sardan, Jean-Pierre
1969 Système de relations économiques et sociales chez les Wogo (Niger). Paris: Institut d'Ethnologie, Musée de l'Homme.

1974 Le Bogu. Mu kaara sani 5:14-17.

1982 Concepts et Conceptions Songhay-Zarma. Paris: Nubia.

1984 Les sociétés Songhay-Zarma (Niger-Mali). Paris: Karthala.

OMVS [Organisation pour la Mise en Valeur du Fleuve Sénégal]
1977 Aménagements hydro-agricoles dans le Basin du Sénégal, rythmes de développement et modulation des crues. Dakar: Organisation pour la Mise en Valeur du Fleuve Sénégal (mimeo.).

ORD de l'Est
1980 Rapport annuel. Fada n'Gourma: Organisme Régional du Développement de l'Est. (République de la Haute Volta).

ORSTOM [Office de la Recherche Scientifique et Technique Outre-Mer]
1973 Cameroun: densité de la population rurale. Calculée par canton d'après le recensement administratif de 1967-1968. Yaoundé: Office de la Recherche Scientifique et Technique Outre-Mer.

1979 Stratégies d'aménagement et de mise en valeur des zones livrées de l'onchocerose en Haute Volta. Mémoire No. 89. Pp. 275-280. Paris: Office de la Recherche Scientifique et Technique Outre-Mer.

Orubuloye, I.O.
1981 Education and Socio-demographic Change in Nigeria. In Women, Education and Modernization of the Family in West Africa. Helen Ware, ed. Pp. 22-41. Canberra: Australian National University.

Ossendowski, Ferdynand
1928   Slaves of the Sun. New York: Dutton.

OTA   [Office of Technology Assessment]
1984   Africa Tomorrow: Issues in Technology, Agriculture, and U.S. Foreign Aid. Washington, DC: Office of Technology Assessment, Congress of the United States.

Ouedraogo, D.
1976   L'Aménagement du bloc de Mogtedo: dans le cadre de la mise en valeur des vallées des Volta. Travaux d'Etudes et de Recherches, Université de Bourdeaux III. Bordeaux: Institut de Géographie Tropicale et d'Etudes Régionales.

1979   Genèse et structure d'un espace enclave: La Haute Volta. Mémoire No. 89. ORSTOM, ed. Pp. 553-559. Paris: Office de la Recherche Scientifique et Technique Outre-Mer.

Owens, Edgar and Robert Shaw
1974   Development Reconsidered. Lexington, MA: Lexington Books, D.C. Heath and Co.

Owusu, Maxwell
1975   Policy Studies, Development, and Political Anthropology. The Journal of Modern African Studies 13(3):367-381.

1978   Ethnography of Africa: The Usefulness of the Useless. American Anthropologist 80(2):310-334.

Painter, Thomas M.
1979   World Bank Dosso Agricultural Development Project: Sociology Working Paper. Binghamton, NY: Institute for Development Anthropology.

1980a Seasonal Labor Migrations and Rural Transformations in Niger, c. 1875 to c. 1975. Ph.D. dissertation prospectus. Department of Sociology. Binghamton, NY: State University of New York at Binghamton.

1980b Adult Literacy and Cooperative Training Programs in the Niamey Department Development Project (Niger Republic): Evaluation of Phase I Development Activities and Recommendations for Phase II. Washington, DC: United States Agency for International Development.

1980c Social Soundness Analysis, Part 1: Overview of the Area and Populations within Project Zones; Analysis. Annexe B in the Niger-Niamey Department Development Project, Phase II (683-0240), Vol. II. Project Paper Annexes. Niamey: United States Agency for International Development. October 27.

1981   "Quel avenir pour le sahel?" - A Response to Guy
       Belloncle. Discussion paper. Binghamton, NY: Depart-
       ment of Sociology, State University of New York/Insti-
       tute for Development Anthropology. January.

forthcoming   Peasant Migrations and Rural Transformations in
       Niger: A Study of Incorporation within a West African
       Capitalist Regional Economy, c. 1875 to c. 1975. Ph.D.
       dissertation. Department of Sociology. Binghamton:
       State University of New York at Binghamton.

Palmer, E.H.
1977   The Desert of the Exodus. Vols. 1 and 2. New York:
       Arno Press.

Partridge, William L.
1984   Training Manual in Development Anthropology. Special
       Publication No. 17. Washington, DC: American Anthro-
       pological Association and the Society for Applied Anthro-
       pology.

Paul, Benjamin, ed.
1955   Health, Culture, and Community. New York: Russell
       Sage Foundation.

Peace Corps
1970   Guidelines for Peace Corps Cross Cultural Training. 4
       Vols. Washington, DC: Peace Corps Office for Training
       and Support.

Peck, Carey
n.d.   Animation Village Life. Dakar: Peace Corps Regional
       Training Resource Office files.

Penning de Vries, F.W.T. and M.A. Djiteye
1982   Le productivité des pâturages saheliens. Wageningen:
       Centre for Agricultural Publishing and Documentaries.

Pelto, Pertti
1970   Anthropological Research: The Structure of Inquiry.
       New York: Harper and Row.

Perrier, Gregory
1985   Comments on Pastoral Network Paper 18c & 18d. In
       Pastoral Development Network Paper 19b. London: Over-
       seas Development Institute.

Person, Yves
1968   Samori. Une revolution Dyula. Dakar: Editions de
       l'Institut fondamental d'Afrique Noire.

Pfeiffer, J. William and John E. Jones
1974 A Handbook of Structured Experiences for Human Rela-
      tions Training and Reference Guide to Handbooks and
      Annuals. 6 Volumes. 2nd Edition. La Jolla, CA:
      University Associates.

Picardi, A.C.
1977 A Systems Analysis of Pastoralism in the West African
      Sahel. *In* Framework for Evaluating Long-term Strate-
      gies for the Development of the Sahel-Sudan Region.
      Annex 5. Center for Policy Alternatives, Massachusetts
      Institute of Technology.

Picardi, A.C. and W.W. Seifert
1976 A Tragedy of the Commons in the Sahel. Technology
      Review 78(6).

Piché, V., J. Gregory, and S. Coulibaly
1980 Vers une explication des courants migratoires voltaïques.
      Labor, Capital, and Society 13(1):77-103.

Pitt, David, ed.
1976 Development from Below: Anthropologists and Develop-
      ment Situations. World Anthropology Series. Chicago:
      Aldine.

Podlewski, André Michel
1966 La Dynamique des principales populations du Nord-
      Cameroun. Paris: Office de la Recherche Scientifique et
      Technique Outre-Mer.

Poncet, Yveline
1974 La sécheresse en Afrique sahélienne (une étude mi-
      cro-régionale en République du Niger: La région des
      Dallols). Paris: Organisation de Coopération et de
      Développement Economique, Centre de Développement
      (mimeo.).

Poulantzas, Nicos
1973 Political Power and Social Classes. London: New Left
      Books.

Purdue University
1979 Proceedings of the First Workshop on Sahelian Agricul-
      ture. Agricultural Economics Department, Purdue Uni-
      versity, West Lafayette, IN (mimeo.).

1980 Proceedings of the Second Workshop on Sahelian Agricul-
      ture. Agricultural Economics Department, Purdue Uni-
      versity, West Lafayette, IN (mimeo.).

Raulin, Henri
   1963   Techniques et bases socio-économiques des sociétés
          rurales nigériennes. Etudes Nigériennes 12. Niamey:
          Institut Fondamental d'Afrique Noire - Centre Nigérien
          de Recherches en Sciences Humaines.

   1969   Communautés d'entraide et développement agricole au
          Niger. L'example de la Majya. Etudes Rurales 33:5-30.

   1971   Sociétés sans classes d'age au Niger. *In* Classes et
          associations d'age en Afrique de l'Ouest. Denise Paulme,
          ed. Pp. 320-339. Paris: Plon.

   1976   Organized Cooperation and Spontaneous Cooperation in
          Africa (Niger Republic). *In* Popular Participation and
          Social Change. June Nash, Jorge Dandler, and Nicholas
          S. Hopkins, eds. Pp. 35-43. The Hague: Mouton.

Raynaut, Claude
   1972   Structures normatives et relations électives: Etude d'une
          communauté villageoise haoussa. Paris: Mouton.

   1975   Le cas de la région de Maradi (Niger). *In* Sécheresses
          et famines du Sahel. Vol. 2. Paysans et nomades.
          Jean Copans, ed. Pp. 5-43. Paris: François Maspéro.

   1976   Transformation du système de production et inégalité
          économique: le cas d'une village Haoussa (Niger).
          Canadian Journal of African Studies 10(2):279-306.

   1977a Circulation monétaire et évolution des structures socio-
          économiques chez les Haoussas du Niger. Africa 47(2):-
          160-171.

   1977b Lessons of a Crisis. *In* Drought in Africa, Vol. 2.
          David Dalby, R.J. Harrison Church, and Fatima Bezzaz,
          eds. Pp. 17-29. London: International African Insti-
          tute.

   1980   Recherches multidisciplinaires sur la région de Maradi:
          rapport de synthèse. Programme de Recherche sur la
          Région de Maradi, Université de Bordeaux II. Paris:
          DGRST/ACC Lutte contre l'Aridité en Milieu Tropical.

Reddin, W.J.
   1970   Managerial Effectiveness. New York: McGraw-Hill.

   1973   The Management Style Diagnosis Test: The 3-D Theory
          of Managerial Effectiveness. 3rd Edition. Fredericton,
          NB, Canada: Organizational Tests, Ltd.

Remy, C.
1972 Donsin, les structures agraires d'un village mossi de la région de Nobéré. Ouagadougou: Office de la Recherche Scientifique et Technique Outre-Mer.

Remy, Gerard
1967 Yobri. Etude géographique du terroir d'un village gourmantché de Haute-Volta. Atlas des Structures au Sud du Sahara. Paris: Ecole Pratique des Hautes Etudes/Mouton.

République du Niger
1977 Projet de développement de l'élevage dans les départements de Maradi et Zinder. Niamey: Ministère du Développement Rural. Service de l'Elevage et des Industries Animales.

République du Niger/Banque Mondiale
1978 Projet de développement rural du département de Dosso. Rapport de la Mission de Préparation Complémentaire. 2 vols. Dosso: République du Niger, Ministère du Développement Rural et la Banque Mondiale.

République du Sénégal
n.d. Création et organisation de la SAED. Dakar: Ministry of Rural Development and Hydraulics. Société d'Aménagement et d'Exploitation des Terres du Delta (mimeo.).

1976a Communication du conseil interministeriel du 12 avril 1976. Dakar: Ministry of Rural Development and Hydraulics. Société d'Aménagement et d'Exploitation des Terres du Delta (mimeo.).

1976b Groupements de producteurs et coopératives de développement. Dakar: Ministry of Rural Development and Hydraulics. Société d'Aménagement et d'Exploitation des Terres du Delta (mimeo.).

1977 Rapports d'activités, 1976–77. Dakar: Ministry of Rural Development and Hydraulics. Société d'Aménagement et d'Exploitation des Terres du Delta (mimeo.).

Rey, Pierre-Philippe
1971 Colonialisme, néo-colonialisme et transition au capitalisme: exemple de la Comilog au Congo-Brazzaville. Paris: François Maspero.

1973 Les alliances de classes. Paris: François Maspero.

Reyna, Stephen P.
n.d. Investment Preference, Stratification, and Welfare. Unpublished manuscript. Durham, NH: University of New Hampshire.

1977   Economics and Fertility: Waiting for the Demographic Transition in the Dry Zone of Francophone West Africa. *In* The Persistence of High Fertility. J.C. Caldwell, ed. Pp. 393-427. Canberra: Australian National University Press.

1980   Impact of Autorité des Aménagements des Vallées des Volta. Abidjan: United States Agency for International Development, Regional Economic Development Services Office/West Africa.

1983   Dual Class Formation and Agrarian Underdevelopment: An Analysis of the Articulation of Production Relations in Upper Volta. Canadian Journal of African Studies 17(2):211-235.

Rhoades, Robert
1978   Peace Corps and the American Development Philosophy. Human Organization 37(4):424-426.

Riesman, Paul
1979   Freedom in Fulani Social Life: An Introspective Ethnography. Chicago: University of Chicago Press.

1980   The Fulani in a Development Context. *In* Sahelian Social Development. Stephen P. Reyna, ed. Pp. 77-186. Abidjan: United States Agency for International Development, Regional Economic Development Services Office.

Roberts, Pépé
1979   The Integration of Women into the Development Process: Some Conceptual Problems. Bulletin of the Institute for Development Studies 10(3):60.

Robertson, A.F.
1980   On Sharecropping. Man 15(3):411-429.

Rogers, Everett
1962   Diffusion of Innovations. New York: The Free Press.

1968   Modernization among Peasants: The Impact of Communication. New York: Holt, Rinehart, and Winston.

Rondinelli, Dennis and Aspy Palia
1976   Project Planning and Implementation in Developing Countries: A Bibliography on Development Project Management. Honolulu: Technology and Development Institute, East-West Center.

Rondinelli, Dennis and Kenneth Ruddle
1976   Urban Factions in Rural Development: An Analysis of Integrated Spatial Development Policy. Washington, DC: Office of Urban Development, Technical Assistance Bureau, Agency for International Development.

Rostow, Walter W.
    1960   The Stages of Economic Growth: a Non-Communist Mani-
            festo. New York: Cambridge University Press.

Rothiot, Jean-Paul
    1984   Zarmakoy Aouta. Les Débuts de la domination coloniale
            dans le cercle de Dosso, 1898-1913. Thèse de Doctorat
            de 3e Cycle. Paris: Université de Paris VII. Juin.

Rouch, Jean
    1954   Les Songhay. Paris: Presses Universitaires de France.

Ruther, Nancy L.
    1979   Goals, Compliance, and Effectiveness in the Agency for
            International Development. M.A. thesis. Public and
            International Affairs Department. Ithaca, NY: Cornell
            University.

Ruttan, V.W.
    1966   Tenure and Productivity of Philippine Rice Producing
            Farms. Philippine Economic Journal 5(1):42-63.

Sahlins, Marshall
    1972   Stone Age Economics. Chicago: Aldine.

Samarin, William
    1967   Field Linguistics. New York: Holt, Rinehart, and
            Winston.

Sandford, Stephen
    1983   Management of Pastoral Development in the Third World.
            Chichester: John Wiley & Sons (in association with the
            Overseas Development Institute, London).

Sarraut, Albert
    1923   La Mise en valeur des colonies françaises. Paris: Payot.

Saul, John S.
    1971   Marketing Cooperatives in a Developing Country: The
            Tanzania Case. In Two Blades of Grass: Rural Coopera-
            tives in Agricultural Modernization. Peter Worsley, ed.
            Pp. 347-370. Manchester: Manchester University Press.

Schaffer, Bernard
    1973   Improving Access to Public Services. IDS Discussion
            Paper #23. University of Sussex, Institute for Develop-
            ment Studies.

Schein, Edgar
    1969   Process Consultation: Its Role in Organizing Develop-
            ment. Reading, MA: Addison-Wesley Publishing Co.

Schumacher, Edward
  1975   Politics, Bureaucracy, and Rural Development in Sene-
          gal. Berkeley: University of California Press.

Schwartz, Norman
  1978   Community Development and Cultural Change in Latin
          America. *In* Annual Review of Anthropology. Bernard
          Siegel, ed. Pp.235-261. Palo Alto, CA: Annual Reviews.

Scott, John C.
  1976   The Moral Economy of the Peasant: Rebellion and Subsis-
          tence in Southeast Asia. New Haven, CT: Yale Univer-
          sity Press.

Scudder, Thayer
  1976   Social Impacts of River Basin Development on Local
          Populations. *In* River Basin Development: Policies and
          Planning. Vol. 1. Proceedings of the United Nations
          Inter-Regional Seminar on River Basin and Inter-Basin
          Development. Pp. 45-52. New York and Budapest:
          United Nations Development Program and National Water
          Authority of Hungary.

Segy, Ladislas
  1975   African Sculpture Speaks. 4th Edition. New York: Da
          Capo Press.

Sénéchal, Jacques
  1973   Espace et mobilité rurale en milieu sudano-sahélien, le
          changement dans l'isolement (Gourma du Nord, Haute
          Volta). Thèse de 3e cycle. Paris: Ecole Pratique des
          Hautes Etudes.

Shaw, Timothy and Malcolm Grieve
  1979   Dependence as an Approach to Understanding Continui-
          ties in Africa. Journal of Developing Areas 13:229-246.

Shenton, Robert W. and Bill Freund
  1978   The Incorporation of Northern Nigeria into the World
          Capitalist Economy. Review of African Political Economy
          13 (September-December):8-20.

Shenton, Robert W. and Louise Lennihan
  1980   Capital and Class: Peasant Differentiation in Northern
          Nigeria. Unpublished manuscript. New York: Columbia
          University Department of Anthropology.

Shenton, Robert W. and Mike Watts
  1979   Capitalism and Hunger in Northern Nigeria. Review of
          African Political Economy 15-16 (May-December):53-62.

Sidikou, Arouna Hamidou
  1974 Sedentarité et mobilité entre Niger et Zgaret. Etudes
        Nigériennes No. 34. Niamey: Centre de Recherche en
        Sciences Humaines.

Skinner, Eliott P.
  1974 African Urban Life: The Transformation of Ouagadougou.
        Princeton, NJ: Princeton University Press.

  1980 A Brief History of the Sahel. *In* Sahelian Social Devel-
        opment. Stephen P. Peyna, ed. Pp. 15-70. Abidjan:
        United States Agency for International Development,
        Regional Economic Development Services Office, West
        Africa.

Smith, James
  1977 Economy and Demography in a Mossi Village. Ph.D.
        dissertation. Ann Arbor, MI: University Microfilms
        International.

SOLAR
  1976 Report of the First Meeting of the Panel on Management
        of Livestock and Rangelands to Combat Desertification in
        the Sudano-Sahelian Regions. United Nations Conference
        on Desertification.

Songré, Ambroise, Jean-Marie Sawadago and George Sanogoh
  1974 Réalités et effets de l'émigration massive des Voltaiques
        dans le contexte de l'Afrique occidentale. *In* Modern
        Migrations in Western Africa. Samir Amin, ed. Pp.
        384-406. London: International African Institute/Oxford
        University Press.

Sorgho, J. and O. Richet
  1979 Les Coûts récurrents d'une installation en culture sèche,
        de 15,000 familles sur des terres nueves aménagées par
        l'Autorité des Aménagements des Vallées des Volta.
        Ouagadougou: Comité Permanent Inter-Etats de Lutte
        Contre la Sécheresse dans le Sahel.

Spencer, Herbert
  1877 The Principles of Sociology. Vol. 1. New York: D.
        Appleton and Co.

Spicer, Edward, ed.
  1952 Human Problems in Technological Change. New York:
        Russell Sage Foundation.

Spittler, Gerd
  1977 Rural Exodus: Urban-rural and Rural-urban Migration in
        Gobir (Niger). Sociologia Ruralis 17:223-235.

Sprey, L. and C. De Jong
1977 Aspects du développement agricole dans le projet de colonisation de l'Autorité des Aménagements des Vallées des Volta. Ouagadougou: Ministère du Développement Rural, l'Autorité des Aménagements des Vallées des Volta.

Staatz, John M. and Carl K. Eicher
1984 Agricultural Development Ideas in Historical Perspective. *In* Agricultural Development in the Third World. Carl K. Eicher and John M. Staatz, eds. Pp. 3-30. Baltimore and London: The Johns Hopkins University Press.

Stavenhagen, Rodolfo
1969 Les Classes sociales dans les sociétés agraires. Paris: Anthropos.

1971 Decolonizing Applied Social Sciences. Human Organization 30(4):333-357.

1975 Social Classes in Agrarian Societies. Garden City, NJ: Anchor Books/Doubleday.

Stier, Francis
1980 Social Soundness Analysis, Part 2: Ethnographic Background, Technical Package, and Use of Animal Traction. Annexe C in the Niger-Niamey Department Development Project, Phase II (683-0240), Vol. II. Project Paper Annexes. Niamey: United States Agency for International Development.

Suret-Canale, Jean
1976 French Colonization in Tropical Africa, 1900-1945. London: Heinemann.

Swanson, Richard
1979 Gourmantche Agriculture. Part 1. Land Tenure and Field Cultivation. Fada N'Gourma. L'Organisme Régional du Développement de l'Est.

Swift, Jeremy
1975 Pastoral Nomadism as a Form of Land-use: the Twareg of the Adrar n Iforas. *In* Pastoralism in Tropical Africa. T. Monod, ed. Pp. 443-454. London: Oxford University Press.

Swift, Jeremy, ed.
1984 Pastoral Development in Central Niger: Report of the Niger Range and Livestock Project. Niamey, Niger: Ministère du Développement Rural (Service de l'Elevage) and United States Agency for International Development.

314   References Cited

Talbot, L.M.
   1972   Ecological Consequences of Rangeland Development in
          Masailand, East Africa. *In* The Careless Technology:
          Ecology and International Development. M.T. Farvar
          and J.P. Milton, eds. Pp. 694-711. Garden City, NY:
          The Natural History Press.

Tendler, Judith
   1975   Inside Foreign Aid. Baltimore: The Johns Hopkins
          University Press.

Thompson, Laura
   1976   An Appropriate Role for Post-colonial Applied Anthropol-
          ogists. Human Organization 35(1):1-7.

Tuden, Arthur and Leonard Plotnicov
   1970   Social Stratification in Africa. New York: The Free
          Press.

UNCD   [United Nations Conference on Desertification]
   1977   Sahel Green Belt Transnational Project. UN Conference
          on Desertification Paper No. A/CONF. 74-29.

Unité d'Evaluation
   1977   Résultats partiels de l'enquête suivi d'exploitation Opé-
          ration Arachide et Cultures Vivrières 1976/77. Bamako:
          Institut d'Economie Rurale (mimeo.).

UNRISD [United Nations Research Institute for Social
Development]
   1975   Rural Cooperatives as Agents of Change: A Research
          Report and a Debate. Geneva: United Nations Research
          Institute for Social Development.

Uphoff, Norman T., John M. Cohen and Arthur A. Goldsmith
   1979   Feasibility and Application of Rural Development Partici-
          pation: A State-of-the-Art Paper. Monograph No. 3.
          Ithaca, NY: Rural Development Committee, Center for
          International Studies, Cornell University.

Upper Volta
   1979   Recensement nationale 1975. Résultats provisoires.
          Ouagadougou: Bureau Statistique, République de Haute-
          Volta.

USAID   [United States. Agency for International Development]
   1973   The Logical Framework: Modifications Based on Experi-
          ence. Washington, DC: United States Agency for Inter-
          national Development.

        1974a Evaluation Handbook. 2nd Edition. Washington, DC:
               United States Agency for International Development.

1974b Project Evaluation Guidelines. 3rd Edition. Washington, DC: United States Agency for International Development.

1975a Guinea Agricultural Production Capacity and Training Project. Washington, DC: United States Agency for International Development.

1975b Annual Budget Submission, Fiscal Year 1977, Yaoundé. Washington, DC: U.S. Department of State.

1977 West Benoué Integrated Rural Development Project Identification Document. Yaoundé: United States Agency for International Development.

1978a Guidance for the Country Development Strategy Statement (CDSS). AIDTO Circular Document 384. Washington, DC: United States Agency for International Development.

1978b Social Soundness Analysis. AID Handbook 3, Appendix 4A, pp. 1-12. Washington, DC: United States Agency for International Development.

1980 Country Development Strategy Statement: Upper Volta. Ouagadougou: United States Agency for International Development.

1981 Guinea Agricultural Research, Training, and Extension Project. Project Identification Document. Washington, DC: United States Agency for International Development.

1985 Need to Redesign the Niger Integrated Livestock Production Project. Audit Report No. 7-683-85-4, February 28, 1985. Washington, DC: United States Agency for International Development.

USAID/FAC
1976 North Cameroon Resource Inventory. Washington, DC: United States Department of Agriculture, for United States Agency for International Development/Fonds d'Aide et de Coopération.

USAID/Niger
1978 1978 Country Development Strategy Statement. Niamey: United States Agency for International Development.

USAID/Senegal
1978 Country Development Strategy Statement. Dakar: United States Agency for International Development.

Valenza, Jean
1975   Les Pâturages naturels de la zone sylva-pastorale du sahel sénégalais vingt ans après leur mise en valeur. Paper presented at the Colloque sur l'Inventaire et la Cartographie des Pâturages Tropicaux Africains. Bamako: International Livestock Centre for Africa.

Vengroff, Richard
1974   Popular Participation and the Administration of Rural Development: The Case of Botswana. Human Organization 33(3):303-309.

Waldstein, Alfred S.
1980   Development for Whom? *In* Sahelian Social Development. Stephen P. Reyna, ed. Pp. 507-603. Abidjan: Regional Economic Development Services Office, United States Agency for International Development.

1983   A Hydro-Agricultural Zone in the Global Economic System; Adaptation to the Constraints on Development in the Senegal River Delta. Ph.D. dissertation. Department of Anthropology. New York: Columbia University.

Wallace, Christine C.
1978   The Concept of *Gandu:* How Useful Is It in Understanding Labor Relations in Rural Hausa Society? Savanna 7(2):137-150.

Wallerstein, Immanuel
1964   Voluntary Organizations. *In* Political Parties and National Integration in Tropical Africa. James S. Coleman and Carl G. Roseber, eds. Pp. 318-339. Berkeley: University of California Press.

1973   Class and Class Conflict in Contemporary Africa. Canadian Journal of African Studies 7:344-354.

1976   The Modern World System: Capitalist Agriculture and the Origins of the European World-Economy in the Sixteenth Century. Text Edition. New York: Academic Press.

1977   Class and Status in Contemporary Africa. *ne* African Social Studies. Peter C.W. Gutkind and Peter Waterman, eds. Pp. 277-283. New York: Monthly Review Press.

Wane, Yaya
1969   Les Toucouleur du Fouta Toro (Sénégal); stratification sociale et structure familiale. Initiations et Etudes Africaines, No. 25. Dakar: Institut Fondamental d'Afrique Noire and the University of Dakar.

Warren, A. and J.K. Maizels
1977   Ecological Change and Desertification. UN Conference on Desertification Paper No. A/CONF. 74-7.

Warren, Dennis M.

1974a A Communication Model for Active Indigenous Involvement in Rural Development and Nonformal Education. Unpublished Proposal. Ames, IA: Department of Sociology and Anthropology, Iowa State University.

1974b Proposal for an Applied Anthropological Component for the ISU AID Project Designed to Increase the Production of Cereals and Legumes in Ghana. Unpublished Proposal. Ames, IA: Department of Sociology and Anthropology, Iowa State University.

1975 The Role of Emic Analysis in Medical Anthropology. Anthropological Linguistics 17(3):117-126.

1976 Indigenous Knowledge Systems for Activating Local Decision-Making Groups in Rural Development. In Communication for Group Transformation in Development. Godwin Chu, Syed Rahim, and D. Lawrence Kincaid, eds. Communication Monographs, No. 2. Pp. 307-329. Honolulu: East-West Center, East-West Communication Institute.

1980 Ghanaian Priest-Healers and Western Health Workers Exchange Techniques. National Council for International Health Newsletter 1(3):1.

1981 The Development Advisory Team (DAT) Training Manual. 2nd revised edition. Ames, IA: The World Food Institute and Iowa State University, USAID Title XII Program, Iowa State University.

1982a The Development Advisory Team (DAT) Training Program at Iowa State University. Practicing Anthropology, 4(3-4):22;24.

1982b International Development Studies: A Masters Degree in the General Graduate Studies Program at Iowa State University. Practicing Anthropology 4(1):10.

1982c The Techiman-Bono Ethnomedical System. In African Healing Systems. P. Stanley Yoder, ed. Pp. 85-105. Los Angeles: Crossroads Press (African Studies Association).

1983 Development Advisory Team at I.S.U. Medical Anthropology Quarterly 14(2):21-22.

Forthcoming. Linking Scientific and Indigenous Agricultural Systems. In The Transformation of International Agricultural Research and Development: Some U.S. Perspectives. J. Lin Compton, ed. Boulder, CO: Westview Press.

Warren, Dennis M. and J. Kweku Andrews
    1977   An Ethnoscientific Approach to Akan Arts and Aesthet-
           ics. Working Papers in the Traditional Arts, No. 3.
           Philadelphia: Institute for the Study of Human Issues.

Warren, Dennis M. and Peter Blunt
    1984   Decentralization in Ghana: The Impact on Organizational
           Effectiveness of Management Training Among District and
           Regional-level Officers. Journal of Contemporary African
           Studies 3(2).

Warren, Dennis M., Steve Bova, Mary Ann Tregoning and Mark
Kliewer
    1982   Ghanaian National Policy Towards Indigenous Healers:
           The Case of the Primary Health Training for Indigenous
           Healers (PRHETIH) Program. Social Science and Medi-
           cine 16:1873-1881.

Warren, Dennis M. and Mary Ann Tregoning
    1979   Indigenous Healers and Primary Health Care in Ghana.
           Medical Anthropology Newsletter 11(2):11-13.

Weil, Peter
    1973   Wet Rice, Women, and Adaptation in Gambia. Rural
           Africana 19:20-29.

White, Cynthia
    1984   Herd Reconstitution: the Role of Credit among WoDaaBe
           Herders in Central Niger. Pastoral Development Network
           Paper 18d. London: Overseas Development Institute.

Williams, Thomas
    1967   Field Methods in the Study of Culture. New York: Holt,
           Rinehart, and Winston.

Wolf, Eric
    1966   Peasants. Englewood Cliffs, NJ: Prentice-Hall.

Wolpe, Harold
    1980   Introduction. cn The Articulation of Modes of Produc-
           tion. H. Wolpe, ed. Pp. 1-44. London: Routledge and
           Kegan Paul.

World Bank
    1974   West Benoué Agricultural Development Project. Yaoundé:
           The World Bank (mimeo.).

    1975a Rural Development Sector Policy Paper. Washington,
           DC: The World Bank.

    1975b The Assault on World Poverty: Problems of Rural Devel-
           opment, Education, and Health. Baltimore: The Johns
           Hopkins University Press.

1976   A Proposed Livestock Development Strategy for West
        Africa. Washington, DC: The World Bank.

1978a   Chad Second Livestock Appraisal Report. Washington,
        DC: The World Bank.

1978b   Rural Development Projects: A Retrospective View of
        Bank Experience in Subsaharan Africa. Report No.
        2242. Washington, DC: World Bank Operations Evalua-
        tion Department.

1981a   Accelerated Development in Sub-Saharan Africa. Wash-
        ington, DC: The World Bank.

1981b   IDA Approves Credit for Technical Assistance to Mali.
        In IDA News Release No. 82/3. Washington, DC: The
        World Bank.

Zolberg, Aristide R.
    1966   Creating Political Order.   Chicago: Rand McNally.

Notes on Contributors

Michael M. Cernea is the Sociology Advisor of the World Bank, Washington, DC. He obtained his D. Phil. at the University of Bucharest and has taught sociology in the USA and Europe. He was a Fellow of the Center for Advanced Studies in the Behavioral Sciences in 1970-71, and of the Netherlands Institute for Advanced Studies in the Social Sciences in 1979-80. In 1974 he joined the World Bank as its first sociologist and has since worked there in operational, research, and advisory positions. His major areas of research and publication are rural development, the sociology of agriculture, family sociology, cooperatives and farmer organizations, rural communities, participation, and agricultural extension. He has carried out sociological research in various countries, principally Algeria, India, Mauritius, Mexico, Romania, Senegal, and Tanzania. Among his recent publications are: Michael M. Cernea, ed., Putting People First: Sociological Variables in Rural Development (London-New York: Oxford University Press, 1985), and Michael M. Cernea, J. Coulter, and J. Russell, eds., Research-Extension-Farmer: A Two Way Continuum for Agricultural Development (Washington, DC: World Bank, 1985).

John Grayzel, J.D. Stanford University, Ph.D. University of Oregon, is an anthropologist and lawyer who has been a Foreign Service Officer for the Agency for International Development over the last seven years. After an initial specialization in psychiatry and law, he returned to graduate studies, conducted his doctoral research among the FulBe in Mali, spent five years with AID in the Islamic Republic of Mauritania and is presently a rural development officer in the Asia/Near East Bureau in Washington, DC. With an emphasis on development theory in general, and agro-pastoral systems and law and development in particular, he strives both to continue his own involvement in applied research and to encourage greater exchange of ideas and information between practitioners and academics through regular conference presentations and occasional publications.

Robert M. Hecht received his Ph.D. from Cambridge University in 1982 for research on smallholder tree crop farming in the Ivory Coast. His articles on the Ivory Coast have appeared in the *Journal of Modern African Studies* and *Ethnology*. He has also worked in West Africa as a consultant to AID, as a postdoctoral fellow of the Rockefeller Foundation, and as a journalist for a number of American and British newspapers. Dr. Hecht is currently employed as a specialist in agriculture and rural development for the World Bank, Washington, DC.

Allan Hoben is Professor of Anthropology and Coordinator of the concentration in development anthropology, as well as Associate Director of the African Studies Center, at Boston University. Between 1976 and 1979 he served as senior anthropologist and chief of the Studies Division in the Office of Evaluation in AID. Following this, he was Visiting Development Fellow at the Overseas Development Council and has been a consultant with the World Bank, AID, FAO, and other development agencies on project design, evaluation, and policy formulation. Dr. Hoben has conducted field work and written on land tenure, agrarian reform, and other aspects of rural development in Ethiopia, Somalia, and a number of other African nations.

Michael M Horowitz, Professor of Anthropology at State University of New York at Binghamton and Director of the Institute for Development Anthropology, has carried out research among farming and pastoral peoples in Niger, Mali, Burkina Faso, the Sudan, Zaire, Rwanda, Zimbabwe, Tunisia, Jamaica, and Martinique. He has been an advisor and consultant to the United Nations Development Programme, the U.N. Environmental Programme, the U.N. Sudano-Sahelian Office, the Food and Agricultural Organization, the World Bank, the Agency for International Development, the Overseas Liaison Committee of the American Council on Education, the Overseas Development Council, and the Board on Science and Technology for International Development of the National Academy of Sciences. In 1974-1975 he served as regional anthropologist and director of applied social science research for AID's Regional Economic Development Services Office for West Africa, and from 1979 to 1984 he was senior social science advisor to AID's Office of Evaluation. He received the Ph.D. in anthropology from Columbia University.

Dolores Koenig received the Ph.D. in 1977 from Northwestern University. She is assistant professor and coordinator of the M.A. program in applied anthropology at the American University in Washington, D.C., and also works as a freelance international development consultant. After finishing her dissertation on salaried working women in Cameroon, she began to work primarily in the rural Sahel, especially Mali. Here she has worked on a variety of projects, including the one on the socioeconomic aspects of agriculture discussed in this volume, on village level energy use, on prospects for the introduction of renewable energy technology, and on resettlement and river basin development programs.

Riall W. Nolan is an Assistant Professor of Anthropology at Georgia State University in Atlanta. He received his D.Phil in Social Anthropology fron the University of Sussex in 1974. Since that time, he has worked almost exclusively as a development anthropologist in Senegal, Tunisia, Papua New Guinea and Sri Lanka. His special interests include project planning and evaluation, social policy formulation, training for development, and urban studies.

Thomas M. Painter is a Research Associate at IDA and a doctoral candidate in sociology and development anthropology at the State University of New York, Binghamton. He has carried out sociological analyses of projects for human resources development, regional agricultural development, and the training of middle-level literacy personnel, and has assisted with the organization and evaluation of adult literacy and cooperative training programs in Niger. Mr. Painter's doctoral dissertation deals with peasant migrations and agrarian change in the Dosso region of Niger, and their relation to capitalist development within a larger region of West Africa.

Stephen P. Reyna is an Associate Professor of Anthropology at the University of New Hampshire. He has taught, conducted research, and participated in development activities in eighteen West and Central African nations. He has written on the economic and demographic aspects of African domestic groups, on social change and the development of inequality in contemporary Africa. He was regional anthropologist for West Africa and the Sahel for AID in 1978–80.

Alfred S. Waldstein is an economic anthropologist, recently with AID's Bureau for Science and Technology. He first went to Africa as a Peace Corps volunteer in the middle 1960s. From 1976 to 1981 he worked as a consultant, mainly with AID, in design and evaluation of development projects in West Africa. In 1981, he became implementation team leader of the Small Farmer Marketing Access Project. The project gives world-wide technical assistance to AID missions in marketing agricultural production from small farms, and is developing an applied research methodology for assessing problems in marketing systems. Waldstein has a Ph.D. in anthropology from Columbia University. The article in this collection was drawn from his dissertation research. A more recent paper, "Where is all that food storage we hear so much about anyway," published in the 1984 Proceedings of the Society for Economic Anthropology Meetings on Markets and Marketing, reflects his current interests.

Dennis M. Warren, B.A., Biology, Stanford (1964) and Ph.D., Anthropology, Indiana (1974), is Professor of Anthropology at Iowa State University. He has lived and worked in Africa in a variety of development capacities for more than a decade and is team leader of the USAID-funded Zambia Agricultural Training, Planning and Institutional Development Project based in Lusaka (1982–85).